INTERNET INVENTION

From Literacy to Electracy

Gregory L. Ulmer
University of Florida

Longman

New York   San Francisco   Boston
London   Toronto   Sydney   Tokyo   Singapore   Madrid
Mexico City   Munich   Paris   Cape Town   Hong Kong   Montreal

Senior Vice President/Publisher: Joseph Opiela
Marketing Manager: Ann Stypuloski
Project Coordination, Text Design, and Electronic Page Makeup: WestWords, Inc.
Cover Design Manager: Nancy Danahy
Cover Designer: Joel Zimmerman
Manufacturing Manager: Dennis J. Para
Printer and Binder: Courier Corporation
Cover Printer: Lehigh Press, Inc.

Library of Congress Cataloging-in-Publication Data

Ulmer, Gregory L.
    Internet invention : from literacy to electracy / Gregory L. Ulmer.
    p. cm.
    Includes bibliographical references and index.
    ISBN 0-321-12692-0
    1. Communication—Philosophy. 2. Internet. I. Title.
    P90 .U43 2002
    302.2'01—dc21
                                    2002034128

Please visit our website at *http://www.ablongman.com*

ISBN 0-321-12692-0

1 2 3 4 5 6 7 8 9 10—CRS—05 04 03 02

"Nowadays," complained Mr. K., "there are innumerable people who boast in public that they are able to write great books all by themselves, and this meets with general approval. When he was already in the prime of life the Chinese philosopher Chuang-tzu composed a book of one hundred thousand words, nine-tenths of which consisted of quotations. Such books can no longer be written here and now, because the wit is lacking. As a result, ideas are only produced in one's own workshop, and anyone who does not manage enough of them thinks himself lazy. Admittedly, there is then not a single idea that could be adopted or a single formulation of an idea that could be quoted. How little all of them need for their activity! A pen and some paper are the only things they are able to show. And without any help, with only the scant material that anyone can carry in his hands, they erect their cottages! The largest buildings they know are those a single man is capable of constructing!"

Bertolt Brecht, Stories of Mr. Keuner

Brief Contents

Detailed Contents

Part III   Entertainment Discourse   125

Chapter 5   INTERFACE IMPRESSIONS   126

Chapter 6   CYBERPIDGIN   155

Foreword

The Writing and Technology Series offers introductory and supplementary textbooks for use in computer-and-writing and communication classes and the Humanities in general. This series will focus on instruction in writing hypertext, on developing electronic journals and multimedia projects, on assessment and evaluation of print versus electronic culture, on Cultural Studies and Digital Studies, the new technology and media, on MOOs as education sites, and on a variety of ever-growing educational concerns and challenges.

Internet Invention is the second book in the series. The book is unique. Basically, Greg Ulmer instructs beginning and advanced students in *how* to make the transition from writing for print cultures to "writing" for and "thinking" in electronic cultures. (Greg is known for making the parallel distinction between literacy and "electracy," hence, the subtitle of the book.) What he does is to explore, systematically and with numerous exemplars, what this new "writing" is coming to be. Greg has taken this issue seriously and devoted his scholarly life to attempting to develop a new rhetoric for the new media. What Aristotle is to rhetoric and poetics, Ulmer is to hyperrhetoric and poetics. He focuses on a variety of discourses: Career, Family, Entertainment, Community, and what he calls Emblems of Widescope. The book closes, or reopens, with the question concerning the "culture wars," which he would see as a form of what he calls "syncretism." For a supplementary web site for *Internet Invention,* go to www.ablongman.com/ulmer.

Victor J. Vitanza
Series Editor

Preface

This book is a textbook for teaching with and about the internet, based on my experience with a pedagogy called mystory first developed in the early 1980s. I have been trying to write this book since I started teaching with computers in the Networked Writing Environment at the University of Florida (1994) and was never satisfied with the results. I decided to try a hybrid form that combined a textbook of readings and assignments with the theory that motivated the pedagogy. We no longer need to include the history of literacy and the theories of Aristotle in our textbooks designed to teach the apparatus of print, since there is a disciplinary consensus about this background and the effectiveness of the practices for turning information found in libraries into knowledge organized as arguments on sheets of paper. It is a different story when it comes to teaching "electracy"—which is to digital media what literacy is to print. How might information stored in databases be turned into knowledge on screens hyperlinked globally and designed with graphics? There is no consensus about new media education, about what skills are needed, what practices are available, for citizens to be fully empowered as native producers of digital texts, authored for the full range of private, personal, social, political purposes as well as for business or professional interests.

Internet Invention is offered as a singular example, representing my pedagogy and curriculum in which I use the website as the medium of instruction and learning in courses ranging from freshman general education composition courses, through courses for upper-division majors in media and cultural studies, to graduate seminars in "Digital English." The "wide image" experiment framing the assignments has been tested not only in such courses but also in workshops with colleagues as well as with students from the Liberal Arts, Fine Arts, and Architecture. This book is a record of and guide to what I actually do in my classes, and why I do it. Although the pedagogy was first developed in a conventional classroom, its primary purpose is for online learning. The book makes no attempt to simulate the Web projects (the few illustrations are personal photographs and drawings, intended to encourage the use of such materials as documents in the projects). Examples of student work and related supplemental materials (syllabi, sample email discussion, commentary, illustrations) may be found at the companion website: www.ablongman.com.

Taking my motto from the Japanese poet Basho, who advised not to follow in the footsteps of the masters, but to seek what they sought, I use the invention of literacy by the Ancient Greeks as a "relay" (heuristic) for the invention of electracy. *Internet Invention* brings the students into the process of invention, in every sense of the word. My optimism about new media for the society as a whole is based on the correspondences among the features of digital hypermedia, the associative logic of creative thinking, and the aesthetics of popular culture. The fears about the *society of the spectacle* based on a culture of images that undermines critical thinking are countered in this pedagogy by the importance of imaging in the creative process and the contribution of imagination and visualization to problem solving.

The best way to learn about the potential of websites and the internet for supporting learning in the Arts and Letters disciplines, is to invent a new practice of writing native to hypermedia. At the heart of this new practice is the old humanities wisdom: know thyself. This book is organized around a project based on the "image of wide scope" discovered by historians of science to exist as a pattern in the careers of the most productive people in our civilization. What if it were possible to discover this "wide image" at the beginning of one's career, rather than waiting for an historian to find the pattern? The project, exercises, and readings take students through a series of Web assignments (the "widesite") designed to produce a version of the wide image organizing their creative imagination.

The convention of many argumentative writing textbooks (organized around controversial issues) is approached from the side of creativity in electracy. The generation of the wide image is framed as an apprenticeship for a virtual consulting agency—the EmerAgency—that places the text-image forms of screen compositions within the global institutional setting of the internet. The EmerAgency proposes through this setting to give education a new voice as a "fifth estate" in community problem solving. The lesson of a century of theory and art is that new forms require new institutional practices. The premise of the widesite (that problem solving in a career domain is guided by one's experience with problems in the other institutions of identity construction such as Family, Entertainment, and Community History) is that the creative wide image is easier to discover in the context of public policy dilemmas. Electracy is not invented in the abstract, but through the formation of a virtual civic sphere. Such is the framing premise of my networked courses.

Internet Invention is a "next generation" textbook for online writing and design that supplements existing print and web primers on HTML and graphics production with a proven pedagogy that puts these tools and techniques to work with a purpose. Designed as a passage from the more familiar rhetoric of the page to the less familiar one of the screen, the book is a hybrid workbook-reader-theory with chapters divided into the following subgenres:

- Studio: An integrated set of assignments and exercises for website authoring, supported by readings, descriptions, and models based on important works of literature, art, popular culture, and critical theory.

- Remakes: In the tradition of rhetorical meditation and arts improvisation, these sections demonstrate how to use the methods of image reason by bootstrapping electracy out of existing classics of arts and entertainment.

- Lectures: Scholarly discussions on the background, context, and rationale for the project and assignments, to share the logic of the pedagogy with students and instructors, in order to invite them to participate in the invention of electracy.

- Ulmer File: Acknowledging that this textbook expresses the pedagogy of an individual rather than a disciplinary consensus, these sections describe and demonstrate my own performance of the assignments, adding to the background on how the pedagogy evolved, not as a model but as a "relay" to orient further work.

- Office: Informal comments, asides, clarifications distributed throughout the chapters, of the sort one would find in email, frequently-asked-questions files, or instructors' manuals, especially addressed to beginning students.

- Companion Website: Correlated with the table of contents, the companion website features student websites composed in my classes, with analysis, commentary, sample email discussions, and step-by-step instructions for the assignments.

Internet Invention expresses much of what I have learned in 30 years of teaching, which means that I have accumulated many debts along the way. The first acknowledgment must go to my dissertation director, Robert Scholes, who got me started. The greatest debt is to the students who attend the University of Florida. They have always responded well to the challenges of experimentation, and I continue to look forward to their projects. You may browse the mystories authored at UF, and catch up on the present state of the EmerAgency by visiting www.nwe.ufl.edu/~gulmer. My work has benefited from the context provided by Robert Ray, through his directorship of film studies and his own heuretic teaching and research. The Florida Research Ensemble (Barbara Jo Revelle, William Tilson, John Craig Freeman, Will Pappenheimer) demonstrated the generalizability of mystory to collaborative group work. I am grateful also to Wolfgang Schirmacher and the students at the European Graduate School in Saas-Fee, Switzerland, who tested the viability of mystory and choragraphy in relation to their diverse backgrounds, interests, languages, and career contexts. Some of the lectures and remakes appeared in earlier versions in *Works and Days; Parallax; Space and Culture—The Journal; Psychoanalysis and Performance* (Routledge, 2000); *Language Machines* (Routledge, 1997); *Interface 3: Labile Ordnungen* (Hans-Bredow Institut, 1997). Thanks to the Power Institute, University of Sydney, Australia, and the EcoDesign Foundation for their sponsorship of a lecture visit in 1994 that gave me an opportunity to test many of these ideas. Thanks finally to Victor Vitanza for his continued support. I am grateful for the support and understanding of my family—Kathy, Ty, and Lee. This book was written with the help of a semester sabbatical from the University of Florida and benefitted greatly from readings and comments provided by a number of colleagues, including David Blakesley, Purdue University; Diane Davis, University of Texas; Michael J. Salvo, Northeastern University; James A. Inman, University of South Florida; and Collin G. Brooke, Syracuse University.

INTRODUCTION: THE EMERAGENCY

Not to follow in the footsteps of the masters, but to seek what they sought.—Basho

HOW TO IMPROVE THE WORLD?

The internet as a medium of learning puts us in a new relation to writing. First and foremost is the fact that someone besides the teacher may read what students write. One of the first things some students want to do is put a counter on their homepage, to keep track of hits on their site. The internet brings into potential communication all the institutions of society. To dramatize that reality I (along with some colleagues in a creative research group called the Florida Research Ensemble) created a thought experiment—a conceptual consulting agency called the EmerAgency—as a framework to motivate the website projects in my classes. The EmerAgency is a consultancy "without portfolio." We imagine it as an umbrella organization gathering through the power of digital linking all the inquiries of students around the world and forming them into a "fifth estate," whose purpose is to witness and testify, to give a voice to a part of the public left out of community decision making, especially from policy formation. The philosopher Wittgenstein once said that even if we could solve all the technical or scientific problems, we would still leave the human question untouched. The EmerAgency approaches public or community problems in terms of this human question, from the perspectives of the humanities and liberal arts.

Reflecting on my own desire to improve the world by means of humanities learning reminded me of a scene that dates from 1964, set in Miles City, Montana, when I tried to explain to my father (a representative to the state legislature from Custer County), and his good friend, Mr. Richards (an area rancher who was also chairman of the Montana Board of Regents), why that spring (my sophomore year in college) I had changed my major from Economics and Political Science to English. That this decision was incomprehensible to them was understandable in that Custer County High School's college preparation track had led me to believe that higher education meant learning a practical trade or profession such as engineering (my father's degree was in Civil Engineering). I actually won a slide rule in a problem-solving competition during a high school recruitment visit to Montana State University in Bozeman.

These adults explained to me that real work added value to the world by taking something and making it useful to society, the way Mr. Richards turned his cattle into beef, or the way my father in his business took sand and gravel out of the hills (deposited thousands of years ago by a retreating glacier and full of the bones of mastadons) and turned them into building materials. What about poetry, didn't poetry add value to life? No, was the unequivocal answer. Poets and people who taught poetry were parasites living off the labor of others—those who turned the stuff of nature into (commodities). "You are wrong," I insisted, "and I can prove it." My proof at the time did not go much beyond the fable of the ants and the grasshopper.

Image Reason

I never won the argument with the patriarchs of my parents' generation but I am still trying to prove something. I mention them to remind myself about the context of writing—the community, the society of which we are a part (nor is it "one," unified, self-consistent). The EmerAgency is an experiment to see if I can make good on my claim on behalf of the Arts and Letters disciplines. The scene of 1964 shows me the poles of my purpose, a tension, contradiction, dialectic between art and instrumentalism. What I intuited in that argument was that art in its purest form had a contribution to make to the practical world. To put it now more strongly: the dilemmas of the practical world are fundamentally resistant to policies that neglect the human question. Nor is it a choice between two different approaches, but the interdependence of arts and sciences. The slogan of the EmerAgency is: Problems B Us.

The second feature that one immediately notices in a networked classroom is that the technology supports graphic imaging along with text: one writes with the whole page, so to speak—text, picture, layout. Moreover, there is an exact correspondence between the cut-and-paste tools and the collage and juxtapositional rhetoric of twentieth-century vanguard poetics. And it is just this fit between technology and aesthetics that constitutes my renewed confidence in the practical relevance of Arts and Letters materials to community problem solving. Electracy is an image apparatus, keeping in mind that "images" are made with words as well as with pictures. I am starting now with one pole of the binary, whose qualities might be found in the opening stanza of "The Lost Son" by Theodore Roethke.

> "At Woodlawn I heard the dead cry:
> I was lulled by the slamming of iron,
> A slow drip over stones,
> Toads brooding in wells.
> All the leaves stuck out their tongues;
> I shook the softening chalk of my bones,
> Saying,
> Snail, snail, glister me forward,
> Bird, soft-sigh me home.

Worm, be with me.
This is my hard time. "

The point I want to make does not depend on this poem in particular. What was the effect when I first read "The Lost Son" in college? The memory of it can only make sense in the context of how surprising to me was everything about "English." Now I understand that there were precedents in my history of learning to read, such as my first encounter with a science fiction story as an elementary student before I knew anything about genre; or when in middle school I discovered at O'Connor's Newsstand my first copy of *Mad;* or the influence of *The Ugly American,* read for a high school book report, on my first choice of college major.

The English Major

When I arrived at the University of Montana in the fall of 1962 as a 17-year-old freshman I did not know that the humanities existed as disciplinary knowledge. Having made this discovery through required general education classes, and learning that it was possible actually to major in English, I enrolled in creative writing courses. Perhaps I was working by analogy with sports: football and baseball were not something I watched or appreciated, but something I did. Literature was not something to be read, but something to be written. I did not want what seemed to be the half-measures of prose either, in my enthusiasm as a convert. I went straight to the essence: poetry. My first poetry instructor was Richard Hugo, and his instructor had been Theodore Roethke.

What did I learn from Hugo? First, that men can be poets. I tell you this good news as part of my exercise in anamnesis recalling the extent of my ignorance and naiveté . . . (mine and the community that educated me). As a young child I believed for a time that dogs were male and cats were female. As an adolescent, to the extent that I thought about it at all, I assumed that engineers were men and poets were women. The canon was a revelation: Hemingway? And the poets at Montana at that time were megahemingways (and perhaps still are). I recognize now the compensation, the overdetermination of the lumberjack brawler stance of some of the Montana writers, as a symptom of that same context that prepared me to be an engineer.

The second thing I learned from Hugo is that my emotions were too raw, too unconditioned perhaps, to work with poetry directly. I am not sure that I am expressing properly this lesson. The way I would say it now is that I went straight from an anesthetic insensitivity to the sublime without passing through beauty. "The roses kept breathing in the dark. They had many mouths to breathe with. My knees made little winds underneath where the weeds slept" (Roethke). An image for it might be the orientation of Uranus, with its magnetic field knocked off the north-south axis that is the case for all the other planets. The solar wind of aesthetically designed language slammed my magnetosphere on its side so that it streamed away from me in the form of a turning curving field. Perhaps this is why I can stand for hours in a bookstore, head cocked sideways to read the titles on the spines of shelved volumes. Theory was as close as I could get to beauty for a long time (imagination in full armor, ready for the joust, requiring a herald of abstraction to recognize the contending parties). Poetry is the calculus of theory in the domain of arts and letters. It is the logic X = Y. The gardening greenhouses of Roethke's childhood = X. He shows us the scene ("scurry of warm over small plants") and suggests "that is me" (Y, the unknown). Here is the logic, the reasoning, to be put to work in the EmerAgency, because it is the basis for the inference system of a digital apparatus.

Perhaps the strange polar dynamics of Uranus tell me something about the poles of my imagination—poetry *applied*. A title of one of my books is *Applied Grammatology*, alluding to Jacques Derrida's *Of Grammatology*. "Ah, the American version," Europeans say when they hear my title. Yes; if it is not *useful*, I am not interested. The kind of uncanny evidence I have learned to trust suggests this possibility, in that the moons of Uranus bear the names of characters from the plays of Shakespeare, including a keyword from my mystory—Miranda. This aesthetic reasoning is not taught in the schools after about the third grade. As a civilization we have preserved the memory of the poetic and we continue sometimes to honor its diviners without knowing why or what purpose might be served by the dimension of language (the remainder) that they operate.

INTERNET INVENTION

The EmerAgency as thought experiment organizes my curriculum. Could it become something more than a pedagogical fiction? Yes, that is my hope and my plan, to be achieved in part by means of this book. The purpose of the course is to approach electracy by trying to invent it (what I call "heuretics"—the use of theory to invent forms and practices, as distinct from "hermeneutics," which uses theory to interpret existing works). It does not matter how a discipline goes online, so long as it gets there, and the sooner the better. The history of writing shows that one of the first uses of a new technology of memory is the recording of the extant works of the culture: the epics of Homer inscribed in Ancient Greece; the Bible printed in Renaissance Europe; the novel filmed in modern America. The content of the new media, Marshall McLuhan observed, is the old media. The consequence of these recordings was a mutation or reformation of one degree or another. Walter Ong and other grammatologists have shown, for example, that school with all its practices such as concept formation and method is the institutionalization of alphabetic writing. Once the move was made from manuscript to print, at least two foundational practices of medieval schooling were abandoned: mnemonic training and scholastic logic. The practices of writing invented by Peter Ramus and others simplified immensely the experience of learning.

In our case, the translation of the literate categories organizing knowledge into cyberspace makes explicit that these categories or specializations (English, History, Sociology, Physics, Architecture, Engineering) are relative to the social machine (apparatus) of literacy and have no absolute necessity. They correspond, that is, to the requirements of the apparatus, not to the nature of the conditions in the real that cause us so much trouble (which we configure as "problems"). While the entire administrative superstructure of literate specialized knowledge will be translated into cyberspace, once there much of it will evaporate. The practices that will replace specialized knowledge remain to be invented. Who will be the inventors? Why not us?

"Diegesis" is a term naming that part of a narrative that persists across all media, all adaptations, translations, remakes. The EmerAgency may help to sort out the diegesis of our disciplines from the accidents of literacy. For example, general education writing courses, staffed by English departments, serve at least the following consensus needs, listed in order of current priority—methods for using the language to learn specialized knowledge; practices of rhetoric and logic required for citizenship in a democratic society; models of self-knowledge for living the examined life. We may assume that these needs continue in electracy, but that they will be articulated differently. The "mystory" genre featured in this book, for example, assumes an inversion of the literate hierarchy: the first communication of an electrate person is reflexive, self-directed. The kind of "belonging together" experienced in electronic culture will not be the same as what was fostered by the novel and print journalism, described by Benedict Anderson in *Imagined Communities*. Taking responsibility for these experiences must be separated from the literate formats of courses, exams, lectures, semesters.

The invention concerns how the new technologies might affect our working conditions and teaching practices, and what we might do to reduce the negative aspects and enhance the positive. The history of literacy shows that we may expect profound changes to result from the changes in the language apparatus of our civilization that have been underway at least since the invention of photography in the early nineteenth century. As I understand it, the one negentropic force in the world is human intelligence (creativity): we should consider this moment as a time for invention. Our discipline, like most others, has neglected the inventive side of its history, but it is present in almost every story we tell.

THE PROGRAM

Internet Invention is divided into five parts, reflecting a basic template of my pedagogy, organized around the composition of a mystory. "Mystory" is the name for a pedagogical genre I introduced in *Teletheory: Grammatology in the Age of Video* (Routledge, 1989). It was a response to a suggestion by Hayden White that if history had been invented in the twentieth century rather than the nineteenth, it would be quite different, reflecting a different science and a different aesthetic: not positivism but quantum relativity; not realism but surrealism. Mystory is a version of this twentieth-century historiography that White proposed.

The Motivating Hypotheses of the Project:

1. that disciplines are organized around paradigmatic problems and their solutions; that the solutions to these problems are important to the society to which the disciplines contribute as a mode of collective intelligence. The

emerging predominance of the image as technology and culture is a problem of the society, which is stated in disciplinary terms as the "spectacle"—the convergence of image and reality into a virtual condition of simulacra. A proper task for English departments in particular, or Arts and Letters programs in general, is to develop rhetorical and composition practices for citizens to move from consumers to producers of image discourse.

2. that there is a promising correspondence of features (isotopy, homology) aligning digital hyperlinked media, the associative "lateral" reasoning described in studies of creative thinking, and the "dreamwork" of entertainment narratives. The imaging condition of the spectacle therefore has a positive side, which is that the new media culture potentially supports and could be designed to augment and enhance individual and collective creativity: that a wired community in principle may be fundamentally "creativogenic."

3. that we propose to test this possibility by organizing a course about the internet and World Wide Web as a workshop devoted to the composition (invention/discovery) of the students' *images of wide scope* (the founding pattern of their signature style of learning and making anything).

Make a Mystory

1. The five parts of the book reflect the steps of composing a mystory. Students map or document their situations or relationship to each of four institutions: Career field or major; Family; Entertainment; community History (as taught in school or otherwise commemorated in the community). The final section is treated separately here but in practice may be folded into the process of the other assignments, the purpose being to interlink the four sites in a way that brings out a pattern. The pattern emerges not at the level of meaning or theme (these may be derived or inferred from the pattern). Rather, the pattern forms at the level of repeating signifiers—words and graphics—which is why each discourse level of the mystory must be documented with details that address the senses. If the History information concerns the Alamo, for example, we want not an abstract discussion of manifest destiny, but Davy Crockett's coonskin cap. Freshmen do the project in four installments, upper classmen in three, graduate students in two.

2. Assignments are stated simply in a sentence or two: "make a website documenting a memory of an incident from your family-entertainment-history background." Then the daily work of students in class meetings and email lists is to use the readings, lectures, tapes, websites as sources from which must be derived the instructions for completing the assignment. Assignments usually include a required "guide" or recipe, collectively brainstormed, that explains the "rules" for making that website, and the maker's

specific plans or proposal for performing the task. Memory is crucial, since we are testing the power of the punctum (Barthes) or memory sting as the connection between personal organic (living) memory and the artificial memory of computing and the Web.

3. An eccentricity of my context in an English department perhaps is the emphasis on the transition from literacy to electracy. In practice this means that the sources for our theoretical rationale and exemplary or model relays of prior work come not from the Web but from Arts and Letters productions. An additional justification for this approach is that the work being produced offline is still superior to work originating online. Certainly there are exceptions to this rule of thumb, and in any case an assumption of apparatus theory is that this difference in quality will disappear as electracy matures. This use of readings and relays is simulated here in the usual way of textbooks, with excerpts and descriptions.

4. I do not provide here discussion questions, instructions on HTML tags, graphics software, Web search engines, and the like. The chief purpose of *Internet Invention* is to provide something to do with the internet either while working out these fundamentals or after they are learned and ready to be applied. There are many useful guides for the skills, and everything students need is available online as well. Mystories are made by students with computer skills ranging from none to expert. For that matter, I taught mystory as a genre for media studies as "paper" assignments in conventional classrooms before the World Wide Web existed.

Narrative Suspense

Once we have established the point of view of the project within the specialized knowledge of the Liberal Arts, the course unfolds as a narrative, with a basic narrative adventure structure (the myth of the hero) providing a literal and figurative outline and guide to lend coherence to the inquiry. A working premise that is an explicit part of the pedagogy is that we are inventing electracy. Electracy does not already exist as such, but names an apparatus that is emerging "as we speak," rising in many different spheres and areas, and converging in some unforeseeable yet malleable way. A benefit of the textbook format providing readings rather than mere citations is that it allows second guessing, alternative emphases, different interpretations, further elaborations. At the same time, the readings address the need for persuasive proof that what we are asked to do is logical, necessary, productive, relevant, possible. The students are helping to invent the future of writing. This attitude and relationship to learning has to be made explicit and encouraged, since students are unaccustomed to working in an experimental way.

A perhaps surprising theme or motif emerges and develops through all the chapters related to the experience and behavior of identity in electracy. The theory predicts that identity behavior or subject formation is as much a part of an apparatus as are technology and institutions. The changing nature of identity in digital civilization is manifested here in the theme of impersonation, both literally in the lives of citizens, or figuratively in the virtual play of media consumption and production. Eric Havelock documented and argued in detail in such books as *Preface to Plato* about the invention of "self" as a byproduct of the experience of interacting with the page. A habitus of reading to oneself caused the voice of thought to move from outside (spirit speaking through nature) to inside (the ghost in me—psyche). Now a habitus of imaging is spreading in which people see themselves on a screen, sometimes literally from the moment they emerged from the birth canal (in home movies) to the present. The subject is observed as "body," surface, gesture, look.

What are the consequences of such a habitus in the long term for human identity both individually and collectively? Oral peoples who experienced thought as spirit were organized collectively in tribes; literate peoples who experienced thought as self are organized collectively in nation states. The heuretic principle suggests that electrate peoples who experience thought as virtual image will organize collectively in some new way that as yet has not come fully into view (but perhaps is glimpsed in multinational corporations). Part of the interest of the book and of the pedagogy is the open question about the coming community (to borrow Agamben's title and phrase). The EmerAgency apprenticeship is quite real in inviting students to participate in testing the claims and possibilities of electracy and in inventing the practices for an electrate virtual civic sphere.

As for the functionality or practicality of the wide image (explained in the next chapter), some students are skeptical. However, the project is explicitly an experiment; its provisions are not to be accepted without question, but only provisionally, for purposes of testing. Students are not asked to "believe" but only to suspend their disbelief while trying the mystory as a genre for *simulating* the wide image. Doubters have literally changed course in the middle of an email complaining that they fail to see any connection between one discourse and another, suddenly (in response to the sheer magic of writing) to be struck by a connection. Is it discovered or invented? Both. That some pattern will emerge through the process is guaranteed due to the very nature of language and design: there will be repetitions. A further guarantee is based on the fact that people's lives have some continuity and coherence, some style, shape. Most students who make a mystory experience some degree of illumination. The pleasure involved in making a self-portrait is as old as the humanities itself: the unexamined life is not worth living. Who knows if composing a version of the wide image in advance will increase the creativity of students? Perhaps. Regardless, the quest for the wide image produces a powerful learning experience, and that is sufficient justification for any pedagogy.

Remakes and Improvisations

The final feature of the book to note is the organization of the chapters into different subgenres.

- *Lecture:* based on previously published articles exploring the theory of electracy, grammatology, chorography, and the rest. Some of this material may be skipped by general education students, or they will need help with it. The lectures remain in the form of arguments conducted in the language and style of specialized knowledge, in keeping with the hybrid nature of *Internet Invention.*

- *Studio:* foregrounds assignments and exercises, with related readings and relays to guide and inform how the websites (projects) are designed. These are stated in simple terms, and may be supplemented and elaborated upon as needed. I have used these assignments in workshops independent of the lectures.

- *Ulmer File:* presents the results and process of making my own mystory—the reasoning, difficulties, decisions, and outcomes.

- *Office:* at the end of each chapter, a few comments addressed to the student about where we are at that point, some background on what has happened. Also the sort of thing one might find in a teacher's manual.

- *Comment:* interventions or asides distributed throughout the chapters, as an extension of "office hours" discussion into the more formal lectures and studios.

- *Remakes:* This mode overlaps with the others, and reflects a heuristic way of generating research writing by starting from some work from theory, litera- ture, the arts, entertainment, or popular culture that is important in some way to the project, and using it as a guide or singular "genre" for generating further thought and insight. This mode reflects at least three sources of in- spiration: postmodern appropriation; the Hollywood practice of remaking American hits or foreign films every so often; jazz structure, which often be- gins with a standard piece and then riffs on it to produce new and transfor- mative versions; theater and stand-up improv routines. Another source is the meditational practice during the manuscript era of selecting and isolating for contemplation and generation of thought certain "gems" of the canon. Distributed through the chapters are meditations on the following gems or relays:

  - "Kubla Khan," poem, Samuel Taylor Coleridge;

  - *Phaedrus,* dialogue, Plato;

  - Meeting the devil at a crossroads, blues legend, Robert Johnson;

  - "Marlboro Man," advertisement, Leo Burnett;

  - "Meeting a remarkable person," essay, G. I. Gurdjieff.

The person or address varies according to the purpose of each of the genres. Stu- dio, Office, and Comments use second person, speaking to you, the one making a widesite, or consulting as an egent. Lectures and Remakes refer to the students or teachers in the third person. The Ulmer File is in the first person and I ad- dress myself.

The larger goal of the remakes, related to the larger purpose of this book, beyond the wide image and the EmerAgency, is to explore and demonstrate the logic native to electracy, that I call "conduction," the fourth inference (adding to the inference methods invented in literacy—abduction, deduction, induction). There is nothing exotic about conduction. The only thing that makes it difficult to follow a work organized conductively is lack of practice or failure to recognize the mode out of context. Conduction puts into logic the aesthetic operations of images (word and picture). Conduction is the inference proper to images.

The EmerAgency is my answer to the position posed to me in 1964 by the patriarchs (the late great fathers). Has the lost son been found? Or are the poets parasites on the working community still? Knowing how to make leaves stick out their tongues *may be* the calculus of electracy. Uncannily, this answer is the same one I gave then, the very same one, except that I only had half the puzzle. "Pipe-knock (who stunned the dirt into noise)." Walt and Mr. Richards were not wrong, exactly, for I take their point: in some ways we theorists, scholars, poets are like those indigenes living among the stone monoliths of Easter Island, having forgotten what the heads were for or how they got there. Or had they? Did not some anthropologist finally get them to move and erect a head, showing that the knowledge was not forgotten but secret? We live in a world of images. Who best can teach us how to make images for ourselves?

WIDE IMAGES

In anticipation of the project to come, I cite here the self-assessments of some upper-division students at the end of a semester, after having completed the mystory search for their image of wide scope (the core image guiding their creativity). While they may make more sense after completing the mystory for oneself, they provide some context for the work to come. What is called the "widesite" in this book was the "noteweb" in the course. The following responses are divided into three parts of a template assessing how an image produces meaning. The parts are (1) the feeling evoked by the image; (2) "metaphysics"—what the image reveals about what the world is like, how things are or how the world works; (3) morality: given the first two points, how one should live (what one must do).

Brent

1. Feeling: always trying to move forward, cover new ground, meet new people, mostly achieve what one's superiors have. In project one, I described the parade of homes, where a bunch of wealthy homeowners vote on the best wealthy home. The guard gate is explicitly described here. In project two, Danny and his father live just off the property of a rich man. He doesn't want them on his property. This is an example of gate keeping. Danny and his father, however, do not have a desire to enter the gate and be part of that group. Further, Danny and his father live in a gypsy caravan. The gypsies themselves faced much gatekeeping, and also chose to exclude themselves. In project three, I have the Lincoln conspirators all given equal punishment, including Mary Surratt. Lewis Paine seems boldly to accept his punishment, but wants to exclude Mary from the group. On the personal side, I aspire to be like my friends (the cool kids) and doing so gets me in trouble.

2. What is: I see things as always separated into groups/cliques/sectors/ whathaveyou. I think people (at least in my cultural atmosphere) generally want to participate in activities while excluding others. This can be seen in all sorts of segregation and persecution, and at all levels of severity. At the smaller levels this segregation can be a great motivational tool (smaller meaning that which is not intense bigotry). At larger levels, this segregation can of course be very dangerous.

3. Morality: I have always felt left out at some points, and have made it my goal to be accepted into whatever specific social group I aspire to belong to. Clearly segregation and bigotry will always exist in some form. While the person on top may be very evil in segregating, the person on the outside trying to get in can certainly use whatever method they have to include themselves in whatever group they wish. Once inside, the ultimate goal is to challenge the system we have entered and mold it to our needs, to set the rules and the trends.

Emily

1. Metaphysics: The Way the World is in Emily land. My life has been marked by long periods of absence and loss. My father's job as a naval pilot included deployments of 3–9 months. These deployments are almost like time markers for my life. Sugarplum Fairy is a reflection on one deployment when I was five. Yet this did not negatively impact my childhood experience. The experience makes my childhood unique. Rather, P-3 jets and airplanes symbolized (and still do) my father, and I have a sentimental attachment to this image. And I continued in the pattern of absence in my family by choosing to go to school 1000 miles away from home. It seems inherent to my life. Autumn leaves, changing composition and texture and departing for a period of time, but returning annually in Spring, signifies how absence was a staple of my childhood. My grandparents on my father's side passed away when I was a young teen, and my heritage on the Carman side is a bit of a mystery to me. While this loss has shaped me in my life, it is more of a fascination with my past than a devastation. My family history is also like a changing leaf of Fall, losing its life and departing from earth, but that always returns in new forms, as I am a descendent of my grandparents carrying on their legacy in the 21st century.

2. My Feeling and its Meaning: I have always known that the sense of absence that marks my childhood was never a negative experience. Absence was rectified through a strong relationship and emotional bond with my parents and family. My mother's family is very close, so there was never an extended family void. Ironically, one finds joy in the midst of melancholy or loss. The colors and visual composition of my notewebs construct a consistent pattern of bright/soft pastels and lush textures. These colors illustrate how the absence in my childhood had a positive impact. Pastels are associated with happiness and spring. I think this metaphor is most

apparent in my second project on the song "What's the Matter Here?". The message about child abuse is contrasted with a light, upbeat tempo (represented with bright colors/happy images). The song cites how important a positive and loving parent is to a child, hence reflecting my positive childhood and feelings (the pastels).

Again, the theme of absence in childhood was reflected in my third project by choosing Chaplin as my historical figure. I used Chaplin's autobiography as a foundation to select a hardship from his life. Although his childhood was marked by tragedy (a departure from my own), he rose to become the first icon of cinema as the Tramp. The themes of his films evoked a sentimental bond to reach out to his audience and connect with them. And, just like Autumn leaves, Chaplin's pratfalls symbolize the act of falling down but always getting up and returning to make more films and garner more laughs. Which is exactly how the season of Autumn, and the trees relinquishing their leaves, affects me. I feel rejuvenated and fascinated by the coming of a colder season (well, if you are anywhere north of Florida) and the loss of life. I am equally enamored with my own loss and absence.

3. Resolution: The Emily moral and how to prevail. The moral of my wide image is that the absence in my childhood is rectified through family bonds and relationships. The periodic physical absence of my father and my grandparents' death left a profound but poetic impression upon me. The time I spent with my father when he was home was wonderful and special, as we enjoy a close relationship to this day. And I am fascinated by my father's side of the family, no matter how ambiguous it is. Thus, the running themes of parent-child bonds, absence, and loss are juxtaposed with the images of falling and rising in pastel colors. And my wide image of the Autumn leaf is an accurate manifestation of my feelings and life. Colors and presence change and depart, only to return every season.

Crystal

1. The world according to stickman: This is stickman. S/he is the most basic and iconic form of my wide image. S/he is the generic human being—small, simple, and alone in the big, busy, and crowded world. S/he has infested my pages looking for refuge. The modern world keeps people apart. How much time in the day do I, or you, stickman, spend in a box? alone in a bedroom? alone in a cubicle? alone in a car? alone in a computer? I have never been a social butterfly. But the people in my notewebs seem to be absolutely isolated by external circumstances. In both of the microfictions I am five years old and entertaining myself. There was no one to play with because I grew up in the middle of nowhere and no kids my age lived down our dirt road. Many of the anxieties in "Ok Computer" are brought on by

the social isolation and relentless individualism of the modern western moment. Finally, because of her gender, Annie Oakley was alone in being a celebrated female marksman. I am, however, rather ambivalent. Frankly, I don't feel that my situation is as dire as this. I feel some connection to this isolation but it's not as if I spend the day without speaking to anyone.

2. How it feels to be stickman: Yes, I am obsessed with stickman. I am obsessed with the simplicity of the figure, the chameleon quality of the figure to represent anyone, the ubiquity of the figure in all variations on bathroom doors and crosswalks. In all of the variations I draw or find stickman, s/he is the same person. Singular and multiple at the same time, stickman only has her-/him-self for company. Isolated in the box, stickman is, essentially, a lonely figure. The low-light blues and grays scattered through the pages suggest melancholia stemming from the fact that these are not welcome, chosen, isolations. Everyone is lonely sometimes, everyone feels disconnected sometimes, and I am no different.

3. What stickman does about it: Stickman is peculiarly modern. S/he is, by definition, isolated and individualist, but s/he seeks the connections anyway— between sea and sky, between natural and man-made, between isolated and networked. In each of the microfictions I am a five year old child, alone. In one I find company in an imaginary friend; in the other I find company in books. I relied on the resources at hand, those within myself, to pass the time. In "Ok Computer," there is a desperate comfort in the double, a person sung to and of throughout the album. In my third project, inner talent triumphed for both Annie Oakley and myself, even though it was a talent we, as women, were not supposed to have, even though it was a talent that contributed to isolation in the first place. Perhaps the reason I am ambivalent about the loneliness is that my moral sensibility that accompanies it seeks to make connections, even if they are indirect, mediated, or even fictional. The solution is not to wallow in loneliness but to realize that no isolation is total.

Kara

1. The image that I am confident in calling my wide image is a highway. More specifically, it is an empty two-lane highway with dotted lines running along the center. I feel this is an accurate reflection. When I am faced with any creative problem, the solution I come up with is almost always in some way or another repetitive. The repetition is usually of the same thing over and over. Even unconsciously I create multiples. If I am sitting with a pen and a piece of paper and my mind begins to wander, I will draw a series of squares running down along side the edge of the paper. The dotted lines in the center of the highway are an enhancement of this doodle. The idea of a highway implies movement, a monotonous repetition of continuous motion.

2. Repeated squares running in a vertical line also signify movement. This image is the embodiment of the way I feel about the world. It represents my atmosphere. I feel the constant desire to move forward, either metaphorically in terms of school or a career, or physically in the sense of moving to another city (I always feel the need to move after I've lived in a city for a few years) or simply just moving down a highway to visit another place. I get satisfaction out of getting in my car and driving 3000 miles by myself. The fact that the lines in the middle of the road are dotted and not continuous probably signifies my insecurity as to where that movement will take me and my constant doubts as to whether or not I have turned the right corner. Perhaps this feeling comes from the fact that my parents moved us so much as I was growing up and the fears I had about going to a new place that the need to constantly move on has now become imbedded in my psyche.

3. I feel that we choose our own path in our lives and that path can change according to what corner we decide to turn. I don't believe that Fate has predetermined our existence. For whichever path we choose, there are a few outcomes that can occur. Our resulting action will cause us to go down one of these paths which then splits to a new set of choices. For me, this means that the actions I take must be chosen carefully. Since the ultimate outcome can vary immensely, I will always be unsure as to whether or not I have chosen correctly and the future will be unclear to me. Yet I continue to strive forward and reach those places to which I have not yet been.

Leigh Ann

1. The image of wide scope that has arisen from this experimental noteweb of my mind is one that I would have never thought of when I first started this project, yet I recognize it as my own. The material image is a lock, more specifically an unlocked lock of a fence. This image encompasses the feeling that was an undercurrent in all three projects, that of wanting to break free, to be released, to let go. I can best sum up this feeling with the words "let me out." Process of Recognition: I had an undeveloped idea early on that my two micronarratives dealt with that feeling of being held back. I was surprised to find this connection because I had selected them independently of one another and only after they were finished did I begin to notice similarities. Both mentioned the idea of play and playgrounds. In the first micro, "The Price is Always Right," I had linked the words "day care" to an image of a chain-link fence. With "House Moving," the image of a fence crept in through words. This connection was interesting, but it didn't seem very important at the time.

I continued to be surprised by the connections as I added to my noteweb with Project 2. The entertainment narrative I chose was *the Goonies,* a movie that centered around a group of kids that went on a real treasure hunt, successfully unlocking the traps of One-Eyed Willie. Project 2 was a big undertaking. I ended up trying to recapture the entire atmosphere of the movie, rather than concentrating on one particular set of details. My goal for that project was to create what I really loved about the movie, the idea of having a great adventure with a bunch of friends. At the end of Project 2, however, I was beginning to doubt that this "wide image" could really exist. It was with Project 3 that I began to zero-in on a wide image. Similar to the effect of Tarkovsky's finding the Soviet Army footage for *Mirror*, the use of the historical figure as a metaphor for my own experience was what made this image become clear. I chose Hamilton Disston without knowing exactly what his metaphorical connection to me would be. I just had a feeling that it was there.

2. I started to make connections all at once towards the end of Project 3. I thought about why the canal lock had always stuck out in my mind. I recognized the function of the canal lock, to hold back and regulate water flow, as central to the feeling of repression that is prevalent in the way that my family always dealt with problems. It was there that I connected to the story of my talk with my dad which was a rare moment of release, unlocking my own true feelings and my dad's in the process. The canal lock is it's own type of fence and I remembered the prevalence of fences in my other projects. When making links throughout the three projects, I knew the fence image worked with my feeling of holding back. Although I used the icon of a small part of a fence to connect the pages, I wasn't settled on the image of a fence alone. For the enhancement, I was able to zero-in on the specific detail of the fence that I recognized—the unlocked lock.

3. Effect of Retrospection: Thinking about the unlocked fence image connected to my first memory ever—looking out from my crib and crying in the dark, wanting to be picked up. This thought led me to remember a quote that stood out from reading Vera John-Steiner in *Notebooks of the Mind*. She discussed children in industrialized societies being raised in cribs and how this affects their need to connect verbally rather than with touch, as is the case for children in tribal societies. Before this noteweb I could never really explain why I have always dreamed about traveling to far away places. But now it seems that part of this explanation relates to this feeling of wanting to unlock and step out of the fences of my everyday life. This feeling of wanting to be "let out" (and now to help others do so) is even at the core of my choice of career, to become an international educator and help get students to study abroad. Although my noteweb isn't quite as cheery as I would have first envisioned it being, it is a true representation of a part of me. And I'll never look at locks and fences the same way again.

Rania

1. Reflection: I attempted to create a feeling of optimism throughout my three notewebs through narrative and atmosphere. Starting from the first project when in both my micro-narratives I show how life for me as a

child seemed to be at its worst yet there was still a way to pull through and at the end everything worked out for the best. In the second project I picked Cinderella as my entertainment story and we all know that her optimism got her the prince at the end. To follow along with this theme (although it was unintentional) in my third project both my personal difficulty and the historical events of the Coptic Church also evoke this theme of optimism. This optimism was revealed to me as I flew through all three notewebs connecting all the images and words that corresponded or resonated. It produced my Image of Wide Scope. As I reflect on my semester of work I must say that all three of those notewebs are me in every sense of the word.

2. Everything happens for a reason. Sometimes people come into your life and you know right away that they were meant to be there, to serve some sort of purpose, teach you a lesson or help figure out who you are or who you want to become. You never know who these people may be but when you lock eyes with them, you know that every moment that they will affect your life in some profound way. And sometimes things happen to you at a time that may seem horrible, painful and unfair, but in reflection you realize that without overcoming those obstacles you would have never realized your potential, strength, will power or heart. You must always look for the good that is hidden underneath the bad. Everything happens for a reason. Nothing happens by chance or by means of good luck. Illness, injury, love, lost moments of true greatness and sheer stupidity all occur to test the limits of your soul. Without these small tests, life would be like a smoothly paved, straight, flat road to nowhere. Safe and comfortable but dull and utterly pointless.

3. The people you meet affect your life. The successes and downfalls that you experience can create who you are, and the bad experiences can be learned from. In fact, they are probably the most poignant and important ones. If someone hurts you, betrays you or breaks your heart, forgive them because they have helped you learn about trust and the importance of being cautious to whom you open your heart. If someone loves you, love him or her back unconditionally, not only because they love you, but also because they are teaching you to love and open your heart and eyes to the little things. Make every day count. Appreciate every moment and take from it everything that you possibly can, for you may never be able to experience it again. Use your own "vehicle" to help you deal with the difficulties that may arise. Finally, create your own life and then go out and live it.

Part I
CAREER DISCOURSE

XANADU–Ulmer at Kanapaha Gardens, near Gainesville, Florida. William Bartram's *Travels* was one of the books that inspired Samuel Taylor Coleridge to write the poem "Kubla Khan."

"I live in Xanadu."

Chapter 1

Mystory

STUDIO
The Image of Wide Scope

The first requirement for becoming a consultant for the EmerAgency is to design a website version of an "image of wide scope." We will call ourselves not "agents" but "egents," since the nature of "agency" (both individual and collective) is undergoing mutation in electracy. The notions of the "wide image" and "themata" were developed by Gerald Holton in his studies of scientific creativity, for which the prototype is Albert Einstein. Holton and other students of creativity discovered the wide image by submitting the lives of especially productive people to close scrutiny. The pattern that emerged from such case studies confirmed the philosopher Friedrich Nietzsche's observation that it is possible to find in a career that secret point at which *the aphorism of thought intersects with the anecdote of life*. Nietzsche was making a similar point when he said that life is the iron hand of necessity shaking a dicebox of chance. One implication of these observations is that everyone's life manifests such patterns: every person possesses a wide or guiding image (actually an interrelated set of four or five primary images) if only in a potential state, as a disposition or propensity. Moreover, all the elements contributing to the pattern of "being"—the state of mind—expressed in the image of wide scope are in place by the time a person reaches the age of eighteen (upon graduation from secondary school).

The first initiative of the EmerAgency as a consulting agency engaged in pedagogy aimed at institutions rather than at individuals (and at individuals through their participation in institutions) is to perform a Copernican Revolution in education. Rather than waiting until after an individual has made a contribution to a knowledge domain, and as a supplement to literate schooling that focuses on verification of what is already known, the EmerAgency is developing a "practice" for helping individuals to generate a version of their wide image before they engage in disciplinary or applied problem-solving in their chosen careers. What if people became aware of and learned how to tap into the wide image as a resource in their career work? To answer this question the EmerAgency proposes to use the internet as an invention bank, using the database and search capability of digital networking to match wide images with problems confronting both specialized disciplinary and public policy arenas. This book constitutes a rationale for and guide to the making of a wide image, or widesite, within the context of an internet public policy consultancy.

General Project: The Widesite

Design a website version of your image of wide scope (a "widesite").

- This project may not be completed all at once, but will be approached through a series of more narrowly focused assignments and related exercises. The first step is to find out more about the wide image and what Holton calls "themata."

- Everything that follows in this book contributes to the process of making the widesite, including not only direct assignments, exercises, and instructions, but also theoretical and historical rationales for the project and examples of work by artists and authors relevant to it.

Gerald Holton on Einstein's Themata

"It is surely significant that these personal 'odd contrasts' have their counterparts in polarities that run right through [Einstein's] scientific work. The most striking of these is the well-known dichotomy between Einstein's devotion to the thema of the *continuum*—expressed most eminently in the field concept—as the basis for fundamental, scientific explanation, and, on the other side, his role in developing quantum physics in which the key idea is *atomistic discreteness*. This merits some amplification. [. . .]

"We can go back even further when searching for the point where the thematic commitment to the continuum was formed. It is well known that, as a child of four or five, Einstein experienced what he called 'a wonder' when his father showed him a simple magnetic pocket compass. It was an experience to which Einstein often referred. His friend Moszkowski reported him in 1922 to have said, 'Young as I was, the remembrance of this occurrence never left me.' His biographer Seelig wrote in 1954 that the compass 'to this day is vividly engraved in his memory, because it practically bewitched him.' In his autobiography, written at the age of sixty-seven, we read: 'I can still remember—or at least I believe I can remember—that this experience made a deep and lasting impression on me. Something deeply hidden had to be behind things.'

"This scene is most suggestive. There is the mysterious invariance or constancy of the compass needle, ever returning to the same direction, despite the fact that the needle seems free from any action-by-contact of the kind that is usually unconsciously invoked to explain the behavior of material things; despite the vagaries of motion one may arbitrarily impose on the case of the compass from the outside; and regardless of personal will or external

Zwang or chaos. If Einstein remembered it so well and referred to it so often, it may be because the episode is an allegory of the formation of the playground of his basic imagination" (Holton, 1973: 357–360).

John Briggs on the Wide Image

"Gerald Holton has discerned that the work of scientific creativity is shaped by clusters of presuppositions and 'gut' assumptions which each scientist has about the universe. He calls these gut assumptions 'themata': themes. For the most part themata are aesthetic qualities like the assumption that the universe is basically symmetrical, or the opposite assumption that it is asymmetrical. . . .

"Holton says, 'My guess is that there's a focusing of these ideas fairly early, in childhood. What is impressive is the stability they show over many years. Once the scientist has committed himself to one particular set of presuppositions, the set doesn't change very much.' The themata are central to scientific process because they are imposed 'on your observations and they often tell you which kinds of experiments to try or not to try.'

"Holton's themata sound like abstractions but they aren't abstractions in the usual sense. They're a concrete feel for the surrounding world. 'Quite a few of the themata have a visual component,' Holton says, 'very often they're not even conscious.' Though he terms them thematic ideas, they might also be called thematic perceptions, for convictions about symmetry or complexity, simplicity, even formalism are convictions about the way things 'look' or should look. . . .'

"Holton believes that that 'direction' Einstein felt, his vision, had something to do with the compass story and a very early commitment to the theme of the 'continuum,' or 'field.' This sense that the 'something deeply hidden' in reality must be a form of continuum, like the magnetic continuum that held the compass needle, guided Einstein in his later work as a physicist. But that wasn't all. For, as the boy had gazed at the amazing instrument that his father had brought to his sickbed, another primitive presupposition must also have been awakened, Holton believes. Perhaps the constancy of the needle that always points north convinced Einstein that there must be a fundamental 'invariance' in nature. Significantly, Einstein first called his theory of special relativity 'Invarianten Theorie.' [. . .]

"Themata are never resolved. Depending on the problems being confronted at any given period of history, some themes may produce real insights into nature and others will not. One could reasonably speculate that great scientists have a much higher commitment to the pursuit of their idiosyncratic ensembles of themes than their less creative colleagues. Colleagues may ignore, even suppress some of their own subliminal thematic perceptions because they are not perceptions that people around them acknowledge" (Briggs, 1990: 26, 32).

Comment

- There is a further biographical factor in Einstein's case. Einstein in retrospect recognized the symbolic value of the compass gift since he of all people became the one to explain the physics of the electromagnetic field that caused the action of the needle. He might also have noted a more obvious personal connection between his aphorism of thought and the anecdote of his life: the fact that his father and uncle operated for a time a small factory in Munich that manufactured dynamos, electric instruments and electric arc lights. The compass anecdote condenses this larger story in which the son of a man who worked in the German electrical industry would be the one to revolutionize the physics of light.

- It is important to note that themata have been found in work produced across the divisions of knowledge and the professions, among artists and humanists as well as natural and social scientists.

- The General Project is to extrapolate from the paradigm (Einstein) to your own case, to ask *what is my image of wide scope?* Einstein's example gives us an idea of what to look for: a childhood experience (the compass memory) expressing an abstract theme (invariance). Extrapolation is central to the project in that every example constitutes a "relay" that helps direct you to your own material. The assumption is that the wide image exists as a potential, a propensity, and that our project is as much an invention as a discovery.

- Keep in mind that the widesite is a simulation of the wide image. You will not know for sure what your wide image will have been until the completion of your career. The methods we are using—the popcycle and mystory—are means to approximate this founding mood in the absence of products or works.

Disciplinary Discourse

Assignment: Career Discourse

Make a website documenting an important discovery, or a (founding) invention, in your career domain (your university major, or a field of disciplinary knowledge in which you have some interest).

- At this point we are not concerned about form and style. The goal is *inventio*—the stage of gathering the materials with which to work. Think of this site as a documentation, a curated display of details related to a discovery, invention, and a figure responsible for it. There is no need to interpret or explain, but just to assemble a collection of details of whatever catches your attention. The figure or invention may be major or minor, so long as it is part of the career field that interests you.

- We will make a series of individual websites, devoted to different areas or institutional experiences, and look for the "constellation" pattern that constitutes the wide image at the end of this process. You likely will notice potential patterns as soon as you start the second assignment, and this awareness of an emergent shape (*eidos*) should be allowed to contribute to the selection of materials to include.

- This first assignment resembles a conventional research topic, except that rather than being asked to form an argument, you are considering the material in terms of your identification with it: an event in a field of knowledge used as a feature in a self-portrait.

- In every case these assignments may also be done on paper, as folders, files, or archives of mixed documentation, using photocopy and assemblage or collage juxtaposition.

Example: Identification with Career—Eunice Lipton, Alias Olympia   Lipton, a professor of art history, influenced by feminism, took a different approach to one of the most important paintings of the nineteenth century—Manet's "Olympia." Rather than undertaking the conventional reading of Manet's style, Lipton identified with the model who posed for the painting, Victorine Meurent. Her book is an account of a search for information about the mysterious beauty, who supposedly had fallen into prostitution and alcoholism, which led to an early death. Lipton finds evidence that Meurent was a painter in her own right, and she composes an imaginary dialogue with her object of study. Meurent's life in the bohemian environment of nineteenth-century Paris represents a fantasy in forming Lipton's choice of career.

If you are just beginning in a major (business, journalism, pre-med) your identification with the field will not be as specific as is Lipton's. Nonetheless, you probably do have some fantasy image or intuition about the career that motivates your choice. The special interest of Lipton's case for us is that she makes explicit the "identification" with her object of study. Of course it is possible to do a conventional biography of Victorine Meurent. What sets Lipton's study apart is her mix of autobiography and disciplinary research. Given the mood of skepticism and objectivity that is the prescribed state of mind for science, most disciplines ignore or deny the importance of identification in education. The wide image, in contrast, emphasizes the subject of knowledge as much as the object of study: the desire to know is prior to any research.

> "I had no idea what the ramifications of the search would be. I didn't even realize that our names were the same: 'Eunice' is a translation from the Greek of 'Evnike': it means 'Happy Victory.' And I certainly didn't *intend* to end up a red-

head. All I knew was that I envied Meurent her autonomy even as I acknowledged the paradox that I was a well-paid American professor in the late twentieth century, and she a working-class model in nineteenth-century Paris. I was
convinced that she had had more choices than I, and that she had acted on
them. The dare of her gaze was the proof" (Lipton, 1994: 16).

Comment

- The discovery or invention may be historical (the work of Copernicus, Darwin,
  Edison), or the site may treat a current question or problem whose solution
  has not yet been found or which is controversial (stem cell research, green-
  house gases). Every field has a history of innovations: advertising (who first realized that marketing was about values and lifestyles rather than products?);
  politics (the Bill of Rights); psychology (the rat maze); law (landmark Supreme
  Court decisions); computers (the microchip). The point for now is to appreciate the difference of disciplinary reason from reasoning in the other institutions that form identity, and to recognize the dynamics of the narrative that is
  already underway when one enters a language. Institutions have default or
  ready-to-wear themata that they offer to their initiates.

- The only formal point to insist on is that the documentation consist of details,
  particulars (both textual and graphic) accessible to the senses and imagination. It should not be homogenized into an abstract explanation, for reasons
  that will become clear eventually.

- These examples (and most of the others throughout this book) are presented
  through verbal descriptions, which of course are not adequate to convey the effect of the works described. Rather, they serve to illustrate the kind of thing
  you could do with your own materials. Translate them into instructions to be
  applied to the details relevant to your own case.

LECTURE
I Am Speaking "Theory"

The purpose for this first installment on the widesite is to foreground the specific features of the discourse in which this book is written. The General Project
is not conducted in some neutral, transparent, or objective way. This book is
composed within a discipline—media studies—in the liberal arts, humanities division of knowledge. Everything we are doing is motivated by my situation, including my stance within the normal science of English department media
studies and rhetoric programs. I am writing not as a scientist or social scientist, nor
as an artist or journalist, let alone as an employee of the entertainment industry
or as a private citizen. This point is obvious yet often overlooked by students.

This first entry into the widesite calls attention to the specific nature of specialized discourse.

The project does not assume specialization in media studies, but only that students have a specialization or career domain. The premise of the wide image is that nothing is created or invented in general, but only within the parameters and paradigms of the disciplines and professions that set the problems and determine the criteria for evaluating proposed solutions. At the same time, it is important to remember that knowledge domains are invented. Part of the story of the wide image is the adventure by which one individual's themata become the paradigm (authoritative example) for a normal science.

Comment

- It is worth emphasizing that a conversation conducted in a classroom is not the same as one carried on at home with the family or in the street with friends. Someone speaking calculus may mention "functions," "rational numbers," "intervals," "derivatives"—all words with meanings specific to mathematics, even if they also have more familiar meanings used in common parlance. This same difference between vernacular and specialized language exists in the humanities and arts disciplines, but it is less obvious.
- Some of the terms we will be using are neologisms, meaning that I invented them. The proof of the value of an invented term is in its use. "Popcycle," "mystory," "electracy," are not in the dictionary, but they may be eventually. Meanwhile, I propose the neologism "neopest," to name a person who makes up words needlessly.

Popcycle

By the time students attend a college or university and undergo initiation or socialization into specialized knowledge they are already native practitioners of at least three and perhaps four or more different institutional discourses. I say "institution" to point out that the "discourse" (all language or meaning-producing activities, verbal and nonverbal, behavioral, all the "practices" of the domain) is moderated by administrative entities with actual powers of oversight, such as (in the case of career domains) professional organizations, journals and presses, licensing boards, accreditation procedures, degrees, and the like. "Popcycle" refers to the ensemble of discourses into which members of a society are "interpellated" (a specialized term in my field). "Interpellation," nicknamed "hailing" or "appellation," refers to the social and psychological processes by which our identity is constructed. A career-day exposition, with representatives of various companies and professions manning information booths and perhaps conducting job interviews exemplifies hailing in practice. One is hailed or called by these booths, and the selection is limited, as are the openings within the selection. The theory of "ideology" (which is to my domain what "evolution" is to the life sciences) classifies our identity into such categories as race, ethnicity, religion, class, gender, sexuality, nationality. We enter into or learn the beliefs and behaviors named by these terms in an interrelated set of institutions. The core or dominant institutions (identified by being capitalized) of the popcycle include:

- Family: beginning at birth in the Home one enters oral culture (orality), learning a native language along with an ethnicity, a gender, and many other features fundamental to one's identity, based on the preexisting commitments of one's parents. Family discourse includes such oral or "simple" forms as the anecdote, the joke, proverb, homily, and the like, embedded in conversation. "Einstein" might occur in this discourse as an insult: "Smooth move, Einstein!" stated in a sarcastic tone. The logic of this phrase is common sense, and the proof that it is true is assumed to be self-evident.

- Community (History): from about age five in school one formally enters literacy, learning the attitudes and some of the methods of science (but not yet the specialized discipline of a career domain). The sponsoring administration of school is the local political community, so that one of the chief lessons is training in nationality, as expressed in the official history of the state (local, regional, national). School discourse takes the form and style of the textbook, translating the established, conventional ideas of specialized knowledge into general literate language. In addition to interpellating children into the beliefs of science and nation, the logic of the curriculum is "cultural literacy," aimed at providing a common body of references or symbolic capital. Proof is by authority. "Einstein" might occur in a textbook as the inventor of the formula "$E=MC^2$," taken out of the context of mathematics and physics and explained as a detail of history, often the history of the atom bomb, despite the fact that relativity theory has nothing to do with the bomb.

- Entertainment: from earliest infancy one enters "electracy," learning the mythologies, dreams, anxieties, and emotional dimension in general of the ruling (hegemonic) values of the society, conveyed through the televisions and radios that are found in virtually every household in the United States. Entertainment primarily hails one into commodity capitalism as a consumer. The forms of this discourse include all manner of narrative genres, from news to advertising. The logic is "mytho-logic," also characterized as "dreamwork," based on the same associative operations of condensation and displacement of terms used in aesthetic practice. Proof is by fashion. Something is hot, or not, cool or a fool. "Einstein" as myth personifies "science" imaged as an eccentric but famous genius or "wise old man" even though Einstein made his discoveries as a young man, working as an unknown patent clerk.

Example: Susan Van Dyne on Sylvia Plath's Interpellation

"In Hollywood cinema of the decade, the female body was pushed in extreme directions, toward voluptuous but vulnerable sensuality and toward an impish asexuality. Underlying both inscriptions is an association of the female body with the child. Feminist film theorists have shown that, even in movies directed primarily at women, what the female viewer reads is not herself but projections of male fantasies. In the antitypes of Debbie Reynolds and Marilyn Monroe, the exaggeration of physical differences becomes synonymous with moral values; body becomes character, and each body has its unvarying script. In the Debbie Reynolds plot, the sunny, ingenuous, freckled heroine is corny but cute, comically inept but always a good sport; she is thoroughly competent, however, in her main project, which is to become a wife, often by tricking her unsuspecting mate into marriage for his own good. Marilyn Monroe, and her dark twin, Liz Taylor, offer erotic gratification without commitment. Sultry, languorous, sexually experienced, and usually undereducated, they can be maternally understanding and yet are rarely rewarded with wifely success. . . .

"Plath saw herself in both figures. As a young wife she viewed all women as her rivals, and in observing Reynolds's defeat she mirrors her own insecurities: 'Liz Taylor is getting Eddie Fisher away from Debbie Reynolds, who appears cherubic, round faced, wronged, in pin curls and house robe . . . How odd these events affect one so' (J 259). In Monroe's marriage, Plath reads her own more ambitious script: 'Marilyn Monroe appeared to me last night in a dream as a kind of fairy godmother . . . I spoke, almost in tears, of how much she and Arthur Miller meant to us.' . . . To Plath, Reynolds is the monitory image, the cautionary tale of sexually inept virgins who are unable to hold onto husbands. Monroe is not punished but rewarded for her extravagant sexual appeal and, in Plath's dream, will gratify Plath's similar aspirations by sharing her beauty secrets" (Van Dyne, 1993: 71–72).

Comment

- Every institutional discourse has its own star icons that function as emblems for scripts of normative behavior, in the same way that Reynolds and Monroe are described as doing in entertainment.

- The experience of the gaze, in which Plath's "self-perception always includes an awareness of herself as spectacle, and her self-representation contains an element of performance" (73), is extended to everyone in electracy, men as well as women.

Two other institutions and their discourses are important—Church and Street—which will be addressed later. For now this brief review of the popcycle is to note that it is the source of the wide image. The term "popcycle" designates the way ideas important to the culture may arise in any one of the institutions and then circulate through the others (invention is an ecological process). The insight that the notion of themata gives into academic learning is that problem-solving in general, and inventive thinking in particular, draw upon all the discourses that one knows. We will find or produce what will at least be a simulation of the wide image by mapping and documenting our own location or position within each one of these discourses. The genre capable of writing with the pop-cycle as a whole is called "mystory" (Ulmer, 1989). The wide image is generated out of a synthesis or syncretic scene that captures holistically a pattern of correspondences that appears when these discourses are brought together and juxtaposed. In subsequent chapters we will work our way through each level of the popcycle, using their forms and logics, in order to externalize and give expression to what we internalized during our first eighteen years of life. The mystory is designed to reveal/compose or "model" our wide image at the beginning of our career education, rather than waiting for it to emerge at the end of our careers as the style running through our accomplishments.

Part of the value of Einstein as paradigm is that his themes are imaged by a compass. The story of his compass becomes a parable for our own search, in that we must find our equivalent of the compass—the scene that we recognize as having this guiding role in our orientation to the world and to life. No matter what object or "prop" might embody our themata, it will serve as our *compass*. The further value of the compass as parable is that it answers at once the question of "determinism": it is true that the needle always points north, but once one has this orientation, one may go in any direction.

Comment

- While you are doing some research on an invention in your career field or major for the first assignment, I will explain my orientation in my own career field. In conventional textbooks it is unnecessary to include the background, orientations, and purposes of the authors, since these are assumed (they express the domain default themata). No such consensus exists regarding electracy, and one purpose of the EmerAgency is to assist in this very invention.

- Throughout the book I will present parts of my mystory, in search of my own wide image. What is the point of intersection between the anecdotes of my life and the aphorisms of thought in my career field of media rhetoric? There is a certain poignancy in the theory due to the possibility that a person's wide image may not be well-suited for the paradigmatic problems of a given field of knowledge. At the same time, this possibility indicates that one practical use for the wide image could be as an aptitude test.

Grammatology (The Ulmer File)

This lecture is part of the Ulmer File because it represents my adherence to a particular school of thought within the liberal arts. Not everyone agrees with this approach. Most textbooks are written in the voice of a disciplinary domain, with the confidence of field consensus about paradigms and themata, problems and methods. *Internet Invention* is a textbook, but it is written in the first person, without consensus. It proposes an institutional practice for electracy, including the EmerAgency, without knowing whether this commitment will have been normal or utopian (*the proof is in the pudding; try it, you'll like it*). The safety net is that the EmerAgency is a practice for invention. Am I the one whose wide image will become the default for a discipline? Is there a fit between my story and the paradigmatic problems of my career domain? Perhaps not. At the same time, I am optimistic about the possibility of the EmerAgency to facilitate the formation of digital rhetoric, even if it is not the rhetoric that I propose, since it does not claim absolutely to be that rhetoric, but rather a means to invent an appropriate internet practice. Meanwhile, I have to explain the disciplinary identifications guiding my approach to the paradigmatic problem of new media culture: *the image.* My own case stands in as the prototype of mystory.

Aristotle   As a professor of English, I work in the only discipline that has not broken with the paradigm of knowledge set by the Classical Greeks. Aristotle's physics has long since been superseded, but his rhetoric still informs every introductory textbook of writing. And for good reason. Aristotle along with his teacher, Plato, and the pupils of the schools they founded (Plato's Academy and Aristotle's Lyceum), invented the institutional practices needed to exploit alphabetic technology. My attitude to the great inventors of literacy comes from the Japanese poet, Basho, who wrote that "one should not follow in the footsteps of the masters, but seek what they sought." My responsibility as a research humanist is not simply to pass along a tradition, but to help do for my society what the founders of my discipline did for theirs. They were confronted with the products of several hundred years of cultural experience with alphabetic writing. Grammatology—the history and theory of writing—uses an analogy with the literate apparatus to set up the terms for the invention of "electracy" (a neologism coined to distinguish the emerging apparatus from the established one). What we are attempting through our projects, then, is not only a practice for the new apparatus, but the very reasoning process of that apparatus in general.

The equivalent for us of the acquisition of the alphabet is the invention in the nineteenth century of a series of new kinds of recording devices, beginning with the camera, capable of registering and manipulating not only the words of a language, but the visual and auditory image of the speaker. The technological dimension of the electrate apparatus consists of this evolving series of recording machines, from the first camera through contemporary digital imaging, an evolution whose end is not yet in sight, but whose fantasy future is figured in the term "cyberspace." In the same way that Socrates, Plato, and Aristotle did not ask how writing might serve the needs of the institutions of orality—religion, ritual, magic—but instead invented a new institution—school—and new practices native to writing (method, dialogue), it is my responsibility (the responsibility of my discipline) to find an equivalent for electracy. The goal is not to adapt digital technology to literacy (anyway, that is happening as a matter of course), but to discover and create an institution and its practices capable of supporting the full potential of the new technology. The EmerAgency is an institutional form, with the mystory as one of its practices, designed to work with the internet as the larger institutional context that will be to electracy what school was to literacy. Literacy shows us by analogy what we are looking for, but it does not give us the answer. The first thing to establish then are the terms of the analogy.

Comment

- To restate the present discussion in terms of your assignment, I am presenting information about an important invention in my field of knowledge, specifically, the invention of writing. This topic is still too broad, obviously, and I will narrow it down eventually. The difference between my purpose and yours is that I am focusing on a specific invention within literacy as a relay for understanding what needs to be invented for electracy.

Literacy   Eric Havelock's account of the invention of the mode of categorization we call "concept" in literacy provides an important analogy for understanding what is happening in our own moment. The implications of the technological ability to record speech by means of the alphabet developed over several centuries, culminating finally in the invention of philosophy: dialectic, method, and their formal teaching in Plato's Academy—itself constituting the invention of a new institution: school. The first concept, the prototype of a new category formation, a new system for classifying the world (the original function of metaphysics), was "justice" (*dike*), extracted from the Homeric epics once they were available in manuscript form.

Eric Havelock on the Invention of "Justice"

"Hesiod affords an initial example of a process which was to gather momentum later, when he chose the term *dike* (usually translated 'justice') as the formal subject of a 'discourse.' The term occurs incidentally and not infrequently in orally preserved speech (as in Homer) but never as the topic of a formal discussion. The narrative laws of oral memorization would discourage such a choice.

"Having made his choice Hesiod cannot conjure the required discourse out of thin air. We could easily manage it today, because we inherit two thousand years of literate habit. He, on the contrary, must resort to the oral word as already known—the only preserved word that is known. He must build his own semi-connected discourse, either some pieces in which the term *dike* happened for whatever reason to occur, or others in which incidents occurred that he felt were appropriate to connect with the word. His decision is compositional (rather than ideological), or perhaps we should say re-compositional.

"If he must do this, he will be forced to continue to utilize the narrative forms which control what he is borrowing from. He still will not be able to tell us what justice is, but only what it does or suffers. He has taken one decisive step toward the formation of a new mentality by inventing the topic to take the place of the person. But he cannot take the second step of giving his topic a syntax of descriptive definition. It will still behave rather than be" (Havelock, 1967: 101–102).

The gathering of disparate materials under the new principle of categorization at first seemed chaotic. When the oral narratives were recorded or written down in the alphabet, it became possible to discern a pattern, a repetition of signifiers that was not perceptible in spoken discourse.

"The psychological push needed to bring this about must have been the use of vision as supplement to hearing. An architectural rearrangement has been performed on language as previously used. The various 'justices' which perform one after the other in Hesiod's account echo each other acoustically to some extent, but they are also all 'look-alikes.' The reading eye has been able to perceive them as located in an oralistic flow that has now been written down in the alphabet, which can be looked at, read, and 'backward-scanned.' Hesiod could have so composed only if he was able to 'read' oral texts of Homer (and perhaps others). The first beginnings of the alphabetic revolution have occurred, in the creation of a topic as a subject of a 'discourse' made possible by the conversion of acoustically preserved memorized speech into materially preserved visible artifacts that are capable of rearrangement" (103).

The First Concept   Hesiod noticed a pattern of words that had been overlooked in the oral performance of the epics. "Whereas it would be an easy matter for oral memory to recollect what Agamemnon or Achilles did or what happened to them, the names of 'dike' and 'hubris' and related terms were buried deep in the oral matrix. To rely on oral memory not only to recollect but to collect what happened to them would be beyond existing capacity. But place the language of the story visibly before the eye, so that the flow is arrestible and the words become fixed shapes, and the process of selection and collection can begin" (Havelock, 1978: 228). Hesiod discovered in the epics a "field" of meaning that he labeled with the abstract term for "justice." Plato completed the extraction of "justice" from its setting in the dramatic action of the epics when he wrote one of his most famous dialogues, *The Republic*. Plato asks after the "being" of "justice," thus undertaking the project that Aristotle later dubbed "metaphysics." Plato assumed that justice, as a universal principle or form, has an essence. To discuss this essence required Plato to separate his discourse from that of everyday life, to create philosophy as the first specialized discipline of knowledge, by introducing a specialized use for the verb "to be," whose normal function was that of copula, connecting subject and predicate.

The enormity of Plato's achievement is perhaps hard to appreciate today. He did not invent philosophy in isolation, of course. Some have said that he is to Socrates what St. Paul was to Christ (founder of the church). Plato founded the first school—the Academy—and introduced the practices of dialogue and method. In the dialogues Socrates's conversations with various sophists and citizens serve as a kind of oral interface metaphor to bring the reader by this more familiar means into contact with the inner nature of writing—dialectic (method). We have to remember in the invention of electracy how basic were the first inventions of literacy. In the first discourse on method in the West—*Phaedrus*—Socrates shows his pupil the procedures of analysis and synthesis: first break a problem or question down into its most basic parts or elements, and then put the parts together in a logical order (an order of intelligibility rather than of mimesis). The practice of definition was introduced and demonstrated in such dialogues as *Euthyphro*, in which Socrates exposed the contradictions in this character's reasoning. Euthyphro accused his father of "impiety," but when asked to "define" or explain this "concept," Euthyphro (egged on by the gadfly's questions) ends up offering conflicting meanings. The lesson is that it might be useful to know what one is doing prior to taking action. Contradictions had not been noticed in oral discourse, which lacked the abstract register and scannable memory equipment that allowed one area of experience or statement to be compared with another. As we know from the fate of Socrates, executed by the State of Athens for corrupting the young, this new practice of argumentation disturbed the status quo.

The Thing

The reason for going into this Classical context in detail is to establish the nature of what we need to invent for electracy (I am explaining how I do my research in the discipline of media studies). What has to be invented is not "only" a new kind of category and classification native to the image, but an institutional practice for learning and applying this category. Aristotle founded his own school, the Lyceum, and extended and codified philosophy into the beginnings of the definitive practice of the literate apparatus: science. Perhaps we have forgotten that Aristotle invented the "thing."

"In two of his early works—in the *Categories* especially, but also in the *Topics*— Aristotle presents a revolutionary metaphysical picture. This picture has had a peculiar fate. Its revolutionary theses are so far from being recognized as such that they have often been taken to be statements of common sense, or expressions of an everyday, pretheoretical ontology. The most stirring and far reaching of those theses is the claim that included among what there is, among the entities, there are *things*. Aristotle, famously, goes on to maintain that these things are ontologically fundamental. All the other entities are by being appropriately connected to the things, for example, either as their features (their qualities, sizes, relations-to-each-other, locations, and so on), or as their genera and species, that is, the kinds under which the things fall. These claims and their interpretation have received considerable discussion. Yet the fundamental one has gone virtually unnoticed. To formulate it most starkly: before the *Categories* and *Topics*, there were no things" (Mann, 2000: 3–4).

When he delineated "things" Aristotle was inventing a world view (metaphysics). "Ontology [the science of being] was born when someone realized that any view of this sort implies a distinction between individual things, on the one hand, and their properties, on the other. Ontology was born when someone realized that there are not only different kinds of individual thing but also different kinds of entity. Plato's theory of forms deals with just these sorts of questions, and we think of it, therefore, as one of the first ontological inquiries" (Grossman, 3). Aristotle continued this project by establishing that which is constitutive of an entity, its essence (what is real about it and that makes it what it is). The task was to determine what something essentially is, as distinct from what it merely happens to be: to distinguish its form from its matter. Aristotle criticized the Presocratics for treating entities as if they were mere heaps of stuff. "Both a heap and a thing are one—for each is unified such as to be one heap, or one thing—the kind of unity characteristic of things is much stronger than that of heaps. . . . Things are genuine unities, whose cause of being one is intrinsic to them, while heaps are merely accidental unities, whose cause of being one is wholly extrinsic to them" (33–34).

Aristotle (continuing Plato's work with the "topic" extracted from epic drama) extended his insights into place (*topos*) from physics to logic, with the invention of the *dialectical topic*. The topic, based on Plato's dialogues, is a mnemonic system for classifying and deploying arguments.

"A topic is a 'head' under which are grouped arguments, or lines of arguments; in a *topos* ('place,' *locus*, 'region') the speaker has a stock of arguments to which he may turn for a particular need. If he knows the *topoi* (regions, places, lines of argument) he will know where to find what he wants for a special case. The general topics, or *common*places, are regions containing arguments that are common to all branches of knowledge; these are the topics of *more and less*, of *magnifying and minifying*, of *past and future*, and of *possible and impossible*—the four commonplaces in the strict sense. . . . The topics or places may be indifferently thought of as in the science that is concerned, or in the mind of the speaker" (Cooper, 154–155).

The Invention of "Definition"

Aristotle's *Topics* is a handbook that teaches students how to argue in a structured debate (Slomkowski, 3). The competition begins with a problem, even an aporia (dilemma, impasse), something about which there is puzzlement and disagreement. A fundamental aspect of the practice is "definition," the procedure of producing "predicables" for the topoi—what may or may not be said of a thing, concerning its proper attributes. The definition, that is, establishes essence. There are four kinds of predicates admitted: definition, property, genus, or accident. An accident is that which may or may not belong to a thing (a given horse may be awake or asleep, brown or white, large or small, without altering its essence, its true nature). "To define a substance means to establish, among various accidental attributes, the essential ones, particularly that one which causes the substance to be as it is" (Eco, 1984: 57).

Example: "Culture"   "Definition" is one of the fundamental practices of literate composition, so familiar to us now that we forgot that it had to be invented in order for alphabetic writing to become functional. We will focus on it not because it is the only aspect of writing that is changing, but because it makes clear the dynamics of change underway. An initial understanding of verbal composition in electracy may be grasped *by contrast* with the established device of definition. A definition of the first concept—"justice"—may be found now in any dictionary, along with many thousands of other concepts and their definitions. Of course Plato assumed he was treating not merely "meanings" of words, but eternal essences. It is useful to review at this point some of the features of "definition," before turning to its electrate equivalent (alternative). Let's look at one dictionary definition—of the word "culture"—and its background to establish in more detail the nature of this practice.

"**Culture**—n. 1. the quality in a person or society that arises from an interest in and acquaintance with what is generally regarded as excellence in arts, letters, manners, scholarly pursuits, etc. 2. a particular form or stage of civilization: *Greek culture.* 3. *Sociol.* the sum total of ways of living built up by a group of human beings and transmitted from one generation to another. 4. *Biol.* a. the cultivation of microorganisms, as bacteria, or of tissues, for scientific study, medicinal use, etc. b. the product of growth resulting from such cultivation. 5. the act or practice of cultivating the soil: tillage. t. the raising of plants or animals, esp. with a view to their improvement. 7. the product or growth resulting from such cultivation. 8. development or improvement of the mind by education or training.—v.t. 9. to subject to culture; cultivate. 10. *Biol.* a. to develop (microorganisms, tissues, etc.) in an artificial medium. b. to introduce (living material) into a culture medium. [ME: tilling, place tilled]." (*The Random House College Dictionary,* 1972).

Raymond Williams gives an essay definition of "culture" in his vocabulary commentary, *Keywords,* in a way that highlights the metaphorical process at work in the formation and growth of terminology.

"**Culture** in all its early uses was a noun of process: the tending of something, basically crops or animals. The subsidiary *coulter*—ploughshare, had traveled by a different linguistic route, from *culter, colter, coulter* and as late as the (early) seventeenth century **culture** (Webster, DUCHESS OF MALFI, III, ii: 'hot-burning cultures'). This provided a further basis for the important next stage of meaning, by metaphor. From (early) sixteenth century the tending of natural growth was extended to a process of human development, and this, alongside the original meaning in husbandry, was the main sense until the (late) eighteenth and (early) nineteenth centuries. Thus More: 'to the culture and profit of their minds. . . . At various points in this development two crucial changes occurred: first, a degree of habituation to the metaphor, which made the sense of human tending direct; second, an extension of particular processes to a general process, which the word could abstractly carry. It is of course from the latter development that the independent noun culture began its complicated modern history" (Williams, 1976).

We are at the core of how discipline works. Robert Hodge and Gunther Kress provide further historical background on culture in particular, and on the historical invention of word meanings in general, when they show the conflicting influence on the term of Matthew Arnold's *Culture and Anarchy* (1869), and Edward Tylor's *Primitive Culture* (1871).

"Arnold and Tylor represent two alternative sets of transformation associated with the word 'culture', enunciated from two different speaking positions in the society. Arnold takes the transformational potential of the Latin *cultura,* its core transformation of peasant or material worker into intellectual work(ers) of various kinds, which he associates in nineteenth-century English society with educators, intellectuals and clergy, including also—and this is a distinct contribution—poets and other artists. But for Arnold, the transformational route is firmly opposed to the work that defines working classes, even though Arnold professes to want to offer 'culture' to the masses.

"Tylor's definition, on the contrary, extends the scope of the original transformation and uses it to establish a chain of equivalences. For him, culture is both material work of all kinds and also intellectual work. The transformational link, instead of being broken as in Arnold, is opened up. Since it is applied to 'primitive' cultures, it includes activities of pre-agricultural peoples, and insists on their fundamental continuity with the various forms of life of modern man. This transformation as a meaning is specifically declared as a basic premise in his style of anthropology: 'There seems to be no human thought so primitive as to have lost its bearing on our own thought, nor so ancient as to have broken its connection with our own life'" (Hodge and Kress, 1988: 190–91).

Exercise: Term Extensions

Using the history of the term "culture" as a model, select a different craft (other than agriculture) and develop its figurative possibilities as a new extension of the meaning of "culture".

- The purpose of this exercise is to gain some experience with the fundamental method of the EmerAgency, which is reasoning by image: figurative inference. The structure of this experiment is to open a new understanding of the "culture" of your career field by figuring it in terms of some craft or applied, practical, physical practice, or process. If human development of learning can be like agriculture, what else might it be like? Or, if human development in general may be tended in the manner of a crop or herd, what about your particular specialized area of work? What sort of craft makes a good metaphor for developing knowledge in your career field?

- In later chapters we will apply this exercise to the practice of "consulting." We need a new term to characterize the EmerAgency approach to public policy formation and problem solving. We will define this deconstructive consulting by the metaphorical extension of a craft practice (a specific kind of music) to name our practice.

Example: Joseph Beuys, from Text to Felt We have forgotten that "text"— the common name for written compositions—derives from "textile," and includes in its etymologies the craft of weaving, just as human "culture" includes the crafts of husbandry. In this example "felt" replaces "textile" as a fabric craft to be developed as a vehicle for the tenor of imaged compositions.

- Joseph Beuys demonstrated how to do theory as sculpture, or rather, as craft, working with felt and fat, researching their reality or "Gestalt": "Actually two elements, fat and felt, are closely related. Both have a homogeneous character in that they have no inner structure. Felt is a material pressed together, an amorphous material, with an uneven structure. The same is true of the nature of fat, and that interested me" (Beuys, cited in Ulmer, 1985: 244). In examining such materials as figures or relays for a theory of social organization ("social sculpture"), Beuys was working out in practice what a philosopher such as Gilles Deleuze attempts as a thought experiment, using the properties of felt as a way to think about certain abstract questions. Fat and felt became auratic in Beuys' context (post-war Germany) because of the association of these materials with the concentration camps and the holocaust.

- Deleuze and Guattari express the difference between a State apparatus and a "war machine" (contrasting notions of social order, and also of science) as the difference between woven fabrics and felt. "Felt is a supple solid product that proceeds altogether differently, as an anti-fabric. It implies no separation of threads, no intertwining, only an entanglement of fibers obtained by fulling (for example, by rolling the block of fibers back and forth). What becomes entangled are the microscales of the fibers. An aggregate of intrication of this kind is in no way homogeneous: it is nevertheless smooth, and contrasts point by point with the space of fabric" (Deleuze & Guattari, 1987: 475).

There may be a disagreement at the level of interpretation (is felt homogeneous or not?) but heuretically the procedure is the same: questioning craft materials for insight into theoretical questions, with both men seeking in nomadic culture (read through its products) a relay for a supplement to the Western frame of mind. For the exercise, an egent would review Beuys' sculpture, and read something by Deleuze and Guattari on nomadic thought, while working during the same period of time on learning how to make felt.

How to Make Felt

"Remember that the wool fiber has scales, like small barbed hooks, which open up at first contact with hot soapy water, then close again during the continued rubbing process. These small hooks attach to one another when they close, and once the felting process is completed, they are firmly anchored. It is this action that produces the compact material called felt. This is why the wool layers have to be put crosswise on top of each other. This also is the reason you must rotate your hands in the same direction when rubbing the wool" (Evers, 1987: 25).

The cohesion of felt literally by "hook and eye" connectors supplies the metaphor for the conductive associations that generated the poetry of Samuel Taylor Coleridge, according to John Livingston Lowes, that will prove central to chorography.

Xanadu as Felt

"Those lines from Bartram [describing a scene in Florida] are in the thick of the pages which Coleridge was ardently transcribing in his Note Book, and the picture which they painted made a profound impression on his mind. For he twice came back to it. It inspired the memorandum in the Note Book, for the 'wilderness plot, green and fountainous and unviolated by Man' is unmistakably the 'blessed unviolated spot of earth' on which Bartram lavished such a wealth of words. . . . Of one thing we may be certain: impressions of Bartram's enchanting little 'Isle of Palms' were among the sleeping images in Coleridge's unconscious memory at the time when 'Kubla Khan' emerged from it.

"But a thousand other impressions coexisted with them there. Did this particular cluster constitute what we have called an *atome crochu*? Had it, in other words, *hooks-and-eyes* which might draw it into the extraordinary complex which was taking form? If it were so equipped, its attraction within the circle was almost inevitable. For it lay, so to speak, just over the threshold of consciousness. Twice already its imagery had recurred to memory and clothed itself with words. And recurrence to memory soon becomes a habit. Conspicuous, now, among its details were 'grassy meadows,' a 'blissful garden,' 'fragrant groves,' and multitudes of trees. And at the moment of the dream, by way of Purchas, impressions of 'fertile Medowes,' conjoined with a 'goodly Garden' furnished with trees, were stirring actively in Coleridge's brain. Clearly then there were sufficient links between the images from Purchas which were sinking into the Well, and the images from Bartram which were already there. And they did coalesce. Here are the lovely lines of the fragment once again:

> 'And there were gardens bright with sinuous rills,
> Where blossomed many an incense-bearing tree;
> And here were forests ancient as the hills,
> Enfolding sunny spots of greenery'" (Lowes, 1955: 333).

Comment

- Mystory is not a text, but a "felt": let us begin to use this word to name our productions, whose overtones suggest the emotional quality of image meaning.
- The method for generating "felt" from "text" may be applied to any term. The procedure is to isolate the metaphor (often a dead metaphor) that may be found in the root or the history of a word. Some important philosophers have used inventive etymology as a strategy for exploring new dimensions of thought or experience.

Paragraph (Composing Definitions) Most composition handbooks place the treatment of definition in the context of teaching the basic unit of essay form—the paragraph. "The building blocks of writing, paragraphs present discussions of single facets of a subject. In isolation, a paragraph describes or explains one idea, but when it is part of a series of paragraphs in a paper, it develops one aspect of a paper's larger idea" (Perrin, 1987: 58–59). "A paragraph of definition, somewhat like a dictionary definition, attempts to clarify the exact meaning of a word or concept that is important in understanding a paper. Such paragraphs should first place the subject in a class and then distinguish it from other items in the same class or describe its notable characteristics. Giving examples and using comparison and contrast are two common methods of explanation in these extended definitions" (79–80). Perrin characterizes dictionary definitions as denotations. He warns about the complexity that results when connotations enter the process in an extended definition. "Connotations, the secondary and sometimes emotional meanings of words, create more difficulties, because the connotations of words create added impressions, ones not always planned on by writers" (287). Working generatively, our task is to find the electrate equivalent that does for the image what the paragraph and definition do for the concept (the thing). Inventing an electrate alternative to the definition (and paragraph) begins with a negative practice, generated by *contrast* with the established convention of writing.

Antidefinition

One of the more famous scenes in this early history of literacy—one that captures the provisional nature of individual inventions within the larger evolution of the apparatus, concerns an ancient alternative to the definition. Aristotle and his students were at work on a definition of "man," and had refined the essence to include the properties "featherless biped." The session was interrupted by the cynic sage Diogenes, who burst into the session holding aloft a plucked chicken, and declared, "Behold, your man!" Diogenes, known as the anti-Socrates, had a different approach to wisdom, different themata, than the one that became the norm. He *performed* his arguments, integrating his daily life and his philosophy. It is reported that he lived in a barrel, and practiced all private bodily functions in full public view. When criticized by a passerby for masturbating in the market place, Diogenes exclaimed that he wished he could satisfy hunger just by rubbing his stomach. Aristotle's pupil, Alexander the Great, admired Diogenes for the freedom with which the latter lived his life. "If I could not be Alexander," the future conqueror of the world declared, "I would be Diogenes." He made his way over to where the sage was sunning himself and asked if there were anything he might do for him. "Yes," was the reply. "Get out of my light." In recent years several important philosophers have returned to Diogenes as the exemplar of a new paradigm, indicating that performance may be to electracy what definition was to literacy. The Greek ancestor of electracy is not Aristotle but Diogenes. The point to emphasize, however, is that electracy is not simply a reversal that turns *topos* back into drama (a return to orality). As Walter Ong observed, postliteracy is *secondary* orality, a hybrid of oral and literate features.

Although the academic discipline of rhetoric, and English departments in general, have remained Aristotelian and ignored Diogenes, the arts and letters community (artists, poets, and philosophers) have been inventing the institutional practices that accord with the technologies of the emergent apparatus, or at least this is how grammatology understands the experiments of the vanguard artists of the nineteenth and twentieth centuries. Electracy was emerging simultaneously in separate dimensions of society, although the artists themselves often understood what they were doing as being opposed to the culture and products of scientific and technological civilization. Nonetheless, their many inventions (often hybrids and syncretisms formed by borrowings and adaptations of practices from oral or non-Western societies) opposed conceptual abstraction and sought direct access to a supposed immediate flow of experience. Our widesite is designed using devices invented by the vanguard arts.

Example: Georges Bataille   A good example of an arts practice specifically devised as a challenge to literate concepts and their definition is the "Critical Dictionary," composed by the Documents group, headed by Georges Bataille in the 1930s. Bataille attempted to break the constraints of literate metaphysics or conceptual classification in this critique of that great achievement of the Enlightenment, the encyclopedic dictionary. "A dictionary's sole purpose is the imposition of form and homology, definition fixes objects in thought, extracts them from the world and pins them to a page. A dictionary is never critical, any element of subjectivity would allow in the formless, that heterological gob of spittle. Formless declassifies and is the negation of definition. . . . An image, a poetic invective, often takes the place of the term in a discourse, something alien to philosophy, and the photographs in the 'Dictionary' perform this same function in a more literal fashion" (Brotchie, 1995: 23). Bataille demonstrates invention by contrast or negation: starting from the principle of the "thing" and *topos* that define according to homogeneity or similarity, Bataille proposed to classify by heterogeneity (creating unstable groupings of incommensurable elements). If Plato invented the first concept, which he preferred to call a form (or an idea), then Bataille is an anti-Plato, proposing a "formless" metaphysics. Here are two entries by Bataille from the "Critical Dictionary."

Georges Bataille on Categorical Accidents

"**Factory Chimney**—When I review my own memories, it seems that for our generation, out of all the world's various objects glimpsed in early childhood, the most fear-inspiring architectural form was by no means the church, however monstrous, but rather large factory chimneys, true channels of communication between the ominously dull, threatening sky and the muddy, stinking earth surrounding the textile and dye factories.

"[. . .] I was not hallucinating when, as a terrified child, I discerned in those giant scarecrows, which both excited me to the point of anguish and made me run sometimes for my life, the presence of a fearful rage. That rage would, I sense, later become my own, giving meaning to everything spoiling within my own head and to all that which, in civilized states, looms up like carrion in a nightmare. I am, of course, not unaware that for most people the factory chimney is merely the sign of mankind's labour, and never the terrible projection of that nightmare which develops obscurely, like a cancer, within mankind. Obviously one does not, as a rule, continue to focus on that which is seen as the revelation of a state of violence for which one bears some responsibility. This childish or untutored way of seeing is replaced by a knowing vision which allows one to take a factory chimney for a stone construction forming a pipe for the evacuation of smoke high into the air—which is to say, for an abstraction. Now, the only possible reason for the present dictionary is precisely to demonstrate the error of that sort of definition.

"It should be stressed, for example, that a chimney is only very tentatively of a wholly mechanical order. Hardly has it risen towards the first covering cloud, hardly has the smoke coiled round within its throat, than it has already become the oracle of all that is most violent in our present-day world, and this for the same reason, really, as each grimace of the pavement's mud or of the human face, as each part of an immense unrest whose order is that of a dream, or as the hairy, inexplicable muzzle of a dog. That is why, when placing it in a dictionary, it is more logical to call upon the little boy, the terrified witness of the birth of that image of the immense and sinister convulsions in which his whole life will unfold, rather than the technician, who is necessarily blind (Bataille, 1995: 51).

"**Formless**—A dictionary would begin as of the moment when it no longer provided the meanings of words but their tasks. In this way *formless* is not only an adjective having such and such a meaning, but a term serving to declassify, requiring in general that every thing should have a form. What it designates does not, in any sense whatever, possess rights, and everywhere gets crushed like a spider or an earthworm. For academics to be satisfied, it would be necessary, in effect, for the universe to take on a form. The whole of philosophy has no other aim; it is a question of fitting what exists into a frock-coat, a mathematical frock-coat. To affirm on the contrary that the universe resembles nothing at all and is only formless, amounts to saying that the universe is something akin to a spider or a gob of spittle" (Bataille, 1985: 31).

Comment

- Bataille is a major figure of electrate theory. "Factory Chimney" is a prototype for an experience of "extimacy" (the outside disaster or problem forms an image of an interior feeling) that is typical of modernist poetic reason, and that shows in a nutshell the method of consulting.
- We will return to "formless" at the end of the project as the name for a new dimension of value associated with electracy. Notice that the invention of an electrate practice of imaging begins with a contrast or opposition: the new practice comes into thought first as something that is not just different from, but opposite to, that which is the established practice. The passage from Plato to Bataille is stated as the opposition between Form and Formless.

Exercise: Counter-Dictionary

Using Bataille as a model, compose an antidefinition entry for his Critical Dictionary.

- The feature of the antidefinition of most interest to us is the way that Bataille establishes a relationship between himself and the "thing." The focus of the account is not the "essential" properties of the chimney ("a stone construction forming a pipe for the evacuation of smoke high into the air"), but the properties or attributes that transform the thing into an image or figure of an invisible, inner condition or state of mind of the child being hailed by the factory system as a way of life. Bataille extends the metaphorical operation at the heart of word formation and growth (the process in "culture" for example of transferring agricultural cultivation into human social husbandry) to include lyrical or poetic figuration, so that the factory chimney becomes an image of his own inner experience of living in an industrial civilization.

- As egents we learn how to bring to bear this kind of reasoning on public problem solving.

OFFICE

The Office sections represent an imagined office hours, a review of where we are at this point. The statements here resemble a Frequently Asked Questions list, attempting to anticipate some of the problems you may be having with the assignments and project.

1. The first quarter of the mystory was introduced: Career. I used to call this quarter "Discipline," but too many of you assumed this term meant "punishment," which is partly true, but the immediate sense here is "specialized knowledge." "Career" has the advantage of being more general, to include not just theoretical knowledge but any field of study in which you might major. Part of the point is to call attention to the fact that our project and my approach to it is legitimate and makes sense only or specifically in the context of specialized knowledge. A better grasp of the peculiar assumptions of my career field may be achieved when you are thinking about the peculiarities of your own major and related career plans. Electracy, grammatology, and the other features of our project are no more part of common sense than are the formalities of law, medicine, engineering, political science, psychology, business, and so on.

2. You should be making the first installment of the widesite, working with a problem, invention, or "star" of your career or major. This project is amenable to production on paper as well, using photocopy for the pictures and graphics. The basic logic of assemblage and collage directing digital cut and paste authoring may be applied in any medium. In my case, I foregrounded the invention of the "thing" and the practice of "definition," by Aristotle.

3. Many of the students in my classes have never made a website before, although most are familiar with the internet and have used email, chatrooms, and the like. Since my courses are not in art or design we do not worry very much, especially early on, about aesthetic quality of layout. We learn the basics of HTML tags, and I introduce most of the graphics tools we have on our system during the first few weeks. My assignments include requirements stated in terms of quantity and feature: the site must be approximately ten "pages" (ten HTML files), a mix of text and picture, and at least one animated gif. We use image searches on the web to find pictures, and these are brought into graphics programs for editing and modification. The idea is to introduce all the tools available right at the beginning, to use them all on the first assignment, to get a

feel for how they work. My evaluation addresses design issues but without lowering the grade at this point for problems, such as failure to account for loading time in the memory requirements of each file.

4. The lectures, examples, and citations simulate the readings and demonstrations presented in my course. Discussion in class and in email is conducted as brainstorming whose goal is to produce a "guide" or "handbook" of instructions induced from the assigned materials. The assumption is that there are many ways to accomplish our goal, but our experiment is taking a particular approach, bringing to bear contemporary theory and arts on our project. You should base your plans and designs on the instructions you are able to extract from the assigned materials, to test their claims and potential. It is an experiment, provisional, and open to question, once the trial is completed.

5. Our project is an experiment in heuretics (the logic of invention). The principle is that any hermeneutics (a way to interpret works) may be transformed into heuretics (a procedure for generating new work). The image of wide scope, for example, began as an interpretation of the lives of a large sample of productive or creative people. The wide image was discerned as a pattern repeated through the works of these makers. Our heuretic premise is that it should be possible to use the wide image principle as a way to make a new work (the widesite). Our minimum claim is that making a widesite provides a significant learning experience, within the humanistic commitment to self-knowledge. The maximum claim is that people who know their wide image may use it to make decisions and solve problems in their professional and personal lives. If you win the Nobel Prize someday, I want some of the credit.

6. The great Russian novelist Leo Tolstoy told the story of an army general who died and went to heaven. Showing the general around heaven, St. Peter inquired if he would like to meet the greatest military genius who ever lived. Of course the general eagerly agreed, and was soon introduced to a Russian peasant, a serf who died in the thirteenth century without ever participating in a single battle. St. Peter then clarified that the peasant would have been the greatest military genius, if he had been given the chance.

Chapter 2
Image

LECTURE
How the Image Becomes Categorical (Electracy)

The description of the invention of the founding practices of literacy in the first chapter provides an analogy for what is needed and where to look for it in electracy. The analogy shows that when the Greeks recorded the words of the epics (*The Illiad, The Odyssey*) in writing, they eventually noticed a pattern of words that had been overlooked in oral performance. Something similar is going on today in entertainment, the institution that so far is making the most of electrate technologies. In its first hundred years of existence, cinema devoted itself to the adaptation to film of the library of classic literature. In principle, the analogy predicts that some quality or feature of this literature that went unnoticed in its printed form would become discernible when recorded in photography. In fact several theorists have noticed a new dimension of order, a category of meaning, in photography in general, and the film still in particular, among them the French theorist, Roland Barthes.

Comment

- While you are still working on the Career quarter of the widesite, I develop the analogy that we are using to invent a writing practice for electracy. This chapter is devoted to describing how the image (both verbal and pictorial) becomes a method, taking up where the antidefinition left off, to become a positive ordering operation in its own right. You will apply this image method in designing the widesite.

Roland Barthes   The grammatological analogy suggests that we may find the beginnings of our image alternative to the definition by observing closely the *photographs of things*. Barthes's discussion of photography was couched in terms of reading or looking at photos, but it may be extended as a relay for *taking* photographs as well. What Barthes discovered or observed emerging within photography is a new dimension of signification that he named with a neologism, *signifiance*, characterized as a meaning that is "obtuse"—a "third meaning," neither literal nor figurative. Barthes' last book, *Camera Lucida,* is devoted to this obtuse signifiance, ("signifierness" in the translation hazarded by Bruce Fink) taking as its primary example a photograph of Barthes's mother when she was a child. This setting links the discovery of the obtuse with the experience of identification and "mourning."

The meanings that are namable in a photograph are called "studium" (constituted by the public encyclopedia of concepts) and the obtuse meanings "punctum"—that which stings or pricks one emotionally. The photograph produces a feeling that we associate with the experience of recognition and epiphany. In relation to the theory of interpellation, studium or "secondary" meanings are the given cultural meanings that we understand at once (or that are public and hence may be established objectively through research). The familiarity of a zombie in a horror film is a studium effect. Nor is there anything esoteric about third meanings. The punctum juxtaposes to ideological (mis)recognition an alternative, a personal memory based not on the public archive but a private repertoire. The subversiveness of this move is not in the content but just in the effect of having two databases to call upon, to slow the fixation of meaning, to interrupt the exchange: two cliches are better than one (the availability of this switch provokes awareness). Whether in reading or in making, one does not plan or intend an obtuse meaning, neither to include nor exclude this dimension.

The material cause of the punctum that stings the viewer is some detail (some accident) in the photograph. In a picture of a family of American blacks, the spectacle of their household interests Barthes, but he is stung by "the belt worn low by the sister," and above all "by her strapped pumps" (being out of fashion, they refer him to a specific date in time) (43). The key to the method, and to the obtuse as an experience, is in the relationship between the detail in the image and the memories and their associated emotions that the detail awakens in the viewer.

> "However lightning-like it may be, the punctum has, more or less potentially, a power of expansion. This power is often metonymic. There is a photograph by Kertesz (1921) which shows a blind gypsy violinist being led by a boy; now what I see, by means of this 'thinking eye' which makes me add something to the photograph, is the dirt road; its texture gives me the certainty of being in Central Europe; I perceive the referent (here, the photography really transcends itself: is this not the sole proof of its art? To annihilate itself as medium, to be no longer a sign but the thing itself?), I recognize, with my whole body, the straggling villages I passed through on my long-ago travels in Hungary and Rumania." (45)

Here is the key to reasoning in the electronic digital apparatus. The language apparatus is a prosthetic memory—an artificial memory that augments and extends the power of living organic human memory. And each apparatus has its own way of performing this supporting function. This power of a photograph *to stimulate involuntary personal memory* is the point of departure for an electrate institutional practice. Every feature of our mystorical search for the wide image follows from this insight. To make a mystory is to record the obtuse meanings of information in each of the institutions of the maker's experience.

The detail in the image attunes Barthes to the setting, objects, characters of the scene in a way mapped by the inside-outside figure of a moebius strip. "The punctum, whether or not it is triggered, it is an addition: it is what I add to the photograph and what is nonetheless already there. To Lewis Hine's retarded children I add nothing with regard to the degenerescence of the profile: the code expresses this before I do, takes my place, does not allow me to speak; what I add—and what of course is already in the image—is the collar, the bandage. . . . Once there is a punctum, a blind field is created (is divined)" (57). The punctum, then, occurs when there is a match between a signifier in the scene (in the photograph), and a scene in memory. Our goal is to develop an institutional practice capable of supporting and augmenting this memorial feature that Barthes called "obtuse."

It is important to remember that the obtuse or "third" meaning has been at work all along, but that the literate apparatus was not suited to exploit it fully. We are speaking of an imaging technology, and the arts never left off making images throughout the epoch of literacy, even if images rarely were granted cognitive, let alone scientific, status. In attempting to communicate his discovery, Barthes returned a number of times to an analogy with one art form in particular—haiku poetry.

> "A detail overwhelms the entirety of my reading: It is an intense mutation of my interest, a fulguration. By the mark of something, the photograph is no longer 'anything whatever.' This something has triggered me, has provoked a tiny shock, a satori, the passage of a void (it is of note that its referent is insignificant). . . . A trick of vocabulary: we say 'to develop a photograph'; but what the chemical action develops is undevelopable, an essence (of a wound), what cannot be transformed but only repeated under the instances of insistence (of the insistent gaze). This brings the Photograph (certain photographs) close to the haiku. For the notation of a Haiku, too, is undevelopable: everything is given, without provoking the desire for or even the possibility of a rhetorical expansion. In both cases we might (we must) speak of an intense immobility; linked to a detail (to a detonator), an explosion makes a little star on the pane of the text or of the photograph." (49)

Michel Leiris on the Verbal Obtuse

The obtuse as a mode of meaning specific to image memory functions also with words as images. Michel Leiris's description of obtuse memory response as the "personal sacred"—with respect to art, places, and behaviors as well as to words—expresses an important feature of chora.

> "I want to speak of certain events of language, of words in themselves rich in repercussions, or words misheard or misread that abruptly trigger

a sort of vertigo at the instant in which one perceives that they are not what one had thought before. Such words often acted, in my childhood, as *keys*, either because surprising perspectives were opened through their very resonance or because, discovering one had always mutilated them, suddenly grasping them in their integrity somehow seemed a revelation, like a veil suddenly torn open or some outburst of truth.

"Some of these words, or expressions, are bound up in places, circumstances, images whose very nature explains the emotional power with which they were charged. I think of the 'Empty Hall,' for example, the name my brothers and I had given a group of rocks forming a sort of natural dolmen, in the vicinity of Nemours, not far from the house where our parents took us several years in a row to spend summer vacation. The 'empty hall'; it sounds the way our voices sounded beneath the granite vault; it evokes the idea of a giant's deserted home, or a temple whose impressive dimensions were hewn from stone of tremendous age.

"A proper name such as 'Rebecca' learned from biblical history, belongs to the strict realm of the sacred, evoking as it does an image that was typically biblical for me: a woman whose face and arms were bronzed, wearing a long tunic, with a full veil on her head, a pitcher on her shoulder and resting her elbow on the well's coping. In this instance, the name itself played in a specific way, making one think, on the one hand, of something sweet and spicy, like raisins or muscal grapes; on the other hand of something hard and unyielding, because of the initial 'R' and especially the '. . . cca' that has some of the same effect today in words like 'Mecca' or 'impeccable'" (Leiris, 1988: 29).

Exercise: Obtuse Meanings

Test Barthes's way of looking at photographs for yourself. Select several photographs to work with, including examples published in magazines and some of your own snapshots. Similarly, write a definition of a word using Leiris's verbal punctum.

- Studium meanings are found in encyclopedias. Punctum or obtuse meanings are images that may be gathered into felts rather than texts.

Haiku Reason

Barthes's analogy—explaining the nature of the photographic image by analogy with a tradition of Japanese poetry—indicates several important points about image reason:

- "image" refers to verbal as well as to pictorial practices.

- imaging is not new in itself, but in electracy it is augmented by the digital prosthesis, and thus acquires a new dimension supporting a new order of thought and expression.

- electracy extends poetic and art imaging into a general practice of language, used by all citizens for quotidian, personal, and specialized thought and expression.

Barthes pursues the implications of his analogy between the photograph and haiku by writing a book on Japan—*The Empire of Signs*. His method for investigating Japan is to treat the nation and its culture as an image, which he studies at the obtuse or third level of meaning. Part of the value of Barthes's example in our context (the invention of the practices of electracy by analogy with the invention of literacy), is that he explicitly contrasts haiku with the practices of literate logic, including the definition, the syllogism, and other forms and procedures invented by Aristotle.

- haiku is not a model but a relay showing how to move beyond the antidefinition of modernist poetics to the use of imaging as a mode of reason. The lesson is not to abandon logic for poetry, but to see that images may be a mode of logic that opens up a different dimension of experience for thought.

- Barthes's turn to Asian arts for this relay continues a practice of the vanguard dating back to the late nineteenth century. For a time such moves away from Western reason to non-Western models was misunderstood as "primitivism" (politically and ethically suspect for overvaluing the traits of non-Western societies that previously had been undervalued during the height of European colonialism).

- in grammatology, "primitivism" is understood rather as "syncretism": a hybrid merging of Western practices with the practices of other traditions and cultures. The West and East (North and South) are mutually undergoing adaptation and crosscultural metamorphosis.

Roland Barthes on Haiku

"What disappears in the haiku are the two basic functions of our (age-old) classical writing: on the one hand, description (the boatman's grass stem, the pine tree's shadow, the smell of fish, the winter wind are not described, i.e., embellished with significations, with moralities, committed as indices to the revelation of a truth or of a sentiment: meaning is denied to reality; furthermore, reality no longer commands even the meaning of reality); and on the other, definition; not only is definition transferred to gesture, if only a graphic gesture, but it is also shunted toward a kind of inessential—eccentric—efflorescence of the object, as one Zen anecdote puts it nicely, in which the master awards the prize for definition (what is a fan?) not even to the silent, purely gestural illustration of function (to wave the fan), but to the invention of a chain of aberrant actions (to close the fan and scratch one's neck with it, to reopen it, put a cookie on it and offer it to the master). Neither describing nor defining, the haiku (as I shall finally name any discontinuous feature, any event of Japanese life as it offers itself to my reading), the haiku diminishes to the point of pure and sole designation. It's that, it's thus, says the haiku, it's so. Or better still: so! it says, with a touch so instantaneous and so brief (without vibration or recurrence) that even the copula would seem excessive, a kind of remorse for a forbidden, permanently alienated definition. Here meaning is only a flash, a slash of light: . . . . What is designated is the very inanity of any classification of the object: nothing special, says the haiku, in accordance with the spirit of Zen; the event is not namable according to any species, its speciality short circuits: like a decorative loop, the haiku coils back on itself, the wake of the sign which seems to have been traced is erased: nothing has been acquired, the word's stone has been cast for nothing: neither waves nor flow of meaning" (Barthes, 1982: 82–84).

Comment

- Barthes reminds us that haiku is practiced within a larger context of a Zen Buddhist worldview in general, and is related in particular to the pedagogy or educational instruction method based on the koan—the riddles, anecdotes, or questions posed by the master to the disciple within a discipline and training whose goal is to achieve enlightenment or satori.

- In haiku, Barthes says, things are treated not as substances but as events. "The haiku never describes; its art is counter-descriptive, to the degree that each state of the thing is immediately, stubbornly, victoriously converted into a fragile essence of appearance: a literally 'untenable' moment in which the thing, though being already only language, will become speech, will pass from one language to another and constitute itself as the memory of this future, thereby anterior" (77). In short, the haiku is an alternative mode of recording "thing." Aristotelian logic prescribed definition as naming the properties or attributes of entities that determine their substance. Western logic, that is, goes behind or below or transcends appearance to locate essence (concept). Eastern reason stays with surface, appearance, accident, and names the attributes that evoke a moment of experience (a mood).

- Barthes's juxtaposition of haiku and logic helps focus on the point that haiku is a relay teaching us a complementary mode of reasoning. "We seek at all costs to construe the haiku's tercet (its three verses of five, seven, and five syllables) as a syllogistic design in three tenses (rise, suspense, conclusion): 'The old pond:/ A frog jumps in:/ Oh! the sound of the water.' (in this singular syllogism, inclusion is achieved by force: in order to be contained in it, the minor premise must leap into the major). Of course, if we renounce metaphor or syllogism, commentary would become impossible" (72).

- The syllogism, also invented by Aristotle, is a calculus of two properties of individual things, allowing four kinds of sentences with respect to these properties: quantity (every, some) and existence (being, not-being). The four sentence types are universal affirmation, particular affirmation, universal negation, and particular negation. The three-line form links two sentences to reach a conclusion: all men are mortal (major premise: every M is P); Socrates is a man (minor premise: every S is M); Socrates is mortal (conclusion: every S is P). Of special interest is the terminology used to characterize the logical status of a statement as a "mood." Medieval scholastics assigned letters to identify the variables of "All = A," "Some Are = I," "None Are = E," "Some Are Not = O." "In the Socrates syllogism, all three sentences are the universal affirmative Type A sentences. The syllogism is thus said to be in the 'mood' AAA. Other moods are EIO, AOO, etc. All in all, there are 4 x 4 x 4, or 64 moods" (Rucker, 1987: 202). "Mood" here is what in dreamwork is called a "switch word" or in haiku a "pivot" word. The pun constitutes an important means of "conductive" inference, guiding movement beyond the given to connect with new semantic domains. The logical "mood" of the syllogism in literacy is supplemented by the poetic "mood" of haiku in electracy. It is worth noting that the *I Ching*, the Chinese Book of Changes, expressing the wisdom tradition that shaped Japanese culture, has a similar combinatorial arrangement, representing all human experience in 64 hexagrams or archetypal situations.

- Another lesson of the haiku relay for our project is that the wide image has no "meaning." It is a primary mood. The effect of recognizing it is that of "insight," related to "illumination."

We are pursuing Barthes's analogy with haiku at such length because it is the best source we have for grasping the possibilities of the obtuse dimension of the image, which grammatology suggests is the key to electracy. We are not interested in haiku for its own sake, but as a relay that helps us understand image logic. We will continue to explore this relay and learn as much as we can from it.

Basho

A brief look at Basho, an exemplar of the "*bhikku*" or spiritual wanderers of Japan, provides further perspective on the context of haiku. Basho's masterpiece, *Back Roads To Far Towns,* is a poetic travel journal recording in a prose poem style ("*haibun*")—punctuated by haiku—his nine-month journey (in 1689) with his companion, Sora, through the mountains and along the sea coast of the region between old Tokyo and Kyoto. "It was to be more a pilgrimage than a case of wandering scholarship: a sight not uncommon even in modern Japan, visiting from temple to temple, seeing old acquaintances, places famed in history or poetry or legend, touchstones for the life lived, the dying to come and what life continues" (Corman, 7).

> "Crossing the Natorigawa entered Sendai. Day of plaiting eaves with blue flags. Found an inn and stayed four or five days. Painter here called Kaemon. Had heard of him as one of not a little spirit and met. For many years he'd hunted up places once famous in the area but now obscure and one day showed us around. 'Hagi' [bush clover, tiny pink or white blossoms] so thick in Miyagi Fields, could sense what fall must be like. Tamada, Yokono, and at Tsutsuji-ga-oka 'asebi' flowers [small white bell-shaped clusters] near peak bloom. Went through pine woods so dense sun can't penetrate, place called Konoshita. Once long ago the heavy dewfall led to, 'Attendants, an umbrella' being written here. Visited the Yakushi-do and Tenjin Shrine, and some other places as sun descended. And he showed and gave us sketches of parts of Matsushima and Shiogama. And added two pairs of straw sandals, cords dyed dark-blue, as 'hanamuke.' So, indeed, was he seen as one of true 'furyu.'
>
> *ah to have blue flags*
> *bound to one's feet*
> *straw sandal cords" (Basho, 67).*

Especially instructive is the talent of the Japanese for articulating their aesthetic categories, classifying the effects and devices that produce them. Basho reveals "state of mind" as the meaning of "mood" in this context. He shows how to bring into an image (a text of word and picture) the mood of a place and time (mood is "obtuse" in its function of connecting the person with things). Basho called "slenderness" the ability "to immerse himself into the heart of an object or an incident and to catch the impersonal mood it shares with the universe" (Ueda, 1995: 160). The experience was that of attunement (but which Basho called "inspiration"): "If you get a flash of insight into an object, record it before it fades away in your mind." The method was to "let there not be a hair's breadth separating your mind from what you write. Quickly say what is in your mind; never hesitate at that moment" (162). The state of mind that Basho sought, as might be expected in the context of his Buddhism, had all the attributes of what stoic sages in the West called "ataraxy"—serenity, quiet, ascetic distancing from desires. "For Basho, sorrow was the word to describe life and the world at large; in his view this life was a 'demoniac world of the lusts' and mankind was 'drowning in a filthy ditch'" (155). The poet did not withdraw from ordinary life, but lived within it unperturbed, to the extent at least that he could sustain the state of mind he called "loneliness"—distinguished from "sorrow" by being an "impersonal emotion." This desired state of mind is *"sabi,"* derived from *"sabishi."*

Loneliness—
Standing amid the blossoms,
A cypress tree.

The effect of *sabi* was achieved by means of "shiori," referring to language that is flexible, supporting productive ambiguity. The verb meaning "to bend" (flexibility) is homophonous with the verb "to wither," and in Basho's poetics the two terms merged, to give the instruction that the sabi mood could be produced by the image of a "withering flower" (158).

Exercise: Haiku Design

Experiment with haiku reason and aesthetic principles in the prose and logic you use in your website.

- Haiku is a good relay for writing on the web. The lesson has nothing to do with the literal use of this poetic form (counting syllables etc.) and everything to do with the principles of brevity and aesthetic design. Think in terms of the "survival" of your words in the flood of language circulating in cyberspace. To be noticed and remembered your writing needs to be "in shape."
- We are not interested in "poetry" for its own sake but as a relay for learning a logic of imaging. We are using haiku as a relay to help us invent the electrate equivalent of the definition and paragraph.

Snapshots   John Frow clarified the links among Basho's poetics, tourism, photography, and the experience of recognition, declaring that "Basho's voyage is precisely a model of contemporary tourism":

> "The writings of the ancient poets establish the formal essence of the tree, and all later seeing is governed by the possibility of conformity to this pattern. Just as the tourist guidebook stipulates an ideal core of interest in the sight, so the authority of a poetic tradition that constantly refashions the essence of the tree, its normative beauty constrains the visitor to a recognition of a conformity between the particular, more or less contingent shape of the tree and its ideal form. The poem by Kyohaku provides a second modeling of the form for Basho, and his own poem confirms (like the tourist's photograph) not an empirical act of seeing but the congruence of the sight with the idea of the sight. The poetic record thus promulgates a form of knowledge that can be recognized in and has a greater force than the appearances of the world. What the traveler sees is what is already given by the pattern" (Frow, 1991: 124–125).

Frow's account shows how a poem and a photograph participate in the dynamic of schema formation (the mnemonic connection between concepts and images, abstract categories and particular embodiments). In the loosening or weakening of the absolute boundaries of conceptual categories that is the philosophical response to the coming electracy, the fact that when people think "dog" they tend to form a mental image of a specific dog, associated with their personal feelings about dogs, is no longer seen as a liability, but an asset. The challenge of electrate reason is to design practices that accept into logic the fact that categories possess an *obtuse* dimension. Literacy supported abstract categories, and electracy supports emotional embodiments.

Wabi-Sabi

Wabi-sabi is the cultural mood of Japan, its default aesthetic, developed over centuries, being to that civilization what the Classical Greek principles of harmony, proportion, and the like are to the West (Koren, 1994: 21). The purpose of following Barthes's analogy to this civilizational level is not to promote *wabi-sabi*, but to propose that the wide image functions for an individual the way *wabi-sabi* functions for a whole culture. Or, to refine the point further, part of finding our own "compass" or wide image involves locating the default mood of our own society and culture. The mediators between cultural default moods and wide images are artists, such as Basho, who show how an established mood may be configured to personal needs (how a shared language may be given creative expression). Our goal of course is not art but an electrate practice. Leonard Koren analyzed the Japanese national mood, showing how to move from particular details of appearance through to a worldview without a detour through "interpretation" or "meaning" in the Western sense (translating an image into an abstract disciplinary code such as Marxism, psychoanalysis, linguistics, or the like). The structure supplied by Koren will become a guide to the elements of the wide image.

The Material Register

1. Things   The image begins in a selection of elements. Basho explains that if you see a man dressed up for a party, and if that man is old, the effect has the color of *sabi*. The peculiar loneliness to which he attends is triggered not by peak states or conditions, but after the peak in moments of decline. Koren explains in his history of the mood that this state of mind became codified in the Tea Ceremony as a reaction against the lavish gorgeousness of Chinese decoration of rich display. Koren's example of an image evoking *wabi-sabi* is that of a nail in a weathered board, showing its age by a streak of red rust. The image may be in words or pictures or both.

Comment

* The egent seeking the wide image must select from all the information gathered from the popcycle the things that repeat across some parts of the popcycle.

2. Material Attributes   The material attributes selected by poets and painters working in the tradition of *wabi-sabi* tend to suggest natural processes. They are irregular, intimate, unpretentious, earthy, murky, simple (41). Anything that shows the effects of wear, whether as a flaw, blemish, damage, or aging, are the features selected for representation. According to Aristotle, such features are not essential but accidental. The essence of a bowl is not affected by its appearance. But the details of appearance convey mood.

Comment

- The things forming the initial pattern of the wide image (the "compass") must be inventoried to produce a list of attributes or qualities, to determine the properties available in the appearance of the things.

3. Atmosphere   The atmosphere evoked by these attributes is characterized as vulnerable, intimate, quiet, humble, unpretentious.

Comment

- The egent avoids interpreting the attributes and instead attempts to locate their objective sense as a setting associated with such features. Thus a bowl (thing) that is worn (attribute) evokes a rustic condition (atmosphere).

The Spiritual Register

4. Feeling   We pass now from the externally ascertainable qualities of things to the inner experience of them. The bridge is the connection between atmosphere and feeling. In this register the responses are more "arbitrary," or cultural. In the case of a national mood such as *wabi-sabi* the responses are codified and perceived by natives perhaps even as inherent in the external conditions rather than as achieved or invented. The emotional state of *wabi-sabi* is one of an impersonal loneliness or sadness experienced at a deeper level as pleasure.

Comment

- The equivalent of this consensus feeling for the wide image is found in the experience of "flow," the state of mind that one enters into when in the process of making or creativity. The premise is that the attempt to recover this core feeling is a strong motivation for creativity. A creative person learns to recognize and take guidance from the "excitement" experienced during making that opens a channel between one's project and one's themata.

5. Worldview (Metaphysics)   An informal or vernacular interpretation is manifested at this level, as the community or person infers from steps 1–4 something about the nature of the world. The *wabi-sabi* worldview based on the observation of nature, framed in Taoist spirituality, is that all things are impermanent, incomplete, imperfect, but that this unrelenting wearing away exists within a cycle of renewal. "What is the universe like? Things are either devolving toward, or evolving from, nothingness. . . . While the universe destructs it also constructs. New things emerge out of nothingness. But we can't really determine by cursory observation whether something is in the evolving or devolving mode. In representations of wabi-sabi, arbitrarily perhaps, the devolving dynamic generally tends to manifest itself in things a little darker, more obscure, and quiet. Things evolving tend to be a little lighter and brighter, a bit clearer, and slightly more eye-arresting. And nothingness itself—instead of being empty space, as in the West—is alive with possibility. In metaphysical terms, wabi-sabi suggests that the universe is in constant motion toward or away from potential" (43, 45).

Comment

- This *wabi-sabi* decision about the nature of the world is a cultural decision, and is based on a long history going back to the ancient Chinese cosmology of the forces of Yin and Yang, expressed in the *I Ching*. The conventional attention to all the nuances of the seasons in haiku (including the prescribed "seasonal term") reflects the influence of one of the two possible arrangements of the *I Ching* hexagrams or situations. The wide image similarly manifests the attitude or state of mind of the egent, although usually this stance is not recognized as a filter or position, but is mistaken for an intuition of objective conditions. Prior to the age of reason one has already made a decision about how the world works, about the nature of things.

6. Morality (Spiritual Value)   Based on the worldview presented, the person or community makes a decision about how one should act (ethics). Again this decision seems arbitrary on the face of it and must be understood within a context of individual or collective history. The question is how we feel about what we know (or believe) to be the case. How should one act in such a world? "Get rid of all that is unnecessary. Wabi-sabi means treading lightly on the planet and knowing how to appreciate whatever is encountered, no matter how trifling, whenever it is encountered. . . . Focus on the intrinsic and ignore material hierarchy. The behavior prescribed for the wabi-sabi tea room is a clear expression of wabi-sabi values. First, as a symbolic act of humility, everyone either bends or crawls to enter the tea room through an entrance purposely designed low and small. Once inside, the atmosphere is egalitarian" (59, 61). In sum, the *wabi-sabi* state of mind is "an acceptance of the inevitable, an aesthetic appreciation of the evanescence of life. All that remains of a splendid mansion is a crumbled foundation overgrown with weeds and moss. *Wabi-sabi* images force us to contemplate our own mortality, and they evoke an existential loneliness and tender sadness. They also stir a mingled bittersweet comfort, since we know all existence shares the same fate (54).

Comment

• It is obvious to someone from a different culture that many other attitudes, emotions, and modes of action are possible in response to this knowledge of inevitable entropy or wearing down of everything. For example in the West one encounters modernist beliefs in progress and improvement, or, alternatively, pleasure-seeking as expressed in the motto "seize the day" (*carpe diem*). Most people accept the default moralities of their culture and society in the same way they accept other aspects of the consensus themata. The discovery or invention of one's wide image gives a greater understanding of one's actions, whether liberal or conservative, active or passive, (and so forth), as well as making apparent the possibility of altering one's stance. This ethical dimension is especially relevant to the EmerAgency as a consultancy addressing civic problems and policy formation.

Comment

• You will recognize in Sections 4, 5, and 6 the template used by the students in the wide image surveys cited in the introduction to this book. The wide image is to an individual what *wabi-sabi* is to Japan.

Voice (Mood)

The haiku analogy shows us something like what we are looking for: a personal equivalent of a holistic mood. The principle guiding our project is that images as such, and wide images specifically, organize reason by means of mood. The issue is not *wabi-sabi* itself but "state of mind" as such, as the feature of mental life fore-grounded in electracy. In practical terms, electrate people reason, understand, and communicate in a manner that at present we see most clearly expressed by designers, such as Jasper Morrison.

Jasper Morrison on Designed Atmosphere

"Consider Industry working without design, what would the result be. Would we have objects which functioned very well? Probably. We'd have efficient objects, we'd have objects which fitted the right price and we'd probably have quite a confusion. For the customers it would become quite arbitrary which product they took. And the problem with all that might be that the objects which filled people's houses, which formed daily life, would definitely bring an atmosphere, because every object brings an atmosphere but would it bring a good atmosphere or a bad one, or a dull atmosphere, or an exciting one? For me Design's role is to improve atmosphere, to improve quality of daily life on the most fundamental level. That to me is the most important issue. And then from that comes a kind of duty to make objects which fulfill that role. . . .

"Sex is to some extent, and probably greater than one realizes, a powerful factor in creativity and that one probably puts into objects a kind of . . . sexual tension. Appreciation of form is also a physical thing and perhaps an object draws on the same level as human sexual attraction and objects can have a kind of eroticism of their own which is put there almost in an instinctive way. A bit difficult to explain. You can look at a garden rake made in this kind of bent wood structure and the way it's split and then rejoined at the end is extremely . . . I hate the word sensual, but let's say sexy, sexy is a better word" (Morrison, in Boyer, 1999: 67, 71).

In the widesite, if not in one's house, every object is designed. To write with images requires an understanding of the atmosphere and aura evoked by things, just as to write with concepts requires knowing the meanings of terms. In the institution and discourse of disciplinary career, we approach this experience of atmosphere through the stylistics of *voice*. The conventional rule for the first meaning of voice is clear: "always write in the active voice." The formulas may be quickly identified in any handbook:

"Direct kinds of sentences, active sentences place emphasis on the people and things responsible for actions and conditions. Passive sentences, on the other hand, are descriptive sentences that deemphasize the actors involved and instead focus on people or things that do not act. . . . Notice that the person completing the action can be totally absent from a passive sentence. . . . Because human choices and actions determine much of what goes on around us, give the credit or blame to the people responsible" (Perrin, 1987: 68).

How is instruction in these and other grammatical categories affected by the theoretical debates surrounding such questions as "who comes after the subject," debates that make it difficult to ascertain who or what is responsible for anything? Roland Barthes noticed that a third category of voice had emerged within experimental literature—a middle voice—based on the reflexive, self-conscious nature of modernist writing that claimed to be knowledge only of language, not of life. In the middle voice one is the recipient of one's own actions: responsibility is neither assumed nor avoided but is discovered as an effect of writing. Mystory is composed in the middle voice. Electracy in general shifts emphasis from the nearly exclusive attention to communication within the "I-s/he" system, to attend more to the "I-I" system. "The place of autocommunication in the system of culture," the Russian semiotican Yuri Lotman observed, "is far more significant than is commonly supposed" (Lotman, 2000: 21).

Comment

- This point should be emphasized, since literacy tends to foreground communication with others. In electracy, we could say that one of these "others" is the "self," except that "self" is the name of the literate experience of identity. What is the experience of electrate identity? We are beginning to explore it through the wide image (in which I learn about me).

Another grammatical category extended into electracy is mood. "Mood, indicated by verb form, refers to the way writers present their ideas and information. Sometimes writers want to stress the factuality of information (indicative mood). Sometimes they want to give commands (imperative mood). Sometimes they want to stress that information is conditional or contrary to fact (subjunctive mood)" (Perrin, 210–211). Voice and mood come together naturally in a literary context:

"It is relatively easy to distinguish between subject matter and mood. A group of poems on the subject of death may range from a mood of noble defiance in Donne's 'Death, Be Not Proud,' to pathos in Frost's 'Out, Out—,' to irony in Houseman's 'To an Athlete Dying Young'. . . . If a distinction is made between mood and tone, it will be the fairly subtle one of mood being the emotional attitude of the author toward his subject and tone the attitude of the author toward his audience" (Holman, 1972: 327).

Tone may include "color," referring to the sound of the words as equivalent to the quality of timbre in music (530). "Voice" is sometimes used as a metonym for "style," as when writers are urged to "find their own voice." In the performative categorization of electracy, voice is considered through all of its meanings simultaneously. Our hypothesis is that the modality of the screen is "virtual." The term evokes the holistic capacity of an atmosphere to accommodate statements that are true-false-secret-lies. Theorists have been discussing for some time the emergence in experimental literature of a middle voice, expressing a condition in which the subject of the sentence is its own object. The question is not "attitude toward" but "state of mind" framing and shaping these intentions. The stand is neither active nor passive but "middle"—reflexive. This reflexivity is made collective (interlinked and amplified) by means of the internet. To compose in the middle voice requires me to notice what happens in my body (emotions) when I introduce materials into my widesite.

State of Mind (Attunement)

We are generalizing now from the initial location of electrate reason in the obtuse power of images to cue memories, through the relay of haiku reason that demonstrated that images organize information through mood, to the "state of mind" as the dimension of human intelligence augmented by the prosthesis of digital imaging. We are applying to the linguistics of "mood" the metaphorical invention process we saw demonstrated with "culture." Jean-Francois Lyotard, in his study of Kant's *Critique of Judgment* (his Analytic of the Sublime), defined precisely the aspect of mentality addressed in electracy.

> "The possibility of universal communication, required of knowledge, must also be required of the 'mental state' accompanying knowledge. For all thought occupied with knowing an object is at the same time affected by its act of knowing and thus finds itself in a certain 'state': for example 'conviction,' which is a delight due to knowledge. By reversing the order, one could even say that this subjective 'condition,' this 'Stimmung,' i.e., the state in which thought finds itself when it knows, is also a 'subjective condition of . . . knowing,' a condition this time in the sense of a condition of possibility. If there were not a disposition of thought about which it was immediately informed and was favorable to its act of knowing, the latter would not exist for thought and thought would not know" (Lyotard, 1994, 100).

The questions that Lyotard pursues in his close reading of Kant are: "How can feelings orientate a critique? Why should the latter have any need for them?" (9). The answer he evolves over an extensive reading is that the "state of mind," a fundamentally aesthetic nuance, constitutes the reflective dimension of judgment upon the object of thought. In literacy, the apparatus split apart these dimensions of thought in the institutional practices, manipulating the object of thought in science, and the state of mind in art. The outcome has been a hypertrophy of the object of knowledge and the atrophy of state of mind (to put an extremely complex history into a simplistic binary). In electracy a state of mind is as writable as the object of thought. To find the wide image we must learn how to write and reason with our state of mind (attunement, Stimmung).

The notion of attunement invoked by Heidegger goes back to *Timaeus* (which in turn was informed by the Pythagorean notion of the "music of the spheres"). In his history of the term "Stimmung," Leo Spitzer noted the importance of *Timaeus* for figuring the world soul as musical. The importance of music in Classical education through the middle ages was based on the idea of morality as a tuning of the individual soul to this world harmony (Spitzer, 34). Heidegger revisited this tradition as part of his return to the Greeks, designating "*Stimmung*" as one of the existentials grounding one's being in the world. It named the ground of feeling that lets us know where we are "at," how we are doing, how things are with us or stand with us (in us), how we find ourselves to be (*Befindlichkeit*—"situatedness" or "state of mind") (Ballard, 1991: 33).

Dread and Wonder In electracy the linguistics of "voice" is extended to include the frame of reference covered by *Stimmung*. Translated as "atmosphere," "ambiance," "mood," "*Stimmung*" (whose root is "*Stimme*" meaning "voice," in the sense intended in studies of style—"tone") calls attention to the attunement of modern people as "dread," according to Heidegger, replacing the Classical Greek attunement of "wonder" (the feeling that gave rise to philosophy). Most importantly, a mood is not private, but is fundamentally a revelation of being-together, of a belonging, an intersubjectivity (hence a politics and an ethics).

> "Attunements are not side-effects, but are something which in advance determines our being with one another. It seems as though an attunement is in each case already there, so to speak, like an atmosphere in which we first immerse ourselves in each case and which then attunes us through and through. It does not merely seem so, it is so. . . . An attunement is a way, not merely a form or a mode, but a way—in the sense of a melody that does not merely hover over the so-called proper being at hand of man, but that sets the tone for such being, i.e., attunes and determines the manner and way of his being" (Heidegger, 1995: 67).

To find the wide image requires sorting out and noticing the singular way in which I relate to the default mood of my culture and civilization. "Which attunement are we to awaken for ourselves today? We can answer this question only if we know our situation well enough to gather from it which fundamental attunement pervades us" (69).

Rilke's "*Weltinnenraum*" was one source for Heidegger's understanding of how Being manifested itself to humans (his notion of the "opening" or clearing was borrowed from Rilke). In a scene of central importance to Heidegger's attunement, Malte Laurids Brigge in his walks around Paris came upon the wreckage or ruin of a house that had been torn down, and the object returning his gaze inspired fear (was a shock).

> "They were houses that no longer existed. Houses that were torn down from top to bottom. What was there was the other houses, the ones that had stood along

side them, tall neighboring houses. They were obviously in danger of collapsing after everything next to them had been removed, for a whole framework of long tarred poles was rammed aslant between the ground of the rubble-strewn lot and the exposed wall [. . .] But most unforgettable were the walls themselves. The tenacious life of these rooms refused to let itself be trampled down. It was still there; it clung to the nails that had remained; it stood on the handsbreadth remnant of the floor; it had crept together there among the onsets of the corners where there was still a tiny bit of interior space. You could see that it was in the paint, which it had changed slowly year by year; from blue to an unpleasant green, from green to gray, and from yellow to an old decayed white that was now rotting away" (Rilke, 1958: 46–47).

Later when Brigge is reflecting upon the experience, he uses the term "recognition." "I've been talking all along about this wall. You'll say that I stood in front of it for a long time; but I'll take an oath that I began to run as soon as I recognized the wall. For that's what's terrible—that I recognized it. I recognize all of it here, and that's why it goes right into me: it's at home in me (48)." Bataille had exactly the same experience of recognition with the factory chimney.

Heidegger showed that mood is the effect of a merger of the outer and inner worlds. He spoke of "attunement" rather than "correspondence" to name the way in which things may be known through moods, as in this example of a book that is "boring." The condition of receiving the instruction from this book in the state of mind of boredom is already a model for the functioning of attunement. "The book must make itself felt, not as an inducing cause, but rather as that which attunes us. This is where the question lies. If the book is boring, then this thing outside the soul has in itself something of the possible, perhaps even suppressed attunement that is in us. Thus, although it is inside, the attunement plays around the thing outside at the same time. . . . It does not cause the boredom, yet nor does it receive it merely as something attributed by the subject. In short: boredom—and thus ultimately every attunement—is a hybrid, partly objective, partly subjective" (Heidegger, 1995: 88). In Heidegger's terms, Basho's haiku mood of *wabi-sabi* is the name of an attunement. It is worth noting that Basho's method is discursive (and not only phenomenological). When he wrote in one of his most famous maxims that "one learns about the pine tree from the pine tree," he was exploiting the pun (also available in English) in which "pine" ("matsu") evokes both "waiting" and "tree" (Hirshfield, 1998: 95). "One learns about 'pine' [to pine] from the pine tree."

Comment

- In practical terms, attunement does for the image something we are already familiar with in argument or narrative. Argument, narrative, and image all deploy a two-part structure: one dimension reports a state of affairs ("content," facts, events, a world), and the other dimension reveals the maker's attitude toward that state of affairs.

- Why so much reference to Heidegger? Because he is a philosopher who credits the poets with bringing ineffable experience into language, making it available for further work. Poets are useful, albeit in a meditative rather than calculative sense.

Epiphany

James Joyce developed the poetic or secularized epiphany as a device for rendering the mood of a city (Dublin). His fiction shares the quality with much other modernist fiction of being an allegory for which no interpretive key exists. "When the material of experience assails us without our possessing its interpretive framework—when we notice that the codes of interpretation can be different, more open, flexible, and full of possibilities, and yet we still don't have the key for using them—then experience must show itself directly in the word" (Eco, 1982: 37). For Joyce this meant that "the form of the story becomes a revelatory image of an entire situation and is, using the categories of Stephen Dedalus, an epiphany. But it is not an epiphany–vision; it is an epiphany–structure" (37). Each story in *Dubliners* is described as one large epiphany: "key moments that arise in a realistic context. They consist of common facts or phrases but acquire the value of a moral symbol, a denunciation of a certain emptiness of existence. The vision of the old dead priest in the first story, the squalid inanity of Corley with his smile of triumph while showing the little coin in 'Two Gallants,' the final crying of Chandler in 'A Little Cloud,' and the solitude of Duffy in 'A Painful Case' are all brief moments that turn moral situations into metaphors as the result of an accent placed imperceptibly upon them by the narrator" (25).

Brecht's concept of the "social gest" is a culmination of this tradition, and is, according to Barthes, "the most intelligent concept ever produced in dramatic theory" (Barthes, 1977: 73). "[The social gest] is a gesture or set of gestures (but never a gesticulation) in which a whole social situation can be read. Not every gest is social: there is nothing social in the movements a man makes in order to brush off a fly; but if this same man, poorly dressed, is struggling against guard-dogs, the gest becomes social." (74). Collectively the moral scene of *Dubliners* is a vision of the city in a state of "paralysis" (Eco, 1982: 33). The wide image is a kind of "social gest" of one's mystory.

The question for the inventor of the modernist image, Baudelaire, was that of the failure of correspondence to function in the social world the way it had for the relationship with the nature in premodern cosmologies. "Nature is a temple, in which living pillars sometimes utter a babel of words; man traverses it through forests of symbols, that watch him with knowing eyes" (Baudelaire, 1964: 36). This experience of reversed observation in which things, events, people seem to look back at the spectator is what Benjamin describes as the effect of "aura." Benjamin's discussion is crucial for the practice of testimonial and theoria. "Experience of the aura thus rests on the transposition of a response common in human relationships to the relationship between the inanimate or natural object and man. The person we look at, or who feels he is being looked at, looks at us in turn. To perceive the aura of an object we look at means to invest it with the ability to look at us in return. This experience corresponds to the data of the 'memoire involontaire'" (Benjamin, 1969: 188). Involuntary memory and aura both involve "the associations which tend to cluster around the object of a perception" (186).

The theory of correspondences, Benjamin suggested, is what enabled Baudelaire "to fathom the full meaning of the breakdown which he, a modern man, was witnessing" (181). Of special interest for electracy is the evocation of the mood of "spleen" in the poems as the feeling of rage caused by the dissolution of correspondences, the loss of aura, the disappearance of meaning from the world, the very closure and shutdown of experience. Spleen is to Baudelaire what ataraxy was to the sages, or *wabi-sabi* to Basho. The following example of epiphany as an experience (as distinct from a literary genre) is doubly valuable since it explicitly involves the experience of the "gaze" as a field of attention. In an epiphany one may experience the gaze of places or things as well as of people.

Example: Jean Genet

"One day, while riding in a train, I experienced a revelation: as I looked at the passenger sitting opposite me, I realized that every man has the same value as every other. I did not suspect (or rather I did, I was obscurely aware of it, for suddenly a wave of sadness welled up within me and, more or less bearable, but substantial, remained with me) that this knowledge would entail such a methodical disintegration. Behind what was visible in this man, or further—further and at the same time miraculously and distressingly close—I discovered in him (graceless body and face, ugly in certain details, even vile: dirty moustache, which in itself would have been unimportant but which was also hard and stiff, with the hairs almost horizontal above the tiny mouth, a decayed mouth; gobs which he spat between his knees on the floor of the carriage that was already filthy with cigarette stubs, paper, bits of bread, in short, the filth of a third-class carriage in those days), I discovered with a shock, as a result of the gaze that butted against mine, a kind of universal identity of all men.

"No, it didn't happen so quickly, and not in that order. The fact is that my gaze butted (not crossed, butted) that of the other passenger, or rather melted into it. The man had just raised his eyes from a newspaper and quite simply turned them, no doubt unintentionally, on mine, which, in the same accidental way, were looking into his. Did he, then and there, experience the same emotion—and confusion—as I? His gaze was not someone else's: it was my own that I was meeting in a mirror, inadvertently and in a state of solitude and self-oblivion. I could only express as follows what I felt: I was flowing out of my body, through the eyes, into his at the same time as he was flowing into mine. . . .

"What I had experienced in the train seemed to resemble a revelation: over and above the accidents—which were repulsive—of his appearance, this man concealed, and then let me reveal, what made him identical with me. . . . I very soon reached the conclusion that it was this identity which made it possible for every man to be loved neither more or less than every other, and that it is possible for even the most loathsome appearance to be loved, that is, to be cared for and recognized—cherished" (Genet, 1985: 108–109).

Example: Maurice Blanchot: "The Disaster"   Maurice Blanchot recorded an epiphany that is at the heart of his *Writing The Disaster.* This "disaster" is important in evoking the dimension of "disaster" that the EmerAgency is designed to address.

"(A primal scene?) You who live later, close to a heart that beats no more, suppose, suppose this: the child—is he seven years old, or eight perhaps?—standing by the window, drawing the curtain and, through the pane, looking. What he sees: the garden, the wintry trees, the wall of a house. Though he sees, no doubt in a child's way, his play space, he grows weary and slowly looks up toward the ordinary sky, with clouds, grey light—pallid daylight without depth.

"What happens then: the sky, the same sky, suddenly open, absolutely black and absolutely empty, revealing (as though the pane had broken) such an absence that all has since always and forevermore been lost therein—so lost that therein is affirmed and dissolved the vertiginous knowledge that nothing is what there is, and first of all nothing beyond. The unexpected aspect of this scene (its interminable feature) is the feeling of happiness that straightaway submerges the child, the ravaging joy to which he can bear witness only by tears, an endless flood of tears. He is thought to suffer a childish sorrow; attempts are made to console him. He says nothing. He will live henceforth in the secret. He will weep no more" (Blanchot, 1986: 72).

Helene Cixous reads this epiphany as a "primal scene" in the Freudian sense, decisive for Blanchot's sexuality and gender, "his resistance to castration put in place by a kind of femininity" (Cixous, 1991: 21). In our context this is to say that the scene registers the subject's experience of interpellation. He knows at age seven that there is no "beyond." This is his "metaphysics," his personalization of the image of the yard of his family home in winter. The event is abstracted from a childhood memory that could be an anecdote for the Family quarter of the mystory.

Exercise: Illumination

Put into epiphany form a scene or memory from personal experience.

- If you have experienced a moment of insight, all the better. Using Genet and Blanchot as relays, describe the situation using sensory details of setting, props, people, event. The insight need not have been profound, but just that it was a moment of understanding or realization about yourself or the world. Even if you do not recall such a moment, use hindsight to recast an event of childhood in terms of an insight (as if you could have known then what you know now).

The Open   The notion of epiphany helps locate the point of entry into electracy attempted in our project. Heidegger's complaint about modernity was that its enframing or apparatus supported only one kind of thinking—the calculative (instrumental, empirical, utilitarian), in short, the kind of thinking applied in conventional consulting. The problem is that there is another kind of thinking, equally important to humanity throughout its history. The kind of thinking neglected in modernity is "meditative" (Heidegger, 1966: 46). The consequence of this neglect and imbalance is, so to speak, the hypertrophy of "outside" existence and the atrophy of the "inside" of individual life. Outside we have the hydrogen bomb, but without a power of thought equal to this physical power in nature. What meditative thinking permits is an experience of "releasement toward things," an "openness to the mystery." "Releasement toward things and openness to the mystery belong together. They grant us the possibility of dwelling in the world in a totally different way. They promise us a new ground and foundation upon which we can stand and endure in the world of technology without being imperiled by it" (55). Releasement is a state of mind related to ancient wisdom, of nonwilling. *"Die Gelassenheit,"* the translator explains, "although used today in German in the sense of 'composure,' 'calmness,' and 'unconcern,' also has older meanings, being used by early German mystics in the sense of letting the world go and giving oneself to God" (54). In the disaster Blanchot similarly discovered what he called "passivity."

Heidegger relied on the poets in general, and on Rilke in particular, for bringing this event of openness to things (the experience of being in the world, rather than apart from it as its master, as in the Cartesian and Baconian worldview) into language. To get a clear sense of Rilke's experience we may turn to Robert Hass's commentary on the "Duino Elegies," and the persona of the angel. Hass comments on this opening passage of the "Elegies."

> "Who, if I cried out, would hear me among the angels'
> hierarchies? and even if one of them pressed me
> suddenly against his heart: I would be consumed
> in that overwhelming existence. For beauty is nothing
> but the beginning of terror, which we still are just able to endure,
> and we are so awed because it serenely disdains
> to annihilate us. Every angel is terrifying.
>   And so I hold myself back and swallow the call-note
> of my dark sobbing . . . " (Rilke, in Hass, 1984: 256).

Robert Hass on Rilke's Angel

"The angels embody the sense of absence which had been at the center of Rilke's willed and difficult life. They are absolute fulfillment. Or rather, absolute fulfillment if it existed, without any diminishment of intensity, completely outside us. You feel a sunset open up an emptiness inside you which keeps growing and growing and you want to hold on to that feeling forever; only you want it to be a feeling of power, of completeness and repose: that is longing for the angel. You feel a passion for someone so intense that the memory of their smell makes you dizzy and you would gladly throw yourself down the well of that other person, if the long hurtle in the darkness would then be perfect inside you: that is the same longing. The angel is desire, if it were not desire, if it were pure being. Lived close to long enough, it turns every experience into desolation, because beauty is not what we want at those moments, death is what we want, an end to limit, an end to time. And—it is hard to think of Rilke as ironic, as anything but passionately earnest, but the Elegies glint with dark, comic irony—death doesn't even want us; it doesn't want us or not want us. All of this has come clear suddenly in Rilke's immensely supple syntax. He has defined and relinquished the source of a longing and regret so pure, it has sickened the roots of his life. It seems to me an act of great courage. And it enacts a spiritual loneliness so deep, solacing in consolation, that there is nothing in modern writing that can touch it. The company it belongs to is the third act of *King Lear* and certain passages in Dostoevsky's novels" (257).

Rilke of course reaches the extreme of the state of mind in question—profound longing—but anyone and everyone experiences it, as Heidegger says of meditative thinking. A more quotidian encounter with this inner space is sometimes recorded when people describe their experience of reading a favorite book in childhood. Sarah Ellis describes one such experience, again in terms that resonate with epiphany. In fourth grade she ordered through a school book club a selection entitled *Beyond The Pawpaw Trees* by Palmer Brown. The story is about a little girl named Anna Lavinia who travels alone to distant realms where she experiences things that happen only in dreams and fantasies. The story is not important here, but its effect on Ellis: "The moment I looked at the cover, with its scratchy drawing of a girl leading a camel across the desert, framed by a border of little objects—book, seashell, pot of gold, hot water bottle, hedgehog, curly-toes slippers—I felt myself going into a room in my head that had always been there, but that I had never before entered" (Ellis, 2001: 44). Ellis notes the miniature quality of the pawpaw territory, and this ability of the illustrated narrative to encapsulate in one graspable diegesis a complete world is an important element of how a wide image is constituted.

Comment

- We may seem to be saying more than you really need to know at this point, and it is true, in that we are running ahead, anticipating what you will not be able to experience until later in the process of making the wide image. You may appreciate why we need so much proof in the form of theory and demonstration, since the claim is that *yearning* or longing is put to work in electracy. *Wabi-sabi* is a version of this feeling, and each national culture has its own default mood of longing. German *Sehnsucht* is perhaps the most familiar Western form. The critic Georg Lukacs suggested that Socrates worked in the mood of *Sehnsucht*, in a dialogue such as "The Symposium," with the love of wisdom having its origins in Eros, the search for the beloved, as for the missing half of one's being. Research and pedagogy in literacy neglected this dimension of the Socratic paradigm, in favor of the dialectic.

The Natural Standpoint

The key point for mystory and the wide image is that interpellation (human identity formation) is possible because (in the terms of the humanities disciplines) there is an inner openness, emptiness, hole, incompleteness, that through introjection or interiorization of the outside (culture and nature) becomes formatted as American or Chinese or French, that is, reproduces the default state of mind of the world into which one is born. What the great majority of people do is line or fill this hole with whatever homiletic or stereotyped readymade stuffing the society supplies, in the same way that they are clothed and then clothe themselves with whatever fashion dictates. It is important to add that the inner clothing is as necessary as the outer for human survival. The introjection of default ego ideals produces the "natural standpoint" of the community, the consensus worldview that allows citizens to go about their daily lives without being overwhelmed by the risks and uncertainties of life. This natural standpoint is ideological in nature; it is all that "goes without saying." It goes without saying not only for political reasons, but for ontological or metaphysical reasons as well.

At the other extreme are the poets (artists, sages) who through considerable training have learned how to leave the hole open. The meditative mood was perfected in Zen Buddhism, which developed epiphany into a practice for achieving satori. "Mind and body dropped off; dropped off mind and body! This state should be experienced by everyone; it is like piling fruit into a basket without a bottom, like pouring water into a bowl with a pierced hole; however much you make, pile or pour you cannot fill it up. When this is realized the pail bottom is broken through. But while there is still a trace of conceptualism which makes you say 'I have this understanding' or 'I have that realization', you are still playing with unrealities" (Dogen, in Bancroft, 1979: 19). The emptiness of Zen mind (no-mind) is rather this openness, and the meditative technique is a means continually to "wipe the mirror clean," so that the circulation between outside and inside is unobstructed.

I am dwelling on this point for now since it sets the terms of our project to overcome the compassion fatigue of the spectacle in EmerAgency consulting and enhance the creativity of individuals and of society. Creativity, Giddens insists, depends upon an atmosphere of fundamental trust, existential security or safety.

Anthony Giddens on Emotional Inoculation

"Trust in the existential anchorings of reality in an emotional, and to some degree in a cognitive, sense rests on confidence in the reliability of persons acquired in the early experiences of the infant. What Erik Erikson, echoing D. W. Winnicott, calls 'basic trust' forms the original nexus from which a combined emotive-cognitive orientation towards others, the object-world, and self-identity, emerges. The experience of basic trust is the core of that specific 'hope' of which Ernst Bloch speaks, and is at the origin of what Tillich calls 'the courage to be.'. . .

"Basic trust is connected in an essential way to the interpersonal organization of time and space. An awareness of the separate identity of the parenting figures originates in the emotional acceptance of absence: the faith that the caretaker will return, even though she or he is no longer in the presence of the infant. Basic trust is forged through what Winnicott calls the 'potential space' (actually a phenomenon of timespace) which relates, yet distances, infant and prime caretaker. Potential space is created as the means whereby the infant makes the move from omnipotence to a grasp of the reality principle. . . .

"The trust which the child, in normal circumstances, vests in its caretakers, I want to argue, can be seen as a sort of *emotional inoculation* against existential anxieties—a protection against future threats and dangers which allow the individual to sustain hope and courage in the face of whatever debilitating circumstances she or he might later confront. Basic trust is a screening-off device in relation to risks and dangers in the surrounding settings of action and interaction. It is the main emotional support of a defensive carapace of protective cocoon which all normal individuals carry around with them as the means whereby they are able to get on with the affairs of the day-to-day life. . . .

"Creativity, which means the capability to act or think innovatively in relation to pre-established modes of activity, is closely tied to basic trust. Trust itself, by its very nature, is in a certain sense creative, because it entails a commitment that is a 'leap into the unknown', a hostage to fortune which implies a preparedness to embrace novel experiences. However, to trust is also (unconsciously or otherwise) to face the possibility of loss" (Giddens, 1991: 36, 38–39, 41).

Chora   This discussion of the epiphany and the image punctum prepares us for the mystory, which is a practice that activates meditative thinking, as an interface for calcuative thinking. Chora names a mediating space that coordinates the inner void, nothing, openness (Being) with the outer order of events (Becoming). Mystory is a genre that maps one's natural standpoint, and directs this co-ordination, with the electrate apparatus in its native nature being attuned to this emotional or mood dimension of human intelligence, in the same way that literacy is attuned to and augments the calculative or analytical dimension. The EmerAgency wide image project is a practice intended to develop digital computing as a *prosthesis* for this "potential space." It tests the premise that one obstacle to problem solving in the community is the natural standpoint, which constitutes a collective blind spot. The widesite as chora materializes this mediating time-space in a virtual mood that allows one to "toggle" between the natural standpoint of security and the open hole of chaos. It constitutes not AI, but AT (artificial trust).

OFFICE

1. These first sections introduce the background, rationale, methods, and assumptions that will prepare you for the rest of the project. The next quarter of the widesite will be introduced in the next section, and the exercises here emphasize our approach—not just to think about what we are learning intellectually, but actually to test the claims and to perform the experiment literally. It is not a matter of "believing" that creativity is dependent upon a person's image of wide scope, but to see what kind of learning is supported by a project designed with this claim in mind.

2. The punctum or sting of recognition experienced emotionally and intellectually when looking at certain images is the principal operating method of this project. We are taking an *image* approach to knowledge in general. The decision procedure for selecting which materials to include in each quarter of the mystory is guided by this experience of the obtuse meaning. This feeling of the relevance of some details of the information in question is partly intuitive, based on an ineffable source of attraction or repulsion, and partly a response to a pattern that begins to take shape in your mystory as you accumulate more materials from the different registers of your lifeworld. It is not only pictures that have a third meaning, but any unit of signification may provide a memory cue that sets in motion an associative chain of recollection, fantasy, speculation.

3. The epiphany or experience of revelation of the meaning or nature of existence is one degree of illumination that exists in a family ranging on a scale from the misrecognition of ideology (one is alienated in an image that comes from the outside and mistaken for one's own authentic being), through the following series of increasingly enlightened insights: recognition, the uncanny, eureka, anagnorisis (tragedy), illumination, satori. There may be some disagreement about the order of this list. The point is that there is such a family of experiences. This series as a whole is a "relay" to call attention to this bodily event of "recognition" that you must learn to notice and enhance.

4. To compose a mystory involves actively developing the epiphany as a form and an experience. The punctum is a methodological use of epiphany. In Genet's example, he discovered what we could describe as the "spiritual" side of his fundamental attunement, or of his wide image. Blanchot, too, describes the illumination as providing his understanding of how things are, the nature of Being. The point to stress is that our examples are relays: the poets and philosophers are to mystory as pedagogy, what professional athletes are to physical exercise. They are experts but what they are performing is possible and necessary for everyone.

5. The "yearning" Hass observes in Rilke's elegies is a universal experience available in daily life that is to electracy what geometry is to literacy: a common denominator, or baseline permitting a shared measure for communication across cultures, languages, civilizations, "differends" (incommensurable standpoints). The grammatological point is that this yearning is put into the apparatus and not left in the body: it is augmented and enhanced in the prosthesis of imaging, and not left to the limitations of organic mindbody, just as literacy did not leave measurement and calculation in organic mentality but augmented them in the institutional practices of school. A useful resource relevant to this mood is Susan Stewart, *On Longing: Narratives of the Miniature, the Gigantic, the Souvenir, the Collection.*

6. The point of the discussion about poets and epiphany is just that the basic device of aesthetic composition (metaphor, to put it in one word), marginalized in literate education, becomes central to electrate learning. The Ulmer File sections of the book should remind you, of course, of my argument with my father and Mr. Richards when I was in college (noted in the introduction). Long before I knew anything about electracy, I wanted the poetic image to be useful in the practical terms these men could appreciate. The argument of this book is addressed to them (they are the ghosts wearing the armor of problema). If this desire motivated my invention, the verification must be in the learning experience of the egents.

Part II
FAMILY DISCOURSE

MAP–Railroad Crossing, Miles City, Montana

"The tracks of the Northern Pacific Railroad make a diagonal slash through the town."

Chapter 3

Home and Family

Act I,1—the subject or protagonist begins in the ordinary world in which everything is normal and according to plan and expectation.

LECTURE
Narrative

The composition of the widesite is a narrative process, whose most familiar form is found in Entertainment discourse (to be reviewed in more detail later). The widesite itself is not a narrative, but the temporal unfolding of the search for the wide image has a narrative structure. Mystory in the context of the EmerAgency brings the egent into an explicit relationship with the process of identity formation, both individual and collective.

> "The existential question of self-identity is bound up with the fragile nature of the biography which the individual 'supplies' about herself. A person's identity is not to be found in behavior nor—important though this is—in the reactions of others, but in the capacity to keep a particular narrative going. The individual's biography, if she is to maintain regular interaction with others in the day-to-day world, cannot be wholly fictive. It must continually integrate events which occur in the external world, and sort them into the ongoing 'story' about the self. . . . Feelings of self-identity are both robust and fragile. Fragile, because the biography the individual reflexively holds in mind is only one 'story' among many other potential stories that could be told about her development as a self; robust, because a sense of self-identity is often securely enough held to weather major tensions or transitions in the social environments within which the person moves" (Giddens, 1991: 54–55).

The form that organizes commercial storytelling embodies the ancient myth of the hero. A guide to mythic structure for storytellers and screenwriters, authored by Christopher Vogler (a story analyst and consultant for Hollywood who evaluated over 6000 screenplays), is based on Joseph Campbell's *The Hero with a Thousand Faces*. Vogler's guide functions as a way to analyze existing screenplays, or to author new ones. It reflects the conventional wisdom of most such handbooks. This discourse, like the other ones in the popcycle, operates around the creation, exploration, and solution of conflicts and problems.

> "Act I, 1—the subject or protagonist begins in the ordinary world in which everything is normal and according to plan and expectation. 2—The call to adven-

ture: the subject is presented with a problem or challenge that will change her destiny. 3—The reluctant hero: the subject experiences fear of the unknown or fear of outside forces. 4—The wise one: a mentor gives guidance and support to the subject.

"Act II, 5—Into the other world/the first threshold: having decided to accept the challenge, the subject enters into action (begins a journey). 6—Tests, allies, enemies: many times the subject is able to glean information pertinent to this other world and to the adventure ahead in out-of-the-way gathering places. 7—The inmost cave/the second threshold: the subject comes to a dangerous place (mythically the land of the dead). 8—The supreme ordeal: at this step the subject must seem to die so that he can be born anew. 9—Seizing the sword: the subject takes the prize (the object of the search). 10—The road back: the subject uses his new wisdom to deal with the consequences of his actions, and declares a desire to return to the ordinary world.

"Act III, 11—Resurrection: the villains make one last unsuccessful attempt to defeat the subject. 12—Return with the elixir: the subject returns with a token of the journey" (Vogler, summarized in Kosberg, 79–83).

This outline maps the route ahead. We begin in Act I, in the ordinary world, the institution of Family—Home.

Comment

- Each chapter from now on progresses through the acts and sections of narrative form, which serves as a kind of interface metaphor controlling the release of information for the unfamiliar experience of making a wide image. Literate narratives are structured as mysteries, regardless of their theme, to the extent that the progress of the plot is a series of enigmas that are posed and solved (will the couple fall in love? will the castaway get off his island and return home?). Each of the readings in the chapters may be considered as a clue in the enigma of the wide image.

HOME(PAGE)SICK

Exercise: Homepage

Make a homepage.

- The first purpose of this exercise is just to introduce the term "homepage," which is to websites what "horseless carriage" is to the automobile. We will be proposing some alternative terms and phrases to name the index.html file in your www directory.

- Use a search engine to gather a representative sample of the personal home-pages to be found on the world wide web (WWW). Inventory the features these sites have in common.

Students come to my classroom with lessons of utility and practicality (calculative thinking) fully inscribed on and in their bodies, learned in the popcycle, including the entry into language and into the Symbolic order as such with its grid of classifications (class, sex, gender, race, religion, ethnicity, nation, and more). All their assumptions are organized in terms of contract and "circulation." They have been hailed by the natural standpoint of America. Perhaps if they were Tibetan, their natural standpoint would be meditative and I would have to teach them calculative thinking.

> "Besides the values of law and home, of distribution and partition, economy implies the idea of exchange, of circulation, of return. The figure of the circle is obviously at the center, if that can still be said of a circle. It stands at the center of any problematic of *oikonomia,* as it does of any economic field: circular exchange, circulation of goods, products, monetary signs or merchandise, amortization of expenditures, revenues, substitution of use values and exchange values. This motif of circulation can lead one to think that the law of economy is the— circular—return to the point of departure, to the origin, also to the home. So one would have to follow the odyssean structure of the economic narrative. *Oikonomia* would always follow the path of Ulysses" (Derrida, 1992: 6–7).

Comment

- Jacques Derrida is a French poststructural philosopher. Note the unusual pressure his vocabulary and syntax puts on his sentences. Of course the previous passage is a translation, but the effect is also felt in the French original. A more vernacular paraphrase might be something like "money makes the world go around." Taken out of context, passages like these function more as aphorisms, whose effect depends as much on aesthetic design as it does on argument. They also provide a certain ethos: proof by the force of reputation (like the effect of Tiger Woods selling golf balls). Philosophical style is to prose what a particle accelerator is to matter. The philosophy throughout the book is not needed to understand *how* to make a widesite, but to understand *why* this project is necessary for electracy. In this case I use Derrida to suggest that the metaphor of *home* in "homepage" is not innocent.

This experience of the circle, in fact, constitutes the nature of subject constructed as a "self" in the literate apparatus. The assumption of the apparatus is that electrate people do not experience their "being" as "selfhood."

The circular journey starts at home. The interface metaphor of "home" is already common parlance, even a dead metaphor, in the terminology of the Web. The point of departure is assumed to be "here and now." The students are to make their own homepages for the internet. The metaphor depends upon the utter familiarity of this "home" as *oikos*. How many times and in how many ways have we been told and shown that life is an adventure, whose prototype is the epic of Ulysses? In how many ways is the current embodiment of the odyssean type (the clever hero) put before us as the model and rule for conduct? This association of the circle of economy—referring to the movement not only of wealth but also of communication and sexual relations—with the story of Ulysses, helps to clarify the relation of the conventional humanities disciplines to capitalist society.

Alienation   The name and title "Ulysses" is a metonym for the canon (now contested) of liberal studies in the academy, a canon telling and retelling the metaphysics (experience of how the world "is") of selfhood. "The child-father analog for the individual soul and its one source," M. H. Abrams explained, "becomes the parable of an internal spiritual journey in quest of a lost home; and in this application Plotinus proposes an allegoric reading of Homer's epic narrative which was destined to have a long and prolific life in European thought" (Abrams, 149). From Homer to the homepage. The better the curriculum of the schools (in literate terms) the students attended before logging on, the more they have retraced the steps of the circuitous journey whose biblical prototype is the story of the prodigal son (164).

The canon provides a theodicy of the feeling that is supposed to be the antithesis of being "at home," whose covering term is "alienation"—the "primal fracture which results when man begins to reflect, and so to philosophize." Within the metaphysics of selfhood, this fracture or contradiction may always be overcome, reappropriated back into the subject. The Romantics, Abrams says, gave wide currency to this secularized version of the fortunate fall, a story into which is packed the composite wisdom of the entire Greco-Roman-Judeo-Christian tradition, which has become "the reigning diagnosis of our own age of anxiety: the claim that man, who was once well, is now ill, and that at the core of the modern malaise lies his fragmentation, dissociation, estrangement, or alienation" (145). The traditional humanistic plot of educational experience is figured, then, as a painful journey of "the conscious subject as it strives—without distinctly knowing what it is that it wants until it achieves it—to win its way back to a higher mode of the original unity with itself from which, by its primal act of consciousness, it has inescapably divided itself off" (191). Alienation in this tradition is felt as "homesickness"—"the yearning for fulfillment is sometimes expressed as *Heimweh*, the homesickness for the father or mother and for the lost sheltered place; or else as the desire for a female [or male] figure who turns out to be the beloved we have left behind" (194).

Homesick   Our point of departure assumes the default state of mind of "alienation." The mood guiding us toward the wide image—the yearning of Rilke's "Open"—is first intuited through the ordinary feeling of homesickness. Our method for bootstrapping into electrate rhetoric is to play on the slippage of meanings, the puns linking "mood" in the linguistic and psychological senses. The two are linked for a certain percentage of freshmen in their first semester at the university by the literal experience of homesickness, defined as a "reversible bereavement." Such studies as exist of this mood have been conducted with beginning college students. Although our culture does not sanction homesickness, which rather is denigrated as "childish" (Fisher, 1989: 26), those who find themselves in this distracted state may in fact be better prepared for the screen than for the page, since electracy includes emotion in its model of reason (Gelernter). This homesickness that within literacy is a distraction, a side-effect that interferes with education and success, turns out to be the most important qualification for the jump into electracy. How many inventions have been delayed by the inability to recognize a disturbance as an insight?

One problem in attempting to bring mood into education is that we have so little formal experience with it. The social scientific view of normal effective behavior is that it involves a decision-making process directed by the coordination of plans and goals. Making a decision is a focused sequence with four elements recalled by the acronym TOTE:

1. a (T) TEST or reality-check of my desires;
2. (O) OPERATE (action selected to resolve the discrepancy discovered in the test);
3. (T) TEST (repeat);
4. (E) EXIST (the stability that follows the resolution of the discrepancy) (Fisher, 1989: 82). This formula describes also the operation of conventional consultants whose job is to help eliminate problems, troubles, disturbances. To the macaronically abled (capable of noticing puns across languages, of the sort Joyce exploits in *Finnegan's Wake*), however, this acronym TOTE echoes disturbingly the German word for "dead." The analogy offered for an effective decision is that of driving a nail flush into a board.

The homesick person is not so efficient. A symptom of homesickness is the cognitive failure known as absentmindedness—a cross wiring or transposing that confuses one set of actions with an unrelated task (84). Something in the present environment triggers a memory (punctum), information from the past intrudes into the present, leading to a hammered thumb. This double consciousness, this "transference" that maps the present by means of the past, this short-circuit switching is just the relationship to decision making that is functional in electracy. An electrate state of mind includes a tolerance for nonutilitarian, inefficient, irrelevant events and experiences.

Exercise: Decision Scene

If driving a nail flush into a board is an image for a decisive state of mind, what is a good image for your manner of making decisions?

- Try to notice and describe the interactive relationship between different environments and activities and your state of mind. Begin with "boredom" and "homesickness." Have you experienced these moods? In what exact circumstances? What are the differences and similarities between these two moods? Make an image (picture and/or words) of each state to show what each one is "like."

- Try to notice and describe the state of mind you are in or enter when you are in such situations as the following: watching a movie in a public theater, watching a movie on TV, attending church, visiting your parents, studying in a library, taking a long trip by plane or by car.

- Homesickness is a vernacular, everyday version of the yearning or longing that we have said takes on logical power in electracy because of the importance of imaging in new media. The point of exercises such as this one is simply to help you notice the way mood and atmosphere are part of your normal experience.

The Two Economies

We need to know something more about "home" in order to relativize further the bias favoring "efficiency" in utilitarian consulting. Students are formed in the home (everything having to do with family and the hearth—"*oikis*"). The motive that brings them to the bricks-and-mortar university is economic in the specialized or "restricted" sense of accumulation, upward mobility, success in every sense assigned to that value by the bourgeois family. Hence they are under some pressure, some stress, some compulsion—their experience is structured by a problem, a conflict: the world resists their goals and plans. These are good students, who will do what is necessary in order to secure the grade, get the credential, become licensed, and move into the productive economy of the society, a situation about which they feel some ambivalence nonetheless. They are not necessarily "true believers" in the commodity spectacle. The modern person inevitably is in an alienated state of mind. Here is a default mood to count on.

In Act I, Career and Home are aligned within what the theorist Georges Bataille called the Restricted Economy. The narrative path ahead (Act II) takes us into a different realm that Bataille called the General Economy. To understand the peculiar stance of the EmerAgency as a consultancy requires an awareness of the relationship between these two economies.

Alastair Brotchie on Georges Bataille's Economies

"The world of accumulation is associated in Bataille's system with profanity, homogeneity and stasis. Monetary economy reduces men and all that is essentially human to the status of objects of exchange, to things, to economic slavery, and to the economically useful. Yet a world in which the sacred, myth, the heterogeneous and sovereignty are accorded their proper due is one in which relations are not based on the useful, but on expenditure and freedom: a world in which codes of immoderation, sacrifice and excess maintain a social structure which accords value to being rather than utility. Its expression is found in 'unproductive expenditure, luxury, mourning, war, cults, the construction of sumptuary monuments, games, spectacles, arts, perverse sexual activity.' This expenditure is the portion of the economy that opposes the forces of production and accumulation. In earlier societies the sacred established social cohesion, but in a society based on accumulation it can only represent its subversion.

"The forces of accumulation—in our day, of capitalism—are engaged in a struggle to increase their share of the economy, of life. They impose an order based on work alone—in which means become ends in themselves (i.e. work)—which is enforced by the imposition of a strict homogeneity upon social relations and activities. The attempt is made to exclude all aspects of the 'useless' from existence, activities are valued not for themselves, but for their accumulative worth, conventionally measured by monetary value alone. 'According to the judgment of homogeneous society, each man is worth what he produces; in other words, he stops being an existence for itself: he is no more than a function, arranged within measurable limits, of collective production (which makes him an existence for something other than itself).' [. . .]

"Bataille gave many instances of heterogeneous phenomena; he recognizes it as everything other or incommensurate, 'a force or a shock that presents itself as a charge.' It is characterized by violence, excess, delirium, and he lists 'the waste products of the human body and certain analogous matter (trash, vermin, etc.); the parts of the body; persons, words, or acts having a suggestive erotic value; the various unconscious processes such as dreams or neuroses; the numerous elements or social forms that homogenous society is powerless to assimilate; mobs, the warrior, aristocratic and impoverished classes, different types of violent individuals or a least those who refuse rule (madmen, leaders, poets, etc.).' (Brotchie, 1995: 22, 23).

We have another version of the distinction between calculative and meditative thinking. The egent must gain an awareness of the General Economy (the sacred and heterogeneous dimension of experience), in order to assess public policy problems from that point of view, and not only from the perspective of the Restricted Economy to which conventional consultants are limited.

Comment

- To say that egents consider policy problems from the perspective of the General Economy may seem to put them in the role of defense attorneys in an adversary legal system, in that in this perspective disasters are necessary and irreducible. Thus if the policy concerned termite inspections related to real estate, the EmerAgency would speak on behalf of the termites. The difference is that the General Economy does not oppose the Restricted one, but marks its limit. Egents have to testify to the existence of this limit, which, moreover, has a positive reality of its own. The paradox is that of the usefulness of the useless.

Mystory

The genre invented to capture a version, a first simulation, of the wide image, as an alternative to the oral epic and literate detective mystery, is called "mystory." Mystory does for postmodern persons what allegory did for medieval persons: allows them to locate their position in the popcycle of their epoch. Fredric Jameson is a theorist who noted the relevance of allegory to contemporary thought. Jameson calls for a "cognitive mapping"—a new collective logic, poetics, aesthetics that reconnects the dimensions of essence and appearance, truth and experience (or, with respect to the haiku relay, the epistemologies of the West and the East). When he mentioned "allegory" and the play of figuration as means of bringing into contact the different levels and scales of reality, Jameson established a context for mystory. He explicitly invoked medieval allegory as a relay for the discursive practice missing from modern society. The epiphany or illumination of insight at work in religious learning, whatever it might have been as an experience, depended formally on allegory. It is worth citing Jameson's description of the four-part medieval interpretive method (hermeneutic), since it establishes a structure whose functionality is not confined to any one cosmology or epoch.

Fredric Jameson on Allegory

"The Old Testament is taken as historical fact. At the same time, its availability as a system of figures, above and beyond this literal historical reference, is grounded in the conception of history itself as God's book, which we may study and gloss for signs and traces of the prophetic message the Author is supposed to have inscribed within it.

So it is that the life of Christ, the text of the New Testament, which comes as the fulfillment of the hidden prophecies and annunciatory signs of the Old, constitutes a second, properly allegorical level, in terms of which the latter may be rewritten. So the interpretation of a particular Old Testament passage in terms of the life of Christ—a familiar illustration is the rewriting of the bondage of the people of Israel in Egypt as the descent of Christ into hell after his death on the cross—comes less as a technique for closing the text off and for repressing aleatory or aberrant readings and sense, than as a mechanism for preparing such a text for further ideological investment, if we take the term ideology here in Althusser's sense as a representational structure which allows the individual subject to conceive or imagine his or her lived relationship to transpersonal realities such as the social structure or the collective logic of History.

"The movement is from a particular collective history—that of the people of Israel to the destiny of a particular individual. It is precisely this reduction of the alien collective to the valorized individual biography which then permits the generation of two further interpretive levels, and it is precisely in these that the individual believer is able to "insert" himself or herself, it is precisely by way of the moral and anagogical interpretations that the textual apparatus is transformed into a "libidinal apparatus," a machinery for ideological investment. On the third or moral level, for example, the literal and historical fact of the bondage of the people of Israel in Egypt can be rewritten as the thralldom of the believer-to-be to sin and to the preoccupations of this world ('the fleshpots of Egypt'): a bondage from which personal conversion will release him or her (an event figured doubly as the deliverance from Egypt and the resurrection of Christ).

"But this third level of the individual soul is clearly insufficient by itself, and at once generates the fourth or anagogical sense, in which the text undergoes its ultimate rewriting in terms of the destiny of the human race as a whole, Egypt then coming to prefigure that long purgatorial suffering of earthly history from which the second coming of Christ and the Last Judgment come as the final release. The historical or collective dimension is thus attained once again, by way of the detour of the sacrifice of Christ and the drama of the individual believer; but from the story of a particular earthly people it has been transformed into universal history and the destiny of humankind as a whole.

"The system of the four levels or sense is suggestive in the solution it provides for an interpretive dilemma which in a privatized world we must live far more intensely than did its Alexandrian and medieval recipients: namely that incommensurability between the private and the public, the psychological and the social, the poetic and the political. While the relationship the Christian scheme projects between anagogical and moral is not available to us today, the closure of the scheme as a whole is instructive:

Anagogical = political reading (collective "meaning" of history)

Moral = psychological reading (individual subject)

> Allegorical = allegorical key or interpretive code
> Literal = historical or textual referent"
> (Jameson, 1981: 30–31).

The registers or levels of our popcycle are different from those organizing medieval experience, obviously, but their nature and function may be understood
by analogy with the medieval example. In mystory the allegorical scheme is appropriated not as a means of interpretation but of invention, production, generation. The expectation is not to live an epiphany, but to write one, by
juxtaposing a modern equivalent of the allegorical levels. The wide image is revealed in this illumination as a pattern that repeats across the discourses of the
popcycle. Mystory is a holistic practice, designed as a way to compose simultaneously in four (more or less) discourses. It is a cognitive map of its maker's
"psychogeography."

Allegory Popcycle

Literal = School (elementary through secondary levels).   The historical fact
that grounds the figuration is not the story of Israel as codified in the text of the
Old Testament, but the history of one's nation, state, or community—the official
version—as codified in textbooks taught in elementary, middle, and secondary
schools. This history represents the memory of the collectivity. People educated
in alternative settings—homeschooled, religious or charter schools—may have
learned a different version of the community history.

Allegory = Entertainment (commercialized information and story).   The
interpretive "key" comes not from the "imitation of Christ" but from identification with celebrity stars. The discourse learned is that of cultural mythology encountered in popular genres (Westerns, film noir, comedies, soap operas)
carried through the media—television, cinema, newspapers, magazines, advertising. The entry into this discourse starts in the early preschool years due to the
ubiquity of television sets in the home.

Moral = Family (biography of the individual).   The individual is considered
in terms of his/her family upbringing, with the language being the one learned
in the home (English, Spanish, Creole) and the discursive regime being the
habits and customs specific to that family, as governed by such things as ethnicity, race, gender and the like.

Anagogy = Career (disciplinary knowledge).   The collective meaning of history is determined in mystory not by Christian theology but by the world view
embodied within the specialized knowledge that one acquires as an expert in
some given career field. This expertise may be disciplinary in the academic or

professional sense—physics, law—or it may be a craft, trade, sport (plumbing, football). This knowledge is the means by which one earns one's livelihood (work), but the knowledge of an avocation may be used instead.

Comment

- To undertake the search for the wide image we need two skills (so far). First, we must be able to notice and make use of our bodily experience as part of our reasoning—to use "recognition." Second, we must be able to use proportional analogies to locate our own position in the mystory relative to the positions of exemplary figures whose lives and works help us map the conditions of the popcycle.

- If I were to try to plug my mystory into Jameson's paraphrasing of the allegorical order, it might read something like this: The *textbook used in the Montana public schools* is taken as historical fact, grounded in the conception of history as the nation's book, which we may study and gloss for signs and traces of prophetic messages. So it is that the *life of Gary Cooper, playing Sheriff Will Kane in the film <u>High Noon</u>,* constitutes a second, properly allegorical level, in terms of which the history *of my home town (Miles City)* may be rewritten. Thus the rewriting of *Custer's Last Stand at the Little Bighorn River as the Sheriff's Showdown with the gang of killers* comes as a mechanism for preparing such a text for further ideological investment. On the third or moral level the literal and historical fact of *the taming of the frontier* can be rewritten as *my* thralldom to the preoccupations of this world (*the competition for personal achievements*): a bondage from which *commitment to scholarship* will release me. In the fourth or anagogical sense, the text undergoes the ultimate rewriting in terms of the destiny of *the society* as a whole redeemed through *the poetic image.* The collective dimension is attained once again, by way of the *detour of Gary Cooper's acting and the drama of my life,* but from the story of *a particular territory* it has been transformed into the story of humankind as a whole.

Example: James Joyce

The author who codified the odyssean circle as an allegory of education for the modern era is James Joyce in *Ulysses*—a novel of a day in the life of Leopold Bloom in modern Dublin, structured to parallel the principal episodes of Homer's *Odyssey.* Joyce with his Irish Catholic identity is a key figure in the transition from medieval to postmodern allegory. He explicitly acknowledges the power of the four-fold schema precisely in rejecting it in favor of its opposite pole—an artist's style. In *A Portrait of the Artist,* his alter ego, Stephen Dedalus, explains to Cranly his decision to leave Ireland: "I will not serve that in which I no longer believe, whether it call itself my home, my fatherland, or my church:

and I will try to express myself in some mode of life or art as freely as I can and as wholly as I can, using for my defense the only arms I allow myself to use—silence, exile, and cunning" (Joyce, in Litz, 1972: 18). Joyce's conscious rejection of the discourses of the popcycle in which he had been interpellated did not alter the fact that the values and practices of these institutions shaped everything he wrote. The effect of his declaration in practice was that he inverted the "anagogical polarity" of his popcycle, so that his destiny was guided not by the Christian cosmology but by his position within language as artist—what Lacan called his *sinthome* (symptom). The four institutions of the popcycle are foregrounded in most accounts of Joyce's stance (with Church replacing Entertainment). One does not have to "like" the popcycle institution for it to have contributed to the wide image. Joyce left it to the critics to describe his mystory, locating a key figure of identification (positive or negative) and the problem embodied in the life and/or work of this person, for each register. The premise of the mystory is that each discourse is organized around the discovery, definition, and (sometimes) solution of exemplary problems. To find our wide image requires a passage through the equivalent of these identifications in one's own popcycle.

THE MYSTORY OF JAMES JOYCE
History (School, Community)

The young Joyce's imagination was captured by the cause of Irish freedom, whose most prominent spokesman at the time was Charles Stewart Parnell, a national hero who suffered a tragic fall. "He was accused of adultery in the divorce suit of Captain O'Shea. At first it appeared that Parnell might weather this scandal, but a coalition of political enemies and devout Catholics ousted him from leadership of the Irish Parliamentary Party, and the rural population of Ireland turned against their hero with savage hatred" (Litz, 1972: 20). At Parnell's funeral crowds tore to shreds the case in which the man's coffin had been shipped in order to have a relic. Soon he became in the Irish imagination the type of the betrayed hero (21).

Church

Joyce's entire formal education took place in schools run by the Jesuit order. His most important religious experience occurred at Belvedere College, "when he was elected Prefect of the Sodality," that is, "head of a group of students who banded together for the purposes of devotion and mutual help." It was his duty according to the Jesuit manual "to excel the other members of the Sodality in virtue and to observe with the greatest diligence not only the rules of his own office but also the common rules, those especially that relate to the frequentation of the sacraments, confessing his sins, and receiving the Blessed Eucharist more frequently than the others, and he should take care to advance the Sodality in the way of virtue and Christian perfection, more by example even than by words" (28). Although Joyce broke with the Church, as Litz observes, this stance carried over to his "view of the artist as secular priest."

Family

Perhaps the defining problem of Home for Joyce was his ambivalence toward his father, whose chief interest in life was "jollification." "The declining family fortune had the greatest impact on James. The inefficiency of Joyce's father and his wasteful habits gradually undermined family finances and family solidarity. When James entered the fashionable Clongowes Wood College in 1888, his family was quite well-to-do; by the time he had reached Belvedere College, five years later, his father had been dismissed from the Rates office on a small pension. The family had now begun a long series of removals to cheaper dwellings" (19). For the mystory some details documenting the family's situation could be excerpted from Joyce's fiction.

Career

At age eighteen Joyce published a review of Ibsen's play, "When We Dead Awaken" in *The Fortnightly Review*. In a letter he sent to Ibsen, the student Joyce explained that while he promoted the dramatist's work at every opportunity, he kept to himself the most important reasons for his admiration. "I did not say how what I could discern dimly of your life was my pride to see, how your battles inspired me— not the obvious material battles but those that were fought and won behind your forehead—how your willful resolution to wrest the secret from life gave me heart, and how in your absolute indifference to public canons of art, friends and shibboleths you walked in the light of your inward heroism" (Joyce, in Litz, 24). A proper mystory would enter Ibsen as a document, represented by details of a scene from one of the plays, focusing on the conflict or problem organizing the story.

Comment

- The figures to represent each discourse are suggestions, to indicate that the popcycle identifications are at work in Joyce's life and art. The institution of Church must be included in the primary popcycle in Joyce's case, in place of Entertainment.

STUDIO
Structural Portraits

Exercise: Frederick Douglass

To gain some practice with locating correspondences or parable-like mappings across different stories, compare the following two excerpts. The first is from the autobiography of Frederick Douglass, telling of an incident during his life as a slave. The second is a summary of a Zen teaching story originally told in pictures. Both involve ox-herding. It is useful to know that Mr. Covey's job was to "domesticate" slaves who were considered by their masters to be "difficult" for whatever reason.

Frederick Douglass

"Mr. Covey sent me, very early in the morning of one of our coldest days in the month of January, to the woods to get a load of wood. He gave me a team of unbroken oxen. He told me which was the in-hand ox, and which the off-hand one. He then tied the end of a large rope around the horns of the in-hand ox and gave me the other end of it, and told me, if the oxen started to run, that I must hold on upon the rope. I had never driven oxen before, and of course I was very awkward. I, however, succeeded in getting to the edge of the woods with little difficulty; but I had got a few rods into the woods, when the oxen took fright, and started full tilt, carrying the cart against trees, and over stumps, in the most frightful manner. I expected every moment that my brains would be dashed out against the trees. After running thus for a considerable distance, they finally upset the cart, dashing it with great force against a tree, and threw themselves into a dense thicket. How I escaped death, I do not know. There I was, entirely alone, in a thick wood, in a place new to me. My cart was upset and shattered, my oxen were entangled among the young trees, and there was none to help me. After a long spell of effort, I succeeded in getting my cart righted, my oxen disentangled, and again yoked to the cart. I now proceeded with my team to the place where I had, the day before, been chopping wood, and loaded my cart pretty heavily, thinking in this way to tame my oxen. I then proceeded on my way home. I had now consumed one half of the day. I got out of the woods safely, and now felt out of danger. I stopped my oxen to open the woods gate; and just as I did so, before I could get hold of my ox rope, the oxen again started, rushed through the gate, catching it between the wheel and the body of the cart, tearing it to pieces, and coming within a few inches of crushing me against the gatepost. On my return, I told Mr. Covey what had happened, and how it happened" (Douglass, 1997: 69–70).

"The Oxherding Sequence" (Zen Parable)

"The ox is probably the commonest domestic animal in China, and is certainly the most useful. This sequence of images, in which ox herding represents the Zen life, was first painted in the Sung period, by a pupil of Lin-chi (Rinzai), and thus its origin is early in Zen thought. In the first picture the boy oxherd searches for a lost ox (his own spiritual life, lost because he has been led astray by his deluded senses; it is typical of Chinese Ch'an/Zen thought to take such a practical animal to represent the spirit). Now he is rootless and homeless; but with the help of the Sutras (second picture) he begins to see traces of the ox despite his own confusion. In the third picture the boy's nature is opened through sound; he sees the ox. In the fourth picture he almost has the ox, but because of pressures from the outside world, the ox is hard to control and struggles to return to its pleasant pasture. The boy has to be very hard on the ox. In the fifth picture the boy is just about controlling the ox, and in the sixth the struggle is over and he is on its back. He is no longer torn by the world of appearances, no longer concerned with gain and loss. He is indescribably joyful. In the seventh picture he recognizes the ox as a symbol and lets it go. He is now whole and serene. In the eighth both ox and man have vanished; the boy's mind is completely clear, and not even the concept of holiness remains. In picture nine the boy remains in immovable mind, seeing that waters are blue and mountains green, but not identifying himself with any change; 'Behold, the streams are flowing—whither nobody knows.' In the tenth and last picture he returns to the world, a free man, doing whatever he does with the whole of himself because there is nothing to gain" (Bancroft, 1975: 95).

Assignment: Family Discourse

Make a website documenting a scene that sticks in your memory from the childhood years of your family life.

- This assignment is the second major one in the composition of the widesite.
- The image pattern we seek for the widesite tends to be found in discourse materials generated around problem issues in each of the discourses.
- When we are born into a family we enter in the middle of an ongoing narrative. We already are a character in the stories of our parents, who have plans, hopes, fears for us that they project into our care or neglect as sons or daughters. The other institutions similarly have a ready-made position for us into which we are hailed as citizen, consumer, professional, and the like.

A good way to locate a productive scene is to use the categories of ideological identity formation as guides to likely sites of conflict or tension. The home is one of the principal training facilities of interpellation, in which the parents pass on to children the cultural and social expectations regarding race, ethnicity, religion, class, gender, sexuality, and the like. Social norms express the preferred values and behaviors associated with each of these categories ("hegemony," which in the United States has been, until recently at least, White Anglo-Saxon Protestant, Bourgeois, Male, Heterosexual etc.). Experience shows however that few if any individuals fit comfortably into these slots, not even the people who appear to be full embodiments of the collective ideals. Some of our stronger early memories often are related to a moment of self-awareness produced by the need to transform our natural inclinations in order to meet an externally enforced expectation.

Snapshots

Example: Annette Kuhn, Family Secrets   The British film theorist and critic Annette Kuhn composed a mystorical study using a series of photographs from her family album as the basis for her memory work. Applying Barthes's method of the sting or punctum, she unified her popcycle allegory around the way she is dressed in the photos, related to relevant images in the other discourses, drawn from entertainment, news, or historical documents. Each photo is "at the heart of a radiating web of associations, reflections and interpretations. But if the memories are one individual's, their associations extend far beyond the personal. They spread into an extended network of meanings that bring together the personal with the familial, the cultural, the economic, the social, and the historical. Memory work makes it possible to explore connections between 'public' historical events, structures of feeling, family dramas, relations of class, national identity and gender, and 'personal' memory. In these case histories outer and inner, social and personal, historical and psychical, coalesce; and the web of interconnections that binds them together is made visible" (Kuhn, 1995: 4). Within this web, supported and augmented in the prosthesis of the World Wide Web, also emerges the wide image. Kuhn provides a list of instructions for doing memory work with family photographs.

> "1. Consider the human subject(s) of the photograph. Start with a simple description, and then move into an account in which you take up the position of the subject. In this part of the exercise, it is helpful to use the third person. To bring out the feelings associated with the photograph, you may visualize yourself as the subject as she was at that moment, in the picture; this can be done in turn with all of the photograph's human subjects, if there is more than one, and even with inanimate objects in the picture.
> "2. Consider the picture's context of production. Where, when, how, by whom and why was the photograph taken?
> "3. Consider the context in which an image of this sort would have been made. What photographic technologies were used? What are the aesthetics of the image? Does it conform with certain photographic conventions?
> "4. Consider the photograph's currency in its context or contexts of reception. Who or what was the photograph made for? Who has it now, and where is it kept? Who saw it then, and who sees it now?" (7).

Kuhn's case histories of the photographs are sorted into the mystorical discourses.

Family   The photos selected to explore this discourse express the problem of gendering. "A mother's attention to the clothing and general appearance of a baby girl is part of the social, cultural, and undoubtedly also the psychical, construction of gender; specifically of femininity" (52). "She entered me in the contests, made the costumes, and exhorted me to display them to best advantage. A frequently expressed conviction of hers had it that costumes she called 'original' (which for her meant conceptual as opposed to mimetic) stood the greatest chance of winning; . . . I did feel exhibited, exploited, embarrassed. Even if I won, there was little pleasure in competing in this way—in being put on display, scrutinized, weighed up, given points, judged. As I grew older, I grew less willing and no doubt decreasingly compliant. A photograph of me wearing the costume for what I believe to be the last fancy dress competition I entered shows me, aged about nine, wearing a long shift to which are attached empty cigarette packets, drink cartons, ice-cream containers, drinking straws, matchboxes: with a head-dress comprised of one waxed Kia-Ora orange juice carton flanked by a pair of ice-cream tubes" (55).

Entertainment   The film that remained in Kuhn's memory after seeing it just once in early childhood is entitled *Mandy*, directed by Alexander Mackendrick for Ealing Studios. It is a melodramatic film telling the story of the problems for a family in raising Mandy who is born deaf. As an adult Kuhn is able to see that Mandy's story is about the difficulty of the "entry into language," of acquiring a "voice," that everyone must go through. As a child, she identified with Mandy completely, and understood her position in her own family by analogy with Mandy's situation. "The narration of the scene in which Mandy first learns about sound draws us into her frustration and rage at not understanding what the teacher expects of her. This short scene is composed of more than thirty shots, some of them, especially during the exchange between Mandy and the teacher around the mid point of the sequence, extremely brief. This latter section is composed largely of shot-reverse shot figures involving the two characters, and includes a series of six shots in this pattern, starting when the sound of the teacher's voice encouraging Mandy fades from the soundtrack and the camera tracks in to a big, distorted wide-angle closeup of the face of the child, disturbed and uncomprehending, as her lips touch the balloon the teacher is using to demonstrate sound vibration. The moment of silence—Mandy's auditory point of view so to speak—is then broken: failing to understand what is required of her, Mandy breaks away from her teacher and starts to scream and cry" (30–31).

History   The photograph linking Kuhn's personal situation to the story of her nation shows her at age seven in the special dress her mother made for her to wear on Coronation Day for the new Queen. In this discourse the personal memory is supplied by the popular, public memory. The community remembers in her place, on her behalf. "In the smaller story, the little girl's frock and its commemoration in a photograph can be read both as a statement of attachment—to a community, a nation—through participation in a ritual; and also as visible expression of an Oedipal drama that is both personal (its cast of very ordinary characters consisting of myself and my immediate family) and collective (the feeling tone, if not the detail, of the story will strike a chord of recognition in others). The ritual meaning of her costume was no doubt largely lost on a young Annette wholly preoccupied by her loathing of the outfit and her discomfort about wearing it. But this in no way detracts from the broader symbolic and cultural meaning of a child dressed up and put on display in this manner. . . . The corollary of this must be the flipside of every Oedipal drama: projection, hostility and disillusion ensue as reality inevitably falls short of the ideal. The loyalty, the wish to belong, claimed in the outward display of a ceremonial dress and a photograph of it are riven with disenchantment: a daughter disappoints, an Empire crumbles" (83).

Comment

- We are introducing the mystory allegory in its complete form, and the examples (Joyce, Kuhn) include all or most of the popcycle stories already worked out. This overview helps anticipate what is to come, although at this stage you are still working on the second installment (the Family discourse).

- Kuhn's relay is helpful in the way she works with family photographs. You should look for the pattern of your wide image in visual and aural materials as well as in words (the image is synesthetic).

Exercise: Family Album

Retrieve some family photographs from home and apply to them the memory work outlined by Kuhn.

- Keep in mind that we are less interested in drama or idea, and more interested in mood and atmosphere. Atmosphere, however, cannot be accessed directly, but emerges out of a combination of material or sensory details.

Endocept

As indicated by the paradigm of Einstein's compass, defining moments that embody one's themata often occur at an early age (preschool years). Memories of this period of life may be few or vague. Attempting to put into an image the attunement of home is good practice for a basic experience of the creative process, which involves noticing and bringing into perceptibility the formless intuitions that appear in a flash and then are lost for those not aware of their potential value. The theorist of creativity, Silvano Arieti, referred to these unshaped private glimmerings as "endocepts," to distinguish and relate them to the public well-defined concepts (Arieti, 1976: 53). These "amorphous cognitions" signal internal processes and are without story or representation. Psychoanalysis refers to "drives," generated from within the body, as distinct from "desires," whose stimulus is external. "Attunement" is the process of coordinating the interaction between inside and outside of "being"—the process of boundary formation productive of identity at both the individual and collective level. One way endocepts come into representation is through an association with a memory of a place or event. Virginia Woolf's wide image exemplifies this endoceptual quality, as recorded in what she said was her first memory:

> "In fact it is the most important of all my memories. If life has a base that it stands upon, if it is a bowl that one fills and fills and fills—then my bowl without a doubt stands upon this memory. It is of lying half asleep, half awake, in bed in the nursery at St. Ives. It is of hearing the waves breaking, one, two, one, two, and sending a splash of water on the beach; and then breaking, one, two, one two,

behind the yellow blind. It is of hearing the blind draw its little acorn across the floor as the wind blew the blind out. It is of lying and hearing this splash and see-ing this light, and feeling, it is almost impossible that I should be here; of feeling the purest ecstasy I can conceive" (Woolf, in Briggs, 36).

Briggs goes on to show how this "mood wave" informs the style, tone, and themes of most of Woolf's fiction. He is interested especially in "nuance," the quality that singularizes and enriches common experiences in the hands of creative people. The bottomless bowl resonates with the example of satori cited earlier. Briggs compares his notion of "nuance" with Holton's "theme."

"These memories become part of the evolving 'theme.' In Woolf's case, the angle of light, the sound of the waves would have activated memories with simi-lar tags or wave forms, like the sound of her mother's footsteps or the ghostly sight of her dressing gown in the wind. Together these would circulate and build as a rich 'theme' of nuance-laced sense data. . . . This 'theme,' circulating mostly below the level of awareness, would contain hundreds of sensory fragments, each impregnated with emotional nuances. . . . What she remembered was not a cognition, but the 'theme' itself with all its nuances. She said the memory sup-ported something you could fill and refill, a bottomless bowl. The memory had for her a 'wonder' and 'incompleteness.' The exact emotion she felt could not be defined in thoughts: it was an emotion that contained wonder, fragility, hap-piness, vastness, security, insecurity—and more. It was a state in which feelings, thoughts, memories and perceptions flowed vividly into each other and were in-separable" (Briggs, 54–55).

Exercise: Memory Glimpse

Put into an image or scene one of your earliest memories. Note especially the details of what you remember. What is the atmosphere of the scene? What details carry this atmosphere?

Anecdote

It is possible to generate material for the documentation of this part of the pop-cycle (and for the others as well) using an informal kind of story—the anecdote. The anecdote is an oral form originally, and is useful for locating sensory details of the home environment that evoke the atmosphere of the place. The following example is by the Swedish poet Tomas Transtromer.

Tomas Transtromer, "Memories Look at Me"

"Hasse, a big darkish boy who was five times stronger than I was, had a habit of wrestling with me every break during our first year at school. At first I resisted violently but that got me nowhere for he just put me to the ground anyway and triumphed over me. At last I thought up a way of disappointing him: total relaxation. When he approached me I pretended that my Real Self had flown away leaving only a corpse behind, a lifeless rag which he could press to the ground as he wished. He soon grew tired of that.

"I wonder what this method of turning myself into a lifeless rag can have meant for me further on in life. The art of being ridden roughshod over while yet maintaining one's self-respect. Have I resorted to the trick too often? Sometimes it works, sometimes not" (Transtromer, 1997: 189–190).

Comment

- The interpretation that generalizes the first-grade school incident into a theme is useful to see how something trivial in itself, if it sticks in memory, may be significant. With hindsight Transtromer can see that he translated "playing possum" from a physical to a psychological approach to problem solving. The mystory does not rely upon this hindsight but only the fact of the memory to locate the most evocative details.

Grateful Dead musician Jerry Garcia collected in his illustrated autobiography what he called "anecdoubts."

Jerry Garcia and Loretta the Parrot

"This tiny room was the parrot's room, and he'd [Pop] open the parrot's cage, insert a piece of sawed-off broomstick (we called it the polly-stick) that the parrot would eye suspiciously and maybe bite once or twice before gingerly climbing on and allowing him to place her gently on top of the cage. Then he'd give her fresh water, refill her parrot food dispenser and change the newspaper that lined her cage. Finally he'd replace her in the cage. This routine of my grandfather's accompanied me from age five through young adulthood. Never once, through years of this daily routine, did the parrot ever really acknowledge Pop. But when he died, Loretta let out a piercing shriek, and then she mourned him, crying like a person until she died of grief.

"The parrot and the parrot routine virtually define 'parrotness' in my life. The parrot's name was Loretta. The story was this—immediately after the big San Francisco earthquake, with the city burning and the dust settling, my Grandma Tillie, a little girl at the time, found this parrot walking down the street! When my grandmother found her, she could say 'prrretty lorrretta.' She never learned anything else speechwise, at least no more English phrases. But she developed a perfectly wonderful vocabulary of environmental sounds, cars passing on Alemany Boulevard, faucets running, toilets flushing and her tour de force, an uncanny imitation of my grandmother's social club. The social club was a collection of Nan's old homegirls from the 'hood who would rotate their meetings from one lady's house to another every Thursday night for an evening of cards and liquor that would get progressively more raucous as the hours passed. The bird could do a perfectly marvelous imitation of the whole deal, cards shuffling, poker chips rattling, ice cubes clinking, old lady voices gabbling, gales of hysterical laughter. It was truly fabulous and absolutely unmistakable" (Garcia, 1995).

Comment

- Garcia illustrates his recollections with many drawings, including a number of sketches of Loretta, that contribute substantially to expressing the atmosphere of his childhood home. It does not matter if you have no skill or training in drawing, as is evident in Garcia's child-like but expressive sketches. The look of these pictures—the lines and colors—produces a particular feeling relevant to Garcia's state of mind.

- Although anecdotes may be highly crafted, for our purposes they do not have to have any "point" other than that they represent a scene or situation that remained in your memory.

Micro Narrative

Exercise: Micro Scenes

To locate some of the features of the home setting that contributed to your themata, compose at least two "micro narratives."

- Based on the collection of micro fictions edited by Jerome Stern, the basic heuristic "rules" for the micro form are:

  1. Length: no more than 300 words.
  2. Situation: establish the key details of a situation (the terms of a relationship). The relationship may be between or among people, or of a person with a place, thing, or event. You may or may not be directly involved with the scene, but it should be "nonfiction" in that the

scene is based on an actual memory (without worrying about the accuracy of the memory).

3. Image: locate and develop some feature of the scene into an image that comments indirectly or figuratively on the scene, in a way that brings out your present understanding of the past situation.

Microfiction: Laurie Berry, "Mockingbird"

"Peter has just returned from Mexico, where his face turned the chalky pink color of Pepto-Bismol. Rachel is at that swooning stage of love, stupid with happiness at his return.

"That evening they drink cold vodka and gossip about a child-laden couple they know, who rise at dawn for work and return home at seven to bathe the three-year-old, console the eight-year-old, and struggle through dinner in time to collapse in bed by ten.

"'Even so they have a great house,' she says. 'And nice things. They make a lot of money.'

"Peter shakes his head and says offhandedly: 'I'd rather inherit it.'

"They are both shocked by the statement. An island of silence bobs to the surface. Rachel swallows the last of her vodka, and with it the realization that she is in love with a man who has just traveled to a third-world nation to play tennis.

"'By the way—' He looks up guiltily, making a game of it. 'Promise me you'll never tell anyone I said that.'

"This makes her laugh, freshens her love. They laugh some more. Talk their slow way toward dinner. Spy on the remarkable albino Mexican boy playing in the yard next door. Make love with the windows open and then lie there listening to the mariachi music that pumps through her Houston barrio neighborhood.

"Everything is soft, very soft. And luck abundant as johnsongrass. The mimosa trees' green canopy. And the mockingbirds, not yet vicious, waiting for the fierce end of summer" (Berry, 1996: 42–43).

Comment

• The situation is organized around an "epiphany," or social "gest." The scene, that is, focuses on Peter's comment ("I'd rather inherit it"), that reveals his attitude toward life. The revelation is "dramatic" (establishes conflict) because Rachel's attitude is equally exposed in her remark about the hard-working couple having "nice things." The seasonal image at the end of the narrative suggests that this relationship is probably doomed.

OFFICE

1. The second installment of the widesite begins here: the Family quarter. The method is almost purely memorial, but the punctum principle is to work with whatever comes to mind without having to think about it for too long. Some students like to talk with family members or friends to gather more information, which is fine, but the signifiers most likely to give access to the wide image are those already (still) there, just beneath the surface.

2. Memories gather around problems, and our premise is that problem solving in your career discipline and in society at large (public policy) revolves around the specific experience of problems and their solutions across the areas of your experience. The problem may be trivial or serious, and anything in between. Divorce is a common traumatic event for many students, although it is more significant for some than for others in terms of finding the best memory material. Some students are embarrassed about how trivial the memory event is that they discover (losing a toy to an aggressive peer in the second grade); others are disturbed by finding they have to deal with a serious situation that they have avoided confronting (bulimia for example). The fact is that our immediate goal—to find the wide image—does not depend on confession or revealing secrets. It is not about "content" but atmosphere, mood. Beyond that, of course, there is therapeutic dimension to self-knowledge detoured through aesthetic form, and the painful pleasure of this process often motivates some excellent mystorical work.

3. The exercises are intended to suggest ways to put the documentation of your experience into some kind of form. The micro narrative gives you some practice with narrative form itself—the structure that is guiding the overall development of the project. The "micro" dimension enacts the haiku principle of brevity, and avoids "confession" since there is so little space for elaboration. It also helps break down blocks such as the false split (for our purposes) between truth and fiction. The wide image is invented as much as it is discovered: it is a simulation, a forcing into appearance of something that is immaterial, a field of energy, an orientation that is an emergent pattern that exists only holistically and not in its parts or elements (it is not "in" any one of the popcycle quarters). The micro is a very short story that evokes the feeling of the domestic scene; what counts is not necessarily any one incident (although there are exceptions to this rule), but the feeling suggested by the story as image.

4. There are quite a few examples in the chapter, all of which serve as relays pointing you to the ingredients of a full mystory. The lesson is not that you have to write a novel, but that you need to locate and select primary documents from each of the popcycle institutions as clues to the mood of your wide image. Part of the argument represented by our subtitle ("from literacy to electracy") is that certain qualities of life persist across every apparatus, but are enacted differently, with different augmentation and power, depending on the nature of the apparatus. People tell stories and solve problems always, but in profoundly different ways. Knowledge of imaging, backgrounded during the epoch of literacy but sustained and refined in the practices of arts and letters, has become central to general electracy in the apparatus of new media. Thus imaging is not just for artists and poets now, but for any person wishing to become electrate. Each example relay poses the same question: What are the equivalents for these experiences in your own situation and circumstance?

5. The "homepage" is neither a home nor a page, but uses these familiar sites and experiences as metaphors to name the point of departure for storing and retrieving information in electronic form. To learn electracy means to leave home, with "home" referring to the familiarity of your "natural standpoint." The structure of narrative, with the call to adventure that takes the protagonist away from the safety of home and into the dangers of the special world, models the shift in attitude, the defamiliarization, that necessarily accompanies your attention to becoming electrate. The mystory method uses allegory to support a holistic understanding, encouraging you to notice correspondences across the levels of your situation: your family relationships, the entertainment you enjoy, the historical record of your nation, the problems confronting your preferred career field. These discourses constitute the ecology of your lifeworld.

Chapter 4

Cosmogram

ULMER FILE
Xanadu

What is the fit between the paradigmatic problem of my career—imaging on the internet—and my own wide image? To include my mystory as a relay for the widesite requires a pass through one of the classic stories of creativity. No one needs to be reminded that the poem "Kubla Khan" is subtitled, "Or, a Vision in a Dream: A Fragment." Nor that it is the product of a legendary (apocryphal) scene of writing, an account of which usually accompanies the poem in publication. The English Romantic poet Samuel Taylor Coleridge had retired to a lonely farmhouse in part to recover his health. Having taken a prescribed "anodyne" (some extract of opium, the historians say), the poet fell asleep while reading a book about the palace of Kubla Khan. While asleep Coleridge dreamed that he wrote a poem, which, upon awaking, he still remembered. He immediately began to transcribe the dream poem:

> "In Xanadu did Kubla Khan
> A stately pleasure dome decree;
> Where Alph, the sacred river, ran
> Through caverns measureless to man
>   Down to a sunless sea.
> So twice five miles of fertile ground
> With walls and towers were girdled round:
> And there were gardens bright with sinuous rills,
> Where blossomed many an incense-bearing tree;
> And here were forests ancient as the hills,
> Enfolding sunny spots of greenery" (Coleridge).

However, the poet soon was distracted by a visitor who kept him away from his writing for over an hour. When Coleridge returned to his page, the memory was gone. Apocryphal or not, this story has been retold in any number of studies of the creative process.

I invoke this scene once again to pose to it a question about the scene of writing appropriate for the computer, the internet, interactive multimedia, hypertext, digital electronic storage and retrieval of information. The potential relevance of

Coleridge to the question of online creativity was established by Ted Nelson, originator of the term "hypertext," who named his vision of globally connected information "Project Xanadu," after Coleridge's poem. This name acknowledged the Romantic quality of the vision, long before it was technically possible, of the "hacker's dream"—total information instantly available to everyone everywhere. Nelson's story is another example of a wide image connecting a childhood memory with a career discovery or invention.

> "'I talk about being in a rowboat with my grandfather rowing—and my grandmother—and running my hands, letting my hands trail in the water, when I was 4 or 5. And I remember thinking about the particles in the water, but I thought of them as places, and how they would separate around my fingers and reconnect on the other side, and how this constant separation and reconnection and perpetual change . . . into new arrangements . . . you couldn't really visualize or express the myriad of relationships.' The chaotic, ephemeral eddies under his grandfather's rowboat are a perfect image of Nelson's style of thought. The inventor suffers from an extreme case of Attention Deficit Disorder. . . . Xanadu, the ultimate hypertext information system, began as Ted Nelson's quest for personal liberation. The inventor's hummingbird mind and his inability to keep track of anything left him relatively helpless. He wanted to be a writer and a filmmaker, but he needed a way to avoid getting lost in the frantic multiplication of associations his brain produced. His great inspiration was to imagine a computer program that could keep track of all the divergent paths of his thinking and writing. To this concept of branching, nonlinear writing, Nelson gave the name hypertext" (Wolf, 1995: 138, 140).

Nelson also suggested that the greatest software designer was film director Orson Welles; or rather Welles would have been the greatest software designer if he had lived in the age of computers. This assertion makes sense in the context of Nelson's view that making a movie is a better interface metaphor for what it is like to write in hypermedia than is the book or desktop metaphors that still tend to filter our access to electracy. The estate that Welles named "Xanadu" in *Citizen Kane* is located in Florida.

Mapping the Diegesis

What is the connection between me and the problem of hypertext set for my discipline by Ted Nelson? A better question is: Where is Xanadu, exactly? The answer, available in both scholarly (Lowes) and popular (Alexander) versions, is that Xanadu is a composite diegesis (just like most Hollywood movies)— "diegesis" referring to the imaginary space and time of the world created in the poem (or narrative). Diegesis names that part of the story world that persists through adaptations, translations, and remakes or retellings of the original narrative. "Xanadu" is a hybrid place made of elements drawn from four locations. These four locations, none of which Coleridge had visited but about which he had read, were four of the most exotic sites of otherness, of "elsewhere," of anyplace-out-of-this-world, available to a Romantic imagination. This use of the exotic as the emblem of curiosity and imagination is important to the Emer-Agency, directed as it is toward global consulting by means of the internet.

Where Is Xanadu?

- An inventory of the sites alluded to in the poem begins with the namesake of "Xanadu" itself, Shangdu, which "lay in what is now the Zhenglan Banner of the Autonomous Region of Inner Mongolia, in northeast China" (Alexander, 1994: xv). It was the capital city of Kubla Khan. The choral significance includes our current relations with China, as distinct from those of Coleridge's day, such as the human rights and democracy issues associated with the Tiananmen Square events.

- The second exotic location alluded to in "Xanadu" is the "holy caves of ice" in Kashmir. The caves in question are near Pahalgam, "at approximately seven thousand feet at the northern end of the Lidder valley, between the junction of the Aru and the Sheshnag, two branches of the majestic Lidder River, which flow through defiles at the valley head" (105). A headline in *the New York Times* on August 21, 1995, for example, updates these sacred caves for the EmerAgency: "Terror in Paradise Keeps Tourists from Kashmir." Kashmir, the Himalayan state that was once India's greatest tourist attraction after the Taj Mahal, now is on the index of the State Department. Muslim separatists held several European hostages there. To show their seriousness, they executed a Norwegian tourist by the name of Hans Christian Ostro, on whose abdomen they carved the signature of their organization.

- The third sacred location referenced in "Xanadu" is Mount Abora, the place about which the Abyssinian maid sang. Located in east central Africa, the holy site in question is Gishen Mariam, in the Ambasel range, forty miles north of Dessie (166). Although much of the news about Ethiopia in the early 1990s dealt with the coups and skirmishes that led to the independence of Eritrea from Ethiopia, the region is still associated in our culture with images of famine.

- And what of the fourth exotic, sacred locale of the poem, site of the mighty fountain itself and the underground river? It is Alachua County, Gainesville, Florida—my place of residence since 1972, and hometown of the University of Florida. As part of her project to visit the four sites composing the diegesis of "Xanadu," Caroline Alexander came to Gainesville, and described it in the same travel journalist prose used to describe her journeys to the other far-flung outposts on the map. Fortunately she does not mention that more tourists have been murdered in Florida than in Kashmir, nor for that matter had *Money* magazine yet ranked Gainesville as the best city in which to live in the entire United States (1995), making it a fit counterpart for Kubla Khan's "stately pleasure-dome."

Coleridge's source for the description of the Gainesville area was Bartram's *Travels*, one of the most popular books of the later eighteenth century, giving an account of the karst topography of northern Florida. Bartram's description of the underground rivers, sinkholes, springs, poljes, and the other features of limestone geology shaped by a semitropical climate is one of the major sources of the language of the poem. The "Ancestral voices prophesying war" is a reminder that the name "karst" applied to limestone topography originated in the region of Bosnia-Herzogovinia whose landscape is the prototype for these features. It is relevant to the conductive network I want to map that Freud was riding on a train in Bosnia-Herzegovinia when he failed to remember the name of the Italian painter Signorelli, an event memorialized in *Psychopathology of Everyday Life*. "The name Signorelli was thus divided into two parts. One pair of syllables (*elli*) returned unchanged in one of the substitutions, while the other had gained, through the translation of *signor* (sir, *Herr*), many and diverse relations to the names contained in the repressed theme, but was lost through it in the reproduction. Its substitution was formed in a way to suggest that a displacement took place along the same associations—'Herzegovina and Bosnia'—regardless of the sense and acoustic demarcation. The names were therefore treated in this process like the written pictures of a sentence which is to be transformed into a picture-puzzle (rebus)" (Freud, 11). This detour from place through names and pictures is a miniature of the logic of electracy.

The experience of realizing that I lived in one of the four most exotic places in the world, according to the Romantic imagination, can be described as "uncanny," to express the encounter of the familiar in the foreign in this discovery. Making a mystory tends to produce uncanny connections, which is just one variety of the larger experience of "recognition" that is central to the practices of creativity. For the remake I applied the Xanadu principle to my childhood hometown, to look for any links or passages between the local and the exotic. A first pass through the popcycle begins in Miles City, Montana.

Comment

- The Ulmer File sections describe my own experience with mystory, to add my personal testimony to the evidence of theory and examples provided to assist you in completing the widesite. I am not asking you to do anything that I have not tried in my own case and with my students. Of course I came to the experiment in midcareer, which accounts for the excessive quantities of career-related materials I include. My basic point is to locate the uncanny moments when I experienced that sense of destiny I understand not as "proof" but more in the style of intuition or even of an omen, signaling that the path or way is open in a certain direction.

STUDIO
Chora (Sacred Space)

I recently learned that Ted Nelson was at Brown University in 1969 (Wolf, 1995), while I was in residence doing graduate work (1967–1972). That modest clue has a stronger formal corollary in the presence of this image in Coleridge's poem.

> *"As if this earth in fast thick pants were breathing,*
> *A mighty fountain momently was forced:*
> *Amid whose swift half-intermitted burst*
> *Huge fragments vaulted like rebounding hail,*
> *Or chaffy grain beneath the thresher's flail."*

Coleridge's reference to the thresher's flail evokes one of the key images of chora in Plato's *Timaeus,* which relates "Kubla Khan" directly to a major area of my career research. In *Timaeus,* Plato addressed one of the profound metaphysical questions of his day—the problem of how being and becoming were related—by proposing a third term, selected from the vernacular and elevated to philosophical status—chora—to name a space of mediation. He characterized this place with a variety of metaphors in order to suggest the effect of this mediation, which was to bring order out of chaos. Metaphors were essential because chora could not be treated directly; it was that which made appearance possible, but itself did not appear. "As, when grain is shaken and winnowed by fans and other instruments used in the threshing of corn, the close and heavy particles are borne away and settle in one direction, and the loose and light particles in another. In this manner, the four kinds of elements were then shaken by the receiving vessel, which, moving like a winnowing machine, scattered far away from one another the elements most unlike, and forced the most similar elements into close contact" (Plato, *Timeaus,* 52d–53a).

Plato's metaphor was a refunctioning of the winnowing basket, which was used symbolically in the Eleusinian mysteries (the dominant religious institution of his day) to carry the stone phalloi during the ritual procession. A sign of the emblematic status of Frederick Douglass's narrative (and of the parable at work in the history of the term "culture") is that the turning point that started him toward his life as a free man began when he collapsed while working for Mr. Covey. "You have seen how a man was made a slave; you shall see how a slave was made a man. On one of the hottest days of the month of August, 1833, Bill Smith, William Hughes, a slave named Eli, and myself, were engaged in fanning wheat" (Douglass, 1997: 75). We should notice the hyperlink between the slave named "Eli" and the syllables (*elli*) in Freud's example, as well as the directly relevant situation of winnowing.

"Chora" is a theoretical invention. The Greeks recognized at least three kinds of space or place—topos, chora, and kenon (Algra, 1995: 39). Topos names the abstract quality of place as a container, and chora names the sacred nature of specific places. "Kenon" is the "nothing" of the atomists that prompted philosophers to pose the originating question of ontology: "Why is there something rather than nothing?" The Greek sense of place took into account all three notions, but with the development of literacy they became separated. Aristotle, in his codification of rhetoric, dropped chora, which still had been important in Plato, and emphasized topos as his metaphor for the places of memory (inventio). Choragraphy, which I developed out of the Derrida-Eisenman collaboration on a design for Villette Park in Paris, is my proposal for a hyper-rhetoric in which chora rather than topos is the kind of space used as a metaphor for the places of invention (for the storage and retrieval of information in electracy) (Ulmer, 1994). Choragraphy adds an identification with a specific location to the mystorical identification with a protagonist in each of the popcycle institutions.

The association of chora with the four elements (in Plato's cosmology chora sorted chaos into the fundamental categories of earth, air, fire, and water) directs the choragrapher to the tradition of the music of the spheres. Another image for bringing the four elements into order is musical: the tuning of a lute. In his history of the term "Stimmung," Leo Spitzer noted the importance of *Timaeus* in figuring the world soul as musical: the importance of music in classical education through the middle ages was based on the idea of morality as a tuning of the individual soul to this world harmony (Spitzer, 34). Heidegger returned to this tradition as part of his return to the Greeks, designating Stimmung as one of the existentials grounding one's being in the world. It names the ground of feeling that lets us know where we are "at," how we are doing, how things are with us. Translated as "atmosphere," "ambiance," "mood," the attunement of modern man is "dread," according to Heidegger. A choral category gathers and holds heterogeneous information in place by means of a shared mood or atmosphere. The widesite is our personal chora, showing the winnowing system of our identity that sorts the world of our experience into a pattern of coherence.

Comment

- There are several ways to understand my use of chora to name the power of images to organize information into categories. In career terms, it is already associated with the differences between Plato (who introduced chora in *Timaeus*) and his pupil Aristotle, with the latter choosing a different Greek term for space—topos—as a metaphor for the way word-concepts organize information into categories. Electracy retains the conceptual topics of literacy and supplements them with the image choras of electracy. As in the case of the shift from text to felt, the shift from topic to chora involves a root metaphor in the abstract term (in this case, a reference to spatiality). So part of what we are learning is just how image space holds together diverse quantities of information.

- In terms of the wide image, my insistence on making chora operational theoretically is due to my emotional investment in it. The genesis of this investment was explained in my previous books, in which I discovered the mystorical correspondence between Plato's metaphor for how choral space participated in shaking chaos into order (it was like the winnowing action of the thresher's flail), and the way my father's sand and gravel plant used vibrating screens to sort out raw aggregate from his quarry in the Montana hills into four sizes of rock and sand. This match between my Family discourse and my Career discourse struck me as an epiphany, and encourage me to continue working with this particular theoretical material, which I call choragraphy.

The Personal Sacred

The revival of choral space in electracy concerns a personal or private experience of the sacred rather than an official or collective version. Mystory is a personalized, secularized cosmogony. The anthropologist and experimental autobiographer Michel Leiris identified the bathroom as a primary site of the sacred in modernity. In the secularized conditions of modernity (and these are the conditions of chora as sacred place in electracy), it was easier to understand the sacred at a personal level ("those objects, places, or occasions that awake in me that mixture of fear and attachment, that ambiguous attitude caused by the approach of something simultaneously attractive and dangerous, prestigious and outcast"— Leiris, 24). To locate the sacred in one's own experience, Leiris looked to memories of childhood, the earlier the better. His family home was organized by a sacred polarity on a right-left axis of parental bedroom and the bathroom. The bathroom served not only its designated function but also doubled as a secret clubhouse where he and his brother collaborated on the composition of fantastic narratives.

"There was something more or less forbidden in what we were doing, which, moreover, brought us scoldings when we stayed shut up in there too long. As if in a 'men's house' of some island in Oceania—the place where the initiates gather and where from mouth to mouth and from generation to generation, secrets and myths are passed on, we endlessly elaborated our mythology in this room, our clubhouse, and never tired of seeking answers to the various sexual riddles that obsessed us. Seated on the throne like an initiate of higher rank was my brother; I, the youngest, sat on an ordinary chamber pot that served as the neophyte's stool. The flushing mechanism and the hole were, in themselves, mysterious things, and even actually dangerous" (26).

Such humble, elemental experiences are overlooked by conventional consultants following the rules of sufficient reason. In a time of emergency, however, that Leiris shared with Walter Benjamin, (they both participated in the College of Sociology conference held in Paris just before the beginning of World War II) a moment when the repressed sacred seemed to have erupted once again directly into political life, it was necessary to take a more inclusive approach to experience, in order to figure out what was going wrong.

Duck Rabbit   An example of the creative operation of the personal sacred through the mystorical popcycle is Wittgenstein's adaptation of the Gestaltist duck-rabbit paradoxical drawing late in his career to discuss his own version of the experience of seeing-as, of recognizing an aspect. The "career" of the duck-rabbit picture puzzle (drawn in such a way as to exploit the schema shared by the two creatures, so that the picture may be seen alternatively as one or the other) demonstrates how ideas migrate or circulate through the economy of the popcycle.

W. J. T. Mitchell on the Duck-Rabbit

"Some day a proper history of the Duck-Rabbit will be written, tracing its migration from the pages of a nineteenth-century German humor magazine that was a favorite of Freud's, to its long sojourn in Gestalt and American cognitive psychology; from its thoroughly canonical and stabilized role in Gombrich's *Art and Illusion* to its surprise appearance in a painting by Jackson Pollock, to its apotheosis in the pages of *Philosophical Investigations*. Wittgenstein's immediate aim with the Duck-Rabbit seems to have been a negative one: the image served to unsettle the psychological explanations that had stabilized the Duck-Rabbit with models of mental picturing in the beholder. For Joseph Jastrow, whose *Fact and Fable in Psychology* first subjected the Duck-Rabbit to scientific discipline, the spectatorial model was explicitly based in photography: 'The eye may be compared to a photographic camera, with its eyelid cap, its iris shutter, its lens, and its sensitive plate,—the retina.' This model of the eye then generates a familiar model of the mind: 'The pictures that are developed are stacked up, like the negatives in the photographer's shop, in the pigeon-holes of our mental storerooms.' The Duck-Rabbit, and multistable images in general, reveal the presence of a 'mind's eye' roving around the storeroom, interpreting the pictures, seeing different aspects in them. 'The bodily eye simply transmits information: the image on the retina does not change', and the identity of the observer, his 'difference' from other viewers, is located in the mental eye: 'physical eyes see alike, but mental eyes reflect their own individualities.' . . .

"Wittgenstein is impatient, vexed with this fable. He warns repeatedly against thinking about seeing in terms of 'internal mechanisms' ('the concept of the "inner picture" is misleading, for this concept uses the "outer" picture as a model'). He shifts the inquiry from speculation on inner visual mechanisms to observations on what we might call the 'grammar of vision,' the language games employed in things like interpretations, descriptive reports, and exclamations prompted by visual experiences. He compares the experience of 'noticing an aspect' to the application of captions or textual labels to a book illustration and, in general, replaces the causal linkages of the 'mental' and 'bodily' eye with the interplay of the visual and the verbal" (Mitchell, 1994: 51).

This capacity for "seeing-as" (aspectuality) is important to the work of "attunement" involved in the shift from literacy to electracy. Meanwhile, the relevance of this example to mystory may not be recognized until it is put together with the biographer's report that Wittgenstein once revealed to a friend a childhood memory to which he ascribed great significance: he recalled that in the lavatory of his childhood home the plaster had fallen off the wall in such a way as to form a pattern that little Ludwig saw as a *duck*. The image, which he associated with the monsters in a painting by Hieronymous Bosch, frightened him (Monk, 1990: 451). The specific painting he had in mind was Bosch's *Temptation of St Anthony*. The association manifested itself further in Ludwig's performances as virtuoso whistler, able to "whistle whole movements of symphonies, his showpiece being Brahms's *St Anthony Variations*" (443). Wittgenstein was addressing a problem in his career field in part through a childhood endocept.

In his last term at Cambridge, Wittgenstein came across the figure of a Duck-Rabbit in Joseph Jastrow's *Fact and Fable in Psychology*, which he introduced into his lectures on "seeing-as," or aspect-seeing, influenced by Kohler's *Gestalt Psychology* (508). "Suppose I show it to a child. It says 'It's a duck' and then suddenly 'Oh, it'a rabbit.' So it recognizes it as a rabbit. . . . The experience only comes at the moment of change from duck to rabbit and back. In between, the aspect is as it were dispositional" (507). In his mystory, Wittgenstein himself is this "child." A sense of relief, a feeling of anxiety reduction accompanied the transformation of a Bosch-like duck into anything else, such as a rabbit, we may suppose, if we take into account the full popcycle diegesis of his genius. He is able to go on to generalize this insight, demonstrating how some basic feeling, or the creation of a specific emotional mood embodied in a concrete gesture or shape, informs the acts of judgment guiding all styles of analytical reasoning.

Comment

- Wittgenstein's example of the intersection of the anecdote of life with the aphorism of thought indicates how the experience of recognition—the resonance of the Gestalt illustration with his childhood memory—may become functional in career decisions or problem formulation and solution. The duck outline carried an emotional feeling tone due to an accident of Wittgenstein's Family setting. When he saw the outline again in his Career discourse, it possessed for him a kind of intellectual synesthesia, which provided a context for the original turn he gave to this meme.

Cosmogram

Walter Benjamin had a four-part psychogeography—or chora or "Xanadu"—as described by Susan Buck-Morss. Benjamin's "home," we might say, was located at the null point of the intersection of two axes: to the west was Paris, origin of bourgeois society in the political sense; to the east was Moscow and the end of bourgeois society; to the south was Naples and the origins of Western civilization in Mediterranean culture; to the north was Berlin, Benjamin's childhood home (Buck-Morss, 1989: 25). Benjamin's *inventio* was grounded in a mood or atmosphere informed by this composite location: Paris-Moscow-Naples-Berlin—the cities that formatted his imagination. A salient feature of this fourfold in my context was the fact that one of the four was Benjamin's "hometown." The wide image is formed at the focal point of this crossroads.

Benjamin supplied a glimpse of the potential usefulness of a mystorical schema for composing the wide image.

Walter Benjamin on Primal Acquaintances

"Suddenly and with compelling force, I was struck by the idea of drawing a diagram of my life, and knew at the same moment exactly how it was to be done. With a very simple question I interrogated my past life, and the answers were inscribed, as if of their own accord, on a sheet of paper that I had with me. A year or two later, when I lost this sheet, I was inconsolable. Now reconstructing its outline in thought without directly reproducing it, I should speak of a labyrinth. I am not concerned here with what is installed in the chamber at its enigmatic center, ego or fate, but all the more with the many entrances leading into the interior. These entrances I call primal acquaintances; each of them is a graphic symbol of my acquaintance with a person whom I met, not through other people, but through neighborhood, family relationships, school comradeship, mistaken identity, companionship on travels, or other such situations. So many primal relationships, so many entrances to the maze. . . . 'If a man has character,' says Nietzsche, 'he will have the same experience over and over again.' Whether or not this is true on a large scale, on a small one there are perhaps paths that lead us again and again to people who have one and the same function for us: PASSAGEWAYS that always, in the most divers periods of life, guide us to the friend, the betrayer, the beloved, the pupil, or the master. This is what the sketch of my life revealed to me as it took shape before me on that Paris afternoon. Against the background of the city, the people who had surrounded me closed together to form a figure" (Benjamin, 1978: 30–31).

The frustrating aspect for admirers of Benjamin has been that he never revealed the *inventio* he used to produce his "figure." The collection of archetypes suggests that every person is in a narrative situation populated with "primal acquaintances." My own version of the exercise turned up not a labyrinth but a mandala. The Xanadu diegesis, that is, shows how to turn Benjamin's exercise into a design method. The method is to "tune" the four (or more) discourses of the popcycle into a composite scene, by finding a thread of whatever sort at whatever level of detail that runs through and crosses the boundaries of these different dimensions of experience. Choral organization collects not by abstract shared features, but by repeating signifiers across conceptually unrelated categories. That is, it uses haiku logic.

The difference between this mystorical "allegory" and the medieval version is that while the latter is held together by totalizing isotopies or absolute homologies attaching the believer's personal existence as a sinner to the salvation of the world by Christ, the former is a turbulent disorder brought into a figure or constellated by the evocative repetition of a few details. The Christian allegory is top-down, ordered by the highest level of generalization (anagogy), while the mystory is bottom-up, ordered by the lowest common denominator (moral). The former is sublime, the latter abject. The social site of the former is High Mass at St. Peter's in Rome. The social site of the latter is watching prime-time TV at home. The goal of the tuning exercise is to identify the figures or primal acquaintances—the historical persons transformed into concepts, or conceptual personae (Deleuze), whose actantial position in the diegesis of Home is that of "donor"—the character(s) who help the protagonist solve the problem of the narrative world. In a mystory the acquaintances are found not only among the people one meets in life but the figures encountered in the other discourses (in stories, histories, specialized knowledge). To these elements must be added the settings whose composite features constitute the chora, whose atmosphere or spirit brings order out of chaos.

Example: Huston Conwill   One lesson of Xanadu as the template for the wide image is that everyone lives in four places (taking four not literally but symbolically). The widesite is a composite diegesis. My present location is always a "psychogeography"—partly physical, partly spiritual. I am drawing on all the discourses of the mystory to negotiate with the world. To make a widesite, of course, one must *extrapolate* from the relays to one's own situation. A good example of a personalized Xanadu are the cosmograms designed by the African-American artist, Huston Conwill.

> **Lucy Lippard, on "The Cakewalk Humanifesto," by Huston Conwill (with Estella Marie Conwill Majoso)**
>
> "The 'initiatory topography' unfolds within three concentric circles. The first is quartered—an ancient image of the cosmos symbolizing power drawn to a center from the four cardinal directions, and the crossroads where blues musicians traditionally gather. The second is a re-

arrangement of the ancient ritual hopscotch game, numbers one through ten guiding the player from heaven to hell. The third is the maze of the Cathedral of Chartres, an ancient dance diagram overlaying Christianity on paganism. Four cities represent the four senses: Louisville, Kentucky, where the artist was born, is the City of Vision, the eye (art); Atlanta, home of Martin Luther King and Conwill's wife, Kinshasha Holman, director of the Studio Museum in Harlem, is the City of Speech, the mouth (leadership); Memphis, where King died, is the City of Balance, the nose (justice); and New Orleans is the City of Grace, the ear (music). At the center of the cosmogram—the mirror in the belly to draw the light and also site of the maypole or earth axis around which the transcendent dance takes place at the end of the journey—is the City of Joy, the Alabama town of Tuscumbia (Choctaw/Chickasaw for 'walking to power,' originally called 'cold water'), where Helen Keller, symbol of communication against odds, was born (water was her first word): 'I was blind and now I see.'

"The pattern is set by directional lines, reminiscent of ancient 'ley lines,' often incorporating ancient Native American sacred sites. The cakewalk dance is the activator. The 'King Line' goes from Atlanta to Memphis, birth to assassination, representing the zone of dismemberment or symbolic death, the chaos that must be passed through to form a new self; the 'Malcolm Line' runs through New Orleans, Louisville, and Detroit. This ideogram is 'a matrix on which to put your ideas—not answers, so much as a way to find the right questions'; around it Conwill has developed a complex iconography almost an independent theological system" (Lippard, 1990: 68–69).

Comment

- This personal cosmogram exemplifies the holistic gathering power of the image as sacred space (chora). It shows how to combine the identifications with protagonists and with place (mystory and chorography).

- Another instruction from Conwill is how to embody the multiple layers of popcycle cultural information in an existing form or forms that are appropriated and refunctioned for this purpose. Conwill uses the Cakewalk dance as his framing device, and refers to his syncretic method as "High Funk." The cakewalk comes from one quarter of the popcycle, and is then elevated to the formal image structuring the relationships among all the other documents in his popcycle assemblage.

- The other framing device is the mandala (cosmogram). These geometric figures map the believer's understanding of the universe. The widesite similarly functions as a map of the infoverse (layering a personal worldview over everything that is). Again, the relays are showing how to put together all four popcycle discourses, although you are working through them one register at a time.

Susan Krane on "The New Cakewalk"

"The work revolves around Conwill's references to the diverse history of the cakewalk, a slave dance performed for the amusement of slavemasters, who awarded cakes (ironically, probably baked by the slaves themselves) to competing dancers. The cakewalk, a series of shuffling movements, is in form strongly related to the holy Ring Shout dances indigenous to Black cultures along the Atlantic, which were derived from ritualistic circle dances of Africa. The cakewalk embodied elements of mockery and subversion, for within the subjugation of this 'entertainment' slaves often parodied the genteel, mannered movements of their oppressors. For Conwill, the dance reflects its sacred roots as a ritual of jubilant release, yet also 'embodies the spirit of survival.' Ironically, it was the first Black dance to be adopted into mainstream white society. [. . .]

"In the installation *The New Cakewalk,* Conwill further extends this fundamental poetic metaphor, and in his hands the subject branches in countless directions. The dance floor of Conwill's cakewalk is a cryptic chart of this highly conceptualized and multifaceted content. The basic ideographic image was formed by superimposing and transforming three cosmological diagrams—the medieval labyrinth laid in the pavement of the nave of Chartres Cathedral, the diagram of the child's game of hopscotch, and the traditional African-American sign for the crossroads, where blues musicians traditionally gathered with their instruments. The quartered circle of the crossroads evolved from Kongolese ceremonial ground drawings, which signified the gathering of energy from the four corners of the universe. . . .

"For Conwill, the cakewalk has become a kind of conceptual architecture. Its interwoven and interdependent iconographical systems reflect a complexity that is analogous in some aspects to the programs of medieval church architecture, diagramming and underscoring a system of beliefs. . . . The work also reveals Conwill's conglomerate interest in inscribing and building meaning, which he always sees bound to specific locations but tracked through layers of time and inhabitations. This attitude of distanced and heightened observation is reflected literally in his persistent use of aerial views, mapping, and city plans. Spirituality, for him, is consistently grounded in locations of human endeavor—those geographical points of energy given significance by the expressions that have emanated from them. Embedded in *The New Cakewalk* are not just the intricacies of its vocabulary and of its fable, but also the artist's order for a spiritual universe. The work becomes to the artist 'a dwelling place for reflection'" (Krane, 1989: 9, 11–12, 16).

Exercise: A Cosmogram

Begin the process of inventorying the documents and scenes generated through your memory work and research related to the two popcycle institutions treated so far—Career and Family. Use The New Cakewalk *as a relay to see how Conwill makes his cognitive map, linking his personal situation as an African-American with the history and culture of his identity group. What are the equivalents in your own case of his sacred places, heroes, and popular entertainment and folk forms?*

Memory Palace

The Xanadu cosmogram updates the memory palaces of manuscript literacy. The all-important difference between manuscript and digital pedagogy is that the memorial practices of the former aided the living memory of orators, while the latter aid the artificial unconscious of egents. The two palaces share the architectural model codified in the classic mnemonic schemas. This schema has an emblematic structure, consisting of a place or "locus," a strong image, and the unit of information being memorized. The ancient and medieval designs recommended the use of actual places familiar to the student, such as a street in one's home town, or the rooms of one's own home. The images are rebuses using visual and verbal puns associated with the information being stored in the place. In terms of the popcycle we could envision the widesite as a memory palace whose foundation was a selective map of one's home places, occupied at significant locations by striking images drawn from works of Entertainment or History, used associatively to recall the information related to the disciplinary problem on which one is working. The key point is that in electracy the interface giving individual's access to civilizational information is not universal and general but customized and idiosyncratic: mystorical.

Example: D. H. Lawrence A relay to guide choral design of the personal sacred cosmogram is tourist sites. Tourism of course commemorates events and people after the fact. Boston has a "Red Line" heritage trail: a red line literally painted on the sidewalk guides visitors on a walking tour of historic sites related to the American Revolution. A map of such a network provides a ready-made memory palace. More mystorical is the adaptation of Boston's trail by the community of Eastwood, England, whose "Blue Line" trail guides visitors around the hometown of the novelist D. H. Lawrence. The trail takes in the four houses the family lived in while Lawrence was growing up, along with eight other sites related to his life and its dramatization in his fiction (Vine Cottage, Felley Mill farm and pond, Greasley Church, Beauvale Priory, Greasley Beauvale School, Old Ram Inn, Eastwood Cemetery, Cossall Village). The blue line painted on the sidewalks of Eastwood is an emblem of how a private themata may impose itself on the collective paradigm of an institution. The mystory takes this passage from the Red Line to the Blue Line one more step, with the Virtual Line of the memory palace: everyone has a Blue Line, and may use it to organize the docuverse, whether or not the figure it draws ever becomes important to the literal community.

Exercise: Mapping Home

Locate an appropriate map and draw your own Blue Line trail, connecting the significant sites of your life. Extract from the map the shape traced by the trail and treat it as an abstract design—a basis for a logo.

Domestic Altars

The apparatus of print made irrelevant the memorial practices of the manuscript apparatus. The memory palaces of oratorical training gave way to the outlines and essays of education based on the printed page. With the coming of electracy and the replacement of the page by the screen, and of libraries by databases, the architectural mnemonics of rhetors become relevant again. The mystory is a secularized updating and "refunctioning" of medieval allegory, one of whose prototypes is Hugh St. Victor's *"arca sapientiae,"* which the scholar Mary Carruthers says exemplifies the whole program of medieval education.

> "'The ark is like to an apothecary's shop, filled with a variety of all delights. You will seek nothing in it which you will not find, and when you find one thing, you will see many more disclosed to you. Here are bountifully contained the universal works of our salvation from the beginning of the world until the end, and here is contained the condition of the universal Church. Here the narrative of historical events is woven together, here the mysteries of the sacraments are found, here are laid out the successive stages of responses, judgments, meditations, contemplations, or good works, virtues, and rewards.' The triple-tiered ark is the triple mnemonic of medieval Scriptural study: 'historia, allegoria, moralia.' This book/ark, constructed by each student, is an 'apothecary' of diverse, yet orderly material" (Carruthers, 1990: 45).

The storehouse managed by digital mnemonics is the internet, and while the resources and concerns now are different, the coordination of multiple discourses and scales, *designed individually by each student* to facilitate storage and retrieval of information, is the same in the mystory as in the ark. Mystory is the practice that manages the resources generated by the search engines of the internet. The medieval students coordinated their personal "morality" with the history (Old Testament) and "allegory" (life of Christ) given in the Bible and expanded through all the institutional matters of Church. The mystorians' "ark" derives *"moralia"* from family upbringing, history from social studies (as taught in secondary school), and allegory from entertainment (lives and dramas of media stars). The chief insight of this analogy is that information management—categorization and classification—may be singular, particular to each user, customized. The widesite is its maker's singular interface access to the global archive. The mystory allows agents to use their wide image as the interface metaphor for their consultations on public policy formation (and for all other uses of information and knowledge).

Example: Amalia Mesa-Bains, "Home Altars"   A contemporary updating of the medieval memorial ark is the practice by women artists of appropriating the tradition of the home altar as a form for cognitive (affective) mapping. The home altar as form shows how to bring the multiple discourses of the popcycle together without relying on narrative coherence or conceptual categories. Amalia Mesa-Bains's popcycle identifications include Career (Frida Kahlo), Entertainment (Dolores del Rio), Family (her grandmother).

Celeste Olalquiaga on Amalia Mesa-Bains

"One of [Mesa-Bains's] recent shows, grotto of the Virgin, consisted of *altares* raised to such unhallowed figures as Mexican painter Frida Kahlo, Mexican superstar Dolores del Rio, and her own grandmother. What is specific to Mesa-Bains's altars is that the personal is not subordinated to a particular holy person. Rather, a secular person is made sacred by the altar format, the offerings consisting mainly of a reconstruction of that person's imagined life by means of images and gadgets. The Dolores del Rio altar, for example, is raised on several steps made with mirrors, bringing to mind the image cults that grow up around Hollywood actors and actresses. This altar is stacked with feminine paraphenalia such as perfume bottles, lipstick, and jewelry, as well as letters, pictures, and other souvenirs of her life. In this way, the image of Dolores del Rio as a 'cinema goddess' becomes literal.

"This secularization of the *altares* is probably due to the importance Mesa-Bains assigns to personal experience. In traditional altar raising, the personal was always secondary to the deity and religious sensibility articulated in the last instance the whole altar. By privileging what were only coding elements so that they become the main objective of her *altares,* Mesa-Bains has inverted the traditional formula. As a result, women and mass culture are invested with a new power that emanates from the sacredness of *altares:* in postmodern culture, Mesa-Bains's work would seem to contend, old patriarchal deities are no longer satisfactory. What she has done is to profit from an established tradition to convey new values. Beyond mere formal changes, her *altares* replace the transcendental with the political. In them, the affirmation of feminist and Chicano experiences is more relevant than a pious communication with the celestial sphere" (Olalquiaga, 1992: 48).

The aesthetics of altar design correlate well with the accumulative nonlinear interconnectedness of hypermedia on the Web. Although we are using narrative allegory as a relay to understand how mystory can collect into one composition the heterogeneous discourses of the popcycle (and in so doing, reveal the outline of a wide image), there is another medieval genre that better describes the result, which is an image (or interrelated set of images—the wide image): speculum, or mirror (Beaujour, 1991: 27). The memory palace, that is, established a series of pictures whose purpose was not illustration or communication but *meditation*. Their religious function was to guide the believer in the practice of worship, including creating the proper state of mind to consider his or her personal salvation and relationship with God. Another function was to generate texts—not just to recall information but to guide the composition of new texts or speeches. A speculum, that is, is not one narrative but a staging area for many narratives. The speculum refunctioned as wide image through the mystory is meant to give its user direct access to his/her mood of creativity (the state of mind or Stimmung that one enters during the creative process of making or problem solving). The artists' use of the home altar shows formally how this effect may be achieved.

Kay Turner on Artists' Domestic Altars

"An inventory of typical symbolic objects can be drawn up from looking at a number of different women's altars. These objects, both individually and in their arrangement as a group, represent and activate the power of relationship. Gathered around the central divine image, there might be any of the following: multiple prints and statues of secondary religious figures; photos, candles, incense, ritual tools, potions, medicine bundles, shells, crystals, coins, mementos, knick-knacks, gifts, offerings, decorative effects, and even seemingly anomalous items, such as a jar of buttons or a door knob. . . .

"The condensed—often intense—focus that the altar provides draws its maker into a stimulating visual field. Rabbi Lynn Gottlieb describes the potency of the visible: 'the visual focus is important . . . it's very hard to create an atmosphere spiritually, internally. The visual aesthetic takes you there right away.' . . . A glance at her altar invites a woman to catalog the relationships represented there. . . . If the first aesthetic goal of an altar is to represent relationship, then the primary artistic move is to set potent images in relation to each other. . . .

"Femmage (feminist collage) utilizes the potential of fragmentation as Lucy Lippard defines it: 'Fragmentation need not connote explosion, disintegration. It is also a component of networks, stratification, the interweaving of many dissimilar threads, and de-emphasis on imposed meaning in favor of multiple interpretations. Fragmentation pervades women's work in all the arts on many subtle levels.' The home altar demonstrates the value of fragments, which, when linked together, provide a center of focus derived not by imposition, but organically through layering and accretion. This process is described by Candice Goucher: 'I think "accumulation" is a good word to describe the process of acquiring objects that begin to have meaning both in and of themselves and in relation to events or people or places or ideas.' . . .

"Such intensification springs from a process of condensing and miniaturizing. What the scholar and poet Susan Stewart considers as only superficially true of the souvenir collection is authentically true of the home altar: it 'offers transcendence to the viewer' by virtue of 'a reduction in physical dimensions corresponding to an increase in significance . . . an interiorization of an exterior.' As Renee Dooley further notes, the altar employs a microcosmic strategy to gain macrocosmic results." (Turner, 1999: 95–101)

Comment

- What the paragraph was to the definition, the fragment is to the mystory. The home altar makes a good relay for the website, in its reliance on the holistic effects of assemblage to achieve a "look and feel" of a mood. Assemblage produces coherence neither through argument nor narrative (although it may contain these literate and oral forms), but through image. The altar evokes an overall look and feel through the accumulation and repetition of sensory details.

- The domestic altar also brings out the personal quality of the sacred in modern choral space.

Exercise: Vernacular Genres

Select some activity, practice, or form common to your Family life, and use it in the way that Mesa-Bains used the home altar (or the way Conwill used the cakewalk) to structure the materials of the mystory Family discource.

- Any activity will work for this purpose. The idea is that a mystory has no "form" of its own, but appropriates a form from one of the popcycle discourses to serve as the mode of presentation for the whole. Think of something that was a regular part of family experience, whether or not you participated in it directly: gardening, card games, garage sales, refrigerator door decoration, for example. Inventory the features of this activity and translate them into design elements for your website. Use this design to display the details you generated to document the Family register of the mystory.

REMAKE (ULMER FILE)
Mapping a Chora (My Xanadu)

Exercise: Mapping the Popcycle

On a map or diagram of your hometown (or wherever the Family discourse is situated), locate the sites that are the local embodiments of the popcycle institutions. Introduce some documentation, details, stories, noting how you experienced each of the institutions.

- This map serves as a preliminary ground of your memory palace.
- Although the mystory and its relays outlined in this chapter (including the case study that follows) pass through the four popcycle discourses, you are responsible to this point only for Career and Family. The form and relays show you what we will work on in subsequent chapters.

I am using my own case as a relay for learning the mystory. The purpose of the following discussion is to demonstrate the path of the flash of spirit, of insight. *Mystory is to insight what electricity is to lightning:* a means to put into a reliable practice a power found "wild" in daily life. This installment shows the connecting paths of my cognitive map that constitute the primary tracks that subsequent "intuitive" reasoning will follow. Such is the prospective nature of the widesite: not to wait for the flash of insight, but to write (design) it. These paths, connecting my personal situation to my collective historical moment, manifest the workings of the fourth mode of inference—conduction—that electracy adds to the modes formalized in the apparatus of literacy (abduction, induction, deduction). The map attempts to trace the circulation of the global world through a specific location in time and space, not abstractly but by following some of the features of the "given" situation in their circulation. The experience is uncanny.

The Phantom Trailer

The year is 1953. My father, mother, sister, and I are in a trailer, a mobile home, parked on concrete blocks on some land beside the Yellowstone River that was part of my father's business, the Miles City Sand and Gravel Company. We are together at the dinner table. It is not so much a table as a counter in the dining area of the trailer. One end of the counter is attached to the wall. A shelf space is recessed into the wall, and on one of the shelves our radio is playing, tuned to the local radio station, KATL. This radio was turned on every waking moment. The playlist was programmed for a week at a time, and it never seemed to change; a certain number of times a week, in a nearly predictable rhythm of repetition, you could hear the Sons of the Pioneers singing "Cool Cool Water." After I got my driver's license and started cruising the drag with all the other teenagers, I could listen at night to KOMA in Oklahoma, which played the new rock music. I used my allowance to go to the Melody Shop and buy 45 rpm singles of the songs I heard on KOMA. I never bought a copy of anything I heard on KATL.

The odd thing about this memory is that we never lived in a trailer. We moved from a rented house to our own home—a three-bedroom, two-bath house with a free-standing garage—when I was in the seventh grade. The mortgage on this house was a financial burden, and the one thing my folks argued about was this expense. The argument consisted in essence of a choice between this mortgaged house and a trailer at the Sand and Gravel, the latter being in a sense "free." In memory these two places have begun to merge—the house and the trailer. I realize now that these dwellings were metonyms for something else, for what distinguished them was not only square footage and building materials. The tracks of the Northern Pacific Railroad make a diagonal slash through the town. Our house was on the right side of the tracks, and the trailer was on the wrong side, the left (out) side, the working-class side. If my father had moved into the trailer as he claimed he wanted to do, he would have moved in without his wife and children: that was my mother's position.

The map of Home for me has these two material axes: KATL-KOMA, crossed by House-Trailer, forming an X. I locate on this grid a particular scene of writing that involved the naming of our cat (to form my version of the composition of "Kubla Khan"). Like almost every cat I have ever roomed with, this one—an orange and white tom—showed up as a stray and moved in. So it was 1953 and we were seated at the kitchen counter in the trailer/house. The cat jumped up onto the counter and began persuading us to adopt it. This was a very persuasive cat. Among its accomplishments was that my mother cooked it scrambled eggs for breakfast every morning of its life, or at least its life with us. How did this happen? She did not cook eggs for the rest of the family every morning. These were not leftovers, an extra egg while she was at it. We ate cereal and toast. The cat had its own schedule, which did not coincide with ours. I never understood how this ritual started. There was a huge scene when my grandmother came to stay with the kids while my folks went on a trip. My grandmother disliked cats, and she was not pleased to learn that part of her duties included scrambling eggs for our cat.

The scene of writing in this home voice (Stimme) has to do with how we named the cat. The radio was tuned to KATL, a station that played the songs of Hank Williams, Sr., on a regular basis. It was 1953, a year when Billboard chart number one for many weeks was "Kaw-liga," and number two was "Your Cheatin' Heart." "Kaw-liga" is about a wooden Indian: "Poor ol' Kaw-li-ga, he never got a kiss. Poor ol' Kaw-li-ga, he don't know what he missed. Is it any wonder that his face is red. Kaw-li-ga that poor ol' wooden head." While the song was playing the cat rubbed up against the radio and started to purr. By whatever process, the family agreed at that moment that the cat could stay, and that it was named Kawliga.

The Baby-Blue Cadillac

The Family voice started the series and led to Hank Williams, Sr., my voice of Entertainment. It is the same mystery as Kawliga's scrambled eggs. I do not know how or when exactly Hank acquired this status. When I was growing up I hated country music and loved the new "rock." I hated the piles of rocks at the Sand and Gravel plant, but I liked the rock music on KOMA that we could hear in Montana at night coming all the way from Oklahoma. Hank's voice in this structure consists of two elements. The first element is his yodel, the way he flipped his singing in and out of falsetto. "If you're tired of breaking other hearts, you can come back again and break mine." On "breaking" the voice flips into falsetto, breaking the word into two parts. The second element in this "voice" is the electric pedal steel guitar. Commentators agree that the signature sound of Hank's music, which included his backup group, the Drifting Cowboys (Cowboys *en derive*) was the sustained wailing glissando that is distinctive to the steel guitar. The opening bars of "Your Cheatin' Heart" are exemplary of this quality. I had forgotten that, as part of Hank's crossover success, "Kaw-liga" was mixed with an orchestral string background. I remember only the yodel and the slide glissando.

"Kawliga Khan" (my remake of Coleridge's poem) focuses on two unknown songs that Hank never finished. Hank was a country romantic, in that his songs exemplify "authenticity." He was a natural, they say. Although he attended school until he was nineteen, he had only made it to the ninth grade. He learned his music in the streets, hanging out with a Black street musician named Rufus "Tee Tot" Payne. Hank was twelve when he started the drinking that made him an alcoholic. His drug use is ascribed to his need for relief from the pains associated with the symptoms of Spina Bifida Oculta, from which he suffered. His songs reflect the hard life he actually lived growing up in south Alabama (Koon, 1983).

The scene of writing for my Entertainment voice is a hybrid of the two unknown songs, both interrupted during the early stages of composition. One is the last song Hank ever wrote. On New Year's Eve, 1952, Hank got into the back seat of his baby-blue cadillac convertible. Heavy snows had grounded his flight to Canton, Ohio, where he was to play in a concert on New Year's Day. There is more to the story, having to do with the drugs prescribed by his quack doctor, his drinking problem, his poor health. The short of it is that when the driver stopped in the dawn hours somewhere in West Virginia to check on his passenger, Hank was dead. He was 29 years old. Clutched in his hand, the story goes, was a new song he had been working on. That Hank was at the peak of his songwriting skills was evident from the two songs completed in his last recording session—"Kaw-liga" and "Your Cheatin' Heart." This new song was, like most country songs, about a problem: *we lived, we loved, you left.*

Not much is known about this legendary final song. To fill in the gap I merge it with a further scene of composition. Hank Williams and the Drifting Cowboys were engaged in 1951 as the featured act of a touring show intended to promote the popular patent medicine, Hadacol. The active ingredients in this medicine were alcohol (12 percent) and laxative. The product sold well in the mostly dry South, but the inventor, Dudley LeBlanc, wanted a national distribution. To gain some legitimacy, LeBlanc engaged some of the biggest stars of the day—Jack Benny, Cesar Romero, Milton Berle, Bob Hope, to name only a few. The stars were to join the main act—Hank and his band—just for a few days each. One of the stars with whom Hank was supposed to perform was Carmen Miranda (Koon, 1983: 36).

Samba Country   Carmen Miranda, whose presence in cinema in the 1940s was a manifestation of the Good Neighbor Policy pursued during the war years, had introduced the samba into American popular culture. Before coming to the United States, Carmen had a successful career as a samba singer in Brazil. I have not been able to find any information about the meeting of Hank Williams and Carmen Miranda on the Hadacol Caravan. The Caravan was cut short after 34 shows when the company folded due to problems over taxes and false advertising (38). Could there have been a phantom song, a syncretic invention crossing country with samba? Elvis did not make his country-blues hybrid until 1954, around the same time that Carmen collapsed and died after a performance on Jimmy Durante's television show. The phantom song that haunts the history of rock, or the song this history forgot, is the one Hank and Carmen might have coauthored or performed. The scene of this collaboration between country and samba may or may not have taken place in 1951, and it is an opportunity whose future remains open (although by now nearly every permutation and combination of forms has been marketed by one group or another in world music). It is worth noting, too, that for her syncretic efforts in Hollywood, Miranda was reviled and abandoned by her former fans when she returned to Brazil for what was supposed to be a triumphant homecoming (Vianna, 1999: 93). Such is often the fate of anything "creole" confronted by the myth of "authenticity."

The original Carnival music of Brazil, before samba, was called "choro" (literally, "sobbing, crying") (Broughton, 1994: 558). This sobbing, crying, is linked with *hanblecheyapi*, lamenting, the vision quest of the Lakota Medicine Man, Black Elk, who first performed his vision just down the road from the Miles City Sand and Gravel. These are some of my primal acquaintances: Hank Williams, Sr., and Black Elk. Hank introduces me to Carmen Miranda, who is associated in turn with Jimmy Durante, thus motivating the appearance of all these figures in my story (a spreading pattern). Their music evokes the mood of my cosmogram. In the same way that philosophy was invented by stripping away everything from the epic except the idea of justice, choragraphy comes into its own by stripping away from music everything except its mood. The experimental arts have taught us how to write chorally, by removing from a text the conventional structuring forms—argument, narrative, character, and finally music (any rhythm of theme and variation for example). Peterson, explaining the way people make sense of texts by calling upon cognitive schemas that are part of their cultural literacy, listed the defaults, the inventory that people go through when they read or view a text, until they arrive at the final default.

> "If viewers are unable to match even quasi-musical schemata to the film's global level, they can still make a general appraisal of the film's overall mood or atmosphere. Viewers may use such 'atmospheric schemata' along with other schemata; a consistent mood, however, may be the sole global schema. In such films, meaning is built up gradually through the connotations of the images, and the order of the images is not especially important" (Peterson, 1994: 50).

Atmosphere created through the repetition of images is the minimal unit of coherence. This accumulation of images to evoke finally a mood is the fundamental structuring principle of the widesite.

Comment

- It is worth pausing in our leisurely pace to emphasize this useful contribution of cognitive psychology or schema theory to our study of how images organize information. Literate people have learned or acquired a set of schemas or ready-made default conventions for understanding any communication they receive. When presented with a message, we tend to assume that it will be in expository form, an explanation, sincerely stated as true, motivated by a desire for direct and transparent exchange of understanding. If this first schema is frustrated, Peterson explains, we move through our other schemas for language processing until we find one that applies, or that at least makes sense. The social setting or institutional frame of the communication also provides clues for which schema is relevant. The following schemas are listed in the preferred order for literate American culture, passing from most highly controlled to loosest mode of order.

    1. argument (exposition)
    2. narrative (story)
    3. character (biography)
    4. musical (theme and variation patterns)
    5. image (atmosphere through repeated signifiers).

  Advertising and art use these schemas in a reverse order of preference, anticipating the categorical importance of imaging in electracy. The nearly complete neglect of imaging in School is understandable, given what has been said about grammatology and the history of the apparatus. However, if schools are to remain relevant in the apparatus of electracy, they must extend education in imaging beyond elementary school and promote it as a method for all disciplines. If schools reject imaging the way churches rejected science in the transition from orality to literacy, then the internet will have to evolve its own institutional administration of electrate knowledge and practice.

String Theory

I am following a thread, or an image of a thread, rather than a story or an argument. A string (*ficelle*). The first mystory I composed, "Derrida at the Little Bighorn," turned up the word "*ficelle*" in the voice of History (School). I found it on the battlefield of Custer's Last Stand, or rather on the map of the battlefield published in the visitor's guide. The five companies that died with Custer were named following military conventions with a letter of the alphabet. The historian who designed the map placed the letters of the five companies on the map to designate the defensive position the units assumed in their last hour of life. C-E-F-I-L. The letters may be read as an anagram of the French word ficelle (allowing for the extra letters that mark gender in French spelling). Ficelle was the term Jacques Lacan used to refer to the loops of string that he tied into knots to demonstrate to his seminars the topologies of the Unconscious (the relationships among the Imaginary, the Symbolic, the Real, and the Symptom). The loops map intersubjectivity at the level of the orifices, the erogenous zones, of bodies in a society.

The word already had a history as a theoretical term, having been used by Henry James, in his preface to *The Ambassadors,* to name those secondary characters included in a novel to meet the needs of the form. Lacan featured a painting by Holbein entitled "The Ambassadors,"—famous for the death's head smeared across its foreground in anamorphic perspective—in one of his seminars. What were these two ambassadors sent to tell me? *Ficelle* means (among other things) "the thread of a plot," a meaning to which James may have been alluding with his choice of terms. Further development of the mystory into choragraphy has helped me understand how I should read the figure in my own carpet, my own diagrammed mandala (labyrinth). The figures that recur in the diagram show me my *superego.* The four voices I found speaking through my popcycle were my father (Family), "General" Custer (School), Gary Cooper (Entertainment), Jacques Derrida (Discipline). A heuristic device for negotiating with this figure is to look for the *ficelle*—the supporting character, for each one of these imagoes. A preliminary incomplete list of my alter-superego (my other) then is: Mom, Black Elk, Marlene Dietrich.

Follow the Inventions   In this remake the string I am following is literally part of a guitar. A heuristic rule of heuretics, useful for locating the conductive path available in the material, is to examine a scene in terms of an invention that might be found in it. One of the inventions prominently displayed in my voices of Family and Entertainment is that of the slide guitar. The provisional contested border of the subject's inside/outside is traced between experience and history, memory and research. What is the status of the slide guitar? In my experience the slide guitar originated in country music. Whatever my tastes were or are, the sound of the pedal steel guitar in the opening bars (bar is a pivot word in my file) of "Your Cheatin' Heart" evoke the essence of Home for me. There is nothing more famliar (more canny) than the steel guitar in my experience. The juxtaposition of this experience with some research produced a shock, an "encounter" or "profane illumination." The most familiar thing turned out to have an unfamiliar register. The steel guitar became uncanny.

The shock is that the steel guitar was invented in Hawaii. I should have known this fact (ATH—foolishness), since steel guitar is often identified in liner notes as "Hawaiian steel." The steel guitar developed from the slack key tunings introduced by Hawaiian musicians, so-called because the tuning of the strings was slackened to achieve an open chord (Broughton, 650). Strumming the strings of a guitar tuned DBGDGD produces a G chord. Placing a finger (barring) or steel bar (the bar) across the strings at the fifth and seventh frets gives the other two chords used for any three-chord song. "The steel guitar developed from the slack key and is played horizontally with the strings facing upward. The steel rod is pressed on the strings with the left hand to produce a harmonious sliding sound. The first electric guitar, a Richenbacher nicknamed the 'frying pan', was actually a Hawaiian lap steel guitar made in 1931" (650).

Slack Key Cosmogram   The different voices of the popcycle are given an open tuning. Slack-key tuning and the resulting style of playing, including the barred chords, give instructions for how to write in choragraphy. They constitute an anecdote of life that forms an X crossing with an aphorism of thought (Nietzsche): slack key tuning + Stimmung. The sound that marks *Heim* and *Unheim* for me is threaded through Hank Williams and Heidegger's Dasein (attunement). Where else does it go? Here is the thread of research, the series that carries me where I would never go otherwise, to produce learning effects whose outer limit is satori. A little more history shows me the larger scene within which my listening to "Kaw-liga" is inscribed. The research is necessary because what is being composed is a cognitive map, a conjunction of private and public stories: library as memory palace, autoportrait within the General Economy, the universal side of unique experience. A worldwide craze for Hawaiian guitar music was launched in 1915 at the San Francisco Panama-Pacific Expo that celebrated the opening of the Panama Canal. The music was featured in the pavilion sponsored by the new territory of Hawaii. The music, and more particularly the style of the steel guitar, became popular worldwide, spread by tours and by the sale of recordings. The records of Jimmy Rogers, who adapted steel style to country, were popular in Africa in the 1930s.

This research, in other words, led me into the area of World Music, and finally to the juju music of King Sunny Ade. Reading a description of the juju sound (juju means fetish) was like finding the place at which the other end of the rainbow touches ground: "I was fascinated by the melding of 'deep' Yoruba praise singing and drumming, guitar techniques from soul music, Latin American dance rhythms, church hymns and country-and-western melodies, pedal steel guitar licks and Indian film music themes, and by the fact that this modernist bricolage could so effectively evoke traditional values" (Waterman, 1990: 2). A word to describe the effect of listening to a CD of juju music is "uncanny"— the discovery of the familiar in the unfamiliar—when I heard floating in over the top of the multiple complex drumming rhythms that predominate in African modes the glissando of the electric pedal steel guitar. I "recognized" this sound as an event of surprise, an illumination. I now pronounce the name of the famous drink invented at the University of Florida after the sound of the last name of the juju king (Gator-Ah-Day). Fetishturgy. Juju-wright. Such is the mental map of my chora.

Comment

* The slide guitar is the thread or string motivating the movement through these different areas of information, joining finally a childhood of Hank Williams with African world music. To gather diverse information or documents into a set using a shared signifier in this way is to use the inference logic of conduction.

Cyberpidgin

My remake as research produced an image: the slack key tunings associated with the steel guitar. It is a question not only of the tunings, but their dissemination. "Common Hawaiian slack-key tunings in C, G, and F—for example, 'taro patch' (5-1-5-1-3-5, ascending)—are identical to tunings used by Lagosian guitarists. The international distribution of such tuning systems along trade routes has yet to be adequately investigated (Waterman, 47). Such images are the basic units of the reasoning suited for the apparatus of electracy with its catas-tropic figures made of syncretic dream packets. The catastrope or *interbody* metaphor for choragraphy is that of World Music. The "trade route" of these tunings figures the inference paths of the mystory, which follows the materializations of the inventions that pass through the different registers of the popcycle. The internet wires these same routes, the way the higher discourses of the popcycle retrace the first entry into language that formatted my creative potential in Family. These wandering associative networks replace in electracy the linearity of literate forms.

World Music includes a more basic version of the interface metaphor— pidgin language. The three terms are interrelated and mutually illuminating— syncretism, World Music, and pidgin. First used in anthropology to describe the symbolic fusion of West African deities with Catholic saints, syncretism was defined as "the tendency to identify those elements in a new culture with similar elements in the old one, enabling the persons experiencing the contact to move from one to the other and back again, with psychological ease" (Waterman, 9). Waterman makes the analogy explicit: "guitar patterns and songs learned from gramophone records were adapted by palmwine performers for use in informal social gatherings. This process involved a schematization of patterns, much in the manner of a pidgin language" (47).

The purpose of the interface metaphor—a postcolonialized version of a pidgin language—is to figure the global dimension of internet interactivity. The metaphor applies to both the inside and outside registers of the design method: to the exchanges across the levels of the mystory within the composers' design; and to the exchanges among all the composers online. Pidgins arose in the special spaces that formed when European traders and colonizers encountered non-Western peoples. What does this phenomenon suggest about the future of a global society in an electronic apparatus? The nature of such a society may be intuited in the syncretic scene of juju invention. "It should be noted that the metaphoric forging of correspondences between musical and social order is not limited to structural analogies. . . . The experiential impact of the metaphor 'good music is the ideal society writ small' depends upon the generation of sensuous textures. An effective performance of juju predicates not only the structure of the ideal society, but also its 'feel': intense, vibrant, loud, buzzing, and fluid" (Waterman 220). Chorography maps the personal equivalents of the trade routes that carried pedal steel around the world (the personal sacred).

Waterman's central point about the moral, political, social lesson of juju has to do with a new attitude toward hybrid formations, to creolization. A postcolonial internet pidgin must abandon the colonialist denigration of the "creole," and the ideological atmosphere in which colonizer and colonized alike favored "purity" whether modernist or traditional, and despised the mixed (75). This exploration of hybrids across cultures and categories sets the program of chorographic research for the immediate future. The link crossing the abyss separating me from Africa consists of nothing more substantial than this uncanny commonality of (creole) pedal steel. But this sound (and the mood it produces) is part of a new syntax or mapping coming into formation (manifesting how the literate apparatus is bootstrapping its way into electracy). The denizens of electrate political formations (whatever replaces the *nation state* and the *self* in the coming community) know cyberpidgin. Pidgin happens. Cyberpidgin is invented and brings an historical phenomenon into an educational practice.

OFFICE

1. The introduction of the mystory previously (with the four-part allegorical structure organizing the popcycle institutions of the lifeworld) and the examples and relays of four-part cosmograms, diagrams, altars, and the like now, provide an overview of the mystory as a whole. You have two of the four popcycle quarters implemented so far: Career and Family. The allegorical structure anticipates for you the "slots" that remain to be filled.

2. The exercises encourage you to begin relating the levels as you work on the widesite. As soon as you have two dimensions to work between, inevitably there will be some repetitions that are formal, coming not from memory but from the signifiers of the documents. It is useful to pay attention to these patterns as pointers about where to look for further information or for the pattern that may eventually become your wide image. Often, more than one area of the discourse is relevant to your experience. A

good criterion for choosing one over the other is that one fits better with material already in the site.

3. It is possible but not necessary to link the sites at this early stage. Against what I said earlier, it is equally useful just to think about each assignment in isolation, without worrying about a pattern. You are guaranteed to produce a pattern within the inference method of conduction, for the same reason that there are puns in language or in imagery: the law of few signifiers supporting many signifieds (only 26 letters in the alphabet representing hundreds of thousands of words, for example). One artist discovered the visual pun when he decided to produce a raygun "multiple" (a large number of a cheaply reproduced object). After putting some effort to making items that looked like at least toy rayguns, he realized that any object that had a right angle in its shape could be a raygun. In this way he could find a raygun thread running through a disparate variety of materials.

4. In the Ulmer File I introduce discussion and examples of my own mystory work, which is intended as a relay rather than as a model or template. Again, it is worth emphasizing that this textbook format requires essayistic prose mostly describing the project, but the widesite itself is not an essay but an assemblage, a collage of heterogeneous, mixed documents of text and picture, that will come together in an aesthetic way, as an image. The widesite is a self-portrait, whose likeness is finally determined by recognition (you step back from it and say: *that's me*). The site is evaluated not for its authenticity however, but for its formal adherence to the principles and relays developed throughout the course. It is possible to fake a mystory, but who would want to? It does not matter if anyone else likes your mystory: it is not art or literature, but a thought experiment. The best and most appropriate response to your mystory is that the visitors get the desire to make one for themselves (to extrapolate in turn and ask: what is that for me?).

5. Every so often in the discussion I summarize the qualities of the wide image or the widesite in an analogy. For example: *In the same way that philosophy was invented by stripping away everything from the epic except the idea of justice, choragraphy comes into its own by stripping away from music everything except its mood.* These analogies serve as aphoristic definitions. I will not single them out usually, but you might watch for them and collect them into a set to use as a reminder of what we are inventing.

Part III

ENTERTAINMENT DISCOURSE

HISTORY–Ulmer with a photograph of George Armstrong Custer, at the Custer National Battlefield Museum, Montana

"Egents are required to work with donors from the full range of possibilities—fool to angel."

Chapter 5
Interface Impressions

The subject is presented with a problem or challenge that will change his/her destiny. The subject experiences fear of the unknown or fear of outside forces. The wise one: a mentor gives guidance and support to the subject.

STUDIO
Beyond Identification

We are entering the discourse of Entertainment, where we encounter the beginnings of explicitly electrate reason. The structure of Entertainment narrative provides an allegorical map for becoming an egent, which explains why the project to make a wide image is performed as learning how to consult on a public policy question. The Entertainment narrative template we are following is based on the archetypal pattern of the hero's quest, which expresses in turn an ancient ritual of initiation—the achievement of individual identity. The motive for leaving home and entering the special world of adventure in this schema is some problem, some excess or lack, some trouble that disturbs the equilibrium of the Family situation. In our use of this schema it will take a couple of chapters to cross the threshold separating home (Family) from adventure (Entertainment).

In EmerAgency terms, the problem that initiates the adventure is the public policy question to be addressed by the egent as consultant. As we shall see, before egents may address this problem they must acquire a "magic tool" (in the terms of the wondertale), which is the wide image. The rationale for our approach (the mystory) is that one's manner of solving problems in a Career discipline is influenced by one's experience of problem solving in the other discourses of the popcycle. The relationship with problems in the home and in the stories consumed as entertainment, not to mention the role of problems and solutions in the historical evolution of one's community, informs the imagination used in applied reasoning in one's work (transfer of learning across the popcycle institutions). We have not yet encountered a current public policy problem. For now, in its place, we will take note of the problems at work in the Family and Entertainment discourses, as we remember them.

Assignment: Entertainment Discourse

Make a website documenting the details of a movie or TV narrative some part of which you still remember from your childhood years (K–12 years).

- This site is the third quarter of the mystory, adding the Entertainment discourse to your cognitive map.

- Some students prefer to use a favorite book from childhood, rather than a narrative from cinema or television.

- The first purpose of the documentation is to record the part of the story that you remember. Once you have inventoried the remains of the work in your memory, view it again (if it is available) and record what you notice in this fresh viewing. The memory is the site of a sting, in Barthes's sense. You are looking for the obtuse meaning of a story—a personal association with some detail in the narrative.

- The second aspect of the memory work is to connect your Family memories and the Entertainment narrative. The connection will most likely not be literal, but figurative. The mystory forms what Roland Barthes called a "structural portrait": the relationship between you and the narrative is that of a proportional ratio. Your position in your family is analogous to the position of the character to his/her diegetic world. The idea is to map one story onto the other. The entertainment narrative figures the atmosphere or mood of the family situation, not its literal circumstances.

- When reviewing the work, note especially the problem or conflict organizing the drama, and the way it is resolved. Memory tends to form around problems, whether the problems are large or small. All narratives are structured by conflict (the protagonist confronts a problem). Use this more clearly defined situation in the story to locate the coherence in your memories of Family.

Examples: Movie Memories   The following examples represent the kind of memories of images that remain long after the details of plot and character have been forgotten. Documentation of such impressions found in memory is a good way to begin work on the Entertainment quarter of the mystory.

1. Sam Shepard on Burt Lancaster

"I remember trying to imitate Burt Lancaster's smile after I saw him and Gary Cooper in *Vera Cruz*. For days I practiced in the backyard. Weaving through the tomato plants. Sneering. Grinning that grin. Sliding my upper lip up over my teeth. After a few days of practice I tried it out on the girls at school. They didn't seem to notice. I broadened my interpretation until I started getting strange reactions from the other kids. They would look straight at my teeth and a fear would creep into their eyes. I'd forgotten how bad my teeth were. How one of the front ones was dead and brown and overlapped the broken one right next to it. I'd actually come to believe I was in possession of a full head of perfect pearly Burt Lancaster-type teeth. I didn't want to scare anyone so I stopped grinning after that. I only did it in private. Pretty soon even that faded. I returned to my empty face" (Shepard, 1982: 14).

2. Barbara Broughel on The Blob

In this interview Broughel named *The Blob,* which she saw when she was eight, as the most memorable film of her childhood. She was asked what frightened her most.

"First—being eaten. When you're a kid, you know you eat, but you don't worry about being eaten. Second, the 'thing' which was the Blob lacked definition. No one in the movie could figure out what they were being confronted by, and so in a sense, it was impossible to focus on it properly, and this really contributed to my confusion. Thirdly, and perhaps most importantly, I was terrified of the idea of outer space—like an asteroid, in what I believe was the opening shot of the movie. I had never been confronted by the concept of space before, and to find out about it in this worst-of-all-possible-ways really threw me into an intellectual and emotional tailspin. Even when the adults in my household tried to convince me that the Blob would not fall from outer space into my own neighborhood, I still got the impression that they didn't really know any more about space than I did, and this made me lose faith in their omniscience—perhaps for the first time, and by implication, I felt that no one—not even an adult—could predict 100% whether another Blob landing might be imminent" (Broughel, 1987: 16–17).

3. John Carson on Darby O'Gill and the Little People

"No matter how corny the characters in the picture postcard parish of Rathcullen, I recognized the fields, I knew the smell of Guinness from drunk men's breath, and my father wore a cap just like Darby O'Gill's.

"I do not recall much of the plot but all through childhood and beyond I have remained haunted by vivid remembered images: little leprechauns in mad underground celebration dancing round pots of gold leaping over plundered treasures; Michael and Katy skipping hand in hand through the fields; the jaunty, laughing, Guinness-swilling devil-may-care Darby with his pub stories, his sideways philosophy and his battles of wit with the wily King Brian of the leprechauns; but mainly, and most frighteningly, the dreaded death coach with its headless coachman come to call Darby's soul on the one-way trip to hell. The thought of it still sends shivers throughout me. Therein is part of the magic of cinema—to implant a visual image so strongly that somewhere in the psyche, the cinematic illusion becomes as real or as powerful a memory as any actual experience" (Carson, 1987: 26).

Comment

- If Carson, for example, were making a mystory he would have to translate this initial memory into a website documentation. He would begin with some representation of the scene of the death coach (ideally grab an image from a tape of the film, or find one on the Web), supplemented by some citation of the script. If no such image is available, then use the Boltanski principle of taking any coach picture and perhaps modifying it in a graphics program. The Garcia principle is also good: make a drawing and scan it in. The signifiers constituting the atmosphere of the scene could then be enhanced, intensified, by further documentation of images and text found on the Web. The switch-object is the hat worn by both his father and Darby. This hat should be documented.

- The documentation procedure for each installment of the mystory should develop as many sensory signifiers as possible that are relevant to the memory, to increase the chances for producing the hook that will catch the eye of another signifier in one of the other quarters to form a "catena" or chain threading together the assemblage into a constellation.

The Method

A good procedure for locating the connection between a family situation and the film (and even for selecting which work among the several that are likely to come to mind) is to borrow some of the techniques used by Method actors to create a role for a stage or screen character. The following passages give an idea of the Method, excerpted from an instruction book for beginning actors.

Anita Jesse on Acting Technique

"The given circumstances make up the environment in which the scene occurs or the particular world in which these events take place. That world includes the physical setting, everything that has happened to the character before the scene begins, and the attitudes shaped by those events. The given circumstances compose the framework within which the action of the scene takes place . . .

"When you determine your point of view—what you assume is true about the way the world works—you are establishing a belief system, a framework in which you operate. We all have belief systems and each of those beliefs is anchored in specific action. Our convictions are either inspired by, or supported by, specific events in our lives. For example, if you believe that all women or men are unfaithful, it is because you were deeply hurt by someone who was unfaithful to you or to someone you loved (probably a parent) and the pain you suffered because of that infidelity taught you a lesson. Every aspect of your outlook on life is directly linked to events you experienced. If you don't know the event that originally established the belief system, at least you remember events that corroborate the point of view.

"Find your character's point of view, and anchor it in action by identifying the specific events in your character-life that have shaped your outlook. If you relive, in your imagination, an event that taught you this belief, you will internalize the belief and avoid posturing. Your character does not choose to embrace these beliefs; your character has learned by experience that this is how the world works.

"In certain instances you will find it advantageous to substitute your own experiences for those that make up the character's given circumstances. Substitutions are particularly useful when answering: Who are the people we talk about? In *All My Sons,* Ann talks about her father and her first fiance, who is dead. The actress must have specific images in her mind of actual people when she says those lines.

"Finding a metaphor for the action in the scene may be the secret to fully engaging your mind and body. For example, the sample scene [you have to persuade your brother to sign a contract for a project that is not in his best interest] could be a courting dance inspiring you to hold in your mind images of a male bird strutting and displaying, showing alternating force and passion" (Jesse, 1994: 101, 103, 112).

Comment

- Note how the actors in the scene or scenes from your entertainment memory performed their role. How did they use their bodies to convey meaning?

- In mapping the popcycle to locate your mystory you are making explicit the *belief system* to which Jesse refers. The belief system often is not explicitly articulated, neither in stories nor in life, but is implicit within the given circumstances of a character or person. Noting an analogy between the circumstances of a character in a story and your own circumstances is a useful way to bring your own belief system into awareness. These beliefs operate through intuitions mistaken for reality itself. Interpellation works in this way, not usually as explicit explanations of concepts, but through the repetition of behavior. A national mood such as *wabi sabi* in Japan may control the taste of an entire culture without being defined. Such is the case with the concept of *shi* in China. François Jullien, in his study showing how this attunement saturates every aspect of Chinese civilization from military strategy to landscape painting, noted that no Chinese thinker ever featured it as an important concept and no formal analysis of it was ever made. This unexamined status of a cultural mood is even more true for the personal attunement associated with a wide image.

Examples

The first example takes a superficial and humorous approach to imperson-ation of a cult or celebrity star. It is useful to notice which features of the persona are the individuating signifiers. These are the kinds of details to look for in doc-umenting your own example.

1. How to Impersonate Famous People

Elvis Presley

"The Man. The Legend. The King. The Pelvis. And now, the Impersonation. Those wishing to clothe themselves in the garb of the late Memphis singer have two choices:

- Early Elvis: tight Levi's, denim shirt, slicked-down hair with unruly fore-lock, sneakers.
- Late Elvis: White studded jumpsuit with turned up collar, pillow down the front, wide studded belts, sideburns, sweat.

"The rest of us will be content with arranging our bodies into four main Elvis-impression modes.

1. The Face: The overriding Elvis facial feature was the Sneer. This involves wrinkling the nose so that a crease forms from the side of one nostril to the edge of the mouth. The eyelids droop slightly, the mouth sneers and the lips purse. Elvis had a small mouth, and by pursing the lips it was squeezed from his face until it looked about to fall on the floor.

2. The Arms: Except for when they are touching a guitar, hands and arms re-main above the head with the fingers clicking like a demented Spanish flamenco dancer.

3. The Hips: The keynote of any Elvis impression. It was the famous 'Pelvic Thrust' movement which originally got Elvis into trouble and resulted in the cameramen on TV's *Ed Sullivan Show* filming the singer from above the waist only. By today's standards it's hard to see what all the fuss was about, the movement being not so much a back-and-forth one as a grinding ro-tary gyration. Swivel your hips as if describing a full 360-degree circle.

4. The Legs: Imagine that while one leg is barely able to support you and is in constant danger of giving way, the other is made entirely of rubber and will hold no weight at all. Keeping the left leg crooked, wiggle the right knee in and out as far as it will go. Try both legs at once, standing on the

balls of your feet. Warning: don't try all of these movements at once or you will fall over.

"The Elvis that people like to remember most existed in the period before he was drafted, leading up to the making of Jailhouse Rock. At that time he appeared dark and sexy, and just a little dangerous. The smoldering looks subsequently vanished in a welter of wholesome and bland beach movies. So grease back that hair, hang down that front forelock, pout, pucker, sneer, and loosen your joints—particularly the knees" (Fowler, 1984: 44–45).

Impersonation as Possession Jean-Paul Sartre, in his study of the psychology of imagination, used the phenomenon of a comedian (Franconay) impersonating a famous actor (Maurice Chevalier), as a point of departure for understanding the nature of images and imaging. His account (part of the discussion of the "analog" effect that enables images to evoke an understanding of that which may not appear) clarifies the nature of a felt composition. If photos and stories of events (disasters) that we browse in newspapers and magazines leave us indifferent, Sartre argues, it is because we fail to fill the signs with our own imagination. Pictures, like words, must be actively read.

Jean-Paul Sartre: The Psychology of Imagination

"The imitation reproduces only a few elements which are, moreover, the least intuitive in intuition: namely the relationships consisting of the rakish angle of the straw hat, the angle formed by neck and chin. In addition to this, certain of these relationships are deliberately altered: the angle of the straw hat is exaggerated, since this is the principal sign which must strike us at first and around which all the others are ordered. . . .

"First I must lend life to these dry schemes. . . . I must execute the movement of the perception backwards, determine the intuition by beginning with the knowledge and as a consequence of the knowledge. That lip was an erstwhile sign: I turned it into an image. But it is an image only in the degree to which it was a sign. I see it only as a 'fat protruding lip'. . . . What I perceive is also what I know; the object can teach nothing, and the intuition is but dull, debased knowledge. . . .

"We can now understand the rule of feeling in the consciousness of imitation. When I see Maurice Chevalier the perception involves a certain affective reaction. This feeling projects on the physiognomy of Maurice Chevalier a certain indefinable quality which we might call his 'meaning.' In the consciousness of imitation this affective reaction is awakened by the intentional synthesis from the very beginning of the signs and the intuitive realization. The affective sense of Chevalier's face will appear correlatively on the face of Franconay. It is this affective meaning which brings about the synthetic union of the various signs, which animates their frozen barrenness, which gives them life and a certain density. . . . Finally, it is in fact this object as an image that we see on the body of the impersonator: the signs united by an affective meaning, that is, the expressive something. . . . A hybrid condition follows, which is altogether neither perception nor image, which should be described by itself. These unstable and momentary states evidently supply the spectator with the most pleasant aspects of imitation. This is no doubt due to the fact that the relationship of the object to the material of the imitation is here one of possession. The absent Maurice Chevalier chose the body of a woman to make his appearance. Thus, primitively, an impersonator is one possessed. Here may lie the explanation of the role of impersonator in the ritual dances of the primitives" (Sartre, 1966: 36–37).

Comment

- The rhetorical lesson is not that you will literally perform an impersonation of a character or star, but that you will use the few gestures, poses, and phrases associated with the star to write the icon of the star.

The remaining examples *reverse the direction of Method acting*, and use the given circumstances of the story character as a metaphor for how the person feels in the Family or personal situation. The entertainment text, that is, is accepted as an icon that already emblematizes a known feeling or condition, and this in turn may be used to illuminate the unknown situation of the egent.

2. Gregg Bordowitz, "Dense Moments"

The Bordowitz example combines the newspaper report with a pop culture event, and presents their intersection with his personal situation (the death of his father in the context of his own positive HIV status) as if a report on the accident that killed his father was mistakenly interpolated into the article reporting Evel Knievel's failed jump over the Snake River. He cites the collaged entries, then makes the metaphor explicit.

Fast Trip, Long Drop

"Evel Knievel tried—but failed—to conquer the Snake River Canyon with his steam rocket in the dust and wind late Sunday afternoon.

"But, Knievel said later, 'to lose to a beautiful canyon and river is not to me a real loss.'

"The rocket fired at 3:44 p.m., about 20 minutes later than scheduled, in front of a jump-site crowd estimated at one-fifth the size expected—about 10,000 people. Perhaps another 10,000 watched from Shoshone Falls, along the rim and from rooftops.

"A California man walking from Shoshone Falls along Falls Avenue late Saturday night, was struck and killed in a car-pedestrian accident. Sheriff's officers said Leslie Hugh Harstein, 30, North Hollywood, a producer of special shows, was killed as he and his wife were walking toward their automobile, which had been left on Desert View Drive.

"Hospital officials said Mr. Harstein was apparently killed instantly about 10 p.m. Saturday. Cloyce Edwards, county coroner, said the man died of head injuries and was dead at the scene. He was struck by a pickup truck and camper also traveling west.

". . . Knievel's wife, his three children and numerous relatives watched the launch from the canyon rim. Linda remained silent, according to an observer, during the takeoff, as relatives shouted 'Oh my god.' When the skycycle disappeared behind the rocks she ran to the edge crying, 'Where is it?'

"Informed by a reporter her husband was alive, 'she just grinned' the reporter said."

"Another strange coincidence—Knievel's wife is named Linda, my mother's name, my father's first wife. I'm his only kid.

Some Fans Felt Cheated

Sunday night a near riot erupted after a group of campers at the jump site, believed to be unhappy over the failure of Evel Knievel to provide free beer, began burning and tearing up concession stand fences and automobiles.

"A disappointed fan, I am my father's absence. Can we be the subjects of the following sentence? I am the author of this story. Now the author faces his own death. He says, I am the beginning of something, the end of another. A vehicle. A failed rocket. There's a void to be leapt. An impossible void. How can I make it? He's gone. Am I here?" (Bordowitz, 1994: 41–42).

Comment

- The effect of the image is just as great if the interpolated story device is fiction.
- Bordowitz makes explicit that the Snake River Canyon is the embodiment in his given circumstances of the void—the hole—in being that is the source of the feeling of longing (*Sehnsucht, Heimweh*). The poets and philosophers have tracked this feeling over the ages, whose basis is simply the fact of the incompleteness of any individual person. The augmentation of this human trait in the digital prosthesis means that its native presence in human intelligence has to be developed through training, just as in literacy the native potential for

analysis was augmented through the practices of logic. The combination of topic and chora in the alliance of literacy and electracy is a collaboration joining reason and emotion.

The next example demonstrates the use of the story memory to pinpoint the precise feeling of the personal problem. The author considers a number of horror or monster films that fit her circumstances, but selects one as the best evocation of her feeling. The example is an essay, but this form should not be used for the website. Rather, key signifiers from each of the two circumstances (narrative and personal) should be recorded and juxtaposed without explicit commentary.

3. Vivian Sobchack, Revenge of the Leech Woman

"Myself a fifty-three-year-old woman, this scary woman scares not only men but also me—although I am ashamed to admit it. Much as I attempt to counter my fear of aging with intellectual rationalization, cultural critique, or humor, I find myself unable to laugh off a recurrent image that truly horrifies me even as I joke about it. The image? It's me and yet her, an Other—and, as her subjective object of a face has aged, the blusher I've worn every morning since I was a teenager has migrated and condensed itself into two distinct and ridiculous red circles in the middle of her cheeks. This image—which correspondingly brings a subjective flush of shame and humiliation to my cheeks for the pity and unwilling horror and contempt with which I objectively regard hers—is that of an aging woman who not only deceives herself into thinking she is still young enough to wear makeup and poorly applies it, but who also inscribes upon her face the caricature of her own desire and of all that was once (at least to some) desirable. . . .

"*The Wasp Woman* is a much simpler film [than *Attack of the 50 ft. Woman*]; Roger Corman, who made it, went straight to the surface of the matter. . . . Janet, however, looks to her own devices and finds a scientist willing to experiment with wasps. Eventually he finds a serum that not only reduces but also reverses the aging process. Watching the rejuvenation of lab animals, Janet does not want to wait for FDA approval, first offering herself as a human guinea pig and then—after she does begin to look younger—stealing into the lab to administer more and larger injections. She looks twenty-two and gorgeous for her stated forty years, but there are side effects. Overdosed with the royal wasp jelly serum, she regularly turns into a Wasp Woman—that is, a woman in a sheath dress and heels, with the head of a wasp and the urge to kill. Eventually, of course, after the non-gender-specific murders of a number of people, she is killed herself. *The Wasp Woman*, then, is a simple but paradoxical little cautionary tale: 'There are some things that woman is not meant to know,' i.e., the secret of rejuvenation; and yet there are some things she must always *be*, i.e., 'young'" (Sobchack, 1994: 80–81, 83).

The work used for the structural portrait may be from any domain, not just popular culture, of course, although for the mystory widesite assignment to which we are committed for now the example must be an entertainment narrative. In the following example, Paul Auster uses Van Gogh's paintings "as an image of his adolescence, a translation of his deepest feelings of the period" (Auster, 1988: 141). In the instance cited, the connection of a specific painting with a specific feeling is motivated by a literal event. This motivation is not necessary for the mystory. Auster could have stated that he recognized in the painting the feeling that he had at that moment in the past.

4. Paul Auster, The Invention of Solitude: A Memoir

"To remember, therefore, a day in April when he was sixteen, and cutting school with the girl he had fallen in love with: so passionately and hopelessly that the thought of it still smarts. To remember the train, and then the ferry to New York (that ferry, which has long since vanished: industrial iron, the warm fog, rust), and then going to a large exhibition of Van Gogh paintings. To remember how he had stood there, trembling with happiness, as if the shared seeing of these works had invested them with the girl's presence, had mysteriously varnished them with the love he felt for her. . . .

"Standing in the Van Gogh Museum in Amsterdam (December 1979) in front of the painting *The Bedroom,* completed in Arles, October 1888.

"Van Gogh to his brother: 'This time it is just simply my bedroom . . . To look at the picture ought to rest the brain or rather the imagination . . .

"'The walls are pale violet. The floor is of red tiles.

"'The wood of the bed and chairs is the yellow of fresh butter, the sheet and pillows very light lemon-green.

"'The coverlet scarlet. The window green.

"'The toilet table orange, the basin blue.

"'The doors lilac.

"'And that is all—there is nothing in this room with closed shutters . . .

"'This by way of revenge for the enforced rest I have been obliged to take . . .'

"As A. continued to study the painting, however, he could not help feeling that Van Gogh had done something quite different from what he thought he had set out to do. A.'s first impression was indeed a sense of calm, of 'rest,' as the artist describes it. But gradually, as he tried to inhabit the room presented on the canvas, he began to experience it as a prison, an impossible space, an image not so much of a place to lie, but of the mind that has been forced to live there. Observe carefully. The bed blocks one door, a chair blocks the other door, the shutters are closed: you can't get in, and once you are in, you can't get out. . . . The man in this painting (and this is a self-portrait, no different from a picture of a man's face, with eyes, nose, lips, and jaw) has been alone too much, has struggled too much in the depths of solitude" (Auster, 1988: 141, 142–143).

Auster's description of Van Gogh's relationship to the room and to the picture he made of it, as well as his *recognition* of his own experience in that relationship, may be generalized to the experience of recognition we are using throughout the mystory, to select and document memories from each of the popcycle discourses for our cognitive map.

Comment

- Since the examples given are relays for your assignment, you should use the literate skill of analysis to itemize the pattern in the technique shared by the group. Make a list of instructions abstracted from the examples for how to write a relationship between a work of literature, art, or popular culture and the life of a viewer. Imitate the style of a freshman composition handbook, with its rules for writing an argument or essay.

- One rule is: write a structural self-portrait, using the given circumstances of a character in a story as a figurative analogy for your given circumstances in your lifeworld. The story provides an image for your feeling about your circumstances. For example: the fate of the Leech Woman in a horror film is how Vivian Sobchack feels as a woman in her fifties.

REMAKE
Plato's *Phaedrus*

What is the historical, the disciplinary, context for these structural self-portraits? They are the basis of an online rhetoric to be practiced by egents. At the beginnings of literacy, the Greek youths who accepted the call to learning were assisted in crossing the threshold by a mentor, epitomized by Socrates. In our narrative map, the meeting with the mentor takes place in Act I, before the hero decides to heed the call: The first discourse on method in the West is Plato's *Phaedrus,* in which he dramatizes a typical meeting between the prototype of a lover of wisdom and his student. Continuing with our practice of bootstrapping ourselves into electracy by remaking or improvising (riffing) on selected touchstone works (gems), we prepare for crossing the threshold into the special world of Entertainment discourse by an updating of Plato's dialogue between mentor and apprentice. The following excerpt from a gloss of the work serves to set a baseline for the session.

Phaedrus

"The *Phaedrus* was probably composed around 370 B.C., after the *Republic* but before the six late dialogues. The dramatic date of the dialogue is about 410 B.C., about ten years before the trial and death of

Socrates. The *Phaedrus* is a direct dialogue; Plato does not use in this dialogue a narrator who retells to some one else a conversation of Socrates. The scene, a walk outside the walls of Athens to a shady spot along the banks of the river Ilissus, is an unusual setting for Socrates. There are only two characters, Socrates and Phaedrus; Phaedrus also participates in two other dialogues, the *Protagoras* and the *Symposium*. . . . The dialogue presents a special method of philosophy, dialectic, which involves collection and division [collection of similars under a single form and the division of generic forms into more specific forms (the Form of Living thing into the Form of Plant and the Form of Animal) are essential to the definition which must begin successful discussion]" (Magill, 1961: 95–96).

"Socrates: So contending with words is a practice found not only in lawsuits and public harangues but, it seems, wherever men speak we find this single art. If indeed it is an art, which enables people to make out everything to be like everything else, within the limits of possible comparison, and to expose the corresponding attempts of others who disguise what they are doing.

"Phaedrus: How so, pray?

"Socrates: I think that will become clear if we put the following question. Are we misled when the difference between two things is wide or narrow?

"Phaedrus: When it is narrow.

"Socrates: Well then, if you shift your ground little by little, you are more likely to pass undetected from so-and-so to its opposite than if you do so at one bound.

"Phaedrus: Of course.

"Socrates: It follows that anyone who intends to mislead another, without being misled himself, must discern precisely the degree of resemblance and dissimilarity between this and that.

"Phaedrus: Yes, that is essential.

"Socrates: Then if he does not know the truth about a given thing, how is he going to discern the degree of resemblance between that unknown thing and other things?

"Phaedrus: It will be impossible.

"Socrates: Well now, when people hold beliefs contrary to fact, and are misled, it is plain that the error has crept into their minds through the suggestion of some similarity or other.

"Phaedrus; That certainly does happen.

"Socrates: But can anyone possibly master the art of using similarities for the purpose of bringing people round, and leading them away from the truth about this or that to the opposite of the truth, or again can anyone possibly avoid this happening to himself unless he has knowledge of what the thing in question really is?

"Phaedrus: No, never.

"Socrates: It would seem to follow, my friend, that the art of speech displayed by one who has gone chasing after beliefs, instead of knowing the truth, will be a comical sort of art, in fact no art at all.

"Phaedrus: I dare say" (Plato, *Phaedrus*, 261e-262c).

Comment

- Socrates, the prototype of the literate pedagogue, is a mentor. This role is played for people becoming electrate by a favorite star or celebrity, who models what it is to become an image.

- Like Phaedrus, we are learning the art of analogy. *Phaedrus* is the first discourse on method in the Western tradition. Our heuretic strategy for inventing electracy is to use the invention of literacy as an analogy: what the dialogue was to the first school (Plato's Academy), something is to the internet. We want to interact with people online, but even if we are using video conferencing, we are not seeing their faces, but representations of faces. We have to extrapolate from the dialogue, to find an equivalent that is functional for the electrate apparatus.

Interface Tables

Table: An arrangement of numbers, words, or items of any kind, in a definite and compact form, so as to exhibit some set of facts or relations in a distinctive and comprehensive way, for convenience of study, reference, or calculation.

In *Phaedrus* Socrates demonstrated for his pupil the method of dialectical reason. In this remake I introduce the image equivalent: a "conductive" ordering of things (tables in this example). The table, along with the list, formula, and recipe, has been described as one of those "figures of the written word" that are native to literacy (Goody 1977, 17). The method of conduction to find an electrate supplement for the literate truth table is to reconsider such claims in terms of the word-thing, to write "table" with its whole set of phrases and shapes.

Richard Bolt (senior research scientist in the Perceptual Computing Group at the Media Laboratory, MIT) gave a presentation at Ohio State University in the Fall of 1993, part of a series on technology and postmodern culture, in which he argued that *dealing with computers will become less like operating a device and more like conversing with another person.* Bolt demonstrated his point by means of a computer program that responded to voice command, gesture (through feedback from a digital glove), and gaze (through feedback from an eye-tracking device). The display contained a chair and a table on which were placed a glass and a pitcher, on a floor covered with black and white tile. To understand how our use of narrative form in Entertainment discourse serves as an allegory evoking the experience of electracy, we need to look more closely at the two central elements of Bolt's performance: the interface metaphor (like conversing with another person), and the demonstration of a virtual (computer-generated) table. The remake will produce a more electrate metaphor: *dealing with computers will become less like conversing with another person, and more like impersonating Elvis.*

Comment

- Here is a point of intervention in apparatus invention for the Arts and Letters discipline: engineers know technology, but not rhetoric. In the project to make an interface metaphor, "metaphor" is just as important as the technology, beginning with the fact, overlooked by Bolt, that "interface" is itself a metaphor. Our method should be familiar by now: to turn to the metaphor operating in a term, and open it up for further elaboration. This procedure is part of what I mean by a logic of the image. There is an image at work in every concept. These images were not particularly useful in literacy, but they are central to electrate reason.

The virtual table brings to mind Plato's three beds (or tables), listed in order of reality from most to least real—the pure form (the idea of the table), the carpenter's table, and the picture of a table made by an artist. The virtual table is considered to be a simulation, which passes beyond representation to constitute a fourth item on this metaphysical list. How should I take the table Bolt displayed? The very insistence on the table—moving it, raising, rotating, and lowering it before the fascinated gaze of the audience—evokes an allegorical effect. The effect of this demonstration does not correspond with his description comparing interacting with a computer to conversing with a person. A starting point is the meaning of this table—a hermeneutic question. To move into an electrate relationship with the table, to learn not what it means but what can be made of it, I put it into a sequence, a series of other tables (the choral table is all tables at once), beginning with the form of which the Periodic Table is the most famous example. In the hybrid circumstances of the webpage, HTML tables show the persistence of literacy during the transition to electracy. Alongside the table as chart is the image of the table with its ability to evoke an associative series.

Bolt's interface metaphor may be contextualized in the history of dialogue, and this metaphor (interacting with a computer is like having a conversation with a person) is a clue that opens up online interactivity to invention. I accept as the terms of our experiment the idea that the future of education in electracy depends upon an ability to extend and adapt the dialogue to computing. What has to be imagined is a dialogue that foregrounds not "communication" (in the sense of the exchange of a message without loss of meaning) but "signifierness" (the "signifi-ance" of Barthes's obtuse meaning). The first thing a quick review of the tradition reveals is the fact that the meanings of the terms are unstable and shift from epoch to epoch. Thus for example "to converse with a person" means quite different things in an oral civilization and in a literate one. I have to assume that when the technology is electronic rather than print or speech (the different media imply dif-ferent institutions contextualizing their employment) both the practice of con-versing and the nature of personhood will undergo a transformation. The task for interface designers is to invent the prototype of an electrate dialogue.

Dialogue

Plato invented the dialogue as the basic practice for his institutionalization of al-phabetic writing in School. As Jan Swearingen has observed:

> "When Plato wrote, dialogue was neither an already ancient literary tradition nor the simple transcription of natural conversation. Instead, dialogue was un-precedented and was inaugurated by Plato's hybrid of oral and written conven-tions, oral genres, and philosophical modes, a blend he termed *dialegesthai*, not just two but many voices crossing speaking or speaking across one another, or spanning or comprehending each other's statements" (Swearingen 1990, 49).

The dialogue actually is part of a collection of interrelated inventions, all of which were designed to take advantage of the material features of alphabetic writing: dialogue, method, and school. Plato's Academy is considered the first school. Method was the practice and dialogue the genre or form in which this practice was tested and expressed in school. *Phaedrus* is a relay, a point of departure for generating its equivalent for the new apparatus. The dialogue was a hybrid—partly oral, partly written—intended as a way to communicate specific to the new institution. What are the elements of the literate-electrate hybrid?

From the old oral culture Plato retained the scene of a face-to-face (F2F) ex-change of two speakers; from the new written culture he accepted the abstract-ing procedures of analysis. When the two are fused in *Phaedrus* (and the other dialogues) the result is "dialectic." The dialogue was a written drama (a narra-tive) showing speakers performing the dialectical method. In the Academy, stu-dents read the dialogues as a basis for further discussion. This discussion was not "conversation" in the form used in daily life, but the peculiar way of talking adapted to the work of specialized knowledge. To converse in school, from Plato's day to our own, is as different from conversing in the home as convers-ing in the home is different from speaking in a ritual ceremony (such as in church).

Oddly enough, this difference, like the technological basis of the practices of schooling itself, is often forgotten or ignored. To make use of the metaphor of conversing with another person for designing the human-computer interface, it is important to remember that the inventors of modern literacy made use of the same metaphor for the human-book interface. Conversation as represented in the tradition of dialogue must be recognized as a response to the possibilities of a new apparatus, including the demand for new institutional practices and new individual behaviors related to the social assimilation of a new technology of language. Plato's invention supplies an inventory of what electracy needs: what are the equivalents of school, method (dialectic), and dialogue (genre, mode) in our circumstances?

Q & A   Between Plato's time and the present the dialogue underwent a complex evolution, marked by at least three distinct moments.

> "Plato's dialogue transcended earlier 'story,' that of epic and drama, with a protocol for conceptual interlocution that was designed to frustrate the technification of thought. Schleiermacher's translation of Plato's dialogues into German came to be the headwater of a massive reform . . . that emphasized natural voices, living speech, union between minds rather than understanding of texts, polyphony, deliberately unsystematic philosophizing in spoken and written dialogues. The modern hermeneutic tradition represented by Heidegger, Ricoeur, Gadamer, and Bakhtin has revived and extended the German romantic template to emphasize the irreducibly polyvocal, interlocutionary elements in all language" (Swearingen, 1990: 68).

The essential shift from Plato to today is the result of the expansion of literacy. Plato's relation to text was prehermeneutic, as reflected in Socrates's complaint in *Phaedrus:*

> "Writing, you know, Phaedrus, has this strange quality about it, which makes it really like painting: the painter's products stand before us quite as though they were alive; but if you question them, they maintain a solemn silence. So too with written words: you might think they spoke as though they made sense, but if you ask them anything about what they are saying, if you wish an explanation, they go on telling you the same thing, over and over forever" (Plato, 1956: 69).

It is the question of voice. Plato feared and warned against the danger of texts being misunderstood in the absence of the author (the text as orphan without its father/author to protect it). Although the methods of interpretation developed in the epoch of literacy proved that the same words could be made to say quite different things, hermeneutics was intended to preserve the presence of the father/author as a spirit accessible by means of the text. "Dialogue persists in evoking the quasi-religious because even when it is not being used in the hermeneutics of sacred texts it invokes the presence of the author" (Swearingen 1990, 69). In other words, the face-to-face encounter of the partners in an oral culture that Plato's hybrid preserved in the written dialogue persisted throughout the entire history of the form, manifesting itself in our own moment as an ethical imperative.

The history of reading in fact may be understood as the exploration of the interface metaphor of conversing with another person. Most of the protocols for reading and writing, developed especially during the era of print, aimed at controlling illocutionary force (to preserve intact the intent of the author during the event of communication) (Olson, 1994: 113). The prejudice against the text is reduced, of course, and the condition of having a relationship with a book is accepted. The Socratic question and answer is transferred to this relationship, as in Gadamer's treatment of the text as an answer to a question: "The reconstruction of the question to which the text is presumed to be the answer takes place itself within a process of questioning through which we seek the answer to the question that the text asks us" (quoted in Crowell, 1990: 345). Gadamer, that is, transferred "voice" to text in order to construe the text as a partner in that dialogue constituted on the other side by the interpreter's (reader's) interrogative activity (343). The ideality of the word and its relationship to truth are not affected by medium or institution in Gadamer's hermeneutics. Reading is interrogation.

F2F (Face to Face)   Plato's invention of the dialogue involves *the invention of an interface metaphor:* writers relate to the written as if they were conversing (communicating) with a person.

Comment

- It is worth emphasizing this point, which is at once obvious and profound: obvious in that clearly when you read a dialogue you are not literally talking with a person; profound in that it calls attention to the key lesson of our analogy. To extrapolate from literacy to electracy, we need to find some popular behavior in our mediated experience that is as familiar to us as having a conversation was to people in an oral apparatus. Elvis impersonation (and by extension, the impersonation of any celebrity figure) is the metaphor we are proposing as a familiar front for ordering access to the electrate equivalent of dialectic.

- In short, we are continuing with the organizing principle of the book, which is to move from the more familiar literacy to the less familiar electracy.

This metaphor is enforced by means of an ethical imperative whose most recent spokesperson was Levinas. "Why does Levinas insist on the irreducibility of the face-to-face? The answer lies in his conception of the face as 'expression': 'The face is a living presence; it is expression . . . The face speaks. The manifestation of the face is already discourse'" (355). This insistence within the modern moment of dialogue on the oral metaphor of conversation reflects a conception of the human subject that, ironically, came into being as part of the apparatus of literacy. The concept and behaviors of "selfhood," as grammatologists such as Eric Havelock have argued, are as much an invention as is the alphabet or school. An apparatus is a social machine. The ethical problem addressed by the face-to-face encounter is a feature of a separating or alienating of the person from the collective people, a unity that is replaced with a subject-object relationship to the world. The methods of abstraction and the experience of individuality both evolved as part of the matrix of literacy.

The invention of the closeup shot in cinema, and the important theoretical discussions devoted to "the face" in media criticism, extend (despite appearances) the ideology of literacy into electracy. Indeed this ethical power of the face is a feature of literacy that lends itself to the peculiar power of the image, as explained by David Moos in his use of a cinema analogy to explain the eloquence of a portrait. His example is a dramatization of the "gaze," the scene in the film *Paris, Texas,* when the husband has tracked down his wife who is working one of the voyeur rooms at the Keyhole Club. Her job is to improvise a performance in response to a fantasy voiced by a man hidden behind the one-way mirror. As the man's "confession" unfolds, the woman gradually realizes that it is her estranged husband.

> "Here the film is crucially focused. As he continues to speak, her face, occupying the full frame, becomes the surface upon which the memory of inter-personal experience is transacted. She no longer looks toward the mirror or directly into the camera. As his voice rolls on her gaze lengthens, head frozen, side-turned toward the infinity of a shattered history. For over a minute her face is thus held.
>
> "Such a vision of the human face—a magnified projection of utter emotion— is unique perhaps to the medium of film. A look crosses her face, the chimera of doubt resolving as fact. The spoken narrative suffuses her face with the movement of thought, recognition and remembrance. Subjective intricacies of a relationship that turned to ashes and that she has buried in her private history now play like so many shadows across her staid visage. A materialist perspective of how cinema obtains union between surface and submerged meaning would regard the 'skin' as inclusive subject of all signification" (Moos, 1994: 21, 25).

What remains to be seen in our discussion is what electracy adds to this look. The ethical dilemma of the relationship between self and other (the problematic of the Other) has dominated and driven the evolution of hermeneutics. The hermeneutic procedure in the modern moment is,

> "characterized by a structure of alienation and return, excursion and reunion or, in Bakhtinian terms, of identification and exotopy. As for Gadamer, in the homecoming of Bakhtin's prodigal Self, the Self becomes 'more' than it was before: after returning home from its long journey, the Self is more itself . . . 'I' can now, upon return in my own unique 'placement' in existence, complete the Other, since I have the Other's vantage point and some extra features to which only I have access" (Daelemans and Maranhao, 1990: 228).

We recognize this hermeneutic circle as the canonical odyssean story of alienation. Part of the difficulty of extending dialogue into the electronic apparatus has to do with the transformation of the apparatus as a whole: not only does the technology change, but so too do the understanding of the person and the behaviors creative of subject formation. How might the process of interface design take into account the wisdom of the ethical imperative of the face-to-face conversation in dialogue without losing sight of the emerging conditions of a new experience of identity?

Comment

- The circular journey of Odysseus, the round trip away from home and back again, permeates the literate apparatus. The quotidian emotional dimension of the founding orientation of literate experience, in other words, is nostalgia. Critics working in the mode of critique sought to root out nostalgia along with identification, related to the general scientific mood of objective distance. Left in the body, without technological enhancement, nostalgia is indeed a limited and limiting mood, just as in oral civilization analysis, left unaided in the body (mind), was limited. In electracy the body mood is augmented in the digital prosthesis and becomes capable of supporting sophisticated intelligence. Our larger project is to develop the educational practices (the rhetoric) for using this prosthesis. A literate person reasons on paper (text); an electrate person feels online (felt).

Death Tables

L. tabula: a flat board, a plank, a board to play on, a writing tablet, a written tablet, a writing, a list, an account, a painted tablet, a painting, a votive tablet, a flat piece of ground, prob. from same root as taberna TAVERN.

The story of Simonides, the inventor of mnemonics, is well known. As reported by Cicero in "De Oratore," Simonides left Scopas's banquet hall just before the roof collapsed, killing all those in attendance. "The corpses were so mangled that the relatives who came to take them away for burial were unable to identify them. But Simonides remembered the places at which they had been sitting at the table and was therefore able to indicate to the relatives which were their dead" (Yates, 1966: 2). The effectiveness of his recall suggested the method of places and images that allowed rhetors to manage the information explosion created by writing, and to give long speeches from memory. "He inferred that persons desiring to train this faculty (of memory) must select places and form mental images of things they wish to remember and store those images in the places, so that the order of the places will preserve the order of the things, and we shall employ the places and images respectively as a wax writing-tablet and the letters written on it" (2).

Like Simonides, interface designers are in the position of having to invent a practice for the use of a new information technology, with the moment of invention being informed by a catastrophe, by a scene of hypothetical massive death. My interface design, that is, must work with the Internet (electronic memory technology), which originated in the ARPAnet experiment to support military research: "in particular, research about how to build networks that could withstand partial outages (like bomb attacks) and still function . . . In the ARPAnet model, communication always occurs between a source and a destination computer. The network itself is assumed to be unreliable; any portion of the network could disappear at any moment (pick your favorite catastrophe—these days backhoes cutting cables are more of a threat than bombs)" (Krol, 1992: 11). The nuclear catastrophe the military researchers had in mind required that the invention of a memory system be accomplished prior to the collapse, rather than after it, as in the case of Simonides. Our new dialogue should take into account and assimilate within itself the anticipation of these conditions of communicating within a ruined interchange.

Truth Tables

Logic: a table drawn up to show the truth-value of a compound logical statement for every possible combination of the truth-values of its component propositions. It is the same as the multiplication table for the numbers 1 and 0. It is also the same as the table for a circuit with two switches in series.

Psychoanalysis shows in the agencies of repression a mind that must think in conditions of censorship whose effect on thought could be imaged in terms of nuclear strikes and middle passages. All sense, that is, has to be extracted from nonsense (nothing abstract that is not first the body), an aspect of thought that it is impossible to experience or to think directly, and which is precisely that part of thought to be augmented and brought into practical service by means of the digital apparatus. "We gave the name 'sublimation' to the operation through which the trace of castration becomes the line of thought, and thus to the operation through which the sexual surface and the rest are projected at the surface of thought" (Deleuze, 1990: 219). Conduction is the translation of psychoanalytic descriptions of dreamwork into a mode of inference.

What occurs between the mouth-ear and brain that allows noise to become speech involves multiple tables, and the project of design is to model the Emer-Agency interface on the frontier of their interaction. This poststructural application of psychoanalytic theory to interface design, however, reveals the misnomer in the terms used to label the experiment: inter-FACE. Getting this term right is important because of the intention to extend the tradition of dialogue into the electronic apparatus (to include the unconscious dimension of the embodied mind). What is the relation of this interFACE with the face-to-face of the dialogic conversation (the model of communication)? The poststructural critique of the philosophy of consciousness supporting the modern moment of hermeneutics is that the face-to-face is an illusion. Or, in psychoanalytic terms, it is a defense mechanism, a denial, a foreclosure of the body. Literacy forgot about the mouth-anus circuit (the abject dimension), but psychoanalysis outlined the family resemblance of the series word-baby-shit (money).

"Not only does the unconscious constitute an unspoken 'inner speech' that only fragmentarily surfaces in the rhetorical tropes of 'oneiric discourse,' but it also constitutes an Other language of the Self, an ex-centric language that is articulated only through rhetorical repressions and tropological displacements onto other (floating) signifiers whose diffractions seep into the discourse of the consciousness. In other words, the internally dialogic operations of the language(s) of the unconscious speak of a knowledge of the Self, which, however, the Self cannot master" (Lacan, paraphrased in Daelemans and Maranho, 1990: 237).

The face-to-face is a displacement of the encounter of genitals. "The phallus should not penetrate, but rather, like a plowshare applied to the thin fertile layer of the earth, it should trace a line at the surface. This line, emanating from the genital zone, is the line which ties together all the erogenous zones, thus ensuring their connection or 'interfacing,' and bringing all the partial surfaces together into one and the same surface on the body of the child" (Deleuze, 1990: 201).

Here is how the body reasons. The direction of displacement passes from the depth to the surface of the body, the surface organized into erogenous zones as an aggregate of letters, given coherence by the priority of the genital zone. "And precisely because castration is somewhere between two surfaces, it does not submit to this transmutation without carrying along its share of appurtenance, without folding in a certain manner and projecting the entire corporeal surface of sexuality over the metaphysical surface of thought. The phantasm's formula is this: from the sexual pair to thought via castration" (218). In receiving this psychoanalytic language in our context we should keep in mind that "castration" is the emblem of "interpellation." Or, in our allegorical system of correspondences, the body is a microcosm of the social macrocosm: the same zoning at two difference scales (fractal rhetoric).

The electrate dialogue must take into account this force of displacement and recognize that the face-to-face has always been a metonym for the interaction of whole bodies. We should keep in mind too that the theory of castration is an account of the mourning process by means of which persons deal with all forms of loss, beginning with the separation from the mother's body. The dead addressed in psychoanalytic dialogue are those figures of the superego, all the authority figures with whom one identifies, introjected to become agencies of unconscious thought. The story of the superego relates how selves (the subjects of literacy) stay in touch with the wisdom of the ancestors.

Dressing Tables

Table (Palmistry): The quadrangular space between certain lines in the palm of the hand. Shirley, Love Tricks (1631): In this table Lies your story; it is no fable. Not a line within your hand But I easily understand.

What do these repeating tables tell us? What instructions may be inferred from this series relevant to our project? What pattern does their juxtaposition reveal?

If theory instructs me to cross the two logics of analysis and pattern (work and play, calculation and meditation) to create a hybrid that will be to the digital apparatus what dialectic was to literacy, it might be helpful to have a scene that condenses and holds the story of pattern as clearly in mind as the Turing test holds the story of analysis. Nietzsche's formula of intersecting aphorism and anecdote tells us where to look for this story, if it is reduced to the term "vita," whose anagram abbreviates the two intelligences (including their institutions, practices, and subject behaviors) converging in a hypermedial Internet: AI and TV. The figure that is to TV what Turing is to computing is Elvis Presley.

> "On September 9 [1956] Elvis Presley appeared live, from Los Angeles, on the Ed Sullivan show, performing four songs—'Don't Be Cruel,' 'Love Me Tender,' 'Ready Teddy,' and 'Hound Dog'—in the more familiar 'Elvis the Pelvis' style (to the delight of screaming fans in the studio) . . . CBS grew nervous over the then-current wave of Presley detractors and when the singer returned in January for his third and final Sullivan show, the cameramen were instructed to show Elvis only from the waist up. This truncating of Presley inflamed proponents of the new rock'n'roll craze who felt their hero was being unfairly treated" (Castleman and Podrazik, 1982: 112).

Elvis the Pelvis. This famous pelvis (the vehicle of funk) is the "strange attractor" that makes sense out of the face-to-face of electronic dialogue, and gives an alternative term for the choral method: *interpelvis design*. In the psychoanalytic session the analyst remains silent, "plays dead," or simulates the status of the "dummy" in a card game while the analysand utters whatever comes into his/her mind, without censorship or any formal considerations. This procedure of the "talking cure" remains recognizable as a dialogue, but one whose rules are nearly the opposite of the Socratic method of interrogation. In psychoanalysis the question is implicit and the analysand confesses everything. The emphasis of psychoanalytic theory on the patient's sexual history and the phallus in particular marks it as a modern way of dealing with the same concerns addressed by the Mystery religions.

Comment

- As the impersonation guide to Elvis noted, his hip motion was not a thrust but a swivel. Elvis did not invent this motion, but he did transform it into an iconic gesture (writing). To understand how Entertainment discourse functions as the site of the emergent apparatus of electracy, you need to notice the connection between the scandal of Elvis the Pelvis and the invention of the hula-hoop (recall the heuretic rule: follow the invention). The hula-hoop was invented in 1958 by Richard P. Knerr and Arthur K. Melvin, owners of Wham-O-Manufacturing Co. Children playing with these colored plastic tubes learned to perform this pronounced pelvic maneuver. Under cover of this game, the Protestant repression of the body in general, and the lower body in particular,

was lifted. This gesture became routine through changes in dance styles associated with rock music.

Detachability (The Gram)

Derrida introduced the notion of the "gram" as a correction and extension of
the semiotic "sign" with its metaphor of the signifier and signified connected
like two sides of one sheet of paper. The gram describes the signifier-signified
relation as a coupling (a "hitch") that allows easy (de)tachment. A better
metaphor for the sign than a sheet of paper (or a phallus) is a dremel tool
(hand operated, with the hose extension and a hundred different attachments,
fit for any job). The detachability and remotivation of parts are the key to a
rhetoric of impersonation. Marjorie Garber has made sense of Elvis impersonation within the general history of transvestism, with cross-dressing marking the
X of dialogue.

> "It is almost as if the word 'impersonator,' in contemporary popular culture, can
> be modified either by 'female' or by 'Elvis.' Why is 'Elvis,' like 'woman,' that
> which can be impersonated? From the beginning Elvis is produced and exhibit-
> ed as parts of a body—detachable (and immitable) parts that have an uncanny
> life and movement of their own, seemingly independent of their 'owner': the
> curling lip, the pompadour, the hips, the pelvis" (Garber, 1992: 372).

The cults formed by fans around certain stars—the likes of Jimmy Dean, Marilyn
Monroe, and in general the finite but ever-growing collection of celebrity icons
(including Carmen Miranda)—echo the scene Plato figured in *Phaedrus*, whose
setting was the site of an Eleusinian ritual. The best linguistics available to account for fan discourse is based on the psychoanalytic theory of fetishism. The
detachable parts that allow the *anecdotal life of a historical person such as Elvis to become an aphorism of thought in a language* are organized by the logic of fetishism.
The detachability that permits transvestism—the deployment of wigs, false
breasts, or codpieces—also allows creolization: the switch that turns a hubcap's
reflection of the sun into a "flash of spirit." In *impersonation* we have the figure
that is to electrate dialogue what conversation was to *Phaedrus*.

"In the Elvis story the detachable part is not only explicitly and repeatedly
described as an artificial phallus but also as a trick, a stage device, and a sham"
(Garber, 1992: 367). In one of his early performances, Garber relates, Elvis
stuffed his pants with the cardboard tube from a roll of toilet paper—an act that
we now recognize as *writing* in pop-pidgin. The logic of the fetish (the double-
ness that both sees and does not see the mother's absent phallus) operates by
dreamwork, pattern formation, displacement, and condensation (the operators
of conduction). The interchangeability of face and pelvis in body thought makes
clear what is involved in the digitizing of dialogue as a face-to-face encounter. "By

a familiar mechanism of displacement (upward or downward), which is in fact the logic behind Freud's reading of the Medusa, 'face' and 'penis' become symbolic alternatives for one another" (247).

The nickname "Pelvis" (replacing "phallus") suggests how to generalize the sex and gender of this displaced face: "pelvis" is gender-neutral. Perhaps we should say "interbody" metaphors to name the design of human access to machine memory. By means of dream reason Elvis as icon can perform the work of the unconscious, that is, deal with those anxiety-producing parts of identity formation unthinkable within the subjectivation of selfhood. All the crossings of the borders constitutive of order and defended by taboos—hence denied to the conscious self—are performed by the Greek chorus of pop icons, thus carrying the liminal function of dialogue into entertainment discourse. "I need to argue for an unconscious of transvestism, for transvestism as a language that can be read, and double-read, like a dream, a fantasy, or a slip of the tongue . . . And that this quality of crossing—which is fundamentally related to other kinds of boundary-crossing in their performances—can be more powerful and seductive than explicit 'female impersonation'" (354).

Table Turning

A final inference about the nature of "interface design" may be drawn from Bolt's interaction with his dynamic table. The demonstration constituted an emblem, combining an image and a sentence. The two elements do not illustrate, but instead supplement, one another. The meaning of his original sentence (interacting with a computer will be like having a conversation with another person) is modified in another way by the projection of the moving virtual table to say: ". . . who is dead." Dealing with computers will become less like operating a device and more like conversing with another person *who is dead*. One converses with Elvis by means of impersonation. In other words, the kind of dialogue conducted by computer is that specialized kind known as a "seance."

A seance is "a sitting held for the purpose of communicating with the dead, an essential requirement being that at least one member of the company be possessed of mediumistic powers" (Spence, 1993: 358). Among the physical phenomena associated with seances, one of the most prominent is table turning, related to "the spontaneous outbreaks of the poltergeist." It is relevant for conduction that the report of a session included in the encyclopedic entry on "seance" is by a "Mr. Home." A description of a typical session begins with table turning. "'After a rather long wait the table began to move, slowly at first,—a matter explained by the skepticism, not to say the positively hostile spirit, of those who were this night in a seance circle for the first time. Then little by little, the movements increased in intensity. M. Lombroso proved the levitation of the table, and estimated at twelve or fifteen pounds the resistance to the pressure which he had to make with his hands in order to overcome that levitation'" (359). The moving table is part of a method of communication, and all the terms related to it are useful for the interface metaphor.

"The *modus operandi* is simple. The sitters take their places round a table, on which they lightly rest their finger-tips, thus forming a 'chain.' In a few moments the table begins to rotate, and may even move about the room, seemingly carrying the experimenters with it. It was, and is, in high favor among spiritualists as a means of communicating with the spiritual world. The alphabet was slowly repeated, or a pencil was run down the printed alphabet, the table tilting at the letter which the spirits desired to indicate. Thus were dictated sermons, poems, information regarding the spirit-world, and answers to questions put by the sitters" (398).

The Eleusinian ceremony that Plato turned into a metaphor of *chora* in *Timaeus* (*chora* sorts chaos into order the way winnowing sorts the wheat from the chaff) involved the display of a concrete thing as the sign of the fertility of nature. The implements and products of the grain harvest (the technology of agriculture) evoked the myth of Demeter and Persephone. The accessories of the Dionysian rites associated with the ceremonies (Dionysus raped Persephone according to the story) were carried in the ritual procession—the phallus and the mask— stored in the winnowing baskets (the metaphor also used by Coleridge in "Kubla Khan"). "It is very likely that in the *cista mystica* [big basket], among the plants that can be seen on representations of the basket, one or more phalluses were hidden" (Kerenyi, 1967: 66). To be admitted to the site of final vision, the initiates performed a rite meant to be kept secret, of "taking things out of the big basket and putting them in the little basket," and then back into the big basket (66).

Comment

• In the same way that the internet finally makes electronic media two-way (the original hopes for radio in this regard never materialized), electracy (in the practices of choragraphy, mystory) makes interpellation two-way. The dead with whom we need to communicate are the figures enshrined as judges in what psychoanalysis calls our superego.

Fortune   A point of articulation between the two logics needed for an electrate dialogue is Alan Turing, whose personal story offers as much guidance for the software question as his professional work did for hardware design. Turing's biographer reported that in the conjectures attempting to make sense of Turing's suicide on June 7, 1954, (two years after his arrest and conviction for homosexuality) one of the most enigmatic pieces of the puzzle was the incident reported by Turing's (psycho)analyst, Dr. Greenbaum. In mid-May of 1954, Turing accompanied the Greenbaum family to an amusement park. On an impulse he went into the tent of a gypsy fortune teller to have his palm read. After half an hour he came out of the tent "white as a sheet." Refusing to speak to the family, Turing went home. It was their last contact with him (Hodges, 1983: 496).

This incident may be read as an episode in the history of method, understood as a continuous evolution of the attempt to master fortune (or chance) by means of system. Divination is marked negatively as the other of computing in this tale. It is the path not taken at the crossroads of history, to which choragraphy returns. Turing himself resisted the turn away from system taken by his colleague Wittgenstein (Turing sat in on Wittgenstein's lectures on mathematics), but his fate now may be read as an example of the X formula Deleuze borrowed from Nietzsche: "We must reach a secret point where the anecdote of life and the aphorism of thought amount to one and the same thing. It is like sense which, on one of its sides, is attributed to states of life and, on the other, inheres in propositions of thought" (Deleuze, 1990: 128).

This dialogical secret point in Turing's case is the famous Imitation Game he proposed as a way to test whether or not a machine could be considered intelligent. The Imitation Game is a kind of dialogue. The exact nature of the Turing Test is sometimes forgotten—the Imitation Game, with its origins in Family discourse (a parlor game), passing into specialized knowledge through Entertainment (a televised interview). "If a person failed to distinguish between a man imitating a woman (via teletype) and a computer imitating a man imitating a woman, then the machine succeeded in the Imitation Game" (Schank, 1986: 1–2). He imagined a game in which an interrogator would have to decide on the basis of written replies alone which of two people in another room was a man and which a woman. In the BBC television program on the topic of intelligent machines, featuring Alan Turing, most of the questions were couched in the form of "gags," as Turing explained in a letter to his mother. What kind of questions could be asked of the machine? "'Anything,' said Alan, 'and the questions don't really have to be questions, any more than the questions in a law court are really questions. You know the sort of thing, "I put it to you that you are only pretending to be a man," would be quite in order'" (Hodges, 1983: 450). In our context the Imitation Game may be recognized as a survival of the rituals leading to dialogue, such as those associated with the Eleusinian Mysteries. It is also a manifestation of the enigma of identity so exploited by advertisers: what am I, a man or a woman?

> "Jane Ellen Harrison remarked on the similarities between Plato's presentation of interlocutors as taking on views they did not agree with, or of being forced to say something they didn't mean, and the Eleusinian rites in which males dressed as females. Transformation and transcendence are effected through deliberate reversal. Harrison asserts that 'Plato's whole scheme alike of education and philosophy is but an attempted rationalization of the primitive mysticism of initiation'" (Swearingen, 1990: 65).

The thread of gender transgression running through our study should be understood as designating similar boundary disorder at every categorical border of the literate apparatus. The relevance of the Turing Test to the new apparatus may be observed in the internet, which is emerging as the "seat" of electracy. The relevant puncept crossing the ideal sense of theoretical vision privileged in literacy with the contact senses (taste, smell, touch) revalued in electracy is "see" in the ecclesiastical sense. A *chora* is a *see,* a place or site of authority, displacing the seeing or visually dominated sensorium of literacy. The experience of the unified self associated with the assimilation of literacy by civilization is being supplemented by a new experience of a distributed identity (terminal identity) forming in the online practices of MUDs and MOOs (multi-user domains with object-oriented programming) and the World Wide Web.

This game of "find the phallus" (fetish work) coincides with the history of dialogue at the point of the Imitation Game, which includes now the phenomenon of Elvis impersonators, and this extension of the lore of artificial intelligence to an entertainment practice marks a passage from literacy to electracy. In learning how to write and reason with hypermedia I have to bring back together the abstract with the concrete *seeing* separated by the history of dialectic in literacy. In the terminology of our interface metaphor, we are working with a "medium." The egent is this "medium" conducting a consultation as seance.

OFFICE

1. You undertake now the third major installment on the widesite, looking for the obtuse features of a work from Entertainment to add to the mystory. The examples provided all make explicit the personal motivation for the selection of the story or scene. This personal motivation is operating in your selection and editing of your work, but it need not be developed to the level demonstrated in the examples. The examples are useful because they show what happens when you have gathered scenes from all quarters of the popcyle. Then through juxtaposition the kinds of figurative transfers across the levels or quarters will happen rhetorically for a reader, regardless of your intention. The atmosphere of the Entertainment work will produce an allegorical connection with the Family story, and so forth. The key in the design then is to be sure to manipulate your selections and combination to produce this effect of recognition for yourself. For now you do not need to hyperlink the separate quarters of the mystory (but it may be helpful in finding the pattern already at work).

2. The remake of *Phaedrus* continues our demonstration of the conductive inferential reasoning through an associative chain that is fundamental to electracy. The Socratic question and answer of the dialogue is replaced in electracy with the creole dance music of the Afro-Caribbean/European hybrid emblematized by Elvis—a feature that will be treated in more detail later. The remake brings out that the operating features of electrate cross-speaking are learned from star icons through impersonation. This impersonation is not intended to be literal, but introduced into the production of image-text writing (authoring) in a virtual modality: the rhetoric of the "gest." To evoke an "Elvis effect" one needs only a few signifiers.

3. Another lesson of the remake concerns the generation of electracy by analogy with the invention of literacy. We are reminded that the dialogue was a *practice* invented by Plato for his new institution—the Academy—and extended by Aristotle in his Lyceum into the "dialectical topics"—a debate performance between students following very strict rules, whose purpose was to produce knowledge of categories and concepts. The rhetoric we are exploring is similarly intended as a practice capable of producing learning and knowledge within the context of the internet as a global institution.

4. Elvis is a relay for how to consider your star actor-character in iconic terms. It may be that the character or scene with which you identify has not been "iconized" in popular culture, in which case you should extrapolate from the Elvis example to locate the set of signifiers that evoke the feeling of your example. It may also be the case that the iconic version of a star differs from your memory or experience. Again, in your widesite you may form your own iconic version of the figure.

5. The conductive link of Bolt's turning table with the seance suggests that the entire rhetoric of "magic" is relevant to the virtual mood. Note how heuretics (the use of theory to generate new ideas, methods, poetics) works: the remake led to the modification of the MIT expert's metaphor to include the spiritualist practice of the seance as a relay for the experience of internet inquiry. What does this mean in practical terms? We do not know, exactly, except that it guides our invention in a certain direction. For example, when communicating with the dead in a seance, the contact with the spirit world is signaled through such material actions as table turning, knocking, and other poltergeist behaviors. However fraudulent these effects might be literally, semiotically they point to the role of special effects in virtual rhetoric. The increase of spiritualist themes in entertainment films (for example, *The Sixth Sense*), is a symptom of the relevance of this marginalized practice to the design of an electrate interbody.

6. Noticing and documenting the problems causing the dramatic conflict in your Family and Entertainment stories anticipate your work with problems in your Career field and in your Community as a consultant. The EmerAgency motto—"Problems B Us"—makes explicit the principle of consultation. Egents testify by finding a figurative (or sometimes a literal) connection between the signifiers of a public problem and the details of their mystory. The point is that the wide image is more readily discovered not in the abstract, but in a situation; not in general, but within the pressures of a specific project. Even if the goal of this book is for you to make or discover your wide image, that discovery must come as a side effect, so to speak, of your intention to become an egent in order to consult on the problems confronting your community. The justification for this stance comes from the structure of narrative: the magic tool the hero uses to solve the problem of the story world is the wide image the egent uses to consult on a public policy issue. We will learn more about this narrative parable of consulting in the coming chapters.

7. "To write is perhaps to bring this assemblage of the unconscious to the light of day, to select the whispering voices, to gather the tribes and secret idioms from which I extract something I call my self. . . . My direct discourse is still the free indirect discourse running through me, coming from other worlds or other planets. That is why so many artists and writers have been tempted by the seance table" (Deleuze and Guattari, 1987: 84).

Chapter 6

Cyberpidgin

Act II, 5—Into the other world/the first threshold: having decided to accept the challenge, the subject enters into action (begins a journey).

LECTURE
Virtual Feeling

We are in the "special world" of Entertainment discourse, scene of the spectacle and of emergent electracy. "Spectacle" names the *literate* (hostile, negative) experience of the electrate apparatus. In the previous chapter we remade the literate dialogue, replacing the interface metaphor of conversation that Plato used to bring his students into contact with dialectic, with the interbody metaphor of impersonation to bring egents into contact with conduction (haiku reason). Dialogue in the new literate institution of School (the Academy) relied on an atmosphere of friendship and trust: participants could set aside their defenses and the need to win the argument in order to learn and discover the true state of affairs. In the new electrate institution of the internet, conditions are somewhat different. The interbody metaphor must mediate a global encounter among strangers in an atmosphere of compassion fatigue, indifference or misunderstanding, perhaps even post-traumatic stress disorder (PTSD). We need to explore further, then, the nature of the iconic or gestural discourse that Entertainment makes available for adaptation or appropriation by the EmerAgency as a new practice for an electrate civic sphere, and electrate experience of identity.

What must an egent learn in order to consult in an electrate way (to syncretize literacy with electracy)? It is not that there is "no communication" in electracy, but that the channel, the connection along with the given circumstances of the senders and receivers, are in ruins; yet within these ruins arises a digital memory palace (Xanadu). What are the working principles of this register? It is useful in this context to review the historical embodiments of the emerging apparatus:

- technology: the internet as a technology of packet-switching, designed to survive a nuclear strike targeting the nation's communications network;
- identity: the rhetoric of the unconscious as described by psychoanalysis, featuring the devices of figurative language or image-making such as condensation, displacement, or secondary elaboration, by means of which a latent thought manifests itself in a fragmentary, encrypted, indirect manner;

- institution: the social corollary of these technological and psychological registers is the survival of African oral culture in the Americas and its syncretism with Western literate institutions: "Voodoo is the African aesthetic shattered and then desperately put back together. More than simply 'put back together,' it has been recreated to serve its people under the shattering impact of slavery and poverty" (Ventura, 1985: 113).

The specific feel of electracy in our time is due in part to its emergence within this shattered and rebuilt matrix. And just as Plato invented the dialogue as a hybrid with oral and literate features, so too now is our consultancy a hybrid selected from oral, literate, and electrate elements. The larger problem holding the place of the public policy issue that calls the egent into a consultation turns out to be historical (a problem of Community, collective history). The name of this issue is "slavery," and the policy is "colonialism." Do we imagine that this policy issue is settled, closed? We make this historical problem explicit as a policy question just to note how we are all carried along in these larger currents of our Community story.

One of the most important facts for the EmerAgency is precisely the global reach of the internet in this postcolonial moment. The virtual dialogue must support interaction, if not "communication," across the cultural and linguistic intervals of global societies. The inference path (filling the gap—fulling) of this interaction relies finally on neither the forms of narrative nor of argument. The narratives and arguments that are involved are organized in turn by pattern, by repetition of material details (signifierness). Conductive logic subsumes the inductive, deductive, and abductive inferences of the interrogator. In conduction the inference path moves from material thing to another thing, from signifier to signifier, without recourse to the abstractions of rules and cases.

Comment

- While you are working on documenting a memorable narrative to represent the Entertainment register of your mystory, we will discuss the function of the remade dialogue with its interbody metaphor in the context of globalization. We will see that the site of intervention of the EmerAgency consultation in policy formation is at the level of values or belief systems of a society. The challenge of the internet consultancy is that policy formation occurs in an international ecology. The crisis of September 11, 2001, illustrates this global ecology. Persuasion in literate rhetoric relied upon appealing to the audience's sense of probability, which meant knowing the other's belief system. In electracy your interlocutor may be unknown, and the consultation may be among singularities whose only point of communication is the recognition of this mutual singularity.

- The quest for the wide image is imagined now as the material of a consultation on the policies of globalization. We are still in the discourse of Entertainment, but it is this discourse that is the most global, the most electrate, site of the emergence of the new apparatus. Community history and problem solving are already present, then, but we still are focusing on what we may learn about imaging from Entertainment. The so-called lingua franca of globalization is not only English, but Entertainment.

From Pidgin to Creole

The global historical situation most relevant to the emerging apparatus is the encounter of literate and oral peoples in the conditions of colonialism. When these incommensurable civilizations met, they learned to communicate in pidgin. Pidgin as a metaphor for internet interbody has already been applied by Thomas Erickson, who suggested the evolution of pidgin languages into creole as a model for the evolution of the Macintosh interface. "The characteristic ways that pidgins evolve into creoles may tell us what properties a linguistic system—or an interface—must have for it to become a powerful communicative device while remaining relatively simple and easy to learn" (Erickson 1990, 13). Erickson does not push the metaphor very far, since the main point of his article is to invite others to use a system of analytical extrapolations from models in order to become more inventive about interface design. The creole model is introduced as an example of how the process might work. Even within the reduced terms of an example, however, the usefulness of Erickson's suggestion is clear and may be appropriated as a relay for our consultancy, imagining an online meeting between strangers and their avatars.

Pidgin begins as a language for doing business in the absence of a common language among different peoples, and evolves into a creole (that is, into a full-featured language) in the speech of pidgin-speaking children, once the pidgin has become so common that it is spoken in the home (14). This analogy has been taken up more recently by anthropologists studying "cyberspace." "The Technology Actor Networks (TANs) of cyberspace are 'Creoles.' . . . Creolization seems to me to be a useful way to think about successful 'technology transfer.' Each time technological artifacts are introduced effectively into a new cultural setting, the resulting TAN is best understood as a syncretic response to the attributes of both the 'spawning' techno-science and the 'receiving' social formation. Their extended capacity for syncretism, increasingly symbolic content, and grounding in more diverse practice make cyberspace TANs even more Creolized" (Hakken, 1999: 85).

Since it is not important for his immediate purpose, Erickson only mentioned in passing that one of the conditions in which creole developed was "a result of the slave trade in the Caribbean, when slaves from the same areas were deliberately separated to reduce the possibility of uprising" (Erickson, 1990: 14). His method of examining the symmetries between two juxtaposed domains (in this case between creole and the Macintosh interface) reveals the fit between the destroyed and dispersed scenario of the Internet design and the conditions of the slave trade that created most creole languages. The choral method of conductive inference, that is, is to consider any figurative juxtaposition in terms of the full semantic domains invoked. The catastrophe of colonialism includes the notorious middle passage in which as many as 10 million Africans were forcibly removed from their native lands and dispersed throughout the New World, a passage which millions of individuals did not survive. A manifesto for creoleness refers to creolization as "the brutal interaction of culturally different populations":

> "Generally resting upon a plantation economy, these populations are called to invent the new cultural designs allowing for a relative cohabitation between them. These designs are the result of a nonharmonious (and unfinished therefore nonreductionist) mix of linguistic, religious, cultural, culinary, architectural, medical, etc. practices of the different people in question" (Bernabe, et al. 1993, 92).

Erickson limits his explicit exploration of the creole interface metaphor to the linguistic dimension (proposing that the Macintosh interface might evolve a greater complexity of syntax, tense, and vocabulary). This analogy may be extended to include Bernabe's, Chamoisseau's, and Confiant's broader understanding of creole as a cultural discourse. Meanwhile, the mnemonic scene supporting and guiding chorography portrays the possibilities of surviving the greatest imaginable destruction—of the internet continuing to function after a nuclear strike; of African culture continuing to function after the diaspora. The creole manifesto makes a good case, moreover, for adopting creole as a relay for interaction in the electronic apparatus:

> "A new humanity will gradually emerge which will have the same characteristics as our Creole humanity: all the complexity of Creoleness. The son or daughter of a German and a Haitian, born and living in Peking, will be torn between several languages, several histories, caught in the torrential ambiguity of a mosaic identity. To present creative depth, one must perceive that identity in all its complexity. He or she will be in the situation of a Creole" (112).

A task of the egents' widesite is first to provide a creole passage between literacy and electracy.

The Liminal   The relevance of creole to dialogue has to do with the fundamental orality of creole (95). The setting of *Phaedrus*—Socrates and Phaedrus hold their conversation on the banks of the river Ilissos—is one that would immediately evoke in Plato's audience the context of the Eleusinian mystery religion, just as surely as the setting of a frontier town evokes the genre of the Western for an American audience. "At the end of the classical period the philosophical imagination set a higher *visio beatifica* above the Eleusinian vision, building on this religious experience, known to almost every Athenian, as on an existing, self-evident foundation" (Kerenyi, 1967: 98). Plato used the mystery religion's ritual practice of moving from a physical to a spiritual *seeing* in a figurative sense, thus preserving a part of oral practice in his hybrid invention. That the genre of the "dialogue with the dead" evolved in antiquity out of the Socratic dialogue may be due in part to this association of the invention of method with the rituals of the Mysteries, participation in which "offered a guarantee of life without fear of death, of confidence in the face of death" (15).

The dialogue form shares with ritual the function of liminality (theorized in the work of Victor Turner [1982]). "From its inception in Plato, dialogue has always been and continues to be programmatically liminal: interstructural, between two states or conditions, essentially unstructured rather than structured by contradictions; because of its deliberate avoidance of closure and finality, it serves perpetually as a vehicle for reformulating old elements into new patterns" (Swearingen, 1990: 47). The creoleness of the dialogue is evident in Plato's understanding of dialogue "as a vast experiment in mixing and mingling discourse conventions in order to bring about optimum understanding, partaking of extant patterns but altering them to fit new objectives. It can, I think, be productively applied to transitional discourses, logics, and literacies today" (67).

The "death" invoked by dialogue includes "the death of one discourse in the birth of another," according to Stephen Tyler. "Its image is 'X,' the coming-together-of-the-crossing-getting-across-crossing-over-crossing-out, the chiasmus within the logos conjuring at one and the same time a bright vision of reason, agreement, consensus, communion, unity, harmony, and mutuality and a darker picture of resistance, disagreement, disensus, opposition, antagonism, and raised voices" (quoted in Maranhao, 1990: 294). This 'X' is the shape (the *eidos*) guiding the design of internet interactivity as well.

Fetishturgy

The analogy between the destroyed network of military command still able to function after suffering a first nuclear strike, and the ruined messages of dream work, scrambled into nonsense by repression yet received and understood in a way by the dreamer, is one of the operative "packets" of chorography. The equivalent ruin at the sociohistorical level is the Black Atlantic—the persistence of African culture through the catastrophe of the middle passage, the diaspora of slavery disseminating individuals throughout the Americas, and the practices of syncretism that enabled the members to reassemble their culture in new forms fashioned out of the materials ready to hand in the colonizing culture. Syncretism—the formation of cross-cultural hybrids in religion, music, crafts, arts and letters—is the dream work, the packet switching, of Afro-Caribbean culture. The defensive powers of fetish charms are still invoked in the American South, for example, even if the flash of spirit is now materialized by a hubcap (a religious readymade) (Thompson, 146–158).

This context suggests that another way to approach the transition from literacy to electracy is as a replacement of dialectic with "fetish" as the logic guiding the design of the widesite. Fetish is another way to take into account the uncanny experience of recognition—the intuitive reasoning—involved in making a mystory. A further (provisional) neologism might be useful to name this practice— "fetishturgy" (thus acknowledging the performance aspect of chorography, with the making of fetish "felts" rather than dramatic "texts") being comparable to dramaturgy: the online composer is a "fetishwright" rather than a playwright. Who is the audience? Whomever is online (the other, the stranger).

(Post)Colonial Fetish   Why "fetish"? Part of the rationale is the global nature of the internet—that the internet is a continuation of the history of colonialism. Part of the task of the EmerAgency is to help reorient the worldwide dissemination of electracy from a colonial to a postcolonial frame. This reframing may be accomplished by thinking about the context of fetish. "Fetish" is a term in the Portuguese pidgin language that developed along the Guinea Coast, the coast of West Africa, in the early 1500s. Pidgins have no native speakers, display reduced or simplified features drawn from the source languages, and arise when peoples of different civilizations with no common language encounter one another. Pidgins may become creoles—evolve into full-featured natural language—among the children of pidgin speakers. "Cyberpidgin" is a neologism naming the effort to appropriate self-consciously the dynamics of pidginization and creolization and apply them to international internet interactivity. Fetishturgy is the means of writing cyberpidgin.

Included within the theoretical rationale for fetishturgy is a reconsideration of the historical status of "fetish" within Western culture. The perspective of cyberpidgin reveals an anomaly in this history. To begin with, when the history of critique is considered from the point of view of fetish, the narrowness of focus of this history becomes more apparent. The intellectual history of the colonial period, that is, could fit in its entirety into the problematic of the fetish. After its origins in the trading language of the Guinea Coast, "fetish" is picked up in early anthropological accounts in the European Enlightenment, then passes to Marx who used it as a metaphor for the commodity, then to Freud who used it as the prototype for the analysis of deviant behavior. The negative inflection of this genealogy reflects the European or Western sense of identity, based on the distinction between the presumed superiority of literate institutions as opposed to the superstition of oral, fetishistic peoples.

Primitivism   The anomaly is that at the same time that a negative use of "fetish" was evolving within Western theory, a positive use developed within Western arts in a tendency known as "primitivism." Many of the controversies and conflicts informing contemporary debates in cultural and postcolonial studies are the result of confusion about this contradictory, ambivalent relationship of Western literacy to the non-Western apparatus of orality. The first step in rethinking this relationship is to reconsider the two strands of theory and the arts together rather than separately as is usually the case, for reasons having to do with the way knowledge is divided up in the current model of specialization that dominates modernist education.

This convergence has already begun to take place in a new phase of the career of "fetish" occurring within feminist-inspired arts and theory (Gamman and Makinen, 1994). Discovering that the defense formations of fetish logic offer a useful strategy for resistance to the dominant ideology of Western patriarchy, the artists and critics associated with identity politics are in the process of continuing the evolution of cultural invention that has taken place in the name of "fetish" in the period of colonialism. Choragraphy draws upon the vitality of this history as a point of departure for cyberpidgin.

The first insight that might come from the contextualization of "fetish" as one word in a colonial pidgin is: what about all the other words that also existed in the pidgin of the Guinea Coast? In principle, some of these other terms should lend themselves to the same kind of elaboration that occurred in the case of "fetish." Or rather, since fetish in particular, and pidginization in general, inform an interbody metaphor as an extended analogy for choragraphy, I infer that cyberpidgin is not only fetishist, but forms a multitude of figures of thought using the natural history of "fetish" as a relay for a more reflexive concentrated fabrication of an online practice. One of the root terms of "fetish," in any case, means "to fabricate" or "to make" something.

Crossroads   Our use of "fetish" reopens or deconstructs the existing uses of this phenomenon as a metaphor in the theories of Marx and Freud. Fetishturgy is more grammatological, approaching fetish as logic. The X *eidos* (idea) at work in dialogue also plays a foundational role in the African cultures that constitute an essential part of the creole mix. In the Black Atlantic world, for example, the god Eshu is widely honored.

> "Eshu came to be regarded as the very embodiment of the crossroads. Eshu-Elegbara is also the messenger of the gods, not only carrying sacrifices, deposited at crucial points of intersection, to the goddesses and to the gods, but sometimes bearing the crossroads to us in verbal form, in messages that test our wisdom and compassion . . . He sometimes even wears the crossroads as a cap, colored black on one side, red on the other, provoking in his wake foolish arguments about whether his cap is black or red, wittily insisting by implication that we view a person or a thing from all sides before we form a general judgment" (Thompson, 1984: 19).

The crossroads, associated with change, were figured in the cosmograms that display the ritual quality of writing in oral culture. According to Wyatt MacGaffey, a scholar of Kongo civilization:

> "The simplest ritual space is a Greek cross, marked on the ground, as for oath-taking. One line represents the boundary, the other is ambivalently both the path leading across the boundary, as to the cemetery; and the vertical path of power linking, 'the above' with 'the below.' This relationship, in turn, is polyvalent, since it refers to God and man, God and the dead, and the living and the dead. The person taking the oath stands upon the cross, situating himself between life and death, and invokes the judgment of God and the dead upon himself" (quoted in Thompson, 1984: 108).

Robert Farris Thompson's *Flash of the Spirit* inventoried the survival and continuation in the diaspora of the different manifestations of the cross from different African cultures into the Atlantic world. All of them have to do with the intersection of two lines associated with the "dia" of dialogue:

> "The quartered circle with four eyes—spiritual communication and enlighten-ment, the core emblem among the signs of the *anaforuana* corpus—becomes, in Abaku masking, a Janus with two eyes seen in front and two implied on a disk at the back of the head. And just as the intersection of two lines in *nsibidi* commu-nicates the intersection of words of one person with words of another, with the same sign the 19th century Abaku masker visually voices the idea of speech. He crosses broom and wand before his body to indicate a desire to speak of things positive and lasting" (262).

The various geometries of the cross were used in practices concerned with mediating the power across worlds, especially between the living and the dead (252). The rituals, that is, served as the methodology for gaining access to the stored wisdom of the ancestors, including a collection of institutional practices such as divination and the making of charms. One of the most elaborate signs in the Abaku "calligraphy of the dead," the sign of the lifting of the plate, refers to the custom of taking up the plate of a dead person from his table, "for no longer will he use it in this world" (268). The Spanish translation of the ritual cited by Thompson— *"levantimiento de plato"*—suggests a macaronic antonomasia between "plato" and Plato that signals the nature of the logic of patterning (conduction) organizing the table series. The purpose of the ritual identified by the ideo-graphic cross of the lifting of the plate, "honoring myriad ancestors simultane-ously" (268), is to preserve in memory the cumulative knowledge of the civilization.

> "Today the function of similar expressions presiding over Kongo graves is the blocking of the disappearance of the talents of the important dead. Lifting up their plates or bottles on trees or saplings also means 'not the end,' 'death will not end our fight,' the renaissance of the talents of the dead that have been stopped, by gleaming glass and elevation, from absorption in the void" (144–145).

Plato is one of our ancestors to be honored in this way, even as he is creolized into a new apparatus, along with Elvis, Marilyn, and all the other pop icons. The passage out of literacy into electracy, ironically, includes a reanimation of the oral portion of the dialogue hybrid.

Logic Switch   Gilles Deleuze provides the theory of this exploration of online interbody as a new dialogue. The assumption of interbody design is that the com-puter is a prosthesis augmenting human intelligence. That intelligence is an ef-fect of a brain located in a body. This embodied mind is positioned within a family, in a culture, a society, a historical moment (the "popcycle"). The person possessed of this mind is sexed, gendered, nationalized, classed, raced, ethni-cized, and so on through all the ideological categories used to describe identity. Deleuze provides a theory that suggests a way to take the full scope of this per-sonhood into account in the metaphor of dialogue (to communicate with a computer *is* *like* impersonating another—dead—person). He shows how to include the unconscious in an electrate model of mind. Electracy adds to orality and literacy the possibility of writing the unconscious (and hence of writing with what we do not know—with our stupidity and with our trust). The question becomes: in what *setting* does this conversation occur?

In *The Logic of Sense* Deleuze shows how to extend method beyond analytical intelligence into the reasoning of pattern, how to go beyond the truth table that brought together logic and the electric switch to solve the problem of hardware, in order to clarify the nature of electracy which concerns the logic that guides the human use of hardware and software. Partly because he is drawing on the Stoic invention of "sense" (a reversal of Platonism), Deleuze echoes many of the terms of the history of dialogue in his account, including the X or crossing lines of *dia*.

> "The Aion is the ideal player of the game; it is an infused and ramified chance. It is the unique cast from which all throws are qualitatively distinguished. It plays or is played on at least two tables, or at the border of two tables. There, it traces its straight and bisecting line. It gathers together and distributes over its entire length the singularities corresponding to both. The two tables or series are like the sky and the earth, propositions and things, expressions and consumptions. Lewis Carroll would say that they are the multiplication table and the dinner table. The Aion is precisely the border of the two, the straight line which separates them; but it is also the plain surface which connects them" (Deleuze, 1990: 64).

Here is the key to a choral dialogue—tables for truth *and for eating*: not one or the other, but both together. The interbody design needed to exploit the convergence of technologies in digital hypermedia may be invented out of this convergence in theory of the truth table with the dinner table (producing the series truth table/electric switch/dinner table). Having poststructural psychoanalysis in his background the way Socrates had Pythagoreanism, Deleuze formulated the orality of conversation in terms of a new dimension. The mouth participates in more than one circuit—not only the circuit with the ear related to voice, but with the anus related to eating: "speaking will be fashioned out of eating and shitting, language and its univocity will be sculpted out of shit" (193). A similar insight motivated Michel Serres's demonstration of isotopies across anthropology, biology, and information theory, coordinated (thanks to a puncept in French) by the "parasite": "In every instance, the parasite disrupts a system of exchange: the disagreeable guest who partakes of a meal and offers only words in return; the organism that physically enters and feeds off of its host; the noise that interrupts messages between two points in an information circuit" (Serres, 1982: 14). The key feature/experience of the "fragment" as a compositional unit that is to electracy what the paragraph is to literacy, is "interruption." "Interruption" is not a thing or an act but a relationship.

First Encounters

To figure what happens when electrate people meet online, we may call upon the experience of colonial encounters as a relay (to remind ourselves how different electracy is from the experience of School). Grammatologists such as Walter

Ong described electracy as a kind of "secondary orality"—as a hybrid sharing features of literate and oral practices, to be understood logically as intervening between and mediating the apparatuses of orality and literacy, distinct from its chronological position as coming after literacy. This characterization suggests that one of the first experiments of fetishturgy should be a remake of the scenes of first encounters between literate and oral peoples that organize so much of the history of colonialism. These remakes are "secondary encounters" after colonialism, aiming at the creation of something similar to the dialectical image theorized by Walter Benjamin (the dialectical image produced by the juxtaposition of the past and present at a particular moment of danger in the civilization).

Treating an interbody metaphor as a dialectical image brings out an important aspect of the rationale for fetishturgy, which is that, seen from the point of view of oral peoples, the page is itself a "fetish." There are many anecdotes recounting the astonishment created among oral peoples when witnessing the workings of writing. One such incident shows a European demonstrating to a native chief the power of writing. The chief whispers his secret name to the European. The European writes the name on a sheet of paper, hands it to an orderly who carries it to another officer some distance away. When the officer reads out the name for all to hear, the chief is stunned, and declares the act to be "magic."

The journalist H. M. Stanley, who went in search of Dr. Livingstone, recorded an incident late in the colonial period (1877) in which natives in central Africa, when they saw him writing in his journal, forced him to burn it. Stanley reported the natives as saying: "Our people saw you yesterday make marks on some tara-tara [paper]. This is very bad. Our country will waste, our goats will die. What have we done to you, that you should wish to kill us?" Stanley actually switched the journal for a copy of the plays of Shakespeare (whose binding resembled that of his journal) and offered it to the natives, who stated: "No, no. We will not touch it. It is fetish. You must burn it" (Greenblatt, 1988: 161). This reference to the paper pages of a book as "fetish," and the sacrifice of an anthology of Shakespeare, indicate the relevance of "fetishturgy" as an interbody metaphor for online design.

In the context of colonialism, then, the page is literally a fetish. The history of fetish proper repays the favor, in that one of the primary functions of fetish practices in both oral and literate cultures is as a defense, protection, or secretiveness—functions that share the attributes of a "screen." In fact, one of the most common functions of a fetish is the protection of the home, indicating thus a compatibility of "home" and "fetish" as metaphors for putting into the widesite that feeling of (artificial) trust. The computer screen in our metaphor is thought of in terms of the magical screening properties of the fetish. The shift from homepage to fetish-screen as the interbody metaphor for online hypertexts opens up a complex, overdetermined group of semantic sets. The interference across these linguistic categories is an important source of creativity in chorography.

Ju-Ju The scenes of secondary encounter are intended as a holistic approach to the design of the practices necessary for exploring the collective identity and behaviors emerging within electracy. If the metaphor is any good, it will help formulate a precise way to deal with the unknowns of the new situation. Or at least it will help map the borders of the given that need to be redrawn within choragraphy. I want to test the diagnostic powers of cyberpidgin by reviewing two stories of first encounters involving fetish, as parables for our postcolonial moment. In these stories I identify with both the colonizer and the colonized. Moreover, in the context of electracy as secondary orality, the low levels of literacy in the so-called third and fourth worlds are understood rather as high levels of orality (and perhaps of latent electracy).

My first exemplary story comes from the autobiography of one Frank Hives who served in a British Colonial office in Nigeria in the early decades of the twentieth century. One of the chief challenges of his service in Nigeria was to suppress the native religious movement known as "ju-ju," a nonnative word that he describes as meaning "fetish," derived he claims from the pidgin French *jeu* (play). Hives considered his role in Enlightenment terms, as ridding the indigenes of a horrible exploitation by local priests, whose rituals included human sacrifice. The central fetish object of the priests was an assemblage made of the skulls of those sacrificed, according to Hives.

Getting a tip from a native informant about a ju-ju ceremony, Hives led a small party of police to a certain village. The villagers, having complete confidence in their gods, protected themselves from intruders simply by blocking the path to the village with a goat, their totem and strongest fetish. No other protection was deemed necessary. Hives, who was heavily outnumbered, won the day with a scientific tactic. When he came upon the goat, Hives butchered, cooked, and ate it. When the ju-ju did not strike him dead for this sacrilege, Hives's gods were assumed to have incredible power, causing the villagers to flee in terror and allowing Hives to capture the priest.

While such an incident is open to a variety of interpretations, the lesson in our context refers to our own confidence in—or rather our fetishization of—our system of knowledge. We have to imagine the shift from literacy to electracy from a point of view that encompasses both sides of the movement, rather than simply from one side or the other. The habit of literacy is problem solving, method, investigation, and inquiry—science, in short. Our habit in discussions of electronic technology is to worry over whether or not we are being critical enough in our collective adoption of the new equipment. What we have to imagine as well is the equivalent of a power that could cook and eat our science, and from whose perspective our science would appear as benighted as does ju-ju religion from the point of view of the British Empire.

Exercise: Fetishscreen

Itemize and represent on your homepage the objects or actions that could be classified as your "fetishes."

- Keep in mind that we are using "fetish" in the sense of something that you possess or do that gives you a sense of confidence and security. A quotidian example of a fetish is a lucky charm. The wide image is an augmented fetish, in that it is an object/theme (thing/word) that has creative power, as emblematized in the "magic tool" of narrative adventure.

Alien Encounters

The second exemplary first encounter is fiction rather than fact, a feature film called *My Step-Mother is an Alien*, starring Dan Ackroyd and Kim Bassinger. Although a work of pure entertainment, this film is an intelligent example of a syncretic intuition in American commercial cinema. It evokes, that is, the pidgin conditions of electracy, in which a foreign person attempts to pass as a citizen of the United States based entirely on what she has learned about American culture from the mass media (the condition Scott Bukatman called "terminal identity," as a variation on "spectacle," whose more serious prototype is *The Man Who Fell to Earth*). In this case, the alien (Kim Bassinger) is from another galaxy. The scientist (Dan Ackroyd) conducted an experiment with a powerful laser that inadvertently threatened Bassinger's planet. She was sent to Earth to find out what Ackroyd did and to get him to undo it. Her assumptions about how to persuade a human male, and the ineptness with which she performs the seduction, themselves constitute an essay on semiotics.

The most suggestive aspect of the film in the context of cyberpidgin, however, concerns Ackroyd's love for the work of Jimmy Durante. He is a Durante *fan*, which is to say he fetishizes Durante. One particular clip of Durante performing a song at a piano is played several times throughout the film. When Bassinger fails at her mission, a council of leaders from her planet (which possesses a vastly more powerful technology) arrive with plans to destroy Earth. A brief tribunal is held at which Ackroyd is given an opportunity to prove that Earth is worth saving. Ackroyd makes his case for Earth by showing the council the Durante number. Ackroyd's tactic is a calculated risk, in that, as most commentators on Durante's career agree, Durante, affectionately nicknamed "Schnozzola," referring to his famously gigantic nose, was the most likable entertainer of his generation. The irresistibility of his act was credited to the purity and goodness of the character expressed in his humor.

In the film what comes through in the clip is the nonsensically absurd charm of Durante's style, with Ackroyd's case resting on a kind of "endangered species" argument: it is not that Earthlings are good for anything, but that they possess a wonderfully unique *spirit*. Unfortunately the council is not persuaded. It goes without saying that the Earth is saved anyway. From the point of view of cyberpidgin, the very ordinariness of this film makes its use of the Durante allusion all the more significant, in that it indicates that entertainment discourse in general is evolving its own manner of complexity. It is learning how to write with its own system, with an intertextual allusiveness of the sort that will eventually give it the same degree of richness produced within literature over its multimillennial history. What "Durante" means is (like "Elvis") specific to imaging, and cannot be "said" in conceptual terms. It is a cyberpidgin signifier.

Pop Syntagms The Durante "number" functions as discourse, as a phrase, a syntagm, a unit of meaning in an electrate pidgin. We noted at the beginning of our project how conceptual thinking was invented by the Greeks over a period of several hundred years, culminating in the dialogues of Plato. As Havelock explained, the effect of being able to review Homer's epics in writing was that readers noticed a kind of halo of terms collected around the characters that had passed unnoticed in the sung version. Havelock demonstrated the process with the term *"dike,"* justice, a term that in its various forms accumulates in the descriptions associated with Agamemnon and other heroes. A quick review of the contemporary scene reveals that a process of category formation is underway in our media similar to the one Havelock described for ancient Greece, this time having to do with images.

The discovery of the equivalent of the abstract terms gathered around the actions of the epic heroes has begun in electracy. The entire tradition of the readymade from modernist collage to the present may be understood as a miming in existing media of the recording properties of the new media: the capacity to write not just with words, but directly with images of objects and actions. Paul Virilio has observed this emergence of electrate writing.

> "From the beginning of the century the perceptual field in Europe was invaded by certain signs, representations and logotypes that were to proliferate over the next twenty, thirty, sixty years, outside any immediate explanatory context, like beak-nosed carp in the polluted ponds they depopulate. Geometric brand-images, initials, Hitler's swastika, Charlie Chaplin's silhouette, Magritte's blue bird or the red lips of Marilyn Monroe: parasitic persistence cannot be explained merely in terms of the power of technical reproducibility, so often discussed since the nineteenth century. We are in effect looking at the logical outcome of a system of message-intensification which has, for several centuries, assigned a primordial role to the techniques of visual and oral communication" (Virilio, 1994: 14).

In the grammatological frame, the decision among many postmodern artists to stop opposing the mass media, and instead to appropriate the icons arising within commercial media as a new discourse, marks a new phase in the invention of electracy.

Comment

- The Duranty impersonation is in the genre of impersonation in general (associated with Elvis as the prototype). The promotion of this "avant-pop" tendency is credited to Andy Warhol and pop art, with the "Untitled Film Stills" of Cindy Sherman being a contemporary extension of the practice (which dates back at least to Marcel Duchamp's readymades). The examples produced in the arts thus far have located the existence of a new unit of meaning, in the way that the Greeks noticed the abstract idea (*dike*) once the story could be scanned visually, but without yet being able to do very much with it directly. This unit of meaning is the "syntagm."

- An example of how to isolate and select a semic series (thus making it available for further elaboration) is Dara Birnbaum's video analysis of *Wonder Woman*—a montage consisting of nothing but repetitions of different examples of the spinning movement by which Wonder Woman transforms herself from an ordinary citizen into a superhero. The tape is not important for what it "means," but for this location of an iconic signifier. What still remains to happen for electracy is the third stage, the equivalent of the invention of philosophy based on the emergent properties of discourse revealed in the recording of the narrative form of the dominant apparatus. For Plato to invent the concept, he had to separate being from doing, category from action, topic from drama. The electrate equivalent of the conceptual topos is chora, and its modality is neither doing nor being, but a mood or atmosphere in which doing and being are written together. An old joke predicted that the metaphysics of entertainment was embodied in an icon such as Frank Sinatra: the issue was not "to do," nor "to be," but "dobedobedoo." In fact, the operating features of chora are to be found in music, thus continuing the "music of the spheres" of choral cosmology.

Exercise: Pidgin Signs

Create a series of pages (files) linked to your homepage that provide a "grammar" introducing visitors to the "pidgin" writing you are using to compose your widesite.

- Use a grammar book as a relay for your sample interbody pidgin grammar (a creole grammar, if you can find one). Adapt the grammatical categories to your needs, as a way to isolate and "formalize" the signifying features of your mystory. Your "grammar" of course is figurative, not literal, since you are working with images, both pictorial and verbal.
- You should extrapolate from the Duranty (or Elvis) relay to your own case. Include in your widesite impersonations of the characters/stars/persons featured in your mystory (the ensemble cast of your superego). Design/write one "number" for each such figure.

Turntable

The structuring unit of cyberpidgin is a "secondary" fetish. The symptoms of this potentiality are plentiful in entertainment—the institution most responsible so far for electracy. Digital technology has made it possible to "sample" the audio-visual record and to create new meanings out of the singularities of existing star texts. The prototype of *readymade* authoring in entertainment is the hip hop club DJ, especially the use of "scratching," the invention of which is credited to Grand Wizard Theodore and refined by Flash (George, 1998: 17). This manipulation of the record turntable within the club dance scene is another item for the "table turning" series initiated in the remake of *Phaedrus*.

Advertisers are digitally introducing syntagms of legendary figures such as Louis Armstrong, Marilyn Monroe, James Dean, and other such icons into promotions, to associate their product with the atmosphere or rather with the aura of the star. One of the purest examples of this practice is the "Think Different" campaign by Apple Computer Corporation. Sampling and digital editing take the old device of the authoritative testimonial into a new dimension when the sound and look of dead celebrities may be used to create the effect of ethos. We are learning from our pop stars in general how to write a persona. George Michael remade his image at a certain point in his career, showing that a leather jacket and a stubble beard constitute a syntagm that millions of people can read. Madonna is famous for making over her image by changing the codes that she evokes (Goodwin, 1992: 118). This writerly personality featured in star texts prefigures the subject formation of every citizen in electracy, just as selfhood, prefigured in Socrates, became the subject formation of literacy.

In the global dialogue of cyberpidgin, America is exporting its celebrities as an iconic discourse. The anecdotes of this process, characterized by literati as "cultural imperialism," are well known in the lore of anthropology: the pygmies whose sacred song turned out to be "My Darling Clementine"; the aboriginal informant who asked the anthropologist about Janet Leigh. This point of departure acknowledges the power differential in many pidgins such as the one that produced the term "fetish." Pidgin, that is, tends to be based on the grammar of the language of the more powerful group. The subordinate group, however, enters into this language, including in the psychoanalytic sense of the mourning process, gaining the ability to negotiate desire at the price of "castration." Once the groups are in "dialogue," as Jack Zipes observed, "I wouldn't bet on the Prince."

Comment

- Cyberpidgin is emerging in the global interchange of cultural materials, with Elvis going from West to East and *wabi-sabi* coming from East to West. Elvis and *wabi-sabi* are important in their own right, of course, but are intended to represent the larger circulation of a quantity of icons and moods across cultures. This circulation is happening on its own, so to speak, and in electracy it becomes self-conscious—a general medium of global "conversation."

Emblematics

What is the grammar of this new discourse? Its prototype may be witnessed in examples of cultural creole noted by Thompson. The transfer to the Americas of the cult of Osanyin, for example, god of herbalistic medicine in Yoruba culture, included a crossing of the African myth with ready-made materials found in the American setting. An important part of the imagery of the cult is "the equation of bird with head as the seat of power and personal destiny" (Thompson, 1984: 45). The sacred metaphor portrayed an "iron bird set upon a single disk of iron surmounting several bells of iron."

> "By 1954 creole transformations had already occurred. The new forms had absorbed Western industrial or cultural fragments—the hubcap of an automobile, a metal rooster from a weathervane or discarded garden furniture, store-bought jingle bells—and invested them with new meaning. The rooster replaced the flattened birds of the elders, the hubcap sometimes became the base, and the jingle bells recalled the agogo gongs" (48).

How to creolize the pop icons operating in television pidgin? One likely answer lies in the development of interface agents, automated browse and search devices personified with the stereotyped gestures and attributes of cult celebrities. The same link (gram) that makes Elvis available for impersonation also makes him available as an information hieroglyph. The personification of information in icons was a standard feature of medieval communication. Medieval education trained students in the mnemonic practice of attaching moral qualities to descriptive attributes. The picture or statue of "Charity," for example, is represented to associate "the head of the statue with the Trinity, the eyes with Jesus' passion, the ears with the Gospels, and so on. The colors of these images are described: scarlet for the blood, black for the passion and death, green for the resurrection, hyacinth for the ascension, purple for Christ's struggles with evil spirits" (Carruthers, 1998: 208).

It is a commonplace by now in pop culture, of course, to describe Elvis and his fans in religious terms (Harrison, 1992). In mystory, these allegorical associations shift from the collective cosmology of society to the personal sacred of the symptom. The modern inversion from collective to personal cosmogony is manifested in Freud's treatment of dreams as "rebuses" (as pictures that signify not as images but as cues for words). The mythological functioning of Elvis in the present information industry may be fused with an analytical functioning by means of a prosthetic unconscious. An important lesson of the medieval relay is that impersonation has a mnemonic function. There is a direct connection between iconology and technology in computer interface design that Bolt demonstrated in his use of dataglove and gesture to operate his magic table.

Ken Hillis on Techno Emblems

"Theorizing bodies as emblems—and I am suggesting that this is the effect of Sun Microsystems' proposal for, and depiction of, a virtual teleconferencing environment—calls to mind connections between a medieval sense of understanding that underpins the affect, or transcendent potential, of emblems, and the power that lies in the contemporary implosion of image, reality, and discourse identified as simulation and made visible in virtual technologies. The body electronic, made 'present' through electronic space as a picture-image with or without supporting spoken text, can be argued to be such an emblem with or without a firm connection to its referent. Writing of former British prime minister Margaret Thatcher's political power and its connection to TV, John Fiske notes that her 'political power is the *same* as her image power, her power to do is the same as her power to seem.' I am assuming here that Fiske assumes her image most often to have had audio accompaniment. Baroque emblematics almost always employed a picture-image, most often incorporating the human body and/or an architectural motif in conjunction with a subtext included to guide and police the viewer-reader's interpretation (Buck-Morss). The English word 'emblem' is quite close to 'resemble', but closer perhaps to the French *sembler*—to seem. When it is recalled that the power of the pre-Enlightened embodied monarchy depended on the seemliness of his physical representation in public, the greater metaphysical effect, or apparent transcendent potential, of seeming rather than merely appearing is underscored" (Hillis, 1999: 67).

It is not only the gestures of the user that must be emblematised so the computer may read them correctly, but that the emblematic gesture also is used to organize electrate rhetoric as well.

Comment

- It is worth insisting on this point, that the reason we are developing impersonation as a part of an electrate rhetoric is because of this capacity of the technology to read formulaic or clearly defined gestures or body movements. The coming equipment will not just have voice-recognition features, but body-recognition features. Not being able to make pop gestures is to be anelectrate (the digital equivalent of illiterate).

Switch Words   Garber makes a case for considering the "transvestite effect" as marking the entry point of the Symbolic order (Lacan's term for that part of the unconscious representing the operations of social institutions). The transvestite, she states, is a good metaphor for writing as such (Garber, 1992: 150). To

become electrate one must learn the gestures of iconic figures that are ana-
logues for the entire range of human potential. If Garber provides us with a case
study, Deleuze provides the grammar of the emerging electrate creole. The dou-
bleness or fuzziness of the fetish structure (a feature of the logic of sense, or of
unconscious dreamwork) forms the same link between pattern and software that
the truth table formed between analysis and hardware. If the truth table made
logic compatible with the electric switch, the fetish does the same thing for the
digital link. "Each of these words," Deleuze writes, citing Michel Butor, "can act
as a switch, and we can move from one to another by means of many passages;
hence the idea of a book which does not simply narrate one story, but a whole
ocean of stories" (Deleuze 1990, 47).

The pun or homophony central to the logic of sense was also fundamental
to mnemotechnique. Carruthers emphasizes, "how fundamental a principle
homophony—punning of all sorts—is to these mnemonics; one encounters
what I have called 'visualized homophony' throughout the history of written
mnemonic advice, both as a principle for forming images and for association
of 'ideas'" (Carruthers, 1990: 105). Typical of the process is a sermon on
Christ's Passion.

> "The preacher elects to divide by fives, a number with evident associations to his
> subject because there were five wounds in the crucifixion. A mnemonic rhyme
> composed of summary catchphrases organizes the main division in five. Then,
> in the subdivision, one remembers the five wounds, imposing upon the struc-
> ture of those five another five, the five vowels, or *voces*, perhaps used because of
> the word's punning association with *voce magna*, the third division of the text
> which deals with the theme *humanitatis veritas'*" (105).

The electrate analogy is extended to pattern in the operation of a paradoxical
word as a switch (such as "table"). One learns about a table from tables (haiku
reason). This compatibility across physics, logic, and language is not surprising
in itself since Bertrand Russell, inspired apparently by Lewis Carroll's Alice
books, started the work that led to the Turing Machine by sorting out the operations of paradox. Rather than trying to reduce paradox to logic as Russell did,
however, Deleuze pushes paradox to its extreme, treating it as an irreducible
logic (or rather dialogic) in its own right.

Deleuze's logic of sense, then, is the postmodern version of the X of dialogical cross-speaking. In electronic dialogue two semantic domains are juxtaposed,
two orders of information are set in motion as two series, which is the equivalent
in pattern of the step-by-step linear sequence of proof in analysis. "The composer's task is to find the entity that produces the X effect: Word = X in a series, but
at the same time, thing = X in another series; perhaps it is necessary to add to the
Aion yet a third aspect, action = X, insofar as the series resonate and communicate and form a 'tangled tale'" (Deleuze, 1990: 67). Such "tangles" hold together
a *felt* (mystory is felt, not text). The "my" in the verbs *myeo* and *myo* (which imply
secrecy) relates these tables to the genre of mystory. "The self-evident first object

of this verb is the subject itself: he closes himself after the manner of a flower. But a second object is also possible, which must be very close to the subject, his very own possession. Such an object is the secret, which is related to the German terms *Geheimnis, heimlich,* and *Heim* (home)" (Kerenyi 1967, 46).

Alice in Cyberspace

Movie stars aren't the only icons: any cultural figure may become an electrate syntagm. Exemplifying the rhetorical possibilities of the icon, *Alice* separated from her specific incarnation in the books by Lewis Carroll to become a feature of contemporary critical theory, used to guide readers through an abstract discourse the way Virgil led Dante through Hell. Luce Irigaray opened *This Sex Which is Not One* with a chapter entitled "The Looking Glass, from the Other Side," moving between an epigraph from *Through the Looking Glass* (Alice trying to remember her identity), through a description of another Alice (in Michael Soutter's film, *The Surveyors*) to her own speculations. Then there is Gilles Deleuze's *The Logic of Sense.* "The privileged place assigned to Lewis Carroll is due to his having provided the first great account, the first great 'mise-en-scene', of the paradoxes of sense" (Deleuze, 1990). The Alice books, juxtaposed with a history of Stoic philosophy, serve Deleuze as a ready-made inventory for a general account of meaning in terms of the relationship between sense and nonsense.

For a variety of essayists, Alice provides a frame, or rather, an interface, a membrane or surface place bringing together a reader with a body of information, as the following introductory sentences from two recent articles attest: "*Alice's Adventures in Wonderland* offers special access to that moment in the history of sexuality when, as Foucault tells it, the normal couple retired from public view, and Western culture began its century-long preoccupation with the sexual behavior of women, children, the mentally disturbed, masturbators, homosexuals, paupers, natives, regional types, and ethnics" (Armstrong, 1990). "When Alice became bored with the drudgery of everyday studies, she wandered a bit from her colorless, pictureless world, taking time off for a little adventure . . . . Habermas had a similar experience" (Trey, 1989: 67). Conduction takes up this device, in turn, deriving from it a basic principle of composition— to appropriate "Alice" (but it could be another figure become mythical, or another work of any sort, for that matter: Sherlock Holmes, Marilyn Monroe, Elvis, The Wizard of Oz, Gary Cooper) as a ready-made organizing device, as if Alice were a kind of index, or a mnemonic system (here is the clue). Alice is not necessarily either symbol or allegory, but "inventio" and "memoria." It is not that she "explains" anything, but that she produces a shape, a coherence.

Having selected Alice as an index of invention, the designer has to figure out how the index works. A conventional skill is brought to bear to find the instructions (analysis) that produces a genre or formula called "Meetings in Wonderland."

Meetings in Wonderland

Ingredients:

1. Alice;
2. an indigene (animal or person). The natives of Wonderland are appropriated from children's popular culture; these familiar figures constitute a "hypotext" (Genette, 1982);
3. a logical and/or rhetorical principle, couched in terms of a fallacy and/or riddle.

Performance:

1. the hyposcene dramatizes a fallacy (rhetorical or logical);
2. in the conversation or action the native takes the logical principle literally or commits the fallacy and sticks to it;
3. the hyposcene is taken up into the hyperscene of *Alice*, in which the riddles posed by the natives to Alice are transformed into jokes—the details of the dramatization are performed as slapstick humor.

This transformation demonstrates a distinction crucial for invention. Andre Jolles classified these two "simple forms"—the riddle and the joke—as being in the same modality (one of his own invention—*silence*) but in different registers (Realist and Idealist, respectively). The riddle is the simple form organizing the code of truth, the hermeneutic code (in Barthes's system of narrative codes), associated with the Realist register, while the joke is the simple form organizing the symbolic code (governing the mythical system of contracts in a culture). The joke, in the Idealist register, is liberated from the demands of truth. This joke in turn models a certain logic: dream work, meaning fallacious reasoning that evokes truth.

The Categorical Joke   The point in our context is to understand the joke as part of conductive reason that does for the image what concept formation did for alphabetic writing. The two kinds of categories are complementary, as manifested in the interdependence of discovery and proof. Silvano Arieti is one theorist who, following Freud, described in detail the correspondence among the kinds of reasoning observed in jokes, dreams, and the like; schizophrenic patients; creativity. The interest of this match is that the "paleologic" or "primary" cognition involved corresponds also to the features of digital imaging. Part of the optimism of the EmerAgency project about the capability of the internet and electracy to support a new kind of consultancy, offering a new approach to community problem solving and public policy formation, is this homology across entertainment forms, creative logics, and digital technology. Arieti distinguishes and contrasts paleologic (joke work) from Aristotelian concepts and definition, which is the appropriate context for using jokework as a relay for inventing electrate conduction. He uses schizophrenics as the prototype for paleologic, leading up to a description of the creative process. It is this similarity of creative and "psychotic" logic, no doubt, that has fueled the myth associating genius and madness. We should keep in mind, too, that Socrates argued on behalf of the mad lover as the best relay to convey the nature of the lover of wisdom (philosopher).

Silvano Arieti, "Creativity"

"It can be seen that patients who adopt paleologic thinking succeed in identifying with objects that otherwise can hardly be used in this way. The patient succeeds in finding at least one element in common between two or more things or persons, and that is enough to warrant the identification. Obviously this type of thinking is absurd from the point of view of a normal person. . . . His capacity [to identify] probably derives not only from the fact that he is particularly receptive to similarities, but also to the fact that he is more capable than the average person of dividing or fragmenting wholes so that the single parts can stand out by themselves. As we shall see later, the same mechanisms occur in the creative process.

"The first psychiatrist who studied this anomaly of schizophrenic thinking and attempted a logical formulation was Eilhard Von Domarus (1944). He enunciated a principle which, in slightly different form, reads, 'Whereas in normal (secondary process) thinking identity is based only upon the basis of identical subjects, in paleologic (primary process) thinking identity is accepted upon the basis of identical predicates.' The predicate that leads to the identification is called the identifying link. Obviously this type of thinking does not follow Aristotelian logic, in which only like subjects are identified. The subjects are fixed; therefore, only a limited number of deductions are possible. For instance, an apple is identified with another apple (both recognized as belonging to the class 'apple'). But in paleologic thinking the apple might be identified with the breast of the person's mother, because the breast and the apple have a similar shape. The breast and the apple become equivalent. In other words, in palelogic thinking, X also becomes non-X—that is, Y—provided X and Y have a predicate (or element) in common. It is the predicate that leads to identification and equivalence.

"Here is the important point. Since the predicates of a subject are numerous, it is not possible to predict what type of identification will take place. Who could have predicted that a patient would have focused on her red hair and identified with her finger? . . . The important thing for our discussion of creativity is that this type of thinking diverges from ordinary paths and opens up a larger number of possibilities. One can find hundreds of predicates in a single subject. Thus the possibilities for originality are enormous" (Arieti, 1976: 69–70).

Comment

- To find the wide image requires the application of paleologic (joke work) to your mystory.

- The connection between impersonation and creativity involves practice with the logic that Arthur Koestler called "bisociation" (related to Deleuze's X-Y crossing of semantic fields). Koestler argued that a good analogy for "having an idea" is "getting a joke." "One of the popular devices of sustained humour is impersonation. Children imitating adults, the comedian impersonating a public figure, men disguised as women and women as men—in all these cases the impersonator is perceived as himself and somebody else at the same time. While this situation lasts the two matrices are bisociated in the spectator's mind" (Koestler, 56).

- The logic of sense (conduction) opens up the linear dialectic of literacy to an entanglement of multiple threads (we are learning more about how a felt works).

- The fact that joke work exploits fallacious (bad) reasoning may pose a kind of logical "sound barrier" to creative thinking, given the reliance of the creative process on joke work. Another way to put this point is that to think creatively requires a temporary suspension of disbelief (suspending the inner critic).

No Guarantees

The virtual mood (modality) supports creativity, then, but the danger of categories formed of items that have but one shared property is that there is no guarantee about the nature of the resulting assemblages. To learn how to adapt this version of informal logic to the new consultancy consider the scene from the film *Monty Python and the Holy Grail* that demonstrates the structure of the joke as a form of fallacious reasoning. The knight helps the villagers determine whether a local woman is a witch by testing whether or not she floats. The script emphasizes the fallacious inference path torturously drawn through the problem. We all laugh. This scene, it turns out, alludes to the life of one Matthew Hopkins, the most famous witch-finder of his day, who traveled the counties of Essex, Sussex, Huntington, and Norfolk, examining females suspected of witchcraft (fetishism). Hopkins's ultimate test was that of "swimming." The hands and feet of the accused were tied together crosswise, after which she was wrapped in a sheet and tossed into a pond. If she sank she was deemed innocent (albeit drowned). If she floated she was deemed guilty and executed. In one year Hopkins oversaw more than sixty deaths by this means. It is a critical joke, pointing out the movement of a "method" from calculation to pattern. The conclusion is not that one is scientific and the other is ideological, but that the scientific and the ideological are irreducibly intermixed, right up through contemporary science and its projection onto policy through conventional consulting.

In the spectacle with its merger of image and actuality, iconic pidgin is extended to the performance of "media events." The most extreme example to date is the September 11, 2001, destruction of the World Trade Center in New York by Islamic fundamentalists who wanted to perform a "critique" of capitalism. The ideal target for the terrorist is one that maximizes both physical and symbolic damage. In our terms, Osama bin Laden represented an oral worldview manipulating the products of science as a rhetoric. The gambit of the Emer-Agency is to virtualize the debate, by democratizing the lesson of Dante: he hated the rulers of his hometown, so he *wrote* them into Hell. Today we see his contemporaries through his eyes. It is not a matter of eliminating hatred from the world (a utopian goal). A challenge for the EmerAgency rather is to make this *virtual* option a viable one for political and ethical action, to help write "murder" out of the equation.

OFFICE

1. Cyberpidgin extends the inferential procedure of filling gaps to the gaps that separate whole cultures, languages, and civilizations. This transfer has always taken place and is called syncretism. The EmerAgency practice is intended to make syncretism even more self-conscious and to augment it deliberately by learning how to reason and write in a syncretic way. An important insight into this creolized inference is a shift in understanding how "communication" works: not as a space to be crossed, but as a field to be occupied or inhabited (not an obstacle but an environment).

2. As usual, the lectures and remakes are intended as demonstrations of methods you should apply to your mystory. You should select and gather details in each of the pop-cycle discourses using the kinds of "resemblances" described and modeled here: look for switch words and shapes.

3. The historical argument is that electracy emerges out of the sheer adaptation of the major literate modes (novel, essay) into image forms and media (movies, documentaries; film, video). The experience of entertainment until recently was a monologue, a one-way reception from the stars to the audience. The dream of dialogue that began with radio and continued in video is beginning to be realized in the internet. With the mystory in particular, you begin to talk back explicitly to the star icons you find in your memory. In the mystory you ask the figures that turn up in each discourse: who are you; what do you want from me? These figures may be avatars of your superego, the force of the social order internalized as your own conscience, morality, ethic.

4. While there are only exercises in this section, the lecture elaborates on the logic of conduction as a gap or interval formation and the associative sequences used to follow the "flash" of insight from X semantic field to Y semantic field. Through the accumulation of remakes and demonstrations you should get a feel for conduction which is the logic of imaging. The wide image formally is generated by creating a field of these X = Y juxtapositions and trajectories or sequences: something in the Family discourse is X, something in the Entertainment discourse is Y, and together they form a figure that you recognize by its sting at the level of atmosphere or feeling.

5. The method of the book is to structure the release of information about electracy in the form of an unfolding narrative. When you get lost you should recall this narrative progress, whose stage or phase is indicated as an epigraph at the beginning of each chapter. For example, at this point you are positioned in the early stages of the second (and longest) act of a three-act structure. This narrative structure is an interbody metaphor, an allegory, guiding our learning of electracy. Thus the crossing of the threshold to enter the special world of adventure in the narrative form evokes in reality the experience of going online or putting your image into cyberspace (so to speak). The colonial and postcolonial references are both literal and figurative. When you go online, even if your body is in Kansas, your spirit is not in Kansas anymore (to allude to *The Wizard of Oz*). The creolization process plays an important role in subsequent chapters.

6. In practical terms, about all we will accomplish at this apprentice stage of becoming an egent will be to put your wide image into the docuverse of the internet. In terms of the politics of electracy, however, being represented in this way is similar to registering to vote in a literate democracy. The historical or grammatological analogy suggests that once a critical mass of materials exists in the technology of the new apparatus, a mutation is triggered whose nature and consequences are difficult to foresee and impossible to control. Our project is an entry point for further work.

Part IV

COMMUNITY DISCOURSE

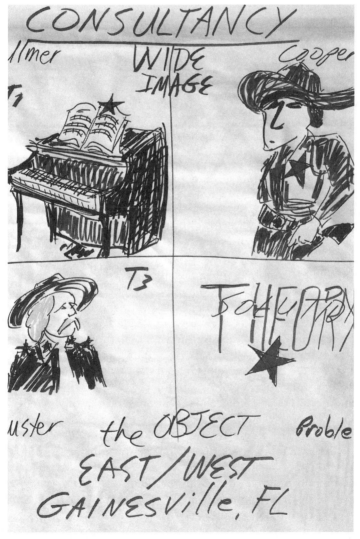

EMBLEM–A flipbook sketch of Ulmer's mystory made during a lecture.
"The mystory entangles the four documentations of the popcycle discourses: Family, Entertainment, Community History, Career."

Chapter 7

History (School)

Tests, allies, enemies: many times the subject is able to glean information pertinent to this other world and to the adventure ahead in out-of-the-way gathering places.

LECTURE
The Donor

The form and experience of narrative are a relay for understanding the combined tasks of consulting and designing the wide image. The protagonists or heroes of tales or stories cannot solve by themselves the problem or conflict that caused them to leave home and enter the special world of adventure. Invariably they find their way to some gathering place—conventionally a bar, saloon, or "watering hole" in the typical Hollywood feature, according to Vogler. Here they meet a character whose function is to test the worthiness of the hero to undertake the quest—their desire and their competence. If the hero passes the tests (answers the riddles, completes the impossible tasks), there is an implicit promise that the "donor" (as this "actant"—character relation—is called) will give the hero the gift of the "magic tool" whose use allows the hero to overcome the villain or obstacle causing the conflict and solve the problem motivating the adventure. It is important to distinguish the donor from the mentor or "helper" roles, since in the larger context of literature, folklore, and mythology, the donor figures are complex and include hostile or reluctant donors as well as benevolent ones. The archetypal donor of mythology is the Sphinx, whose changing function from orality to literacy is represented in the transitional form of the tragedy of *Oedipus Rex*, by Sophocles. The Slavic Witch Baba-Jaga, whose preferred meal was little children is an important donor figure in the Russian wondertales that provided the data for the structuralist theory of narrative introduced by Vladimir Propp. The donor-hero relationship is a parable for the EmerAgency consultation.

This moment or segment of narrative structure is of central importance to the invention of electracy, and to the apprenticeship of the egent. To undertake the work of the virtual consultancy requires egents to work with donors from the full range of possibilities—monster to angel. Perhaps more difficult to understand is that while one makes the wide image from the position of hero, one consults in the position of donor. To get a sense of how the hero-donor relationship works in contemporary entertainment narrative, we will consider one example—*The Silence of the Lambs*—the novel by Thomas Harris, adapted in a screenplay by Ted Tally for the film directed by Jonathan Demme (1991). The following reading describes *Silence* in terms of the mythical journey that Vogler showed operating in most entertainment narratives, thus providing a case study (and mise en abyme) of the path that we are following in the quest for the wide image. The focus of our immediate interest is on Hannibal Lecter's relationship as donor (which Voytilla calls "shadow-mentor") for the apprentice FBI agent Clarice Starling.

Stuart Voytilla on Myth and the Movies

THE SILENCE OF THE LAMBS
The Journey

"The FBI Academy in Quantico is the ORDINARY WORLD of Cadet Clarice Starling. Determined and smart, Clarice aspires to work for Jack Crawford in the FBI's Behavior Science Division after her graduation, her OUTER PROBLEM. She worshipped her father, a town marshal, and felt abandoned when he was murdered when she was ten. Clarice's INNER PROBLEM is to come to terms with her father's death by accomplishing a worthy deed.

"Crawford offers Clarice an 'errand,' to convince convicted serial killer Hannibal Lecter to fill out a questionnaire. She willingly accepts his CALL.

"Clarice meets Dr. Chilton, a THRESHOLD GUARDIAN, who quickly drills the Rules for communicating with 'the Monster' Lecter. Although Clarice impresses this SHADOW MENTOR, she fails her errand; Lecter refuses to fill out Crawford's questionnaire, rejecting Clarice from the SPECIAL WORLD. As Clarice leaves, an inmate flings semen in her face. An incensed Lecter apologizes and offers Clarice advancement with a TEST: to see one of his old patients, Miss Mofet.

"Before Lecter will reveal more, he offers a psychological profile of Buffalo Bill, in return for a room with a view away from Dr. Chilton, Lecter's OUTER PROBLEM.

"Back at the Academy, Clarice watches the news report announcing that Catherine Martin has been kidnapped by Buffalo Bill. The stakes are raised, forcing Crawford (using Clarice as his agent, making a swift bold APPROACH) to make a deal with Lecter: a room with a view in exchange for a profile on Buffalo Bill. Lecter accepts on the condition that Clarice answer his questions, quid pro quo. She must tell him things about herself, allowing Lecter to get into her mind. She accepts, confessing her worst childhood memory: the death of her father.

"Dr. Chilton reveals the FBI's bogus deal to Lecter, and kills Clarice's relationship with Lecter, an ORDEAL. In a move to RESURRECT their relationship, Clarice gives Lecter back his drawings as an apology, but she also stands up to her MENTOR and demands the truth. Lecter directs her to the case files. He presents one simple revelation about Buffalo Bill's nature: we begin by 'coveting what we see every day.' Before he will tell more, Lecter gets her to confess her childhood ORDEAL, when she failed to save the spring lambs from slaughter. She still wakes up in the dark with the screaming lambs and admits that if she could save Catherine, the screaming would stop, her INNER PROBLEM (Voytilla, 1999: 96–98).

Exercise: The Quest Schema

Look again at the entertainment narrative you represented in your mystory. See if you can locate in its plot the stages of the initiation quest, as demonstrated in Voytilla's description of Silence.

- Keep in mind our use of narrative form to map the steps of becoming an egent (and acquiring the wide image).

Comment

Jame Gumb

- The serial killer Jame Gumb believes that he is a transsexual, but according to Lecter's diagnosis this belief covers a psychosis that manifests itself in Gumb's motive for killing and skinning his victims: he is sewing the skins into a "body suit" that he hopes will allow him to pass as a female. This horrific plot element typifies the logic of entertainment, which tends to represent life problems in terms of their most extreme or worst-case potential. Transgressions of sexual and gender norms are dramatized here as monstrous, which in our context may be read as a defense against the emerging mutation in identity experience associated with electracy (becoming image). "Bill has been turned down by at least one reputable hospital that does sex-change operations, yet he still believes that he is a transsexual to the point where he is driven to kill and flay women. Perhaps we are to believe he is simply insane and there is no explanation for his behavior, apart from his assumed abuse as a child. Ultimately, however, the filmmakers seem to dodge the issues of homosexuality and transsexualism, opting to leave the question of fundamental motivation vague in order to sidestep the volatile issue of gender altogether" (Thompson, 1999: 121).

Detective Mystery

- The grammatologist Walter Ong observed that narrative is transformed in literacy from the epic form of oral cultures to the detective story. Semioticians such as Roland Barthes have shown that every literate narrative is structured as a mystery, regardless of the themes or contents of the particular story. The action of literate plots, that is, is organized by a "Hermeneutic Code." Information is released over the course of the tale in terms of "enigmas" that must be resolved; scenes and props provide details configured as clues, triggering the use of inference by characters within the diegesis, and by readers. The prototype is Sherlock Holmes, whose solutions to crimes rehearses and celebrates the three modes of inferential reason: abduction (starting with a clue at the scene of the crime, Holmes uses his knowledge of his culture and of human behavior to discover the "rule" that makes the clue intelligible); deduction (based on this rule—stating what in principle is most probable—Holmes formulates a case that explains the event, the crime); induction (Holmes tests the case against reality, to see if his hypothesis is correct). That so many of our narratives are framed as crime stories, including journalism as well as fictional stories, is an expression of the literate frame of mind, whose analytic stance addresses experience in terms of problem solving.

Hannibal the Cannibal

- In this mythological context, the fact that Hannibal Lecter is a cannibal is entirely conventional: cannibalism is as much an archetypal trait of the donor as beauty is a trait of the "object" of the quest (the King's daughter). Lecter in his jail cell evokes Baba Yaga in her hut: "The hut of this cunning old hag lies in the darkest reaches of the forest. Propped up on hens' feet, it is enclosed by a fence of human bones crowned with skulls. The gateposts are human legs, the bolts are arms, and the lock is made of teeth. Every fairy-tale hero knows that this witch delights in eating young children and drinking their blood. The fiends and villains of Russian folklore are no less bloodthirsty than French ogres, British giants, and German witches. When Baba Yaga cackles, 'Foo! Foo! I smell Russian flesh!' she strikes terror into the heart of the tale's hero" (Tatar, 1987: 188). The German name for this character type is *Menschenfresserin* (devourer of humans).

The mythological frame of the hero's quest reveals that a basic function of narrative is to rehearse the stages of an initiation ritual. Narratives allegorize the experience of achieving identity, of individuation, or of subject formation that is specific to each apparatus. We are borrowing this structure in turn as a relay for becoming an egent. The test is the requirement to compose the wide image. The wide image is the magic tool that allows the egents to confront the problem, the obstacle, the trouble of their world.

Fredric Jameson on the Donor

THE PRISON-HOUSE OF LANGUAGE

"The basic tale begins with either injury to a victim, or the lack of some important object. Thus, at the very beginning, the end result is given: it will consist in the retribution for the injury or the acquisition of the thing lacked. The hero, if he is not himself personally involved, is sent for, at which point two key events take place.

"He meets the donor (a toad, a hag, a bearded old man, etc.) who after testing him for the appropriate reaction (for some courtesy, for instance) supplies him with a magical agent (ring, horse, cloak, lion) which enables him to pass victoriously through his ordeal. . . .

"The donor is therefore the element which explains the change described in the story, that which supplies a sufficiently asymmetrical force to make it interesting to tell, and which is therefore somehow responsible for the 'storiness' of the story. Thus, the satisfaction and the completeness of the tale comes not from the fact that the hero manages to rescue the princess in the end, but rather from the means or agent given him to do so (a bird who tells him the right word to say to the witch, a magic cloak that lifts him to the tower). This is to say something a little more than that what interests us in a story is the how rather than the what: what Propp's discovery implies is that every How (the magical agent) always conceals a Who (the donor), that somewhere hidden in the very structure of the story itself stands the human figure of a mediator, even in those more sophisticated forms in which he is concealed beneath more rational motivation.

"We may restate the necessity for the existence of a donor in yet another way by pointing out the fact that in the beginning the hero is never strong enough to conquer by himself. He suffers from some initial lack of being: either he is simply not strong enough or not courageous enough or else he is too naive and simple-minded to know what to do with his strength. The donor is the complement, the reverse, of this basic ontological weakness. . . . The basic interpersonal and dramatic relationship of the narrative tale is therefore neither the head-on direct one of love nor that of hatred and conflict, but rather this lateral relationship of the hero to the ex-centric figure of the donor" (Jameson, 65–68).

THE POLITICAL UNCONSCIOUS

"We can better appreciate the usefulness of actantial reduction, if we reflect, for instance, on the 'character' of Heathcliff in *Wuthering Heights*, a figure whose ambiguous nature (romantic hero or tyrannical villain?) has remained an enigma for intuitive or impressionizing, essentially 'representation,' criticism, which can only seek to resolve the ambiguity in some way (for example, Heathcliff as 'Byronic' hero). In terms of actantial reduction, however, the text would necessarily be read or rewritten, not as the story of 'individuals,' nor even as the chronicle of generations and their destinies, but rather as an impersonal process, a semic transformation centering on the house, which moves from Lockwood's initial impressions of the Heights, and the archaic story of origins behind it, to that final ecstatic glimpse through the window, where as in the final scene of Cocteau's *Orphee,* 'le decor montre au ciel' and a new and idyllic family takes shape in the love of Hareton and the second Cathy. But if this is the central narrative line of the work, or what Greimas would call its principal isotopie, then Heathcliff can no longer be considered the hero or the protagonist in any sense of the word. He is rather from the very beginning—the abrupt introduction into the family of the orphan child, 'as dark almost as if it came from the devil'—something like a mediator or a catalyst, designed to restore the fortunes and to rejuvenate the anemic temperament of the two families. What is this to say but that 'Heathcliff' occupies in some complicated way the place of the donor in this narrative system: a donor who must wear the functional appearance of the protagonist in order to perform his quite different actantial function. . . .

"Hence the complex semic confusion between good and evil, love and money, the role of the 'jeune premier' and that of the patriarchal villain, which mark this 'character' who is in reality a mechanism for mediating these semes (Jameson, 1981: 126–127).

Comment

- The confusion caused by the ambiguity of Heathcliff's position in *Wuthering Heights* is found also in commentaries on Hannibal Lecter's function in *Silence of the Lambs.* Marina Warner associates him with the villains, "the mass murderer, the kidnapper, the serial killer: a collector, as in John Fowles's novel, an obsessive, like Hannibal Lecter in *The Silence of the Lambs*" (Warner, 269). Kristin Thompson notes the complexity of Lecter's role and concludes, "what we have in *Silence* is a rare case of a film with parallel *antagonists*" (Thompson, 1999: 104). Nonetheless, she goes on to inventory the "Socratic" style of Lecter's "interrogation" scenes with Starling, in which he turns the tables on the interrogative mood of the conventional third degree (124). In our context, this style marks their relationship as "literate."

- Lecter's "quid pro quo" contract that requires Starling to reveal her most personal secrets—death of her father; her failure as a child on the farm to save the lambs from slaughter—in exchange for clues to help capture Buffalo Bill (Gumb), is a quality of the Turing dilemma of interrogation in the Imitation Game and in his personal problem. The introduction of personal material in the mystory is conducted rather in the mood of haiku, and not that of the third degree: not the third degree, but the third meaning, appropriate to the epistemology of imaging. Testimony, not confession.

- The basic event of all narrative is a transformation from one situation to another (from X to Y). The event of the EmerAgency story is the transformation of the apparatus from literate to electrate.

- *Silence* is a relay allegory for how a wide image is applied to a disciplinary problem (the relationship between the problems in the outer and the inner worlds of the protagonist).

Value

The first insight to be drawn from Jameson's analysis of the donor "actant" (relational position in the narrative structure) is to look outside any particular narrative, and, in our context, outside the institution of Entertainment, to another dimension of the popcycle—History—in order to understand the forces shaping the diegesis or dramatic world of the story. Greimas, the theorist Jameson refers to, articulated the deep structure of narrative in terms of several axes or vectors that control the dynamics or economy of the story. The three axes include the relations of subject and object (the goal or desire of the hero); helpers and opponents (the counterforce or conflict, the obstacles to the goal and the resources that support the quest); sender and receiver.

This latter axis of sender and receiver is called the axis of "communication," suggesting the role of narrative in the mutation from literacy to electracy. This dimension is the "lateral" relationship Jameson discusses between the donor and the hero. This relationship is central to the operation of the EmerAgency and the creation of a consultancy capable of dealing with the problem of the spectacle in an electrate way. As Greimas explained, the sender function is the source of value or values in the narrative world. The dramatization within the diegesis of tests given and passed, followed by the awarding of the magic tool, is "isotopic" with the framing condition that determines the "aspectuality," focalization, or point of view that the "discourse" level of the narrative takes to the dramatic action of events. Every narrative is told from a point of view, and this point of view is ideologically overdetermined. The relation of donor-hero locates the channel and flow of value through the popcycle (the society). The task of the egents in composing the wide image is to map their individual relationship to this force, this source of value.

Hannibal Lecter's way of combining the functions of sender and donor may be seen in his motives for helping Agent Starling. The traditional qualifying test for the hero in any case usually involves "etiquette"—whether the applicants know how to behave properly, with humility, honesty, and courtesy. The larger lesson for us is to notice that our use of narrative form as an allegory for the consultancy may be becoming counter-intuitive: the relay for the egent's position is not only that of "hero," but rather the relationship among all the actants.

Readings on the Sender

1. Mieke Bal, Narratology

"The intention of the subject is in itself not sufficient to reach the object. There are always powers who either allow it to reach its aim or prevent it from doing so. This relation might be seen as a form of communication, and we can distinguish a class of actors—consisting of those who support the subject in the realization of its intention, supply the object, or allow it to be supplied or given—whom we shall call the power. The person to whom the object is 'given' is the receiver. . . . 'Sender' suggests an active intervention or an active participation, and this does not always apply; that is why 'power' is perhaps a better term.

"The power is in many cases not a person but an abstraction: e.g. society, fate, time, human self-centeredness, cleverness. The receiver may also be embodied in a person. Thus a typology of fabulas might be related to the concretization of this actant: in fairy tales the 'sender' is mostly a person, often a king who under certain conditions gives his daughter in marriage to the aspiring subject. In psychological novels, a character trait of the subject itself is often the power which either facilitates or blocks the achievement of the aim. In many so-called 'realistic' nineteenth-century novels the class structure of bourgeois society is decisive—one is determined for life by one's social background. It is also possible that several powers are in play at the same time. A combination of a character trait (ambition) and a social power (the division into rich and poor) may conflict as positive and negative power" (Bal, 1997: 198–199).

2. Bob Foss, Filmmaking

"It is impossible to treat a subject without making value-choices; values lie behind every choice of camera angle, every cut, every sequence of shots. . . .

"We may formulate the stance adopted by the filmmaker toward the subject of the film in terms of a central idea. Like the main subject, the central idea must be formulated in words; it can be said to be the shortest possible formulation of what the filmmaker is trying to say. The central idea expresses the essential insight that the filmmaker wishes to impart to the spectator. It is not and can never be an incontrovertible scientific truth; it is always based on overt or covert values.

"The central idea lends the key to the structure of the program. It determines what we are going to emphasize and what is to be ignored; it determines the order of the various parts, how we use the various narrative elements, how we begin, develop, and end the program. . . .

"In dramatic productions the central idea is often called the premise. The drama promotes the central idea or premise through action that substantially (on the Plane of Events) 'proves' the premise. The premise always has two constituent parts: it formulates (a) preconditions and (b) consequences. It says, condition X leads to consequence Y. In other words, the premise is dynamic. It sets action in motion. The premise is inherent in the development of the action.

"Example: The subject of Ibsen's *A Doll's House* can be said to be 'moral inequality in marriage.' There can be various opinions on this theme. For example, one might think that men are morally superior to women and that a wife should therefore submit to her husband's moral judgment. Many people believed so when the play was written (some still might even today). Ibsen, however, was not of this opinion. His position vis a vis the subject was expressed in the play and can be formulated thus: 'Moral inequality in marriage leads to the destruction of marriage.' . . .

"What the writer/filmmaker chooses to emphasize is of the utmost importance to our understanding the 'message' or the 'moral' of the film. Consequently, starting from the subject/object axis, [Gabold] sets out a third (horizontal) axis, where he tries to decide what it is that determines whether or not the dramatic aim is achieved. He calls this a 'giver/recipient' axis or an axis of communication. This axis shows who or what makes it possible for the recipient to achieve the objective (the dramatic aim)" (Foss, 1992: 144–145, 151).

3. Mark Turner on Parable and Values

"Analogy places pressure upon conventional category structures. A successful analogy can, through entrenchment, earn a place among our category structures. The assault of an analogy on conventional categories is often expressed in the early stages by a blend-construction that draws its noun from the source and its modifier from the target. 'Same-sex marriage,' for example, asks us to project the scenario of marriage onto an alternative domestic scenario. People of violently opposed ideological belief will freely agree that the generic space of this projection carries information applicable to both scenarios. It might include people living in a household, dividing labor, protecting each other in various ways, and planning together.

"What is at issue is not the existence of this information but rather its status. Those whose conception of conventional marriage has a requisite component 'heterosexual union' and has as its prototype 'for the sake of children' will regard this abstract generic information as merely incidental or derivative in the story of traditional marriage. In their view, 'same-sex marriage' will remain an analogical projection whose blended space is as fantastic and conflicted as any we have seen in Dante or Shakespeare, but which nonetheless draws legitimate abstract connections—however inessential—between one kind of story and an entirely different kind of story.

"But others may regard this abstract information in the generic space as the central information in the story of traditional marriage. They may regard 'heterosexual union for the sake of children' as merely incidental information in the traditional story. For these people, 'same-sex marriage' is not an aggressive analogical construction, it simply refers to a subcategory of marriage in the way that 'light wave' refers to a kind of wave. . . .

"In a situation of ideological tension over category connections, there is always the opportunity to reject the projection and invert the relative status of the two input spaces. . . . What is at issue here is of course not any particular ideological view but rather the fact that all ideological views use parable to judge and reason. Parable is an instrument of thought and belief and consequently of argument.

"The cultural tussle over the analogical pressure of 'same-sex marriage' upon conventional category structures provides daily journalistic copy and stirs passions. It is an example of the role played by blended spaces in our understanding of cultural and social reality, and of our place in that reality" (Turner, 1996: 93–95).

4. Greimas on the Sender's Gift

"We have already seen the extent to which mythical thought—and probably in a very general way all of our imaginary activity—was reluctant to recognize the *ex nihilo* status of ambient values and preferred to substitute an axiological elsewhere for that status, thus postulating the possibility for some communication between these two universes. Given that senders, in their role as possessors of transcendent values, can be considered as subjects that are at the same time both real and transcendent, it is possible to conceive of their communication with receivers functioning in their own right in the immanent universe, that is, in their role as immanent and virtual subjects. This is at least valid for their original, first state. It is as subjects that they can be included in communication, and it is as subjects that their status can be described in terms of canonical utterances.

"The difficulty in describing this transubstantiation of transcendent values into immanent values, using the structure of communication, is first caused by the fact that the very definition of communication (understood as a transformation bringing about, in a solidary way, the disjunction of the object from one of the subjects and its conjunction with the second subject) is not always applicable to the relations between sender and receiver. The existence of a relation of unilateral presupposition between the presupposed sender-term and the presupposing receiver-term makes communication between them asymmetrical. . . . Let us take the case of the sender that, as a transforming subject, ensures that a gift is given to the receiver: If the transformation results in the attribution of a value to the receiver, that attribution will not thereby be in a relation of solidarity, as we might have expected, with a renunciation on the part of the sender. The object of value, while still attributed to the receiver, remains in conjunction with the sender.

"There are many examples of this unexpected phenomenon. For instance, in verbal communication, once the knowing of the sender is transferred to the receiver, it remains a shared knowing. The sender is not deprived of it. Even when the queen of England has one by one delegated all of her powers to duly constituted bodies, she remains the supreme sovereign. You might say this is a nice fiction, but without it you cannot found the concept of sovereignty" (Greimas, 1987: 102–103).

Comment

- Everything said about narrative actants applies to our own life situations and to the consultancy dealing with the narratives forming the imagined community of the nation. The mystory maps the powers sending the values we received (interpellation); the EmerAgency intervenes in this interpellation process.

- Turner's example is especially important for seeing how an understanding of imaging in electracy is relevant to public policy debates. The point of intervention for the egent is the metaphor or figure operating in the language/scene of the debate.

- "Value" is the name for what is described in the latter part of the *wabi-sabi* image template: feeling, metaphysics, morality. Arguments, stories, policy decisions, reflect these elements—a feeling or mood informed by an idea of how the world is or ought to be, that justifies certain actions. To take an extreme example, a religious fanatic has a feeling of righteousness, based on a belief that the world is an unfolding of God's will, that justifies actions that assist the realization of this will in society. The point to stress is that values are not whims or tastes, but worldviews grounded in interpellation (identity constructed in institutions).

STUDIO
Receiver

Exercise: On the Premises

Do an analysis of your Entertainment narrative in terms of sender and receiver. Try to describe the value/power working in the diegesis, using the form of premise and central idea. How does the dramatization prove the premise? Relate the premise to the ideological categories of identity you noted in your Family story.

- We are learning electracy by analogy with literacy. We are familiar with the fact that every story is told from a point of view, even if it is harder sometimes to locate point of view in a movie than in a novel. Critics use the terms "story" and "discourse" to sort out this quality: Story is what happens; discourse is the teller's attitude to what happens. Point of view in narrative is often indirect, whereas in a documentary or essay, it may be directly or explicitly stated. An argument is not just information about a theme, but a claim about that information the writer tries to prove. The equivalent for the image of discourse or claim is state of mind (mood).

Assignment: Community Discourse (History)

A mystory helps the egent map the sources of value coming from the community as Sender. Add to your widesite the documentation of an exemplary story from your community, that is a story about a person or event that your community identifies with and tells about itself in its celebrations, festivals, naming practices (of streets, buildings, parks), memorials.

- The official history of the community is recounted in textbooks used in schools in required courses in the middle and secondary levels to teach the history of the state and nation. The identification with this history is not experienced in the same way that one experiences Family and Entertainment at the level of conscious awareness and memory. The collective history is preserved "outside" the subject, in the archives, rituals, and practices of the public sphere. The goal of this assignment is to notice how the community in which one was raised focalizes the story of its founding and existence. The idea is to find the point of view that expresses the values of the community. The "moral" of the history narrated in this way convey the "power," that is the values that the community promotes.

- What problems and solutions are significant and important to your community? What historical figure or event do you recall studying in middle or secondary school? The criterion for selecting the material to put into the mystory is not that you "liked" the person or event, but that you remember it (punctum). We have been using the history of colonialism as a national problem as a default to fill this slot.

- It is often the case that once we become intellectually aware, by the time we enter college, for example, but sometimes earlier, we consciously reject or at least question the heroes or ideals of our community. The purpose of this part of the mystory, however, is to locate the interpellation, what the community thinks for us, and prior to us, on our behalf. The wide image is a compass, as we have said: once we know the orientation of our fundamental state of mind, we may use it to go in any direction.

- It is also possible to work with "secondary" identifications: to work with persons or events with which we consciously identity, in the same way that we identify with parents or characters in stories.

- It may be the case that one has no "home town." The "primary identifications" relevant for the School (History) part of the popcycle do not depend necessarily on a local community, since the story of the nation is promoted in similar terms in every community. However, it is also possible to define "community" not as nation but in terms of religion, race, or ethnicity, when those collective stories that one grew up with took precedence over the story of the nation and state told in the public schools.

Examples: Relating History and Family

1. Glenn Ligon: "To Disembark"

This reading is excerpted from a pamphlet provided as part of an exhibition held at the Hirshhorn Museum, Smithsonian, November 11, 1993, to February 20, 1994. As is always the case, the examples provide a relay, not a model. The idea is to observe the relationship established between the maker and the historical figure or event (in this instance), and also the formal devices used to express and document this relationship. The mystorian must adapt the materials, to find the equivalent in one's own case. Similarly for the formal devices: how might a museum exhibition format be adapted to the Web?

Phyllis Rosensweig (Curator)

"In this exhibition, which has four discrete elements, Ligon continues to probe issues of self-definition. Wooden boxes, using international symbols that define fragility, emit barely audible sounds (a heartbeat, Billie Holiday singing 'Strange Fruit' and 'Traveling Light,' disco music by Royal House. The boxes vary slightly in size and construction method, but all take their proportions from the one in which a slave, Henry 'Box' Brown, was shipped from Richmond, Virginia, to freedom in Philadelphia in 1849. In the same gallery are lithographs imitating 19th-century advertisements for the return of escaped slaves. All name and describe the artist himself (he asked friends to describe him without giving a reason and used their descriptions to create the prints). In another part of the exhibition, three quotes from an essay by Zora Neale Hurston, which Ligon had also used in a series of 1990 paintings, are stenciled directly on the walls. Accompanying them are etchings with chine colle (a process by which a thin piece of high-quality paper is glued to a less-expensive backing paper) that mimic frontispieces of the 19th-century narrative published by white abolitionists in which former slaves re-counted their lives under slavery and the stories of their escapes. Ligon has re-placed the Bible verses and anti-slavery poems that often appeared on the title pages of the narrative with quotes from contemporary authors such as Hilton Als, bell hooks, and others. Like the runaway posters that describe him, these narratives tell the story of the artist. As Ligon expressed it: 'The show seems to be coalescing around the idea of absence and presence. How is identity construct-ed? What are the narratives of one's own life, and, for Americans, are those nar-ratives by necessity formed against the background of slavery? Who are the other 'masters' from which we flee?'" (Rosenzweig, 1993).

Glenn Ligon (interview)

"These things came together when I read Henry Brown's narrative and I began to organize the exhibition around the idea of the box, the missing slave, and the slave telling the story of his escape. Nineteenth-century traveling shows put on by abolitionists restaged the escape of slaves from the South, but my aim was never to recreate Henry Brown's escape. I was interested, to paraphrase Stuart Hall, in how I positioned myself and was positioned by these narratives of the past, I am positioning myself against a certain historical experience and trying to find the connections between it and who I am'" (Rosenzweig, 1993).

Comment

- Ligon's installation recalls Conwill's cosmogram, or the domestic altars noted previously. To extrapolate from installations to websites, the objects literally presented in the museum or gallery would be represented in pictures, graph-ics, or text in hyperlinked files on the internet.

2. May Stevens: "Ordinary Extraordinary"

Also an exhibition by a visual artists, "Ordinary Extraordinary" juxtaposes images of Alice Stevens (1895–1985), the artist's mother, with those of Rosa Luxemburg (1871–1919), the Polish/German revolutionary.

Melissa Debakis on May Stevens

"In 'Two Women', Stevens creates an interplay between Rosa and Alice through visual interconnections and thematic overlays. Both women are presented with a chronology of their lives: at age twelve, at maturity, and at death and dying. As children, the women share the same wide-eyed innocence, yet in subsequent photographs, it is clear that Alice—holding her first-born (the artist) tenderly, awkwardly, and tentatively—is entrapped in a domestic sphere that would ultimately suffocate her. As the artist recounts,

> 'Sexism and classism, male authority and poverty-and-ignorance were the forces that crippled my mother; the agent in most direct contact with her was, of course, my father. But the equation cannot be written as two equal forces of sex and class focusing their oppressive powers through one man onto my mother. . . . She was taught to be good. She was a good student. She was always good—until she painted the kitchen red in the middle of the night and screamed at passing cars.'

This image of Alice is juxtaposed to Rosa, who in 1907, the date of the photograph, was at her height of power in the Social Democratic Party. Elegantly dressed, a privileged middle-class upbringing clearly apparent, she addressed the world with confidence and vigor. But at the same time, Rosa would have envied Alice her children and their love—an intimate need never fulfilled.

"These four images, iconically frontal, are distinct from the image of Rosa's bloated corpse, pulled from the river several months after her murder, and that of the elderly Alice, institutionalized since the early 1950s, seated before a window. They form a diagonal, moving directly out into the viewer's space. They speak of death—of the injustice of lives cut short. . . . In "Tribute to Rosa Luxemburg," it is the revolutionary to whom Stevens pays homage. Overlaid with excerpts of Rosa's private writings are images associated with her imprisonment and murder. Stevens appropriates three photographs: a 1917 prison letter from Rosa, secretly written in urine on a page of poetry; her cell in Wronke, which as a political prisoner she was allowed to furnish with her own belongings; and members of the Freikorps guard who celebrated after murdering her. The historical references are not arbitrary, but described by the captions that accompany each photograph. Rosa's words speak clearly as Stevens restates her letter: 'See to it that you remain a human being . . .'" (Dabakis, 1988: 20–22).

Comment

- As was the case with the relays used to help with the Entertainment part of the mystory, these relays demonstrate a relationship between History (a Community problem), and Family (personal problems associated with identity, such as race or gender). Keep in mind that your mystory also works in these terms, in that the obtuse sting is a recognition of the relevance of a situation in one of the other popcycle discourses to your Family situation (the structural portrait). For the assignment you do not need to include the personal situation each time, but just document the details of the situation specific to that discourse (in this case, Community History). Any new Family materials discovered to be important during this process may be added to the Family part of the widesite. Of course, ultimately, once all the registers of the popcycle have been documented, you will look for ways to interlink them.

Ficelle

Jameson suggested the strategy of displacement away from the hero to the supporting cast—what Henry James called the "ficelles"—in order to find an alternative to the ideological or interpellative default mood of a text. Slavoj Zizek made the connection between Henry James's ficelle and the concept of the "point de capiton" or quilting point in Lacan. The role that Maria Gostrey plays in *The Ambassadors* (and this title in itself evokes Lacan's use of Holbein's painting by the same title as an example of anamorphosis), is played in anti-Semitic ideology by "the Jew": "The criticism of ideology consists in unmasking traditional allegory as an 'optical' illusion concealing the mechanism of modern allegory: the figure of the Jew as an allegory of Evil conceals the fact that it represents within the space of ideological narration the pure immanence of the textual operation that 'quilts' it" (Zizek, 1991: 18, 19). It is the old story of the scapegoat, whose sacrifice creates the border of inside-outside, safety-danger. The formula for the syncretic project of electracy is to locate the ideological other quilting or suturing ("sutra") together one's cultural point of view, and then switch the dominant focalization (usually so familiar that one does not even experience it as such) for an unfamiliar one associated with the ficelle.

This possibility of detaching and reattaching signifiers from signifieds marks the agency of the letter in the unconscious (also the *gram*, the structuring principle of General Writing: every level of order—logical, psychological, social). For now, the EmerAgency consultation on public policy—a "writing of the disaster"—comes together in all its dimensions (creativity, ontology, psychology) around the interior hole filled by a catachrestic metaphor, or by a lost object of desire. "The gaps of the real become a kind of refuge within the universalization of knowledge for the particularity of the subject. From the gaps of the real emerges a text, like the strands of a web out of a spider's belly. By exploiting the ambiguities inherent in languages, a literary text may trace the contours of those gaps and bring out the places of singularity in which the subject may live" (9). Lacan names this "singularity" by means of an archaic version of "symptom"—*sinthome*—a relay for which is the "style" specific to an artist's work. Agamben calls it the "whatever," and all these terms are relays to the wide image. "Recognition" as an experience signals that a border exists articulating outside/inside in a correspondence between an outer situation and my inner condition. The first work of an egent is to testify and bear witness to this correspondence, thus registering for oneself the slogan of the EmerAgency: "Problems B Us."

Riddles of Sense

The donor tests the hero by posing riddles. The logic of riddles manifests the basic structure of conductive sense through which the hero may receive the magic tool. "There is a riddle form which in a sense is a 'meta-riddle'; the question 'what is the difference between X and Y?' To this the answer is 'I do not know', and the answerer receives a retort which puts him to shame. ('What is the difference between the behind of a horse and a mailbox?—I do not know.—Then you should not take letters to a mailbox.') The question can be read: Can you make a riddle metaphor of X and Y?" (Maranda, 1971: 136). The legacy of structuralism is a treasure house of poetics: all those analyses of modes, genres, and works amount to a rhetoric for making more texts (or rather, more felts). The Marandas for example show the poetics of making a riddle, beginning as follows:

1. Riddles are metaphors that establish, on the basis of an initial insight, the equivalence of two sets.

2. The greater the initial opposition between the two sets, the more effective the riddle metaphor.

3. The initial insight is based on the identity of one function shared by the two sets (Maranda, 138).

Conductive inference is essentially aesthetic, operating by means of metaphor.

> "What makes metaphor or simile-metaphor work is what might be called the unlike factor between the two things being compared. Without the unlike factor there is no metaphoric action at all, just a simple (if sometimes odd) statement of fact. It would be the kind of statement you would have if a boy said of his girlfriend, 'My love is like a girl,' words lacking impact and real meaning unless his sweetheart was in fact rather old. Second, notice some of the ways 'luve' connects with 'rose' [in Robert Burns familiar line, 'Oh my luve is like a red, red rose']. For instance, the girl the poet is writing about might be soft, sweet, fresh, and pure, smell nice, bloom, blush, and have a certain intensity (the intensity of 'red, red') as well as sharp thorns (so be careful how you handle her), and more. . . . So the metaphor's dynamics operate as follows: 'my luve' (X) + 'a red, red rose' (Y) = a set of new meanings that are not specifically spelled out, a relationship to be discovered by the reader. In 'Oh my luve is like a red, red rose' the X and Y terms are compared: X is like Y. But metaphoric terms can be juxtaposed (laid side by side) in other ways that also force the mind to bring them together: For example, the juxtaposed terms can be identified, contrasted, or associated with one another" (Briggs and Monaco, 1990: 4).

Example: High Concept   A manifestation of the X-Y dialogic of the riddle in entertainment practices is known as "high concept," the one-liner captions used to pitch and even to write narratives, whose invention is credited to Barry Diller and Michael Eisner (one-time heads of Twentieth Century Fox and Disney respectively).

Robert Kosberg on High Concept

"The essence of high concept is that it is both brief and provocative. It piques the imagination and promises that big things are going to happen out of an ordinary situation. In the comedy *Some Like It Hot,* for instance, two men also dress up as women, with hilarious consequences. The same goes for the humorously provocative *Tootsie,* based on a similar device of 'cross-dressing.' Out of the top ten movies every year, most of them are raised from a high-concept premise. . . .

"If you break down the meaning of the term, the literal translation is that there is a high amount of concept in the movie, or that the concept is high above the rest of the movie's components. All of the action is hinged on that one critical point. It's sometimes referred to as a hook, a twist or a gimmick. The hook in a song, for example, is the key line that is repeated throughout the song. When you hear that key line, you're hooked on the song. When you hear the hook of a movie, you should immediately know what it's about. You're hooked and want to see the movie. . . .

"Say you wanted to pitch *Amadeus.* You could play someone fifteen seconds of the best composition Mozart ever wrote and then ask the question: *Who would want to kill a man who makes this kind of music?* Or how about *The Graduate? How do you tell the girl you're in love with that you're sleeping with her mother?* . . .

"Try the trick of taking your situation to the *n*th degree. What is the absolute most impossible wish for a character in your situation? The absolute worst fear? The kookiest, wildest fantasy? You want to take the premise from the original thought and exaggerate it to outrageous proportions. What is the worst thing that could happen to a babysitter? She loses the kids. From *Adventures in Babysitting,* of course, something like this could happen, and probably has. . . .

"X meets Y. Remember my project about a floating campus? By describing it as '*Love Boat* meets *Animal House,*' anyone can get the whole picture and everyone can laugh. I used the tag line '*Rear Window* meets *1984*' when pitching *Closed Circuit.* By merging two contemporary movie titles that are immediately recognizable—X meets Y—you come up with a brand new brainchild, a high-concept Z" (Kosberg, 1991: 60, 62, 64).

Comment

- The mystory is a high concept meeting of discourse figures whose only connection is you. High concept is Hollywood haiku. The title of my first attempt to compose a mystory reflects this quality: "Derrida at the Little Bighorn."

Exercise: High Concept

Review the documentation of the three main assignments (treating the discourses of Career, Family, Community History). Select one person or character who appears in the documents for each discourse and state their relationship in the style of high concept.

THE ULMER FILE: VISION QUEST
Medicine Ficelle

I test the ficelle or high concept generator in my own case by following a line of displacement away from the protagonist of the History of my community—George Armstrong Custer—to one of his opponents at the Last Stand. Black Elk was just a teenager in the summer of 1876, and he took his first scalp at the Battle of the Little Bighorn. As soon as he had his scalp he raced back to the village and showed it proudly to his mother. Black Elk's tribe camped near the mouth of the Tongue River, where the Tongue empties into the Yellowstone, which became the site of Miles City in 1876 because it was the farthest point navigable by river boats. The boats were used to supply the garrison at Fort Keough (named for the commander of one of Custer's companies, whose horse, Comanche, was the sole survivor of the Last Stand). The frontier photographer Huffman, who used Miles City as his headquarters in the last two decades of the nineteenth century, took a picture of Spotted Eagle's village at this place where some of the Sioux were wintering. Black Elk mentioned that they often camped at the mouth of the Tongue. The winter Black Elk camped on the future site of my home town "a medicine man by the name of Creeping went around among the people curing snowblinds. He would put snow upon their eyes, and after he had sung a certain sacred song that he had heard in a dream, he would blow on the backs of their heads and they would see again, so I have heard. It was about the dragonfly that he sang, for that was where he got his power, they say" (Neihardt, 1961: 14).

Creeping's power was relatively small, a gift from the dragonfly, in contrast with the world vision given to Black Elk that included all the great animals sacred to his culture (horse and buffalo). Creeping triggered in me a memory of winter, from the last year we lived in North Dakota, before moving to Miles City. I remember the year because the event in question happened when I came home from school, and I only went to one year of school in North Dakota. I was five years old. We lived on a hill on what was then the outskirts of Mandan. A road cut deep into the hill at a steep angle connected the school at the bottom with my house at the top. A strong wind blew through the cut with such force that when I walked downhill to school I could lean with all my weight out into the air without falling. Returning I could catch the wind in the arch of my back with the effect of a spinnaker and nearly fly straight up the hill. One day I entered the house after this exhilarating scramble and I knew instantly by the silence that something was different. My mother was not home. Dad was gone during the weekdays, working on the dam being built near Minot. Mom was always at home after school, but this day she must have taken my sister somewhere. The only sound was the wind circling the house, pushing back and forth between the prairie hills and our windows. I got behind a couch in the living room and waited for my mother and sister to return. That was when I heard a voice calling, almost imperceptibly, from a distance, but then more insistently: help. Help! HELP!

Comment

- The mystory functions as cognitive map, to make explicit how "Problems B Us." In my case, I am examining my own participation in colonialism—the settling of the frontier. How did my Community (that is, how did I) solve the problem of conflict with Native Americans? War and the reservation system. That solution is part of what constructed my identity. An important part of the mystory is to acknowledge how one's intuitions or body is coded or formatted with values or ideologies that one does not necessarily agree with once one becomes an adult. Einstein's compass is useful as our paradigm for the wide image in this respect. The needle pointing always north allows me to navigate in any direction. The needle of your wide image always points in the same direction, but once you learn how to use it, you may think and imagine otherwise. To deny the original conditions of your attunement (from any of the popcycle areas) breaks the compass.

- Recently the Palestinian leader Yasser Arafat attempted to apply something like Turner's parable technique in a speech addressed directly to the American public. He said that the relationship of the Palestinians to Israel was structurally similar to that of the founders of America and England (thus placing himself in the position of George Washington). Unfortunately a closer examination of the history of the state of Israel suggests that a more accurate application of the figure would put the Palestinians in the position of Native Americans in the parable, with Arafat's character oscillating among such figures as Chief Joseph, Sitting Bull, and Geronimo.

Lamenting (Hanblecheyapi) Is it possible for me to identify with Black Elk now, the way I identified with cowboys (and Custer) as a child? Cyberpidgin includes both star icons and states of mind, with much more attention given (so far) to the former. The mystorical method proposes the possibility in my own experience of a *secondary encounter* with an oral state of mind. To do so produces an event of learning, and reveals the temporal or historical distance that has to be negotiated to cross the gaps of cyberpidgin. The difference is the untimeliness between living and telling. In telling the story I know that the series filling (fulling) the gap makes an itinerary linking different intensities and orders of a feeling (felt) with different status and standards between two apparatuses, literate and oral. On this side is the feeling of longing in its abject condition of homesickness. On the other side is the Native American vision quest, and the ritual called "hanblecheyapi." The passage from one side to the other (the secondary encounter) is created by means of the uncanny as an experience of (mis)recognition. The riddle is stated: what is the difference between "Heimweh" and "Hanblecheyapi"?

Black Elk's camp by the Tongue (he performs his dream vision for his people); Mandan (hearing the shout in the wind); Gainesville (writing a book). Together these moments form the time of deferred action—"Nachtraglichkeit." "The subject revises past events at a later date, and it is this revision which invests them with significance and even with efficacy or pathogenic force. . . . It is not lived experience in general that undergoes a deferred revision but specifically whatever it has been impossible in the first instance to incorporate fully into a meaningful context. The traumatic event is the epitome of such unassimilated experience" (Laplanche and Pontalis, 1973: 112). This reworking of memory Lacan referred to as retroaction, a logical time of three moments: the instant of seeing; the time for understanding; the moment of concluding (Evans, 1996: 206). Today I am recording the peculiar procrastination that characterizes mystory.

The act of writing offers its own version of deferral and aftereffects. I start a series, sequence, chain, recording one of my earliest memories. The time of understanding is narrative time. "We ought not therefore to continue to speak of time but of temporalization. This distension is, in fact, a temporal process that is expressed through the delays, the detours, the suspense, and every strategy of procrastination in the quest" (Ricoeur, 1985: 47). This experience of procrastination may be the one shared point between living the quest and telling about it. Writing is an action that triggers retroaction. "Writing is per se already (it is still) violence," said Blanchot in *The Writing of the Disaster*. "The rupture there is in each fragment, the break, the splitting, the tearing of the shred—acute singularity, steely point" (Blanchot, 1986: 46). To map my case of "Nachtraglichkeit" is to write a disaster (understanding as catastrophe—in the theatrical and mathematical senses together). This rupture teaches us the organizing structure of the fragment.

"Recognition"—the moment of understanding—is the experience of "anagnorisis." "A 'recognition plot' is one in which the principal reversal or 'peripety' results from the acquisition by one of the characters of knowledge which was previously withheld, and which, known, results in a decisive change of course for the character" (Holman, 1985: 440). Recognition plots may produce the effects of either tragedy or comedy, but in either case the discovery scene relies upon some contrivance that violates verisimilitude. "The emblem of this trivial aspect of recognition is of course the birthmark, the scar, the casket, the handbag—all those local and accidental details on which recognition seems to depend yet which seem unworthy of serious attention" (Cave, 1988: 2). Anagnorisis is to identity what Eureka is to invention.

Comment

- Lamenting or Crying for a Vision is another example of the longing or yearning noted at the beginning of the book as a primary mood of imaging that gives it its categorical or universalizing power (a source of the ability of images to classify experience and hence to operate as a metaphysics).

Orality

What is the difference between becoming a person of learning in an oral apparatus and in a literate apparatus? "I think I have told you, but if I have not, you must have understood, that a man who has a vision is not able to use the power of it until after he has performed the vision on earth for the people to see. You remember that my great vision came to me when I was only nine years old, and you have seen that I was not much good for anything until after I had performed the horse dance near the mouth of the Tongue river during my eighteenth summer" (Neihardt, 1961: 208). Black Elk, the Oglala Holy Man, made public his vision near where the Tongue river runs into the Yellowstone. The name of this place (the mouth of the Tongue) signals conductively that it has a message for me. I visited this area many times growing up since it is a good fishing spot. The horse dance took place a short distance from my father's Sand and Gravel Plant. At the time I lived there I knew little about the horse dance, Black Elk, or of anything else having to do with the Native Americans who walked that ground before me. This "Tongue" and "mouth" should have been enough to alert me sooner to the relevance of Black Elk's vision to mystory.

My oral education was neglected. At some point in my literate schooling (a redundancy) I acquired a taste for knowledge that set me on a path east to the Ivy League and Paris. Along the way I learned a great deal about writing—from Plato to Grammatology. And yet, Jacques Derrida's notion of "differance" is as alien to me, conceptually, as is Sioux "hanblecheyapi." It is not a question in any case of a literate person undertaking a fundamental practice of the oral apparatus. Rather, my question is: What *syncretic* formation might combine the "vision" in "theoria" and "hanblecheyapi" (Lakota "crying for a vision")—the literate and oral modes of insight?

Spirit When Black Elk later converted to Catholicism, he was christened Nicholas. Another Black Elk, named Wallace, a contemporary Oglala medicine man, believes that the power of the sacred pipe is for everyone. Wallace, like Nicholas before him, did some research into Wasichu power. "I went inside this communication (English language) to study the white man. It was like walking up to the Statue of Liberty. You go inside everywhere. I went into the heart. I went into the head and even looked out through his eyes to see what he sees, how he observes things. What I learned was that the white man has a real keen sense of eyes. They see values, so I give them credit for that. But what they don't see is the spirit" (Black Elk, 1990: 13).

We don't see the "spirit" in Wallace's sense any more than he sees the "self" in our sense, in that these terms refer to the identity formations of distinct apparatuses. Spirit and self are mutually exclusive possibilities in this sense. What remains of "spirit" for us, due to the nature of our apparatus, is the "concept," as in the notion of "Stimmung" central to Heidegger's account of being-in-the-world. We always live out of some frame of reference or expectation, according to Heidegger, which is our attunement ("Stimmung") to the world. "'Stimmung' fundamentally reveals facticity, thrownness, the 'already there' of the there. In attunements, in sadness or joy, Dasein 'finds itself' in the face of its already-there of the world and of itself. All understanding is imbued with a disposition which situates it, anchors it, or makes it remember its anchorage. . . . Phenomenologically speaking, 'Stimmung', the atmosphere, emanates from the things themselves and not from our subjectivity or from our own bodiliness. In 'Stimmung' the world presents itself as what touches us, concerns us, affects us. If we were not thus accosted, struck, surprised 'by things' we could never experience feelings of security or dread, nor even discover the differences among things" (Haar, 1993: 37). The mood is not in us, but we are in it, in Heidegger's account. An entire epoch may have a dominant mood: Ancient wonder; Modern dread. Such are the attunements of Western civilization. What about the attunement of Lakota civilization, who live in a condition in which thought is experienced as a voice spoken by a bird or stone? Attunement is a crossing point, an action of encounter.

Writing is violent, as Blanchot observed, because through writing one may overcome the common tendency to avoid the uncanny call of Dasein (what remains of spirit in modernity). Picking up on the meanings associated with voice in "Stimme," Ned Lukacher noted the "calling" that is part of attunement in an explicit connection between the Heideggerian and Freudian uncanny state of mind. "In response to 'the call of conscience,' Dasein discovers, to its amazement, that no one is on the other end of the line. Like the conscience of the criminal, Dasein's conscience is silent. The telephone rings, but when Dasein finally brings itself to answer, there is only an indecipherable noise. The 'call' is decisive for Dasein because it 'gets its ontological understanding of itself in the first instance from those entities which it itself is not but which it encounters within its world, and from Being, which they possess. It is the purpose of the call that it says nothing which might be talked about, gives no information about events.' What Dasein instinctively feels in this fearful confrontation with the 'fading' of the voice, is guilt and anxiety" (Lukacher, 1986: 79). Heidegger's inquiry into what is "called" thinking may be juxtaposed with the call received by a potential shaman in an oral culture. My secondary encounter opens the possibility of syncretizing these two calls, these two dreads—Dasein and spirit (the syncretism is not at the level of individual sages, but of civilizational apparatuses). EmerAgency Medicine. The "call" is a paradoxical case in the logic of sense applied to this syncretic meeting.

Poetic Image   The community in me. This inside/outside experience is named "extimacy" in Lacanian psychoanalysis, another version of "epiphany." Interpellation: first there is language (the entry into language, castration) and the chain of signifiers that produces the "exterior at the heart of me." The signifier introduces a hole into the Real (a metaphysical gap). The hole that connects the shaman to "the other side" migrates to the chain of signifiers in literacy. "It was the power from the outer world, and the visions and ceremonies had only made me like a hole through which the power could come to the two-leggeds," as Black Elk put it. This is how Black Elk experienced his identity, his subject: not as "self" but as "spirit." The experience of thought in orality is that of *hearing a voice outside*, as spoken by a god. This ghost migrates inside the body in the experience of literacy: *psyche*—literally, the *ghost in me*. What is it like to have the outside inside? Lacan's image for representing how extimacy produces an identity for a subject is the effect of anamorphic perspective. Describing the mirrored tube used to view anamorphic illustrations, Lacan explains: "It is any kind of construction that is made in such a way that by means of an optical transposition a certain form that wasn't visible at first sight transforms itself into a readable image. The pleasure is found in seeing its emergence from an indecipherable form" (Lacan, 1992: 135). The subject emerges into coherence through this relationship of the hole and the Thing ("das Ding," the "objet a") that fills it temporarily. The mirrored tube rhymes with the toilet-paper roll with which Elvis stuffed his pants.

Tragedy as a transitional form between orality and literacy, exemplified in *Antigone,* mapped the location of this border, the boundary line of the interface between the inside and the outside (between the state of mind and its object). "Tragedy is that which spreads itself out in front so that the image may be produced, " Lacan says (273). The central word of Antigone's drama is "*ate* " (ATH) Lacan says, using this basic term of tragedy that when referring to an individual means "foolishness," and to the collective means "catastrophe," "calamity." From small individual errors may come community disaster. "It is an irreplaceable word. It designates the limit that human life can only briefly cross" (263). "Without going into the optical definition of the phenomenon (of anamorphosis), one can say that it is because an infinitesimal fragment of image is produced on each surface of the cylinder that we see a series of screens superimposed; and it is as a result of these that a marvelous illusion in the form of a beautiful image of the passion appears beyond the mirror, whereas something decomposed and disgusting spreads out around it" (273). This stain opens itself to writing in the virtual mood of the internet. The purpose of my exercise in cyberpidgin with Black Elk is that this border is moving again in the transition from literacy to electracy: the "ghost in me" is neither spirit nor psyche now, but is becoming image.

Primitivism   The EmerAgency seeks a new way to understand ATH (foolishness, catastrophe), as part of extending the exchange between literate and oral societies into electracy. The generic name for this process of exchange in the era of colonialism—the rejection of the dominant mood of Western society and the embracing of the moods of non-Western societies—is primitivism. Within the perspective of the culture wars, primitivism seems "racist," in that it amounts to a celebration of the same stereotypes of the "savage" that the colonialists denigrated. Lucy Lippard located the real problem of primitivism in the neglect and disparagement on both sides of the issue of the process of syncretism or creolization (Lippard, 1990). Her recommendation is to avoid the false choice of having nothing to do with the moods of a different culture, or to embrace the pre-Colombian versions of the non-Western. Instead, she encourages us to participate in the syncretism modeled in the work of contemporary minority artists.

Syncretism is crucial to the mapping of "ate" at both the individual and collective levels (the levels of blindness and of disaster). In this spelling, too, we see the puncept, the repeated syllables, that link ATH with the past tense of "to eat" (a conductive link). The task of the EmerAgency could be described as attempting for electracy what the inventors of tragic theater achieved for literacy. "That is the first purpose of theater, in its Greek origins as tragedy: to structure the vision of an audience. That the act of seeing had become problematical is implicit in the very creation of theater—a place for seeing institutionalized in an art that attempts to assist the 'naked' eye. We recognize, what is in itself remarkable, that dramatic vision attempts to draw some nobility from the ruins of remembrance" (Hermassi, 1977: 18–19). The challenge is to construct the practice—the equivalent of the tragic drama or the anamorphic perspective—capable of bringing the repellent scramble into intelligibility (to write my own blindness).

The relay for my secondary encounter is the artists throughout the century who imported non-Western states of mind in a quantity and with an effect on Americans similar to the exporting of Hollywood images to the Third World by the entertainment industry. There are at least as many "Buddha impersonators" in the West as there are Elvis impersonators in the East. A good example that might stand in for a host of syncretic cases is Jack Kerouac. "In 1954, Kerouac's reading of Thoreau's *Walden* led him to pursue a serious, self-taught program of Buddhist study, and his affinity for the teachings was immediate. Both Kerouac's sense of compassion for the down-and-out, the beat, who populated his novels, and his revolutionary method of 'spontaneous bop prosody' found full expression in Buddhist thought. The *Surangama Sutra*, for example, affirmed Kerouac's own commitment to spontaneity; in the sutra, the Buddha counsels: 'If you are now desirous of more perfectly understanding Supreme Enlightenment and the enlightening nature of pure Mind-Essence, you must learn to answer questions spontaneously with no recourse to discriminating thinking" (Tonkinson, 1995: 24).

Comment

- Our interest in the states of mind operating in non-Western cultures or in societies other than one's own is first to note how common are such states and what an important role they play in daily life. Second, the point is not to mimic the foreign state of mind (*wabi-sabi* or hanblecheyapi) but to use it as a relay to locate one's own default or cultural state of mind. A third possibility is the syncretic one: to form a hybrid out of the two threads, such as in this case, the attitude to "voice" of Black Elk and Heidegger. "Voice " in cyberpidgin belongs neither to America or to Africa (for example), but to the internet (to electracy).

Identity Ritual

In the tradition of Native American medicine, the vision quest was meant to answer the question "what do I want to be," and the answer, received in the form of a dream or vision, although it might come spontaneously, usually required a ritual of considerable hardship. The books written by anthropologists as well as those recording the stories of various Lakota holy men and women often mention foolish Wasichus who demonstrate the pitfall of primitivism when they attempt the quest literally. I have come to understand the possibility, instead, of a practice between literacy and orality, that syncretizes, for example, the rock in Lacan that represents an absolute resistance to meaning, with the stone in Black Elk, which becomes eloquent during the vision quest. Fools Crow explained how the "yuwipi" ceremony works. "The yuwipi stones talk. They tell what the illness is, if a person has been shot with something, and what medicine to get. I don't know myself. The stones say. They tell me what to do, like ghosts. A dead boy or girl may hang around the house, annoying. It is because the ghosts want to say something" (Lewis, 80). The purification or "sweat" lodge is called the "stone-people-lodge."

As Wallace Black Elk explained, the rocks have songs. "Like the rock I wear around my neck, it has a song. All the stones that are around here, each one has a language of its own" (Black Elk, 34). These rocks told him how to make the colored paints needed for the rituals. Afterward Wasichus scoured his hills breaking many rocks with their hammers looking for the colored paints, but to no avail. "'Hanhepi' is the night," Wallace says in relating his experience of "hanbleceya". 'Ble' is where it is quiet. That is where a person comes with pain and tears to plea for something" (62). The ritual quest, crying for a vision, is called also "lamenting." "In the old days, we all—men and women—lamented all the time" (Black Elk, in Brown, 1971: 44). This "lamenting" resonates with the "yearning" associated with the Open in Rilke.

If the quest is successful the seeker makes acquaintance with spirit helpers who are the real medicine men. Such helpers (donors) gave Wallace his stones. "A flash of light came right through the lodge and somebody jumped in. He said, 'I am a stone-man. I give you this power.' So I carry this little medicine. It attracts electricity. It attracts lightning. So when I use this stone, these lights come. They talk like little radio waves" (62). The syncretism is already at work in Wallace's explanation of how he recalls the "power of the Four Winds" that is the source of his wisdom: "Everything that I see, hear, smell, taste—I have a little color TV back there that records it. Everything I saw and everything I heard was recorded in there, and I could rewind it and replay that little picture" (9–10).

Wallace made his first contact with the stone-man when he was nine. He heard heavy footsteps coming, then a hooting of an owl. "Then it was like my whole body became hollow, and that sound echoed up and down inside. I heard the spirit say, loud and clear, 'I am coming'. It was like the hooting was on the outside, and his voice was on the inside. Then he hooted a fourth time, and I felt a finger poking me in the top of my back, kind of pushing me" (11). After that the spirit came around, sat down, and conversed with the nine-year-old Wallace for some time. When it departed, a stone was lying there. The two keywords of the Sacred Pipe ("Chanunpa") are "health" and "help" (41).

Comment

- "Rock" is a switch word or pivot term guiding the conductive inference I am using to move from my familiar world to the unknown world of an oral practice (Hanblecheyapi). The X logic of crossing follows a signifier that repeats on both sides of the threshold.

A Missed Encounter

Rock (gravel) is an important "thing" in my story. Here is one story from "Derrida at the Little Bighorn," about the Sand and Gravel Plant, in order to focus on a fetish object—a stone.

> "There was this huge pile, a mountain, of oversize rock that came off the side of the washer. Too big for anything, unless we had a crusher, which we could not afford. So it just sat there and piled up over the years, always with a few rockhounds climbing over it, looking for agates. You could get a full cubic yard, over a ton of this rock, for two dollars. One day the hired man, George, came back from lunch with a present for Walt, a birthday present, something he found at the drugstore. Walt opened it and there was this box and inside the box was a pet rock. Now there was no difference between this pet rock and the rocks in the oversize pile, except that the pet one had a face painted on it, sort of a frown, as I recall, and it came in a little box. And the pet rocks sold for two dollars *each*. Dad stared at that rock, and this look came over his face" (Ulmer, 1989: 237).

Theory is little help with the power of this pet rock in my story (this fetish sitting now on my desk). Wittgenstein, for example, asserted: "Could one imagine a stone's having consciousness? And if anyone can do so,—why should that not merely prove that such an image-mongery is of no interest to us?" (Wittgenstein, 1968: 119). This lack in one tradition, however, may be filled by an excess in another. Two rocks, two holes, two visions, two dreamings, two focalizations: Lacan

(Heidegger, Wittgenstein) and Black Elk. Brown clarifies in a footnote in *The Sacred Pipe* that the term "fetish" is misapplied.

> "The Indian actually identifies himself with, or becomes, the quality or principle of the being or thing which comes to him in a vision, whether it be a beast, a bird, one of the elements, or really any aspect of creation. In order that this 'power' may never leave him, he always carries with him some material form representing the animal or object from which he has received his 'power.' These objects have often been incorrectly called fetishes, whereas they actually correspond more precisely to what the Christian calls guardian angels, since for the Indian, the animals and birds, and all things, are the 'reflections'—in a material form—of the Divine principles. The Indian is only attached to the form for the sake of the principle which is contained within the form" (Brown, 45).

The search for the wide image is a vision quest. The history of "fetish" as a pidgin term is one misunderstanding after another (noise versus message), and this is the source of its shaping power. The important point of the syncretism for choragraphy is the connection between the "fetish" and voice. Black Elk heard his first voice ("Stimme") when he was four. "It was like somebody calling me, and I thought it was my mother, but there was nobody there. This happened more than once and always made me afraid, so that I ran home." When he was five, a kingbird that he was about to shoot with a little bow and arrow spoke: "The clouds all over are one-sided," it said (Neihardt, 19). The bird called his attention to the sky where two men slanted down toward him coming like arrows. Then they were gone, and "the rain came with a big wind and a roaring. I did not tell this vision to anyone. I liked to think about it, but I was afraid to tell it." The first contact with spirit happens in early childhood.

I recognize (anagnorisis) in Black Elk's story, however distantly, my memory of North Dakota, the wind whistling, and the extimate voice saying HELP. Scene of a missed encounter (a definition of ideology). Like Black Elk at the same age, I never told anyone of hearing the voice. As I reflected on this memory from time to time over the years (the time of understanding) I assumed either that I was hearing things or that someone was injured somewhere in the hills behind our house. Why did I hold on to this memory, one of the few that survived from that time (or is it a "screen memory")? I did not think about the extimacy of the whistling outside and the voice inside as coming from the stone people. Why must the call come at age four or five? "It was a good thing I didn't get educated in school," Wallace explained. "Otherwise I would have lost this gift. I might have even gone against it" (Black Elk, 1990: 9). Is one implication of Wallace's warning about the interference making oral and literate knowing incommensurable that to become fully electrate requires avoiding school? Perhaps since I did go to school, along with every other cause associated with living in one apparatus rather than the other, It never occurred to me, no never (*ate*), that the voice was not asking for help. Perhaps if I had learned sooner the keywords of the Sacred Pipe ("health" and "help"), the event would not now seem so uncanny. The voice was not asking for help but (impossibly) *offering it*.

OFFICE

1. In this studio you begin the final quarter of the mystory—the History or Community story. The sting of memory or punctum in this discourse works somewhat differently than in the others. Here the recognition is not an experience from inside, but an admission intellectually that you are inside the belief system of the community in which you were raised. Some students find this observation to be obvious, but others have not accepted responsibility or seen the continuity between the values that informed the past of their community and their present attitudes and behaviors. The point of the cognitive map is to clarify such connections, to locate the borders and networks that conduct thought through the popcycle of your situation.

2. In researching and documenting your community story the primary criterion for selection is not your immediate identification with the story but the simple association of the story with your place in the world. The story may be central or marginal, as long as it is factually present in the community in which you went to school. School is the institution that selects and preserves the stories entrusted with group identity. However, other institutions also contribute importantly, such as tourism (Entertainment), religion, and the like. You will decide in the final phase of the project how this quarter relates to your wide image.

3. Comparisons between your Entertainment narrative and the historical narrative of Community are helpful in locating the voice or position of power, the sender actant, that mediates as donor between the "outside" (the value reserves and resources of the civilization) and the "inside" (the identity situation). This domain of mediation is the site of contention, valuation, and transvaluation of values, which is the focus of EmerAgency consulting. The mystory with its comparison of discourses provides perspective on the frame itself of your experience.

4. My inquiry into Black Elk as a ficelle for the Miles City story revealed to me the difference between the levels of drama and discourse, events and stand point, in the history narrative. Using Black Elk as a prototype for oral identity formation revealed the major importance in his experience of hearing a voice or being addressed by nature. When I meditated on my memories of a similar period in my life, when most shamans are first contacted by spirits, I discovered several such approaches, only one of which I recorded here (the wind in Mandan). Wallace's point about schooling preventing him from communicating with the spirit world, in the context of apparatus theory, is easy to explain as the different attunements or focalizations of a civilization. Native Americans had a complex religious institution in place to notice and augment the "endocepts" of childhood experiences of nature. Literacy still has religion as an institution, but it has been displaced and subordinated in favor of a utilitarian frame of mind in which animals and stones cannot speak. The point is not to prefer one over the other, but to recognize that this aspect of the apparatus is changing again: the ghost is on the move, into the machine.

5. The default frame for the rite of passage in literate narrative is that of "detective"—solving a crime (a problem). The implication is that electrate individuation rites will be neither those of shaman nor detective. The discussion of Heidegger, meanwhile, in the context of Black Elk was to explore the possibility of thinking electracy through a syncretic hybrid of the two "calls"—those of shaman and those of philosopher. The "Open" referred to by Heidegger adds to our understanding of the "gap" that is chora (the winnowing place).

6. As was the case with the first installment of the mystory—the Career discourse—you will have to do some research of a conventional literary sort to locate relevant documents and details for the Community history. The sting or obtuse principles of image meaning still applies, however. In this effect we see how "nostalgia" operates as rhetoric. I recognized Black Elk simply because of his association with the geographic region of my home town. It is a relationship of contiguity. The entanglement of his story with the past of my community lends Black Elk an aura. When I read Black Elk's autobiography, the account of something that is a common experience for an oral person, but a marginal one for a literate person—being addressed by spirits, having a vision—triggered a memory (an obtuse connection) that in this context could be reconstrued in spiritual terms. Another anecdote I could have used concerns the two shmoos I saw in my backyard when I was four (this also happened in Mandan). A shmoo was a creature in the comic strip Li'l Abner, drawn by Al Capp, which was popular at the time.

Chapter 8

The Bar (Street)

The bar can be a microcosm of the Special World, a place through which everyone must pass, sooner or later. Bars also play host to a number of other activities including music, flirting, and gambling.

STUDIO

Following the logic of the ficelle, we turn our attention away from the encounter of donor and hero, sender and receiver (performing the gift of the magic tool) to consider more closely the site, the scene in which this encounter most often takes place in entertainment narratives—the bar or "watering hole." The forward progress of narrative development is arrested in this chapter. What may be learned from this setting itself about the special world of electracy? In turning the focus of our allegory away from the plot line to the atmosphere or mood of the setting we are locating the place of transformation, of transition from literacy to electracy.

Comment

- While you are completing the fourth part of the mystory (documenting an historical problem solved or commemorated by your Community) we will work through the most important and most difficult part of the theory of electracy.

Last Call (Reliable Sources)

Of the two dimensions of the egent apprenticeship—the wide image and the consultation on a public policy issue—so far we have emphasized the wide image. The narrative allegory showed us that a magic tool (the wide image) is acquired only within a situation, specifically, that of dealing with conflict or solving a problem (the public policy question). The default policy question we have used (but not emphasized) is the historical one of colonialism, considered in the context of our post-colonial moment. The reason for tying the collective problem to a policy issue is to

ground or anchor the question to an institutional setting. We are interested in colonial policy, for example, not as a topic (or not only as a topic) but as a chora (the
image mode of categorization). A chora appears in the world as a literal place, a site
and setting that manifests the "cosmology" or ordering operations of a society. Each
of the popcycle discourses is grounded in an institution that occupies a particular architectural site (home, school, cinema, the workplace). The reason for lingering
now at this moment, still in the second act of our narrative allegory—the setting of
the bar where the hero meets the donor—, is that in the corresponding world of
daily life, the bar and the institution of which it is the seat (which is called "Street" in
the popcycle, derived from the term "streetwise") has become a chora: a place that
manifests what is happening at a global level of events. Therefore, I will introduce a
policy question related to human behavior specific to the institution of the bar.

Once you are an egent, this is how a consultation begins. The egent receives a
call from the daily news (is stung, the punctum). The consultation takes the form
of testimony, even a testimonial. As consultants we may testify to the desire of so
many potential protagonists to enter bars, especially underage protagonists (such
as the daughters of President George W. Bush). The following reading is typical of
many newspaper stories calling attention to the "problem" of drinking—an issue
of public policy.

"Binge Drinking Worries Parents"

—COLLEGE CAMPUSES ACROSS THE NATION ARE BATTLING ALCOHOL PROBLEMS

BATON ROUGE, La.—The bars line each side of Louisiana State University's campus, offering free shots and other drink specials. So many choices, but Rebekah Monson knows the secret—drink fast and move on.

"As college students head back to school, an American Medical Association survey released Wednesday shows binge drinking is among
their parents' top concerns: 95 percent said excessive drinking is a serious threat to their children and 85 percent said easy access to alcohol in
college communities contributes to the problem.

"'We can no longer treat binge drinking as a rite of passage. It's a
major health threat not only to binge drinkers but also to the people
around them,' said Dr. J. Edward Hill, AMA's chairman-elect.

"Binge drinking often is described as four drinks within an hour for
a female or five drinks in an hour for a male. An estimated 44 percent of
college students admit to binge drinking, and nearly one-fourth of those
binge frequently.

"'Four drinks in an hour? That's when I'm taking my time,' said Monson, a 20-year-old junior at LSU. 'That is a lot but that's pretty average for
a lot of college students. When I go to bars, I don't see people nursing
beers. I see people throwing back shots and chasing it with beers.'

"College students don't seem dissuaded by drinking-related deaths, including several fatalities during the last school year. A university of Michigan student celebrating his 21st birthday died after downing his 20th shot in 10 minutes. An Old Dominion University student choked to death on his own vomit during a pledge-week drinking binge. A Colgate University student is facing four years in prison after crashing into a tree during a night of drinking, killing four students.

"'Most students get here and think, "Oh, it's freedom. I can do whatever I want without mom and dad finding out,"' said Kelly Hill, a junior at Michigan. 'A lot of them don't know what their limits are'" (*The Gainsville Sun*, August 30, 2001: 6A).

Comment

- One inference from the article is that what is important in the setting of the bar is not the drinking itself, but the rite of passage.

Exercise: Policy Research

Make an inventory of the conventional policies and proposals regarding drinking laws and drinking etiquette circulating in society in general, and in your local community, college, or school in particular. Tell a brief story or anecdote about an experience you have had at a bar or similar establishment. Collect an alphabetized list of the names of the bars in your community.

Comment

- We want to explore in this call the paradoxes of virtue and vice, distinguishing between the official and unofficial systems of value. This split is a symptom of the unconscious, and of fetish logic. In the official order, the abuse of stimulants of any kind is condemned as a vice; in the unofficial or "Street" order the abuse of stimulants is attractive and even admired. The dilemma or "aporia" that structures a fundamental obstacle in your narrative as creator and consultant is the operation of this contradictory value system in the economy of the popcycle.

REMAKE

A Blues Legend (*Robert Johnson at the Crossroads*)

Street is an institution on the margins of the dominant popcycle in America. The creative transformation of any civilization tends to arise on the margins, and the emergence of electracy is no exception. Everyone notices the technology of electracy invading and transforming the literate apparatus. But an apparatus is also institutional formation and identity behavior, which also contribute to the invention process. The purpose of this remake is to learn more about the magic tool that the hero receives from the donor in the bar. The key to the nature of this magic tool (and hence to the wide image) is not only the plot action or the primary institutional purpose of dispensing alcoholic beverages or the socializing associated with leisure. Rather, it is the music that is played, setting the mood for all these other activities and behaviors. Here is the key, the pivot point, the fulcrum supporting the movement from one apparatus to the next. Both dimensions of our quest, then, may be explored through an improvisation on a blues legend—the midnight bargain Robert Johnson struck with the devil at a crossroads (and the previous chapters have prepared us to recognize the larger cyberpidgin significance of this place). The scene is represented in an unproduced screenplay for a film dramatization of the life of the great bluesman. An interesting and relevant twist in Alan Greenberg's script is that Johnson originally meets the "devilman" in a movie theater showing "The Painted Desert," a Western starring Clark Gable.

Alan Greenberg: from Love in Vain

"EXTERIOR. CHARLIE'S TRACE. MIDNIGHT

"A road sign reads: 'Charlie's Trace.'

"The camera slowly dollies down the ghostly, dirt-paved artery. Anonymous black men walk or stand stationary at points along the way.

"Now the road becomes barren. At a dark crossroads we behold Robert Johnson, picking on his guitar nervously, delicately. It is out of tune. Then, footsteps, up the road.

"The devilman weaves and stumbles into view. He never looks at Robert, only at his guitar. He takes it, tunes it, turns around and plays an extraordinary guitar part. He hands it back and starts to go.

"DEVILMAN

"'I's so broke, can't even buy my dick a doughnut.'

"Robert fishes in his pocket, then tosses a coin onto the dirt road. The devilman stoops to pick it up. He tips his hat, stumbling off into the night.

"DEVILMAN

"'Talk some shit, man, talk some shit—'

"Silent Image: Robert, on his knees at crossroads, in the midst of a furious riff on his guitar.
"DISSOLVE" (Greenberg, 1994: 49–50).

Comment

- This scene of writing and creativity emblematizes the original Pythagorean metaphor of the harmony of the world soul as the tuning of a lute (philosophizing with a hammer, in Nietzsche's phrase, referring to the pitches of the hammered anvils that is part of the Eureka story of the mathematics of strings). We suppose that it is an open tuning, for playing slide or barred chords.

The blues tend to foreground a personal situation and leave implicit the underlying social construction of that situation. "In his 'Crossroads Blues,' Robert Johnson cries out to someone to save him as he stands at a crossroads trying to get a ride. There is nowhere for him to go. He doesn't know of any women living nearby. In desperation he calls to someone passing to tell his friend Willie Brown, another singer from Clarksdale, that he is 'sinking down.' The reason for his desperation is that he is in a Mississippi county that jails any Negro found on the roads after dark. But instead of an explanation he only cries out in his fear, and it is the intensity of his cry that gives his blues its poetic strength" (Charters, 1999: 359). Johnson's most original composition and performance is said to be "Hell Hound on My Trail" in which the blues are falling down like hail (Guralnick, 1998: 45).

Edward Kamau Brathwaite, "Blues"

Here is an example of a lyric that dramatizes the typical blues situation (problems of love).

"*i woke up this morning*
sunshine int showin through my door
i woke up this mornin
sunshine int showin through my door
'cause the blues is got me
and i int got strength to go no more

i woke up this mornin
clothes still scattered cross the floor
i woke up this mornin

clothes still scattered cross the floor
las night the ride was lovely
but she int comin back for more

sea island sunshine
where are you hidin now
sea island sunshine
where are you hidin now
could a sware i left you in the cupboard
but is only empties mockin at me in there now

empty bottles knockin
laugh like a woman satisfied
empty bottles knockin
laugh like a woman satisfied
she full an left me empty
laughin when i should a cried

this place is empty bottles
this place is a woman satisfied
this place is empty bottles
this place is a woman satisfied
she drink muh sugar water
till muh sunshine died"

(Brathwaite, in Meltzer, 1999: 55)

The Modernist Brothel

One sign of the significance of the bar in our civilization is the prestige and attraction it holds for American youth. Another symptom that there is something important about the bar, beyond its manifest function in daily life, is the place it holds in important works of modernist art and literature. In these works the scene is of a particular kind of bar—a brothel or bordello. The value, as a poet once said, is to "be drunken," to disturb the body and senses, by any means necessary. Walter Benjamin, in his commentary on the first poet of modernism—Charles Baudelaire—found the figure of the prostitute turned into an allegory of the commodification of everything in the industrialized metropolis (Buci-Glucksmann, 1994: 79). "Brothel" or "bordello" are switch words linked conductively to "border," which is the clue to their importance as emblem for inventing the category formation of imaging.

> "Laura Kendrick has called attention to how the Anglo-French word *bo(u)rdure*,
> or 'border,' can help to account for marginal images of play of all kinds, whether
> of games or musical instruments, via a set of puns or words related to the noun
> *bo(u)rde*, 'play, jest, have fun.' The puns also include the verb *bo(u)rden*, meaning
> 'to joust' or 'tilt at the quintain,' and we see many scenes in English borders of

jousting and tilting knights, or creatures dressed as knights. *Bo(u)rde* includes the meaning of sexual intercourse, and it has long been observed that marginal scenes can be bawdy: in addition to the sexual meaning of *bo(u)rde,* a variant fifteenth-century form of 'border' is *bordel,* a homophone of the word for 'brothel,' *bordel*" (Carruthers, 1998: 162).

The bar (and especially the brothel) is a liminal location on the borders of established society. The anthropologist Victor Turner defines "liminality" as "the midpoint of transition in a status-sequence between two positions" (the positions of roles and their status in a community) (Turner, 1974: 237). Every society has liminal regions where rites of passage occur. The purpose of the following series describing or citing a sample of modernist bar scenes is to note the atmosphere or mood evoked by this setting in our culture. The bar is an allegorical place.

Comment

- To apply the term "remake" to these sections is to speak loosely, or figuratively. I begin with a familiar or important work, such as Johnson's blues, and use it to frame a meditation or improvisation. The original serves as an image category, lending its coherence to the gathering of an extended heap of mixed materials. In this remake we follow the thread of the blues right into cyberspace.

Examples

1. James Joyce, "Night Town," *Ulysses*

"The Mabbot street entrance of nighttown, before which stretches an uncobbled trainsiding set with skeleton tracks, red and green will-'o-the-wisps and danger signals. Rows of flimsy houses with gaping doors. Rare lamps with faint rainbow fans. Round Rabaiotti's halted ice gondola stunted men and women squabble. They grab wafers between which are wedged lumps of coal and copper snow. Sucking, they scatter slowly. Children. The swancomb of the gondola, high-reared, forges on through the murk, white and blue under a lighthouse. Whistles call and answer.

> *The Calls*
> *Wait, my love, and I'll be with you.*
> *The Answers*
> *Round behind the stable.*
> *(A deafmute idiot with goggle eyes, his shapeless mouth dribbling, jerks past,*
> *   shakes in Saint Vitus' dance. A chain of children's hands imprisons him.)*
> *The Children*
> *Kithogue! Salute.*

The Idiot
(Lifts a palsied left arm and gurgles.) Grhahute!
    The Children
Where's the great light?
    The Idiot
(Gobbing) Ghaghahest.

(They release him. He jerks on. A pigmy woman swings on a rope slung between the railings, counting. A form sprawled against a dustbin and muffled by its arm and hat moves, groans, grinding growling teeth, and snores again. On a step a gnome totting among a rubbishtip crouches to shoulder a sack of rags and bones. A crone standing by with a smoky oil lamp rams the last bottle in the maw of his sack" (Joyce, 1966: 429).

2. Edward Fry on Pablo Picasso, "Demoiselles d'Avignon"

"In 'Les Demoiselles' Picasso posed and attacked many problems at once, some of which he was to resolve only during the course of the following seven years. The subject, a brothel scene, recalls Picasso's interest, during his previous blue and pink periods, in episodes from the lives of those on the margin of society, as in fact he himself lived during his years in Montemartre, beginning in 1904. But while the brothel as a theme appeared frequently in late nineteenth- and early twentieth-century painting, Picasso's version is as far removed from the spirit of irony or pathos of his predecessors as it is from the empathy and restrained lyricism of his own earlier painting.

"But what makes 'Les Demoiselles' truly revolutionary work of art is that in it Picasso broke away from the two central characteristics of European painting since the Renaissance: the classical norm for the human figure, and the spatial illusionism of one-point perspective. During the year previous to the completion of "Les Demoiselles," Picasso had turned to various sources in his search for a new approach to the human figure, the most influential of these being Iberian sculpture, El Greco, and the work of Gauguin, particularly his carved sculpture. But the decisive influence on his thinking was African sculpture. . . . This new approach appears most clearly in "Les Demoiselles" in such details as the reduction of human anatomy to geometrical lozenges and triangles, as well as in the abandonment of normal anatomical proportions. African influence is even clearer in the mask-like faces of the two right-hand figures" (Fry, 13).

3. Michael Chekhov, "Improvisation"

In the autumn of 1941 Michael Chekhov gave a series of lectures and exercises explaining and demonstrating his development of the Stanislavsky style of Method acting. He used the principles of "going from yourself"—the psychological gesture, emotional memory—and the other Stanislavskian ideas for creating the effect of real life on stage. His innovation is the emphasis he gives to "atmosphere" as a holistic means to organize and give coherence to the entire performance, individually and collectively. His understanding of atmosphere resembles Heidegger's idea of Stimmung: the atmosphere is not an emotion internal to the actor, but is an attunement between the person and the environment. Advising an actor about getting into the character of King Lear by remembering his grandfather, Chekhov insists upon locating and extracting just the atmosphere as the connection between life and art. "If we accumulate enough experiences from our 'grandfathers' and then forget them, we will not need to remember our 'grandfathers.' You need only to remember the atmosphere, to have a spark of anticipation of what it should be, laughter, sorrow, and so on. The same 'grandfather,' if he has been forgotten and gone his way, will return as an artistic emotion. I am speaking against remembering things which are still too personal. . . . If, for instance, we imagine King Lear, we can imagine him only because we are already rich enough inside ourselves with all the 'grandfathers' which we have forgotten. But we cannot imagine King Lear if we have a concrete grandfather who is still tearing our physical nerves and heart to pieces" (Chekhov, 1985: 42). The interest for us is this singling out of atmosphere as the unit of coherence, and the fact that the scene that Chekhov used as the point of departure for building a play by means of improvisation is that of a tavern.

Atmospheres for the Sketch

"The first atmosphere will be the following one: Early morning—very early—before dawn, in a tavern which is very dirty, very low. All the people are very drunk—they have been drinking the whole night. Everyone is tired and exhausted—prostitutes and sailors. Everything that could happen has happened. They are exhausted, unbridled, weak, over-tired—it is like a nightmare. Somewhere there are attempts to sing the songs which have been sung during the night—disharmony everywhere. Satiety. Drinking goes on very lazily—some exclamations, some attempts to sing, nothing reasonable, tired, stuffy. This is the atmosphere.

"Try to imagine it around us—don't try to *feel* anything. We will feel as soon as the atmosphere is there. When you imagine the atmosphere around you, allow yourself to be open to it. Don't force yourself to be open—just open yourself to this heavy atmosphere. Now try to move a little in harmony with this atmosphere" (56).

Comment

• This sequence is a sampling of representative canonical works in several media that foreground the brothel as the setting of a modernist sensibility. The point is to notice the place and its atmosphere. The synthesis of all such works, each with its own nuance, manifests a state (or states) of mind that we will name eventually. Image categories write states of mind.

Song

We are building a series, performing the narrative transformation from literacy to electracy. Our narrative quest for the wide image is suspended at the station of the donor—the bar—in which the donor tests the hero and gives the gift of the magic tool. We already know that the magic tool gives access to the wide image, but we are working toward learning exactly what that means. The transformation occurs through a step-by-step shift of focus away from the plot line, away from the transaction between the donor and hero, to the environment of their encounter, the honky tonk, saloon, tavern, barrelhouse, bar. Vogler reminded us that the bar setting often includes a band playing music that helps to set the atmosphere of the scene. We are in transition now from the general environment of the bar, continuing the displacement away from the plot to the setting (scenes of eros and violence) and now within the setting the music played in the bar.

This displacement of attention is also a "reduction," following the terms of the analogy with the invention of the dialogue. Plato's dialogues may be understood as following the lead represented by Oedipus in his encounter with the Sphinx—to retain the intellectual trial and reduce or eliminate the tests of blows and caresses. The drama of blows and caresses persisted in narratives of all types. The type we are focusing on now is that of song, in order to bring out the symbiotic relationship between the bar and a certain kind of music—the Afro-Caribbean music that emerged from the syncretism of Western and non-Western cultures during the Colonial Era (slavery and the Black Diaspora that created the "Black Atlantic" in Paul Gilroy's phrase). Samba is the version this syncretism took in Brazil, paralleled in Argentina by Tango and the United States by Jazz, to name some of the most important variations.

Comment

- Let me summarize here the point of the long series of descriptions and readings coming up. The readings on the modernist brothel demonstrated the atmosphere associated with the "bar" in the arts. Now we turn to the music played in the brothel/bar and its atmosphere. Why this focus? You will recall how Plato invented philosophy, noted in the first chapters. Through the power of alphabetic writing he was able to isolate the concept (a categorization specific to literacy) from the epic. He culminated a Greek tradition that gradually stripped away from the epics (*Illiad* and *Odyssey*) all dramatic action, to leave only the abstract notion of "justice" (*dike*) first noticed for itself in the pattern of words used to describe the action of the heroes. Using our grammatological analogy, we are looking for a similar effect when our novels are put into photography (Barthes's third meaning). It turns out, however, that the practice most relevant to the obtuse order of meaning, most revealing of mood and atmosphere as categorical states of mind, is music. The point for electracy is not the music as such, or does not stop with the music. Rather, as our analogy shows, the electrate dimension is not the music but the mood it supports and evokes. In the same way that Plato stripped away drama from epic to arrive at idea, so are we stripping away music from song to arrive at mood. In literacy it is possible to write concepts directly (justice); in electracy it is possible to image moods directly. To understand mood as such requires a review of some of the national musics that have most clearly established categorical moods. All these moods are variations and nuances of yearning.

The most famous samba of all is "Aquarela do Brasil," by Ary Barroso, known internationally simply as "Brazil." It is the opening number of *The Gangs All Here* (1943), perhaps Carmen Miranda's best film, directed by Busby Berkeley.

In Terry Gilliam's *Brazil* (1985) "the song represented a vision of beauty and freedom to the protagonist, trapped in a futuristic, totalitarian society" (McGowan, 35). Not that it is possible or even desirable to try to translate samba into a concept. Indeed, its resistance to "conceptuality" is what recommends "samba" as the relay for a new category based on mood. The dancing is figurative, a figure of thought. "It is common for Cariocas to say, rather ironically, that everything ends up in samba. If things go wrong there's always samba to lift peoples' spirits. Samba is many things: solace, celebration, escape and abandon, plus philosophy, culture, and tradition" (28). The effects of samba are summed up in the word 'saudade' ("longing or yearning for something or someone"). "It's a certain poignance, a soulfulness, coming from what Brazilians call 'saudade'—a kind of bittersweet longing, which means, in a way, 'glad to be feeling.' (We have no word in English for this concept)" (Paul Winter, in McGowan, 9).

The fundamental happiness underlying the sadness of samba is to be distinguished from the melancholy of the Argentine tango. "Argentines think of themselves as reluctant to give in to exuberant emotion, much less to its display. Proudly in control, yet sometimes, for precisely this reason, trapped in themselves, Argentines channel their characteristic combination of inhibitions and introspection into a particular form of brooding that amounts to a national institution: *el mufarse*. The mood relates closely to the tango. *Mufarse* involves bitter introspection, but Argentines add to this emotion a clear sense of self-indulgence when they give in to a *mufa*. It is a depression, but with a cynicism about the depression itself, an awareness that it can feel good to throw practicalities aside, have a *vino tinto* or one of the demitasse coffees over which many a tango was written, and contemplate one's bad luck and its universal implications" (Taylor, 1998: 4).

4. Marta E. Savigliano on Tango (Mufarse)

Marta Savigliano brings out the complex "dialogic" struggle of interpellation—colonization and decolonization—taking place around and within these hybrid musics. In most of the Americas, there is a struggle for "ownership" or for dominance in controlling the meaning of music as a practice among individual citizens who use it for personal reasons (including for resistance or rebellion), by the state appropriating it for the politics of national identity, and by the corporations who treat it as a commodity for the purposes of profit. Electracy is emerging within this complex history, and to locate the precise nature of this emergence we continue to follow our trajectory (using narrative structure as an allegory of a quest for the wide image) of displacement from the bordello to the blues, and from the blues to the categorical image.

A Tango Tableau Vivant

"At dusk, La Moreira would go with other women to the 'bar' of La Pichona where she 'worked' as a prostitute, as a lancera, as a go-between for clients and other prostitutes, and as a dancer. As a lancera because she stole wallets from the drunk distracted clients and from the immigrants who had money; as a go-between because she was associated with her 'husband' in that business of deceiving poor souls and selling them as 'novelties'; as a dancer, because she was a great one and because La Pichona's 'bar' was one of the places that helped to give the tango its fame and its association with prostitution. At night, she was a tango-woman. Brave gypsy blood ran through her veins, and, even though she was apparently very feminine and quite beautiful, in her dark endeavors she showed great 'courage' in throwing the dagger, and that is where her name came from. She usually carried a knife, but when she had to wander alone at night in the outskirts or in dealing with 'difficult' business—just think of the resentment of the less successful ruffians, lazy and cowardly, but nonetheless dangerous, whose women she took away—she wore high boots, almost up to her knee, and in the right one she carried a dagger or saber. Do not forget that the outskirts of the city saw times of violent madness and lust. Her looks: Not too tall, perfect figure, sensuous voice, like her face; like her walking" (Savigliano, 1995: 51).

Whether in its "ruffian" or "romantic" version, the tango story told in the lyrics and performed in the dance is one of love, seduction, power, violence, and loss, as recorded in the lyrics of *Always the Same Story* (1925). The story is usually told from the point of view of the ruffian or thug, who makes "a whiny confession" of his troubles with women and his competitors (other ruffians, or wealthy men).

> *"When she was at the door she said: 'In any case*
> *wherever I choose to go I'll be better off.'*
> *The guy arrived tired from his job and making*
> *a tremendous effort, he read on the page:*

'Because I've had it up to here with living in pain,
I decided to leave you. Forgive me. Margo.'
The blow was so strong that his confused mind
stopped instantly, as if mortally wounded.

Suddenly he reacted, he was going to go after her,
but being a streetwise guy, he checked the impulse.
It's always the same story: a lost broad
and a poor hope preserved in alcohol" (49).

The mood evoked through the combination of setting, lyrics, music (including the sound of the signature instrument, the box-shaped button accordion or bandoneon), and the dance, is described as a profound melancholy. The feeling carries homesickness into another dimension of passion.

> "Tango and exile (in the sense of 'being away from home' for whatever reason) are intimately associated. On a personal level, it is more than common for any *argentino* living abroad to connect the experience of longing and nostalgia to the tango. It is a recurrent pattern, even for those of us who do not consider ourselves connoisseurs or fans of the tango, to be affected by the tango syndrome after being deprived for a while of our *argentino* 'environment.' The tango syndrome can affect one in various degrees: paying attention to the word 'tango' whenever it is mentioned; reading whatever pops up about tango in newspapers and magazines or on posters; attending every tango performance we possibly can; recalling some fragments of lyrics in order to name puzzling situations we go through; viewing ourselves in the same shoes as some of the characters in old tango movies; and in some extreme cases, like my own, deciding to learn about it in a more or less systematic way" (xiv).

The master of the bandoneon, Astor Piazzolla, pushed tango into a concert mode. "Traditional tango captures the dislocation of the immigrant *porteno,* the disillusionment with the dream of a new life, transmuting these deep and raw emotions onto a personal plane of betrayal and triangular relationships. Piazzolla's genius comes from the fact that, within the many layers and changing moods and pace of his pieces, he never betrays this essence of tango—its sense of fate, its core of hopeless misery, its desperate sense of loss. Piazzolla translated the philosophy expounded by tango poets like Enrique Santos Discepelo, who, in 'El cambalache' (The Junkshop), concludes the twentieth-century world is a filthy place, an insolent display of blatant wickedness, onto the musical plane" (Broughton, 1994: 582).

The movement we are tracing passes from the plot line of love and death through the music to this atmosphere and mood, on the way toward electracy. W. C. Handy, whose "Memphis Blues" was the first blues song to be published in America (1912), noted in his account of the composition of "The St. Louis Blues" that he had been listening to tangos and recognized the African quality (later learning that "tango" derives from African *tangura* referring to the "tom

tom beat." "The tango was in vogue. I tricked the dancers by arranging a tango introduction, breaking abruptly into a low-down blues." The idea for the song came, he said, from overhearing "a drunken woman stumbling along a dimly lighted street in St. Louis mumbling, 'My man's got a heart like a rock cast in the sea'" (Murray, 1976: 139–140).

Exercise: Lyric Evaluation

Write down the lyrics of a favorite song and analyse the relationship between the narrative situation of the lyrics and the atmosphere of the music. Make explicit what the music style is saying about the theme expressed in the words.

"Storyville"   The "invention" of tango "among the pimps and prostitutes of the bordellos and bars of the *arrabal* and *orillas* (slum districts) on the outskirts of Buenos Aires," in a "melting pot of European immigrants, local Criollos, blacks and natives" (Broughton, 1994: 577), has its equivalent in the United States in the invention of jazz in New Orleans. "In 1897 town officials rope off a district for prostitution, gambling, and the new music that seems to go with these: the District, the players called it ('Storyville,' to us). Here [Buddy] Bolden solidifies his rule, moving nightly through his domain of halls and cabarets: Perseverance Hall, Globe Hall, Come Clean, Big Easy, Few Clothes, Drag Nasty, Funky Butt, Spano's, Tuxedo. At each of these Bolden plays the numbers he has made famous, 'Make Me a Pallet on Your Floor,' 'If You Don't Shake, You Don't Get No Cake,' and his theme, 'Buddy Bolden's Blues'. As in the days of Congo Square which Buddy can see from the bandstand at Globe Hall, this is music for the dancers, and there is an electric sympathy between those on the floor and those on the stand" (Turner, 1994: 27).

The invention and evolution of jazz is a good example of how innovations arise and circulate through the different institutions of the popcycle.

> "The questions of how Haitian Voodoo came to the continental United States, and the question of why jazz originated in New Orleans, are in fact parts of the same question. Jazz and rock 'n roll would evolve from Voodoo, carrying within them the metaphysical antidote that would aid many a twentieth-century Westerner from both the ravages of the mind-body split codified by Christianism, and the onslaught of technology. The twentieth century would dance as no other had, and, through that dance, secrets would be passed" (Ventura, 1985: 120).

The ritual behavior of the slaves in New Orleans' Congo Square, including everything from music to sex and violence, when transposed into the frame of entertainment in Western culture, was institutionalized in the bordellos of Storyville. As commentators on this history insist, the relationship between blues, jazz, and the bordello is circumstantial rather than essential. The genealogy is from black folk practices, evolving to the city streets—played by local bands in parades celebrating various occasions, from carnival to funerals—while being invited into the pleasure clubs to provide entertainment. Street is the name of a popcycle institution of which the bar is the unofficial "seat" or "see." Street is administered loosely by gangs, and its logic or proof is violence (Anderson, 1999). The unofficial values of the society enter the popcycle through the institution of Street. That the mafia boss Tony Soprano uses a burlesque or strip club as his base of operations in the HBO series *The Sopranos* dramatizes the politics and economics of Street and its alliance with entertainment. The code of the street regulates an unofficial system of values, organizing the "special world" of alternative, underground, outlaw, or countercultures. In the history of artist "bohemias" such as Montmartre in Paris, artists, proletarians, and outlaws rubbed shoulders in cabarets such as *Le Chat Noir*.

The Tables are Turned

In the story of the invention of the blues (and its incorporation into jazz) the negative valence of African religion found in Marx (his use of fetishism as the worst thing he could think of to say about the commodity) is inverted (the legendary meeting of Johnson with the Devil at the crossroads,) marking one of the fundamental shifts (post-Enlightenment) that distinguishes electracy from literacy. The passage through the popcycle from Enlightenment condemnation of colonized civilizations through the "primitivism" of the avant-garde (Picasso's reference to African masks) to the multiculturalism of postcolonial politics and the simulation of Hip-Hop within the teenage population of White suburbia, traces the emergence of a new paradigm. It is the same trajectory that brought together the masters and slaves of a previous epoch—Rome and Jerusalem from the crucifixion of Christ to the conversion of Constantine. This context reveals another entry in the "table turning" series, expressed in the phrase "to turn the tables." Within choragraphy the perspective usually used to frame the problematic of colonialism is shifted from politics to invention. The phenomenon looks the same from either position (saving the appearances) but the plans of action called for by the respective cases are different (policy formation).

Comment

- The reason for using slavery and colonialism as the default policy questions is now clear. In the various debates pitting one popcycle institution against another (School and Family, for example, against Entertainment and Street), the EmerAgency consultation would testify to this historical process of syncretism, whose vehicle is Afro-Caribbean music.

Who is (or will be) the Saint Augustine of electracy? Augustine's name signs the previous principal moment of syncretism in the Western tradition, bringing together a hybrid out of the Greco-Roman and Judeo-Christian civilizations. "Traditional Western thought was largely though not exclusively composed of a blending of biblical and Greek concepts. The admixture of the intellectual frameworks of Jerusalem and Athens reached most explicit expression in the famous 'Christian synthesis' of medieval philosophy" (Kearney, 1988: 114). Kearney adds that "It was Augustine in the fourth century who first succeeded in forging a sustained and systematic concordance between Judeo-Christian theology and Greek ontology" (116). The apparatus of electracy will be described similarly as a continuation of the syncretic growth of the Western tradition, admixing the onto-theology of the Greco-Roman-Judeo-Christian state of mind that informed the apparatus of literacy with the magic and orality of Black Atlantic into a Funk synthesis (syncretism) of electracy.

A function of this image as part of the deconstruction of method is to interrupt and supplement the instrumental mood of "anomaly/solution." Conventional consulting works in a kind of booster mood of progress. Inventional consultants, rather, frame problems in the mood of "the blues." The individual tuning of a problem zone specifies the image within this frame. To open "problem" with its empirical state of mind to the realm of Arts and Letters in this syncretic frame is to integrate the practical politics of public policy formation with the emotional wisdom of the Afro-Caribbean musical and dance traditions (related with the syncretic religious traditions of the Black Atlantic) whose different names in different regions and nations reflect the different nuances of creolization that have occurred historically.

In the United States, the creolization of the Judeo-Christian-Greco-Roman West with the Black Atlantic has developed in the mood of blues. The Emer-Agency goal is to fashion a consulting practice that combines literate method with the lessons of "blutopia," referring to the two major impulses of African-American music: "a utopian impulse, evident in the creation of imagined places (Promised Lands), and the impulse to remember, to bear witness, which James Baldwin relates to the particular history of slavery" (Lock, 1999: 3). "Blues" is not feeling "bad," but what you do about bad feelings.

Stephen Diggs on Blues

"I have built a cultural narrative about the transformation of Western consciousness through African-American music by focusing on color and alchemy. In *Shadow Dancing in the USA* (1985), Michael Ventura arrived at many of the same conclusions by constructing a historical narrative about jazz and rock 'n' roll that focused on a return to the body through the 'loa' or spirit possession of the musician and listener/dancer. The bluesmen are the secular carriers of the Hoodoo or Voodoo religion which is a hybrid of traditional West African religions and Christianity. As such, bluesmen and women tend to spirit and psyche in a manner handed down from Africa to Hoodoo; spirit possession.

Where the Northern soul, from shaman to Christian priest, operates dissociatively, leaving the body to travel the spirit world, the African priest, the Hoodoo conjurer, and the bluesmen ask the 'loa' to enter bodies and possess them. It is through this possession that the 'loa' is known and expressed. . . .

"Blues lyrics have tremendous breadth, within which are two core streams, depression and libido. The depressive quality of the blues is the most recognizable to the majority of people, an example of which is the lament for being 'done wrong' by a lover. But the blues is also highly sexual and at times exuberant. There are many 'happy' blues about good time fun, including the joys of food and dance. The blues is about the passions of the flesh. Where the pathological Western mind tended to create dirty movies out of this blue, blacks turned these libidinous hurricanes into the huge body of art called the blues. . . .

"It is fascinating to note that in addition to the lyric content of the blues, its music and performance practices also worked to transform the dissociative consciousness. Harmonically, the blues is based on the tritone interval which is considered the most dissonant of all intervals and thus full of tension. In Renaissance times this interval was known as the 'Diabolus en musica' and for a time its use in performance was actually illegal. In the blues almost every chord contains the tritone, even the tonic. The problem of union of the opposites is managed in the blues by permeating the music with the tension of the tritone. The Christian Devil is everywhere, the dream of salvation nowhere" (Diggs, 1997: 35).

The point to stress in our trajectory toward the magic tool present/present in the bar is that, as one bluesman put it, "We gave the blues that seventh [the 'blue note']. But it can be in anything. It's up to the individual to know how and when to bring it out" (Meltzer, 1999: 43). The quarter tone, in any case, is indigenous to African music and preceded the state of mind of melancholy that became associated with the sound in the American hybrids. The quarter tone is the moment of liminality in the musical structure. This location of the essence of blues in mood continues in jazz. "Jazz isn't music merely, it is a spirit that can express itself in almost anything. The true spirit of jazz is joyous revolt from convention, custom, authority, boredom, even sorrow—from everything that would confine the soul of man and hinder its riding free in the air. The Negroes who invented it called their songs the 'Blues,' and they weren't capable of satire or deception. Jazz was their explosive attempt to cast off the blues and sorrow. And that is why it has been such a balm for modern ennui. It is the revolt of emotion against repression" (8).

Cyber Duende

Jazz may be in anything, and its "elementals" are found in dances around the world: "It is in the Indian war dance, the Highland fling, the Irish jig, the Cossack dance, the Spanish fandango, the Brazilian *mixise,* the dance of the whirling dervish, the hula of the South Seas, the *danse du ventre* of the Orient, the *carmagnole* of the French Revolution, the strains of Gypsy music, and the ragtime of the Negro" (9). While jazz is as expressive of America "as the movie and the dollar" (8), this elemental spirit is universal and as such is the relay for the global apparatus of electracy. One of the best accounts of this "spirit," of the "blue demons" that are the soul of "jazz" is the description of "duende" by the Spanish poet, Federico Garcia Lorca. Lorca agrees that this spirit is not specific to any one time or place, even while he attempts to locate the qualities of its Andalusian variant. It has nothing to do with witchcraft or the "devil" of the Catholic church, he says; it is distinct from both the muse and the angel (even Rilke's angel) and is related to the daemon that Socrates often consulted when he had an important decision to make (when consulted meditatively, it either was silent, or said 'no'). This connection with the Socratic daemon marks a thread of continuity through the apparatuses (oral, literate, electrate).

Comment

- Having outlined the features of mood and atmosphere associated with syncretic music, we now review the connection of this civilizational movement with new media. Everything to do with "cyberspace" we take as an attempt to theorize a rhetoric of imaging.

Readings on Duende, Cyberspace, and Allegory

1. Federico Garcia Lorca, "The Duende"

"Once the Andalusian singer, Pastora Pavon, 'the Girl with the Combs,' a sombre Hispanic genius whose capacity for fantasy equals Goya's or Raphael el Gallo's, was singing in a little tavern in Cadiz. She sparred with her voice—now shadowy, now like molten tin, now covered over with moss; she tangled her voice in her long hair or drenched it in sherry or lost it in the darkest and furthermost bramble bushes. But nothing happened—useless, all of it! The hearers remained silent.

"There stood Ignacio Espeleta, handsome as a Roman turtle, who was asked once why he never worked, and replied with a smile worthy of Argantonio: 'How am I to work if I come from Cadiz?'

"There too stood Heloise, the fiery aristocrat, whore of Seville, direct descendant of Soledad Vargas, who in the thirties refused to marry a Rothschild because he was not of equal blood. Pastora Pavon finished singing in the midst of total silence. There was only a little man, one of those dancing mannikins who leap suddenly out of brandy bottles, who observed sarcastically in a very low voice: 'Viva Paris!' As if to say, 'We are not interested in aptitude or techniques or virtuosity here. We are interested in something else.'

"Then the 'Girl with the Combs' got up like a woman possessed, her face blasted like a medieval weeper, tossed off a great glass of Cazalla at a single draught, like a potion of fire, and settled down to singing—without a voice, without breath, without nuance, throat aflame—but with *duende*! She had contrived to annihilate all that was nonessential in song and make way for an angry and incandescent *Duende*, friend of the sand-laden winds, so that everyone listening tore at his clothing almost in the same rhythm with which the West Indian negroes in their rites rend away their clothes, huddled in heaps before the image of Saint Barbara.

"The 'Girl with the Combs' had to mangle her voice because she knew there were discriminating folk about who asked not for form, but for the marrow of form—pure music spare enough to keep itself in air. She had to deny her faculties and her security; that is to say, to turn out her Muse and keep vulnerable, so that her *Duende* might come and vouchsafe the hand-to-hand struggle. And then how she sang!" (Lorca, 1983: 46).

Comment

- The point to note for now is the experience of emotion in the body described in terms of possession by a god or spirit.

- The great authority on American folk music of all kinds, Alan Lomax, once referred to blues as America's *cante hondo* (Spanish deep song) (Lomax, 1993: 9).

2. Marcos Novak, "Liquid Architectures in Cyberspace"

Keeping in mind that our narrative is an allegory evoking an understanding of electracy, we are prepared now to appreciate the claim made by Marcos Novak in the collection *Cyberspace: First Steps* that the design and navigation of the databases of cyberspace—inhabitable information—must be organized by means of poetic logic that he calls "liquid architecture" and that we have called conduction. His reasoning is based on the principle that the human-computer interface must be designed rather (in our terms) as an "interbody"—that the dualism of mind-body will be abandoned in the new apparatus. Hillis agrees, arguing that the Cartesian mind-body dualism accords primacy to sight and in general hierarchizes the sensorium in a way that "minimizes recognition of synesthesia and the interpolating role of metaphor in human understanding of sensory experiences. The eye-hand coordination that Jonas admits as leading to a higher-order understanding of the world is part of a corporeal intelligence based on an interplay of sensory differences that the Cartesian tradition pulls apart for analysis. This process makes it difficult even to acknowledge corporeal intelligence, for conceptually it has ceased to exist" (Hillis, 1999: 94).

A virtual diegesis must take into account the embodied nature of human intelligence, since in cyberspace many of the constraints of daily life are irrelevant: it is a realm in which the omnipotence of wishes, dreams, desire, fantasy (summed up as magic) may be given free reign. It is not just that the complexity and speed of cyberspace as a technology require a practice based on the speed of human intuition (insight, the flash of spirit), but that a new metaphysical condition of subject formation and identity exist in the new apparatus. "For it is clear that our reality outside cyberspace is the metaphysical plane of cyberspace, that to the body in cyberspace we are the mind, the preexisting soul. By a strange reversal of our cultural expectations, however, it is the body in cyberspace that is immortal, while the animating soul, housed in a body outside cyberspace, faces mortality" (Novak, 1991: 241). We enter cyberspace by becoming image. The dimension of the body that comes with us is not the flesh, but the duende.

He makes this observation in the context of wondering what happens in the event of cyberlove and cybersex. "Friendships and associations of surrogates that only meet in virtual worlds are inevitable and have already been observed in on-line networks as well as in early implementations of consensual worlds. Suppose now that two entities meet in cyberspace and choose to produce offspring. Assuming that behind these two entities are humans who are in a very real sense the 'souls' of these entities, we are now faced with the question of where to find a 'soul' for the offspring. Will this be a friend of the humans in the real world? Will it be an applicant on a waiting list for cyberspace? Will it be an artificial intelligence?" (240). His attraction to Lorca's *duende* as the interface metaphor is due to his understanding that cyberspace is experienced from the point of view of the blue demon. "Lorca's *duende* is therefore not only a poetic description of an attitude toward the construction of cyberspace, it is also a tangible reality in the sense that every entity in cyberspace, and cyberspace itself, is somehow animate" (240).

"The *duende* is a spirit, a demon, invoked to make comprehensible a 'poetic fact.' An 'hecho poetico,' in turn, is a poetic image that is not based on analogy and bears no direct, logical explanation (Lorca). This freeing of language from one-to-one correspondence, and the parallel invocation of a 'demon' that permits access to meanings that are beyond ordinary language permits Lorca to produce some of the most powerful and surprising poetry ever written. It is this power that we need to harness in order to be able to contend with what William Gibson called the 'unimaginable complexity' of cyberspace.

"How does this poetry operate?

"Concepts, like subatomic particles, can be thought to have world lines in space-time. We can draw Feynman diagrams for everything that we can name, tracing the trajectories from our first encounter with an idea to its latest incarnation. In the realm of prose, the world lines of similar concepts are not permitted to overlap, as that would imply that during that time we would be unable to distinguish one concept from another. In poetry, however, as in the realm of quantum mechanics, world lines may overlap, split, divide, blink out of existence, and spontaneously reemerge. Meanings overlap, but in doing so call forth associations inaccessible to prose. Metaphor moves mountains. Visualization reconciles contradictions by a surreal and permissive blending of the disparate and far removed. Everything can modify everything. . . .

"Cyberspace stands to thought as flight stands to crawling. The root of this fascination is the promise of control over the world by the power of the will. In other words, it is the ancient dream of magic that finally nears awakening into some kind of reality. But since it is technology that promises to deliver this dream, the question of 'how' must be confronted. Simply stated, the question is, 'What is the technology of magic?' For the answer we must turn not only to computer science but to the most ancient of arts, perhaps the only art: poetry. It is in poetry that we find a developed understanding of the workings of magic, and not only that, but a wise and powerful knowledge of its purposes and potentials. Cyberspace is poetry inhabited, and to navigate through it is to become a leaf on the wind of a dream. Poetry is liquid language." (228–229)

3. Angus Fletcher on the Allegorical Daemon

"The hero [of allegory] is either a personified abstraction or a representative type, which amounts to much the same thing, and in either case what is felt as a narrowed iconographic meaning is known to us the readers through the hero's characteristic way of acting, which is severely limited in variety. We must return to the allegorical hero's behavior for our answer. We find that he conforms to the type of behavior manifested by people who are thought (however unscientifically) to be possessed by a daemon. This notion may be hard to accept, but only because the present common idea of a daemon is of a wild, unkempt, bestial, monstrous, diabolic creature, whereas ancient myth and religion recognized many mild and beneficent daemons, The *eudaimoniai*. Between the extremely good and the extremely bad daemons there are all the intermediate stages of good and evil, so there is no shortage of patterns for any and all allegorical types, at least on the score of moral or spiritual status.

"Daemons, as I shall define them, share this major characteristic of allegorical agents, the fact that they compartmentalize function. If we were to meet an allegorical character in real life, we would say of him that he was obsessed with only one idea, or that he had an absolutely one-track mind, or that his life was patterned according to absolutely rigid habits from which he never allowed himself to vary. It would seem that he was driven by some hidden, private force; or viewing him from another angle, it would appear that he did not control his own destiny, but appeared to be controlled by some foreign force, something outside the sphere of his own ego.

"Take moral allegory, for example. It is concerned chiefly with virtue, and one might assume that virtues were a sort of habit of good; one might assume that they transcend differences in relative power. Virtue might be conceived without regard to the original sense of *virtus*, meaning 'manliness' or 'power.' If moral allegory is the narrative or dramatic rendition of contests between virtues and vices, however, it will inevitably be a contest between warring powers. By equating daemonic and allegorical agency, I believe we shall be able to explain the relationship between virtue in its Christian sense of 'purity' and in its original pagan sense of 'strength'" (Fletcher, 1964: 39–41).

William Gibson on CyberVoodoo   The relevance of Vodun in particular to the invention of cyberspace is confirmed by the novels of William Gibson, who invented the term "cyberspace" in the prototype of cyberpunk fiction, *Neuromancer*. While working on the next book in what became his trilogy, Gibson read in his doctor's waiting room a *National Geographic* article about Haitian religion. He recognized at once the value of spirit possession as a metaphor for the experience of "jacking-in." What is it like to think with the total knowledge of "the matrix," the Unconscious, the Symbolic order, which is extimate for me? It is like spirit possession.

William Gibson, Count Zero

"'Bobby, do you know what a metaphor is?'

"'A component? Like a capacitor?'

"'No. Never mind metaphor, then. When Beauvoir or I talk to you about the loa and their horses, as we call those few the loa choose to ride, you should pretend that we are talking two languages at once. One of them, you already understand. That's the language of street tech, as you call it. We may be using different words, but we're talking tech. Maybe we call something Ougou Feray that you might call an icebreaker, you understand? But at the same time, with the same words, we are talking about other things, and that you don't understand. You don't need to.' He put his toothpick away.

"Bobby took a deep breath. 'Beauvoir said that Jackie's a horse for a snake, a snake called Danbala. You run that by me in street tech?'

"'Certainly. Think of Jackie as a deck, Bobby, a cyberspace deck, a very pretty one with nice ankles.' Lucas grinned and Bobby blushed. 'Think of Danbala, who some people call the snake, as a program. Say as an icebreaker. Danbala slots into the Jackie deck, Jackie cuts ice. That's all.'

"'Okay,' Bobby said, getting the hang of it, 'then what's the matrix? If she's a deck, and Danbala's a program, what's cyberspace?'

"'The world,' Lucas said.

Comment

- Allegory and the emblem are not "mimetic" or motivated by verisimiltude or a realist aesthetic. They are coherent in relation to the "idea" rather than to lived experience. The guiding effect of the wide image is properly rendered by this force of "destiny" that makes the allegorical heroes' behavior legible.

- For the EmerAgency wide image, poetry is a relay. We may study poetry to see how liquid architecture works, but the goal is conduction (a method of inference for moving through information): electrate reason. The gathering of blues, duende, daemon, allegory, and cyberspace suggests the nature of electrate rhetoric and design. The coherence principle is the "tangle" of felt (hooks and eyes of signifiers). Novak's allusion to the "overlap of the world lines" of concepts is another version of tangle as form.

LECTURE
The Bar as Such

We are in a slow-motion enlargement of the transfer of the magic tool from donor to egent. With Novak's help the donor scene has been traced to the *duende* of the musical performance underway in the background, and this "duende" in turn has been equated with the devices of poetic discourse, proposed as the logic of cyberspace. We could have asserted this trajectory in one sentence but it would not have been persuasive. Media theory allows us to push this series one more step in order to locate the magic tool in its purest form. In popcycle terms, we are aligning actual taverns (represented by the community problem of underage and binge drinking), historical honky tonks (sites of the invention of jazz in all its versions worldwide), entertainment narratives (represented by stories of donors testing heroes), with disciplinary knowledge. The "bar" at issue in all the discourses is defined in theoretical terms as the articulating relationship between signified and signifier, in short, the structure of signification as such (the gram).

Comment

- This lecture demonstrates how the logic of conduction works as inference. Inference is a reasoning procedure carried out in the prosthesis of writing that allows you to move from what you know to what you do not know and would never think of on your own (normally). One of the basic devices of conduction is the pun (puncept) or "choral word" (writing with all the meanings of a word at once). If you are already familiar with the puncept or choral word you will not be surprised, once I began to make a fuss over the bar as saloon or brothel that eventually I would be talking about the bar-as-such, referring to the slash (/) of division that is the operating gesture of articulation, separating and relating signified to signifier in the sign. I could just assert this connection, but this book is not only a textbook but also a theory attempting to demonstrate and prove that the EmerAgency project is not just interesting but *necessary*. If you are willing to take my word for it you may skip this lecture, although it adds some further functionality to imaging.

In Jacques Lacan's structuralizing of Freud's discovery, his assimilation of the logic of dreamwork to the operations of rhetoric (condensation and displacement as metaphor and metonymy), Lacan made it possible to write a matheme or formula in which the unconscious is represented as a bar in an algebraic formula. "The sign—placed between ( ) represents the maintenance of the *bar*—which, in the original formula S/s marked the irreducibility in which, in the relations between signifier and signified, the resistance of signification is constituted" (Lacan, in Lemaire, 194). The symptom is an unconscious metaphor (198). "Bar" as a verb names the operation of repression: "Foreclosure never conserves what it rejects; it purely and simply crosses it out or bars it" (231). This bar marks the split in the subject: "The 'I' of discourse is radically separated from the Other of the subject, the unconscious. As a mediator, language distances the 'I' which speaks and believes itself to be telling the truth about its essence from the unconscious reality which founds it in its truth" (215). It is this unconscious condition that produces the effect of the gaze, and which is made accessible to manipulation through the prosthesis of cyberspace.

A happy feature of English is this naming of the subject with the "pipe," the upright bar of the letter "I." It is not "me" but the signifying slash who writes. This gap between truth and knowledge may not be closed or filled (a condition that constitutes the fundamental aporia of knowledge), although it may be jumped. At the same time, the Gap of all gaps makes possible what it prevents: the inferential orientation directs me, albeit asymptotically, toward learning. The split subject, my stupidity, creates the gaps negotiated by the logic of sense whose proof is surprise. Surprise is inevitable and irreducible because I am not omniscient. This surprise is a spark, the flash of spirit, the shock required to awaken thought to the possibility of invention. The uncanny is one form of access to this surprise. The blue note is the sound of the bar. The internet as a technology and institution is the built form of this gap; cyberspace is the prosthesis of the gram.

Whatever

The theorist Giorgio Agamben helps transfer Novak's insight to the problem of the spectacle. In the spectacle we do not encounter "The Girl with the Combs," but her animated image. Agamben uses an example of a TV advertisement to focus the entire question of what he calls "the coming community" (the title of his most important book), or what we are calling "electracy" (the new apparatus). His example and its theoretical framing will allow us to finalize our *antidefinition* of the EmerAgency project and the wide image.

Agamben, "Dim Stockings"

"In the early 1970s there was an advertisement shown in Paris movie theaters that promoted a well-known brand of French stockings, 'Dim' stockings. It showed a group of young women dancing together. Anyone who watched even a few of its images, however distractedly, would have a hard time forgetting the special impression of synchrony and dissonance, of confusion and singularity, of communication and estrangement that emanated from the bodies of the smiling dancers. This impression relied on a trick: each dancer was filmed separately and later the single pieces were brought together over a single sound track. But that facile trick, that calculated asymmetry of the movement of long legs sheathed in the same inexpensive commodity, that slight disjunction between the gestures, wafted over the audience a promise of happiness unequivocally related to the human body.

"In the 1920s when the process of capitalist commodification began to invest the human body, observers who were by no means favorable to the phenomenon could not help but notice a positive aspect to it, as if they were confronted with the corrupt text of a prophecy that went beyond the limits of the capitalist mode of production and were faced with the task of deciphering it. This is what gave rise to Siegfried Kracauer's observations on the 'girls' and Walter Benjamin's reflections on the decay of the aura.

"The commodification of the human body, while subjecting it to the iron laws of massification and exchange value, seemed at the same time to redeem the body from the stigma of ineffability that had marked it for millennia. Breaking away from the double chains of biological destiny and individual biography, it took its leave of both the inarticulate cry of the tragic body and the dumb silence of the comic body, and thus appeared for the first time perfectly communicable, entirely illuminated. The epochal process of the emancipation of the human body from its theological foundations was thus accomplished in the dances of the 'girls,' in the advertising images, and in the gait of fashion models. This process had already been imposed at an industrial level when, at the beginning of the nineteenth century, the invention of lithography and photography encouraged the inexpensive distribution of pornographic images: Neither generic nor individual, neither an image of the divinity nor an animal form, the body now became something truly *whatever*. . . .

"The task of the portrait is grasping a unicity, but to grasp a whateverness one needs a photographic lens. In a certain sense, the process of emancipation is as old as the invention of the arts. From the instant that a hand drew or sculpted the human figure for the first time, Pygmalion's dream was already there to guide it: to form not simply an image of the loved body, but another body in that image, shattering the organic barrier that obstructs the unconditioned human claim to happiness. . . .

"Today, in the age of the complete domination of the commodity form over all aspects of social life, what remains of the subdued, senseless promise of happiness that we received in the darkness of movie theaters from dancers sheathed in Dim stockings? Never has the human body—above all the female body—been so massively manipulated as today and, so to speak, imagined from top to bottom by the techniques of advertising and commodity production: the opacity of sexual differences has been belied by the transsexual body; the incommunicable foreignness of the singular *physis* has been abolished by its mediatization as spectacle; the mortality of the organic body has been put in question by its traffic with the body without organs of commodities; the intimacy of erotic life has been refuted by pornography. And yet the process of technologization, instead of materially investing the body, was aimed at the construction of a separate sphere that had practically no point of contact with it: What was technologized was not the body, but its image. Thus the glorious body of advertising has become the mask behind which the fragile, slight human body continues its precarious existence, and the geometrical splendor of the 'girls' covers over the long lines of the naked, anonymous bodies led to their death in the *Lagers* (camps), or the thousands of corpses mangled in the daily slaughter on the highways.

"To appropriate the historic transformations of human nature that capitalism wants to limit to the spectacle, to link together image and body in a space where they can no longer be separated, and thus to forge the *whatever* body, whose *physis* is resemblance—this is the good that humanity must learn how to wrest from commodities in their decline. Advertising and pornography, which escort the commodity to the grave like hired mourners, are the unknowing midwives of this new body of humanity" (Agamben, 1993: 47–50).

Comment

Punctum (Sting)

- The first point to establish is that Agamben's use of the term "whatever" throughout *The Coming Community* (CC) is an extension and augmentation of Roland Barthes's discovery of the third or obtuse meaning in the photographic image, experienced as a "sting" that triggered memories of personal experience, thus creating a relationship between the artificial memory of the photograph and the living memory of the individual. Agamben extends the obtuse effect, understood as specific and native to the photographic image ("to grasp a whateverness requires a photographic lens") from memory to "happiness," which stands in for "state of mind" or attunement in our context. The human experience that Agamben associates with the obtuse is "desire," ultimately "love" (thus alluding to another of Barthes's works, *A Lover's Discourse: Fragments*). That aspect of the photograph that affects and supports human "state of mind" (whether happiness of some other state of mind) Agamben names "whatever." The wide image has this whatever power to put its maker into the state of mind that constitutes his or her themata.

Thing

- In terms of the apparatus, whatever is the name Agamben gives to the categorical operation of images, to distinguish the classifying capacities of new media from those of literacy. At the beginning of our project we noted that the Classical Greeks invented the category of "thing" as the classification practice native to alphabetic writing. "Things" are created through the method of "definition," the craft of deciding which "features," or "properties" or "attributes" of an entity constitutes its "substance," its "essence" or true nature. All other properties (and the number of namable features is potentially infinite) are considered to be "accidental" (their presence or absence does not affect the substance of the thing). Barthes's use of haiku poetry as an analogy for the obtuse dimension of the photograph shifted away from essential to accidental properties (the rust on the nail, the crow in winter) to account for the capacity of the image to support state of mind (*wabi-sabi*). Now Agamben pushes this trajectory further by insisting that whatever may not be understood in terms of properties. Or rather, the properties of an entity are used not to establish an abstraction (a concept), but a singularity: not the category that an entity belongs to, but its being-such.

The difficulty Agamben has then in theorizing this dimension of the photographic image is that since it is electrate, or falls outside the reach of conceptual definition, it is useless to define it. His strategy is to call upon the imaging power of language to make whatever intelligible in an obtuse or indirect way. He begins by turning to an obsolete philosophy, medieval Scholasticism, to find a name for the electrate category. "The coming being is whatever being. In the Scholastic enumeration of transcendentals (*quodlibet ens est unum, verum, bonum seu perfectum*—whatever entity is one, true, good, or perfect), the term that, remaining unthought in each, conditions the meaning of all the others is the adjective *quodlibet*. The common translation of this term as 'whatever' in the sense of 'it does not matter which, indifferently" is certainly correct, but in its form the Latin says exactly the opposite: *Quodlibet ens* is not 'being, it does not matter which,' but rather 'being such that it always matters.' The Latin always already contains, that is, a reference to the will (*libet*). Whatever being has an original relation to desire" (1).

Theological discourse is rich with examples of attempts to articulate the peculiar nature of the spiritual, of God, and Agamben appropriates a number of these religious accounts for the secular purpose of rendering intelligible the new dimension of order coming into practice within the electrate image. The theological notions of spiritual place or space that Agamben transfers to image space include "Limbo," "Demonic," "Halos," "Gehenna," "Shekinah." The 19 numbered sections of CC develop analogies from other discourses as well: "Ease" from Provençal poetry, "Manner" from logic, "Homonym" from linguistics, "Tiananmen Square" from politics, "Chora" from philosophy.

Chora Stanza

Elsewhere Agamben developed in more detail the relationship of whatever to chora, in a way that integrates all the terms we have been tracing. In relation to electracy and cyberspace it is important to emphasize that whatever is a new kind of space. All 19 items put forward as analogies develop a notion of a peculiar spatiality that accompanies the image and that is the place of mediation between the inside and outside worlds of experience. It is an "adjacent" place. "According to the Talmud, two places are reserved for each person, one in Eden and the other in Gehenna. The just person, after being found innocent, receives a place in Eden plus that of a neighbor who was damned" (23). "One can think of the halo as a zone in which possibility and reality, potentiality and actuality, become indistinguishable" (56).

In *Stanzas*, Agamben relate all such topologies to Plato's notion of chora, the third kind in his cosmology whose purpose was to mediate the relationship between being and becoming (existence). Both *whatever* and *stanza* name the dimension of reality that humanity creates within language (or we might say "discourse," to clarify that it involves all media and modes), related to Novak's designation of cyberspace as an attempt to technologize the *duende* effect of "poetic" making. "From this vantage one can speak of a topology of the unreal," Agamben says. "Perhaps the *topos*, for Aristotle 'so difficult to grasp' but whose power is 'marvelous and prior to all others' and which Plato, in the *Sophist,* conceives as a third 'genre' of being, is not necessarily something 'real.' In this sense we can take seriously the question that Aristotle puts in the fourth book of the *Physics:* 'Where is the capristag, where the sphinx?'" (Agamben, 1993a: xviii). Agamben proposes a kind of Rosetta Stone capable of tracking this spirit (which he equates with love) across all apparatuses, in his outline of correspondences among the sphinx, the fetish, and the emblem. All three are incarnations of whatever, or chora, which are in turn theories that account for the bar of articulation, of language, as such.

Thus the riddles of the sphinx, the emblem arts of the Renaissance (based on a misunderstanding of Egyptian hieroglyphic writing), and psychoanalytic descriptions of "fetish," all provide relays for chorography (and conduction). Freud, of course, used the story of Oedipus as a theoretical parable to explain his new science, and, as Agamben says, Freud's description of the "language of the unconscious" amounts to a reassignment of the emblem tradition to the category of psyche. All these practices Agamben categorized as "apotropaic" (working by indirection, obtuse). "The human is precisely this fracture of presence, which opens a world and over which language holds itself. The algorithm S/s must therefore reduce itself to simply the barrier (/) but in this barrier we should not see merely the trace of a difference, but the topological game of putting things together and articulating (*synapseis*), whose model we have attempted to delineate in the apotropaic *ainos* of the Sphinx, in the melancholic profundity of the emblem, in the *Verleugnung* of the fetishist" (156).

Agamben: "Oedipus and the Sphinx"

"In modern semiology, the forgetting of the original fracture of presence is manifested precisely in what ought to betray it, that is, in the bar (/) of the graphic S/s. That the meaning of this bar or barrier is constantly left in shadow, thus hiding the abyss opened between signifier and signified, constitutes the foundation of that 'primordial positing of the signified and the signifier as two orders distinguished and separated by a barrier resisting signification,' a position that has governed Western reflection on the sign from the outset, like a hidden overlord. From the point of view of signification, metaphysics is nothing but the forgetting of the originary difference between signifier and signified. Every semiology that fails to ask why the barrier that establishes the possibility of signifying should itself be resistant to signification falsifies, with that omission, its own most authentic intention. . . .

"The origin of this dissimulation—effected by the expressive unity of signifier and signified—of the fracture of presence was prefigured by the Greeks in a mythologeme that has always held a particular fascination for our culture. In the psychoanalytical interpretation of the myth of Oedipus, the episode of the Sphinx, although, necessarily of essential importance for the Greeks, remains obstinately in the shadows; but it is precisely this aspect of the life of the hero that must here be put in the foreground. The son of Laius resolves in the simplest way 'the enigma proposed by the ferocious jaws of the virgin,' showing the hidden meaning behind the enigmatic signifier, and with this act alone plunges the half-human, half-feral monster into the abyss. . . .

"What the Sphinx proposed was not simply something whose signified is hidden and veiled under an 'enigmatic' signifier, but a mode of speech in which the original fracture of presence was alluded to in the paradox of a word that approaches its object while keeping it indefinitely at a distance. The *ainos* (story, fable) of the *ainigma* is not only obscurity, but a more original mode of speaking. Like the labyrinth, like the Gorgon, and like the Sphinx that utters it, the enigma belongs to the sphere of the apotropaic, that is, to a protective power that repels the uncanny by attracting it and assuming it within itself. The dancing path of the labyrinth, which leads into the heart of that which is held at a distance, is the model of this relation with the uncanny that is expressed in the enigma" (137–138).

Comment

- Putting this apotropaic protection into the design of the widesite is intended to build into this externalization of your creative heart the feeling of trust or safety needed before the risks of invention may be ventured.

- Part of Agamben's importance for us is his placement of the Sphinx in relation to an historical sequence passing through the Baroque emblem and the modern fetish. Since other scholars have associated the Sphinx with the complex donor figure of archetypal narrative, we are able to integrate into one scene of consultation most if not all of the ideas and practices circulating in our project. We may infer, for example, that the appropriate form in which to represent the magic tool/wide image is the emblem. *Eureka.* As an egent you will not be authoring statistical studies or empirical reports, but offering enigmatic emblems as testimony. The force of these emblems is in the collective state of mind they produce, augmented through connectionist technology.

The Task

The plague that afflicts Thebes when Oedipus arrives at the place of the Sphinx is a relay for the problems and policy issues that consultants are invited to address by their communities. When conventional consultants arrive at "Thebes," they are not even aware that there is a sphinx, let alone that it poses to them a riddle. The EmerAgency supplements the conventional instrumental response to these demands within the state of mind of jazz blues. When the blue demons begin to swarm, Albert Murray states, we are in the position of the hero of *Oedipus Rex,* 'which begins with a chorus of suppliants lamenting a curse that hangs over the city-state of Thebes and beseeching the hero/king to seek out and dispatch the menace and restore good times. As in the Wasteland episode in the medieval romance of the quest in which the knight-errant comes into a region whose inhabitants are suffering under a blight because their ruler, known as the Fisher-King, is apparently bewitched and his impotence extends not only to the housewives but also to the cattle, the fields, and even the streams. As in Shakespeare's *Hamlet,* in which the young prince is charged by the ghost of his late father to rid the kingdom of Denmark of the evil forces that dominate it. Also always absolutely inseparable from all such predicaments and requirement is the most fundamental of all existential imperatives: affirmation, which is to say, reaffirmation and continuity in the face of adversity" (Murray, 5–6).

Blues music is an antidote to the conditions that cause depression and despair. "The blues counteragent that is so much a part of many people's equipment for living that they hardly ever think about it as such is that artful and sometimes seemingly magical combination of idiomatic incantation and percussion that creates the dance-oriented good-time music also known as the blues. . . . Hence in consequence the fundamental function of the blues musician (also known as the jazz musician) the most obvious as well as the most pragmatic mission of whose performance is not only to drive the blues away and hold them at bay at least for the time being but also to evoke an ambiance of Dionysian revelry in the process" (16–17).

Agamben has another version of this response to the call of disaster and problem. In it we see his own metaphysics and ethics (his view of how things are, and what action we should take). "The Irreparable is that things are just as they are, in this or that mode, consigned without remedy to their way of being. States of things are irreparable, whatever they may be: sad or happy, atrocious or blessed. How you are, how the world is—this is the Irreparable. . . . The root of all pure joy and sadness is that the world is as it is. Joy or sadness that arises because the world is not what it seems or what we want it to be is impure or provisional. But in the highest degree of their purity, in the *so be it* said to the world when every legitimate cause of doubt and hope has been removed, sadness and joy refer not to negative or positive qualities, but to a pure being—thus without any attributes" (Agamben, 1993: 90, 91). From this stance Agamben gives us an assignment that is a task, a test, and an enigma (an aporia or dilemma to which we shall return in the Conclusion).

Agamben's Test (If We Wish to Accept it)

"The fact is that the senselessness of their existence runs up against a final absurdity, against which all advertising runs aground; death itself. In death the petty bourgeois confront the ultimate expropriation, the ultimate frustration of individuality: life in all its nakedness, the pure in-communicable, where their shame can finally rest in peace. Thus they use death to cover the secret that they must resign themselves to ac-knowledging: that even life in its nakedness is, in truth, improper and purely exterior to them, that for them there is no shelter on earth.

"This means that the planetary petty bourgeoisie is probably the form in which humanity is moving toward its own destruction. But this also means that the petty bourgeoisie represents an opportunity un-heard of in the history of humanity that it must at all cost not let slip away. Because if instead of continuing to search for a proper identity in the already improper and senseless form of individuality, humans were to succeed in belonging to this impropriety as such, in making of the proper being-thus not an identity and an individual property but a sin-gularity without identity, a common and absolutely exposed singularity—if humans could, that is not be-thus, in this or that particular biography, but be only the thus, their singular exteriority and their face, then they would for the first time enter into a community without presuppositions and without subjects, into a communication without the incomunicable.

"Selecting in the new planetary humanity those characteristics that allow for its survival, removing the thin diaphragm that separates bad mediatized advertising from the perfect exteriority that communicates only itself—this is the political task of our generation" (64–65).

Exercise: Being Singular

Try to sort out your experience and behavior along the lines of the predominant mode asso-ciated with each apparatus, to notice group feelings (oral), individuality (an inner private self, "character"), and what Agamben calls "singularity" (behaving as an image?).

- To demystify Agamben's language, just recall the discussion of the definition and the antidefinition in the first part of the book. In the context of electra-cy it is possible to see that Agamben is asking us not to think about "humans" or "the human" in terms of concepts—categories based on properties that determine the essence of a thing. At the same time he warns about the com-ing categories of imaging (the coming community of the new apparatus). He is anticipating the mutation in identity (subject formation) that is part of the apparatus shift. He proposes that a person who becomes image experi-ences identity not as "individual" but "singularity."

OFFICE

1. What happened to the consultation on policies relating to binge drinking? We never concluded anything in this respect, but the exercise gives some practice with consulting

on a policy issue and public problem relevant to the college community. We used the issue for now just to show the grounding of the wide image in quotidian experience. The historical review of syncretism underway through music provides a context for what is going on in the alliance between Street and Entertainment. A practical implication is that the new behaviors associated with "teen spirit" and the like are not a breakdown of morality or the decline and fall of the West, as some might have it, but a symptom of apparatus shift. There is a transformation of values, but the direction is not "down" but "elsewhere."

2. Part of the point is to notice the cognitive map that situates us and our behavior, beliefs, values, within the mythology and history of the community. The dissociation and isolation of the different discourse institutions in the literate apparatus changes in electracy in which we begin to experience ourselves as images. The exercise is meant to stimulate thinking about the interface(body) between your daily life and mythology, to notice how behavior includes several invisible dimensions. The binge drinker is not "thirsty," but is performing his/her image of a certain mood, to be discussed in the next section.

3. An extra difficulty for young people is that, unlike oral civilization, we do not admit that there are rites of passage still enforced. The sacred is now personal more than collective (despite the popularity of attending church). The connection between the wide image and the consultancy is the slogan "Problems B Us." What experience have you had with rites of passage? Where are these passages located in our society? A metaphor might be white water rafting: where is the white water (the rapids) in your social and psychological experience?

4. This remake pushes our project narrative to a point of revelation, a point of passage from one apparatus to another. The motif of the gap or interval that we have worked with in a variety of ways is revealed now as the most fundamental dimension of language as such, in itself: the bar (barre) of articulation. When the bar is written by itself (/) as Agamben writes it, without the S (signifier) and s (signified), it may be called the "gram" (of grammatology). The barroom scene of narrative structure provides through allegory the nuance and complexity of the power available through this magic tool (writing). It also helps remind us of the cognitive map: the barre operates at every dimension and plateau of existence and being: it articulates mentality, society, cosmology. The whatever is Agamben's name for this alignment between you and your world through the gap of language. Within the frame of entertainment as allegory, the light sabers in *Star Wars* allude to this bar or gram.

5. The chapters of this book have a narrative structure supporting an argument. The assumption is that the narrative allegory and the theoretical argument supplement one another: sometimes you will understand one mode more than another, and each may be used to help interpret the other. Still, the intellectual grasp of the rationale for the project is likely to be incomplete. No matter, since the success of the project depends less on understanding and more on performance: the proof is in the practice of making the widesite and the learning that this entails, especially at the level of emotional experience in taking responsibility for the self-portrait and the cognitive map. Thus Agamben's test remains partly a riddle, whose answer will come through the performance of the final phase of the project. We have to take Agamben's assessment personally. He is talking about us, you and me, when he addresses the planetary bourgeoisie.

6. By the end of Part Four you have completed all four registers of the mystory: you have selected details, expressed in words and graphics, to document what you recognize in the discourses of Career, Family, Entertainment, and Community. Each installment was made independently, although as soon as a pattern begins to emerge it is good to take it into account in making decisions about what to include or exclude. The point to keep in mind is that the mystory is an autocommunication, addressed first to yourself, as a self-portrait. The next step is to juxtapose all four tracks (parts of your website) and make links between any signifiers that repeat. This is the first step to designing the wide image, remembering that the wide image is not a thing, but a mood. Einstein's compass memory was not the cause of his theory of relativity, but a sampling of his wide image at the age of four, in Family; relativity was a sampling in his early twenties, in Career.

7. I will give one example of the pattern I found at this stage, the first time I tried the mystory. The puncept "gall" repeated through the four levels, associated with the four figures of my superego or internal Mount Rushmore. To find these figures I first wrote or cited anecdotes showing my place in each popcycle institution. This produced the following figures: Family—my father (died of gall bladder cancer); Community— George Armstrong Custer, died at the Little Bighorn in a counterattack led by Chief Gall (along with Crazy Horse and one other warrior); Entertainment—Gary Cooper, whose acting style was described by some critics as "cheeky" (cheek = gall); Career— Jacques Derrida, French (Gallic) philosopher (modern France = ancient Gaul). The puncept is: gall bladder; Chief Gall; cheeky gall; Gaul. This pattern does not "mean" anything, but it orients me in a certain way. My next step was to research the pattern, to find out what semantic possibilities might be stored in it. The early results are recorded in *Teletheory* (Ulmer, 1989).

8. Music dictionaries define "quodilibet" (whatever) as a humerous type of music characterized by the quotation of well-known melodies or texts combined in an incongruous manner—a kind of musical collage-montage. Agamben's *Coming Community* is a textual quodlibet.

Part V
EMBLEMS OF WIDE SCOPE

HAPPINESS–Ulmer (seated, on the right) with friends, near Madrid, Spain, 1965.

"The question of the happiness promised through the whatever of the image."

Chapter 9
Emblem

7—The inmost cave/the second threshold: the subject comes to a dangerous place (mythically the land of the dead). 8—The supreme ordeal: at this
step the subject must seem to die so that he can be born anew. 9—Seizing
the sword: the subject takes the prize (the object of the search).

STUDIO
The Second Threshold

In terms of the narrative path guiding our quest for the wide image, a great deal
happens at this stage of the project. The raw material of the mystory provides the
makings of the magic tool that is the immediate "object of the search" (the wide
image). Once we put the mystory into a form, to make it legible and trans-
portable, we will be in a position to consult for the EmerAgency (to perform as
Sender/Donor). In this chapter we return to the template of haiku reason, derived from the *wabi-sabi* mood, to fill in the blanks for ourselves (the wide image
is to its maker what *wabi-sabi* is to Japan).

Assignment: The Wide Emblem

Design an emblem that evokes the look and feel of your mystory.

- The method of asking you to do something before you know how to do it
  continues in this assignment. Posing the assignment at the beginning of the
  chapter provides a practical motive for working through the readings, relays,
  and arguments. You want to know what an emblem is, and how to make one.
  The rule of extrapolation applies: Everything that is said about the emblem
  is there as a relay for your own composition/design. You should always ask:
  What is that for me?

- In some cases other popcycle institutions may be important to a mystory,
  such as Church or Street. In the case of Church, there may be a coexis-
  tence or conflict with Entertainment, depending on the tenets of the religion involved. Most people have some experience of Street, which tends
  to conflict with Family and School, while it is in (reluctant) alliance with
  Entertainment.

- Keep in mind Agamben's observation of the equivalence among the emblem, the fetish, and the Sphinx's apotropaic discourse (a poetics of indirection and defense). The function of the fetish in oral civilizations is protection, safety, security. The widesite in electracy performs this function in its own way, as a virtual "potential space" that augments the basic trust or ontological security needed in order to be creative. The ability to read and write this space digitally has the potential to do for the emotional body what the ability to write concepts did for analytical reason.

- At the same time, remember Agamben's point that this sphinx or fetish quality of the emblem is not merely a disguise but is an irreducible quality native to imaging. He is not saying that images are not intelligible or legible, but just that they mean in an obtuse way different from and resistant to conceptual naming.

- This emblem is a version of your wide image. It should evoke the mood of your "themata." Remember that this project to find the wide image is an experiment. The design of the emblem leaves considerable room for choice and judgment in working with what the mystory gives you. The mystory documents were selected largely through the sting of memory. Putting these details into a form is a more calculated formal or aesthetic procedure.

That the quest for the wide image and the initial task for the EmerAgency are conducted simultaneously is due to the fact that the image must be sorted out or winnowed from the collective moods and themes circulating through the popcycle. "The Althusserian concept of interpellation of the subject by ideology and/or language," Jean-Jacques Lecercle points out, "is aptly expressed by a conception of the shaping power of ideology and of meaning (the subject's meaning) as the object of a Freudian compromise between the speaker's expressive needs and the mastery of ideology/language in the shape of ready-made discourse, cliche and polemical positions" (Lecercle, 1990: 228). The "miracle" of language is that it is an "open system," such that it is possible to "say" something original and still be understood (the interdependence of tradition and creativity).

In our context interpellation may be understood as the provisional acceptance of the default or ready-made images and themes of the popcycle. When one "enters a language" (is hailed, interpellated) one takes up a place assigned in advance by that discourse (language promises/speaks me). Lecercle proposes that the operation of this default positioning may be experienced in miniature in reading a novel: when reading, "we are not only hailed by a striking new voice, but given a modicum of background information and asked to share a mood" (249). The task of finding the wide image is both easier and harder than it might seem: easier because it turns out that mood or state of mind is not something alien to us but is an inherent part of our experience as socialized individuals; harder because the default mood has been internalized as our very own personal state of mind.

We will undertake the winnowing process, sorting out defaults from signatures, by improvising on another media "gem." Since Agamben recognized a promise of happiness in an ad, it is useful to try to replicate the insight in our own case.

Exercise: Patterning

Review the documentation recorded in the previous assignments and make links connecting any signifiers that repeat between any two (or more) registers.

- The mystory entangles the four documentations of the popcycle discourses generated in the previous chapters: Career, Family, Entertainment, History (Community/School). The pattern created by the repetition of details or signifiers across some or all of the discourses expresses a *simulation* of the wide image, one that you will want to revise and track as your career develops. What your actual wide image will have been cannot be determined until the end of your career, as expressed in the pattern of lived events and works, whatever they might be.

Advertising Emblems

The mystory has no innate form of its own. The wide image itself (or themselves) is an embodiment of themes or "themata" (abstract orientations) that we propose to locate through mood. We are evoking it as an emblem because of the connection of that form with allegory. A Renaissance scholar has demonstrated the continuity between the emblem tradition of the sixteenth and seventeenth centuries and modern advertising (Daly, 1988: 350), which is important since advertising, working within the institution of Entertainment, is a principal site of the invention of electracy. This connection helps focus the task or test assigned by Agamben: To remove "the thin diaphragm that separates bad mediatized advertising from the perfect exteriority that communicates only itself."

Peter Daly on the Emblem Form

"The emblem is, properly speaking, a mixed form comprising a motto, a picture and an epigram. The motto introduces the emblem and usually indicates the theme, which is embodied symbolically in the picture that depicts one or more objects, persons, or events. Beneath the picture is printed an epigram or short prose statement that interprets the picture and elucidates the theme. Alciato's emblem is a typical example. The emblem begins with an abstract statement in the motto 'Fortuna virtutem superans' [Fortune overcoming virtue]. The picture shows Brutus about to fall on his sword. The epigram relates briefly that Brutus had been overcome by Octavian's forces, and that he had seen the river Pharsalia flowing with the blood of his fellow citizens. There upon he committed suicide. The significance of the action is summarized in Brutus's own words, lamenting that Virtue follows Fortuna, i.e. fortune and not virtue rules the world.

"The Brutus emblem is characteristic of the genre in so far as a general message or moral is enunciated in the motto, embodied in the picture through the particular fate of Brutus, which in turn is elucidated in the epigram.

"The function of the emblem is didactic in the broadest sense: it was intended to convey knowledge and truth in a brief and compelling form that will persuade the reader and impress itself upon memory. In this process the choice of picture symbol is essential, since it encapsulates visually the meaning of the emblem. . . . Not unlike the Renaissance emblem, modern advertising is an exercise in communication and persuasion, and like the emblem much symbolic advertising may be considered a form of exemplary discourse" (350).

Daly goes on to explain the effect of the emblem as that of creating an enigma in the relation between the motto and the picture, which is then resolved by the epigram (351). The epigram, which could be in either prose or verse, often quoted learned sources. The success of the emblem or ad depends upon the use of codes shared by the audience. E. D. Hirsch called these shared codes "cultural literacy"—a superficial knowledge of an encyclopedia of information which, he said, it was the job of the public schools to teach. Emblems assumed a knowledge of the classical tradition, for example, including an awareness of the "stock images" selected from the tradition and fixed into iconic poses and gestures. The historical literary stories are miniaturized in the emblem into one pose that expresses the fundamental significance, and atmosphere, of the narrative.

The audience had to be familiar with this context associating certain figures with specific virtues or values in order to read the emblem. "Such figures stand paradigmatically for abstract notions: Ulysses for prudence, Brutus for virtue vanquished, and David for the healing power of music. In every case the emblem writer refers to a personage well known to his readers, who are persuaded by the argument of exemplary instance. The emblem seeks to persuade by referring to symbolic figures who are beyond doubt and question" (358). Advertisers similarly use "famous contemporary personages who endorse a range of products and services," with the assignment of celebrities or other icons to products carefully restricted according to "appropriateness," to maintain credibility (359).

How to Compose an Emblem   During the Baroque Era it was fashionable to treat emblematics as a game to be played by any literate person. One author provided basic instructions for a "conversation-game of emblems."

1. by naming a thing as the basis for an emblem;
2. by choosing a picture and inventing a motto;
3. by choosing a motto and inventing a picture;

4. by illustrating chapters of the Bible;

5. by going through nature and making emblems

6. by choosing suitable sayings from the poets as mottoes.

"Among the many mottoes discussed by the conversation group is the following: 'A Happy end to the Misery of War.' Various pictures are suggested to embody this motto: a dove with an olive branch flying over a calm sea; a garden in which the 'Eisenkraut' (literally, 'iron plant') has withered and a central 'Friedelar' (from the root 'Friede,' meaning 'peace') flourishes; the temple of peace at Rome, a hieroglyphic combination of a crown hovering in the air above a flourishing olive tree at the base of which are scattered broken weapons of war. Thus motifs from classical and biblical tradition, nature lore, and simple metonymic symbols provide the graphic details in these *picturae*" (Daly, 1998: 96).

Daly notes that the complete word emblem contains both a pictorial and an interpretive element. "The simplest forms of emblems are compound nouns and genitive noun constructions," such as this example from the poetry of Greiffenberg: "that my rock of faith were a clear stream of joy" (113). This basic X + Y combination was usually contracted (leaving the interpretation implicit), extended, and made complex (by including multiple motifs), as in Southwell's "The Burning Babe":

> "*My faultlesse breast thy furnace is,*
>   *The fuell wounding thornes:*
> *Love is the fire, and sighs the smoake,*
>   *The ashes, shame and scornes;*
>
> *The fewale Justice layeth on,*
>   *And Mercie blowes the coales,*
> *The metall in this furnace wrought,*
>   *Are mens defiled soules"*
> *(118).*

The emblem is a specific device used within the allegorical mode. In the Baroque Era the compositions were guided by the religious worldview of the time, or by the anagogical level in terms of the allegory form. As Walter Benjamin pointed out in his study of Baroque drama, the modernist image secularizes the mode. The appropriation of allegory in mystory, as we have seen, replaces the traditional religious cosmology with the "personal sacred." The mystorian may not construct the emblem in the same way as the allegorist, who knows the moral in advance, has the concept anagogically provided in advance for which a suitable image must be found. The mystory inverts this process, beginning with the mapping of the popcycle, locating a repeating pattern across the discourses, and isolating the signifiers found in this pattern. The emblem then is composed by means of these signifiers, in order to discover the metaphysics and morality they evoke. Formally or compositionally, however, the allegorical and mystorical emblems are similar.

Mark Turner on the Word Emblem

"As an example of how grammar gives us guidance in space building, space blending, and projection of generic spaces, consider the *xyz* construction, whose syntax is deceptively simple:

NounPhrase(x) be NounPhrase(y) of NounPhrase(z)

as in *Vanity is the quicksand of reason.* This simple syntax has a complex semantic and pragmatic interpretation: Construct a set of spaces and projections with the result that x in a target is the counterpart of y in a source, and z in that target is the counterpart of an unmentioned fourth element w in that source. In 'Vanity is the quicksand of reason,' w is the traveler who travels toward a goal. As quicksand stops the traveler, vanity stops reason. The grammatical information is minimal and highly abstract—find a mapping and a missing element. The rest is left to the cognitive competence of the user, who must construct an implicit generic space and an implicit blend, in which a single element is simultaneously reason and a traveler" (Turner, 1996: 104–105).

Comment

- This form is easy to parody, as in this example by the columnist George Will. "In life, as in baseball, we must leave the dugout of complacency, step up to the home plate of opportunity, adjust the protective groin cup of caution and swing the bat of hope at the curve ball of fate, hoping that we can hit a line drive of success past the shortstop of misfortune, then sprint down the basepath of chance, knowing that at any moment we may pull the hamstring muscle of inadequacy and fall face first onto the field of failure, where the chinch bugs of broken dreams will crawl into our nose." I wish he had said, "our nose of remorse."

The Readymade

The emblem form stripped of both its theological and commercial anagogies (cosmologies, rationales) is practiced as pure language in the vanguard arts in a way that reveals and codifies its formal properties.

Marcel Duchamp, "Apropos of 'Readymades'"

"In 1913 I had the happy idea to fasten a bicycle wheel to a kitchen stool, and watch it turn.

"A few months later I bought a cheap reproduction of a winter evening landscape, which I called 'Pharmacy' after adding two small dots, one red and one yellow, in the horizon.

"In New York in 1915 I bought at a hardware store a snow shovel, on which I wrote 'In Advance of the Broken Arm.'

"It was around that time that the word 'readymade' came to mind to designate this form of manifestation.

"A point which I want very much to establish is that the choice of these 'readymades' was never dictated by esthetic delectation.

"This choice was based on a reaction of visual indifference with at the same time a total absence of good or bad taste . . . In fact a complete anesthesia.

"One important characteristic was the short sentence which I occasionally inscribed on the 'readymade.'

"That sentence instead of describing the object like a title was meant to carry the mind of the spectator towards other regions more verbal.

"Sometimes I would add a graphic detail of presentation which in order to satisfy my craving for alliteration, would be called 'readymade aided.'

"At another time wanting to expose the basic antinomy between art and readymades I imagined a 'reciprocal readymade': use a Rembrandt as an ironing board!

"I realized very soon the danger of repeating indiscriminately this form of expression and decided to limit the production of 'readymades' to a small number yearly. I was aware at that time that for the spectator even more than for the artist art is a habit forming drug and I wanted to protect my 'readymades' against such contamination.

"Another aspect of the 'readymade' is its lack of uniqueness . . . The replica of a 'readymade' delivering the same message; in fact nearly every one of the 'readymades' existing today is not an original in the conventional sense.

"A final remark to this egomaniac's discourse.

"Since the tubes of paint used by the artist are manufactured and readymade products we must conclude that all the paintings in the world are 'readymades aided' and also works of assemblage" (Duchamp, 1973: 141–142).

Comment

- The readymade is the prototype of all procedures of "appropriation," in which an object, image, text, is selected, decontextualized, recontextualized in combination with other selections, to form an assemblage. The Pop Art mode, such as the silk-screened portraits of movie stars and other celebrities made by Andy Warhol, continues this procedure, while making explicit that the readymade is a generalization of the photographic principle, a hybrid of photography and writing. In electracy it is possible to write not only with recordings of the spoken word (the alphabet) but with recordings of the look and actions of the whole human body (including the interaction of the body with the world). Conduction is a logic for authoring with readymades.

Example: How to Make an Interval

Martin Kippenberger, "Rameau's Nephew"

"It is a cardboard box used by movers to transport books; legibly inscribed upon it are the name and address of the ROGGENDORF movers. The top is open and the flaps are casually held up by the moving company's tape which adds height to the box. The walls and bottom of the interior are lined with orange and white checked wallpaper that has the motif of a man sitting on a park bench huddled over a plate of food he seems to be eating with two pigeons at his feet. Under the motif a sentence appears in several languages, for instance, in French, 'Ne me regarde pas manger' ('do not watch me eat'). That is all" (Frey, 1989: 88).

The gap created is between the cardboard mover's box and its name or title ("Rameau's Nephew"). I think at once of Diderot, the author of the work alluded to in the title, or his hybrid essay/fiction, and experience a certain emotion of recognition. Nothing is communicated to me, no message at least, but I am oriented in a certain direction. *Juxtaposition.* X + Y. It would be easy enough to multiply examples of this piece, to make them myself, literally or conceptually.

Exercise: Automatic Emblems

Test the productive effect of the gap by composing a readymade word-thing of your own. Your selections should be made arbitrarily, but use something from one of your mystory discourses. Choose a material object from Family, Entertainment, or History, and assign to it a title of an important text in your Career discourse. Document the object with photographs and detailed descriptions of its features.

- See how many steps it takes to create a connection between the object and the text. Keep notes on the learning effect associated with the process. One result of working through the cultural encyclopedia using conventional research procedures to construct this path of associations is a powerful learning effect, especially for one who knows nothing about Diderot or Kippenberger (but even for those who do). The chain of associations maps a "flash" path an insight might take.

REMAKE
Neocowboys (Marlboro Man)

Leo Burnett's Agency   In 1954 Philip Morris Corporation sought an advertising agency to design a campaign that would allow men to smoke a filtered cigarette in public without embarrassment. At the time, filtered cigarettes were associated with women. Leo Burnett (the Burnett Agency) did some research to determine the most "virile" male image in American culture, which not surprisingly turned out to be the "cowboy." The original "Marlboro Man" ads first appeared in January, 1955, depicting a portrait closeup of a square-jawed man wearing a cowboy hat and smoking a cigarette. Subsequent ads included more of the figure and setting, displaying more of the iconic costume (vest, horse). Burnett also designed the package—deep red with a "V" of white space. This campaign ran for over two decades and was one of the most successful in the history of advertising (Lorin, 2001: 68).

A typical Marlboro ad is readily described as an emblem.

- The *motto* (slogan, caption, *inscriptio*) reads, "Come to where the flavor is. Come to Marlboro Country." It is inscribed in the lower right-hand corner of the frame.

- The *picture* is a photograph of a cowboy: a rugged-looking man with a mustache, visible from the waist up, wearing a white cowboy hat low over his eyes, head at three-quarters face, eyes squinting into the distance, leaning forward, elbows resting on the pommel of his saddle, the horse only suggested in the darkness at the bottom of the frame. The motto and picture together compose an "enigma," which is resolved by the epigram.

- The epigram (*subscriptio*) includes the following material: a small inset picture of two cigarette packages in two sizes, with three filtered cigarettes protruding from the top of the smaller pack. Beneath the packs some small print reads, "Marlboro Red or Longhorn 100s. You get a lot to like." The Surgeon General's warning is superimposed as a label with a white background on the lower left-hand border of the frame.

Our remake places the ad within the project of the EmerAgency consultation on the problem of the spectacle. In light of previous discussions we understand that the ad is positioned in civic discourse (the public sphere) in the role of Sender, creating a narrative that taps the symbolic resources of the nation, the imagined community, to circulate an object of value that is a "charm bundle" binding the sign value of the cowboy with a commodity (the filtered cigarette). "The intermediate object [the cowboy] in representing a value [masculinity, manliness] which becomes attached to the product [Marlboro cigarettes], is thus a sort of currency. Currency is something which represents a value and in its interchangeability with other things gives them their 'value' too" (Williamson, 1978: 20). The task assigned by Agamben is to untie this bundle, separate the body image from the commodity, and to experience in its place the bar or *barre* as such—the nature of our being-in-language (or of becoming-image). The difference between the EmerAgency project and something like Adbusters is that the latter provides literate critique of ads, exposing the ideological interpellative effects (which is indeed useful and important) while the former proposes to show how to write with sign value oneself, and even, through the wide image, to create new sign value by introducing private themata into the public realm.

The premise is that the ad form is a kind of "haiku," meaning that it is a "simple" or primary form whose operation is a mise en abyme for image authoring at more complex levels as well. Placing the ad form in the series of emblem-fetish-Sphinx clarifies that there is nothing inherently commodified in the form, but that ads are a version of conduction, using the X + Y logic of the poetic image. A first step in expanding chorography from the reduced micro-site of the barre (/) out into the internet and the spectacle is provided by the frame of the ad form, emptied of its propaganda and considered as a genre for the mystory. The following discussion uses the example of a film star testimonial for a perfume, which is easily adapted to the cowboy type and a cigarette.

Judith Williamson on Ad Structure

"Catherine Deneuve's face and the Chanel bottle are not linked by any narrative, simply by juxtaposition: but there is not supposed to be any need to link them directly, they are as it were in apposition in the grammar of the ad, placed together in terms of an *assumption* that they have the same meaning, although the connection is really a random one . . . ; the link is in terms of what Catherine Deneuve's face means to us, for this is what Chanel No. 5 is trying to mean to us, too. . . . So what Catherine Deneuve's face means to us in the world of magazines and films, Chanel No. 5 seeks to mean and comes to mean in the world of consumer goods. The ad is using another already existing mythological language or sign system, and appropriating a relationship that exists in that system between signifier (Catherine Deneuve) and signified (glamour, beauty) to speak of its product in terms of the same relationship; so that the perfume can be substituted for Catherine Deneuve's face and can also be made to signify glamour and beauty.

"Using the structure of one system in order to give structure to another, or to translate the structure of another, is a process which must involve an intermediate structure, a system of systems or 'meta-system' at the point where the translation takes place: this is the advertisement. Advertisements are constantly translating between systems of meaning, and therefore constitute a vast meta-system where values from different areas of our lives are made interchangeable.

"Thus the work of the advertisement is not to invent a meaning for no. 5, but to translate meaning for it by means of a sign system we already know. It is only because Catherine Deneuve has an 'image', a significance in one sign system, that she can be used to create a new system of significance relating to perfume. . . .

> "Only the form and structure of the referent system are appropriated by the advertisement system; it is the relationship and distinction between parts, rather than the parts themselves that make an already-structured external system so valuable to advertising. The links made between elements from a referent system and products rise from the place these elements have in the whole system rather than from their inherent qualities. Thus Catherine Deneuve has significance only in that she is not, for example, Margaux Hemingway" (Williamson, 1978: 25–26).

Comment

- The Marlboro ad may be mapped onto the mystory allegory frame:

    Anagogy = Capitalism

    Moral = The consumer

    Allegory = The Cowboy

    Literal = Philip Morris Corporation

- A first step in extrapolating from the emblem/ad form to the mystorical emblem (wide image) is just to put yourself in the position of a commodity. You are the tenor of the figure, the unknown Y (like Chanel perfume in Williamson's example). When this Y is juxtaposed with a vehicle, some known X, such as Deneuve (or any film star or celebrity), there is a transfer of meaning in your favor.

Lifestyles

An advertising agency is rather like a corporate Sherlock Holmes in that it knows a great deal about the "rules" or codes of culture. Agencies use research to establish the VALS (values and lifestyles) of consumers, in order to hail them directly in the ad. We ourselves, Williamson argues, are the transformational space of the ad (44). The commodity creates a "totemic" group through identification. We recognize ourselves as the sort of person who would use that product, through the feeling that the product promises to provide. The ad offers a "lifestyle kit" with which to create our self-image (70). Market research has identified the default range of ready-made lifestyles. The typology is based on various psychological and sociological schemas, such as need and drive hierarchies, and inner/outer-directed distinctions. The list is arranged developmentally from the most "impoverished" personality type to the most mature integrated personality, with the assumption that persons may move through the typology and achieve integration (Leiss, Kline, Jhally, 1986: 256). The types (with percentage of the population in that type noted in parentheses, as of 1980) are:

"Need-Driven Groups:
  Survivor lifestyle (4%)
  Sustainer lifestyle (7%)
Outer-Directed Groups
  Belonger lifestyle (35%)
  Emulator lifestyle (10%)
  Achiever lifestyle (22%)
Inner-Directed Groups
  I-Am-Me lifestyle (5%)
  Experiential lifestyle (7%)
  Societally Conscious lifestyle (8%)
Combined Outer- and Inner-Directed Group
  Integrated lifestyle (2%)" (256).

As a relay for mystory, the ad starts in the right direction, in that it promises the possibility of becoming "artists of ourselves" (Williamson, 1978: 70). In the X + Y transfer space I am the product, and the cowboy is my "objective correlative," Williamson says, borrowing T. S. Eliot's term: "'The only way of expressing emotion in the form of art is by finding an 'objective correlative': in other words, a set of objects, a situation, a chain of events, which shall be the formula of that particular emotion; such that when the external facts, which must terminate in sensory experience, are given, the emotion is immediately evoked'" (31). It must be added here that Eliot's formulation is representative of the poetics of modernism as a whole, from Baudelaire to Rilke, with different poets giving their own names to this effect. Advertising and art work at opposite poles of meaning creation, however: advertising persuades individuals to adopt a ready-made norm, while art persuades a collective to accept a private or personal theme as having collective or universal relevance. In the ad this objective correlative is in fact not an artistic image, but a cliché; the metaphor is dead; it is only the "idea of a feeling," not the mood itself, which is why the commodity cannot make good on its promise of happiness or well-being. The mystory must turn from the ad to the artist to learn how to design an emblem for the wide image. But first we need to look closely at how the ad initiates the link between the sign value and the individual subject. This technique is the key to the effect of compassion fatigue in the spectacle.

Comment

- In studying the ad form as a relay for designing our emblem, you are also casing the area of your intervention as a consultant on policy issues. The Emer-Agency does not so much provide solutions for problems, as identify the value sources that control the whole problem-solution process. Ads are a reliable guide to the nature of contemporary values.

Richard Slotkin on Mythology

"Myths are stories drawn from a society's history that have acquired through persistent usage the power of symbolizing that society's ideology and of dramatizing its moral consciousness—with all the complexities and contradictions that consciousness may contain. Over time, through frequent retellings and deployments as a source of interpretive metaphors, the original mythic story is increasingly conventionalized and abstracted until it is reduced to a deeply encoded and resonant set of symbols, 'icons,' 'keywords,' or historical chichés. In this form, myth becomes a basic constituent of linguistic meaning and of the processes of both personal and social 'remembering.' Each of these mythic icons is in effect a poetic construction of tremendous economy and compression and a mnemonic device capable of evoking a complex system of historical associations by a single image or phrase. . . . Sooner or later defeat in war, changes in modes of production, internal imbalance in the distribution of wealth and power produce a crisis that cannot be fully explained or controlled by invoking the received wisdom embodied in myth. At such moments of cognitive dissonance or 'discontent,' the identification of idealogical principles with the narratives of myth may be disrupted and a more or less deliberate and systematic attempt may be made to analyze and revise the intellectual/moral content of the underlying ideology. . . . The historical development of the culture's repertoire of genres is driven not only by social and cultural change but by the specialized discourses of artists and producers who work in that form" (Slotkin, 5–6).

Slotkin's argument locates a point of intervention for the EmerAgency in the space of spectacle. The effect of advertising is exemplary of the effect of myth in the spectacle in general: to introduce the actual problems of life, but then to invoke the psychic defense mechanism of fetishism and conduction, by displacing the threatening, anxiety-producing possibilities of the problem toward a sense of well-being, reassurance, safety. The ad creates or initiates an associative series of moves along a chain of signifiers, which is to say that the ad uses the conductive inference of dreamwork.

This is indeed the logic of electracy, but here it is used to stop thinking by immediately channeling the energies (drive and desire) provoked by a scene or situation into the ready-made or "homiletic" clichés of ideology. The problem is raised, but the "consultation" or advice provided by advertising (or the spectacle as a worldview in general) gives the default solution, based on the hegemonic norms of the culture. The Marlboro man is a prototype for masculine identity. The "problematic" that motivates the consumer at a deep level in this case is the fundamentally unanswerable question, "am I a man or a woman?" (180). In terms of the two economies, the consumer in the Restricted Economy may be worried about his health, but in the General Economy he is worried about his image. Fetish logic allows the two to coexist in the formula, "I know these are bad for me, but nevertheless, am I not a man?" A person of either sex could use this reasoning.

Haineault and Roy locate in advertising a moment of choice created when an ad touches on authentic sign value or currency, when it enters into one of the problematics of collective and individual identity (which are irreducibly unstable). We recognize in the scene the "gap," "hole," or "void" that marks our necessary incompleteness, our limitation, our dilemma or aporia as human beings (what psychoanalysis sometimes calls "castration"). In this metaphysics, our identity is constructed through introjection or internalization around this central void or traumatic wound of separation and individuation. The difference between advertising and art is that the former uses conduction defensively, to move us away from the trauma to the ideological (mythological) solution to the dilemma, while art carries on deeper into the dilemma, locates and surveys the field of the wound (Rilke's Open). The imagined community, at least as constructed in the literate apparatus, produces the mood of belonging by eliminating difference, excluding the "other," forming a homogeneous community around what is the "same" (154). Art in this view transgresses the readymade or default mood to locate an alternative but lonely encounter with the outside, the real, or with what Agamben called "the irreparable." The history of the emblem shows how the irreparable gap in being (the incompleteness of an individual or a society) has been stopped up, plugged with God in the Baroque Era, and with the Commodity in the modern period.

Comment

- It is this capacity of the emblem to express (and hence to locate) the spiritual gap and its stopper that makes it also a promising form for the widesite—a prosthesis for the imagination that allows its maker to leave open the hole in being.

Haineault and Roy on the Different Functions of Advertising and Art

"It is important to note right away that the three advertising thematics we have considered—nostalgia (Bell Telephone), difference (Carlsberg beer), and pleasure and necessity (Urgo)—could each constitute the problematic of a major motion picture, one that is profound, moving, and pertinent. [. . .]

"What one could not imagine from a film made on one of these themes is that it might *deconstruct itself* just as rapidly as it starts, that it might evoke its subject no sooner than to repress, to annihilate, it.

"Fellini or Bergman would leave us with one or more real questions, would have us see that we both differ from and resemble one another or that distance evokes separation but also is what unites us. When *Scenes from a Marriage* sketches the love drama of both solitude and real sharing, one does not especially feel as spectator, shielded by the screen. On the contrary, one is confronted by a real void, but a manifest gap so subversive that it sends us back to ourselves and suggests that we make sense, all of us for ourselves, of this void. . . .

"Carlsberg divides the screen but reunites all its protagonists around a single beer. Difference no longer exists. Or, more exactly, after having drawn in desire, difference is metamorphosed into a resemblance that denies desire. The hole, the void, the yawning gap by which the subject, eventually, would have been able to accede to the necessity for it to take on meaning, is sealed before being able to exert its subversion.

"Just as in the Rothko painting, it is the interstice, the flux, from the lack of representing from which the freedom of the cinematic work of art is born, it is from the hole or the void between the sequences that subversity is born. The fullness of advertising presents itself, on the other hand, as a stopgap against authentic desire, as a blinder, but above all as an avenue of perversion.

"In short, the work of art invites us to transgress meaning and the signifier in order to take up signification again on its own account: to kill Laius, empty oratory, and discourse in order to come to *its own way* of speaking.

"Advertising films, thanks to the commercial principle to which they owe their existence, have to block this transgression, at least partially, in order to entrust to another object the trouble of making sense. It is around this axis that their construction pivots" (110).

The "void" stands in for that unnamed mood or state of mind that is the feeling of our being. The goal of the mystorical emblem is to find a match in the world "outside" for this "inside." The widesite draws upon the lessons of both promotional and artistic uses of the image as relays toward the wide image.

Exercise: Ad Art

Select an advertisement, define the issue or problem that it treats, and trace the alternative paths available that avoid or confront the real social or psychological difficulties touched on by the ad. Test Hainault and Roy's claim that the theme of an ad might also provide material for an art film.

Art: Tarkovsky

An example of how an artist works with a default mood of his culture may be seen in the films of Russian director Andrey Tarkovsky. A profound feeling of homesickness or *nostalghia* is to many Russian artists what *wabi-sabi* is to the Japanese or *saudade* to Brazilians. "Nostalgia means literally the pain for return: it is the traveler's ailment—the condition of exile. Yet in its peculiarly Russian form it is complicated by being part and parcel of its opposite, a sort of necessity for journeying that issues from Russia's enclosedness" (Le Fanu, 1987: 109). The mood of sadness and longing that is at the same time the pleasure of "glad-to-be-feeling" associated with *wabi-sabi* is also characteristic of Brazilian *saudade* and could be applied to all the "blues" or demons of *duende* that we have considered. What recommends Tarkovsky's exploration of "nostalgia" is his film poetics in which, like Barthes, he uses Japanese haiku, and its mood of *wabi-sabi,* as a relay for how images function in general.

Tarkovsky on Haiku Poetics and Film Image

"In his account of Japan the Soviet journalist Ovehinnikov wrote: 'It is considered that time, per se, helps to make known the essence of things. The Japanese therefore see a particular charm in the evidence of old age. They are attracted to the darkened tone of an old tree, the ruggedness of a stone, or even the scruffy look of a picture whose edges have been handled by a great many people. To all these signs of age they give the name, saba, which literally means 'rust'. Saba, then, is a natural rustiness, the charm of olden days, the stamp of time. [—or patina—A.T.]

"Saba, as an element of beauty, embodies the link between art and nature. In a sense the Japanese could be said to be trying to master time as the stuff of art" (Tarkovsky, 1986: 59).

"If time appears in cinema in the form of fact, the fact is given in the form of simple, direct observation. The basic element of cinema, running through it from its tiniest cells, is observation.

"We all know the traditional genre of ancient Japanese poetry, the haikku [sic]. Eisenstein quoted some examples:

> *Silent in the field*
> *A butterfly was flying*
> *then it fell asleep.*

"Eisenstein saw in these three-line verses the model for how the combination of three separate elements creates something different in kind from any of them. Since this principle was already there in haikku, however, it is clearly not exclusive to cinema.

"What attracts me to haikku is its observation of life—pure, subtle, one with its subject.

> *The dew has fallen,*
> *On all the spikes of blackthorn*
> *there hang little drops.*

". . . And although I am chary of making comparisons with other art forms, this particular example from poetry seems to me close to the truth of cinema, with the difference that prose and poetry use words by definition, while a film is born of direct observation of life; that, in my view, is the key to poetry in cinema. For the cinema image is essentially the observation of a phenomenon passing through time" (66–7).

Tarkovsky approaches cinema as a poet rather than as a storyteller or essayist. He is more interested in using images to evoke a state of mind, an atmosphere, than to dramatize action. Of course he includes drama, action, character, and all the other features of narrative cinema, but these are organized by an overriding image to create an atmosphere, which is why he makes a good relay for learning electracy. An act of pure cinema, he said, would be to represent a person's life in 90 minutes. The principle of selection governing what to include would follow the workings of memory, which preserves only in a partial way, with certain central events "standing out like a tree in the mist." "The cinema has to be free to pick out and join up facts taken from a 'lump of time' of any width or length" (65). These bits of sequential facts are not intended as symbols. When he shows on the screen in close detail "those long, dreary, persistent rains that are typical of the Russian landscape," he says, there is no "point," other than to show his world as he sees and feels it: "I am recreating my world in those details which seem to me most fully and exactly to express the elusive meaning of our existence" (213).

This elusive meaning (accessible only through the image) for Tarkovsky is precisely the reality of "time." "How does time make itself felt in a shot? It becomes tangible when you sense something significant, truthful, going on beyond the events on the screen; when you realize, quite consciously, that what you see in the frame is not limited to its visual depiction, but is a pointer to something stretching out beyond the frame and to infinity, a pointer to life" (117). Any art produces an "allegorical effect" by an insistence, an intensification through repetition and variation, of certain details. Tarkovsky's emblems are not conventional allegories, he says, like those of Eisenstein's montage that are riddles with word-for-word solutions. Their meanings, we could say in our context, are not those of studium, but of punctum. A brief review of several of his films shows the pattern of how he works with images. I will focus on those aspects of the film that reveal how Tarkovsky uses mostly landscape images to personalize the default mood (nostalgia), and how he uses a mystorical structure to introduce a singular nuance into a collective default attunement.

Comment

- Tarkovsky is useful as an example, even if you have not seen his films, in that he is a filmmaker who confirms Roland Barthes's use of haiku poetry as a good analogy for the rhetoric of the photographic image.

Tarkovsky Examples

Mirror (1974)

An autobiographical film, made up of a mosaic of "facts" remembered from different parts of Tarkovsky's life. Applying to himself his conviction that, "if somebody tells us of his impressions of childhood, we can say with certainty that we shall have enough material in our hands to form a complete picture of that person" (57), it was shot in part on the location of his childhood home, which was rebuilt completely since the original had been torn down. Central memories from childhood are dramatized, such as the fire that destroyed the barn, along with key incidents in the life of the parents, as well as dreams and visions experienced by the young Andrey. Andrey's relationship with his mother and wife (played by the same actress!) is a recurring theme. The setting is explored in great detail, including various sounds typical of the environment (dripping water, the creaking sounds of the house at night, the wind in the trees).

The mystorical potential of the film is evident in the juxtaposition of the family scenes with other cultural materials: the child looks through a book of drawings by Leonardo da Vinci; he is asked by a ghost-woman to read aloud from a famous letter that the great poet Pushkin wrote in the nineteenth century to a former guardsman and mystic, Chaadayev, arguing that Russia occupies a middle way in the world, between Europe and Asia; a series of newsreel clips showing scenes from a disturbance on the Chinese-Soviet border during the Maoist period, a sequence from the period of the civil war in Spain. The most important interpolation in this way, establishing the historical dimension of Tarkovsky's popcycle, is footage from World War II of Soviet troops pushing their artillery across the shallows of Lake Sivash.

"I was beginning to despair of being able to draw this hotchpotch together in a single time-sense, when suddenly—quite unheard of for a newsreel—here was a record of one of the most dramatic moments in the history of the Soviet advance of 1943. It was a unique piece; I could hardly believe that such an enormous footage of film should have been spent on recording one single event continuously observed. When, on the screen before me, there appeared, as if coming out of nothing, these people shattered by the fearful, inhuman effort of that tragic moment of history, I knew that this episode had to become the center, the very essence, heart, nerve of this picture that had started off merely as my intimate lyrical memories.

"There came onto the screen an image of overwhelming dramatic force—and it was mine, specifically my own, as if the burden and the pain had been borne by me. The scene was about that suffering which is the price of what is known as historical progress, and of the innumerable victims whom, from time immemorial, it has claimed. It was impossible to believe for a moment that such suffering was senseless. The images spoke of immortality, and Arseniy Tarkovsky [the director's father] poems were the consummation of the episode because they gave voice to its ultimate meaning. The newsreel had aesthetic qualities that built up to an extraordinary pitch of emotional intensity. Once imprinted on the film, the truth recorded in this accurate chronicle ceased to be simply like life. It suddenly became an *image* of heroic sacrifice and the price of that sacrifice; the image of a historical turning point brought about at incalculable cost" (130).

This footage, in other words, functions as an *emblem* of sacrifice (this meaning is inherent in the situation, but assumes the viewer's knowledge of history). It functions mystorically in the blended space of the film in that the emotion of self-sacrifice is transferred to Andrey's life, to evoke his state of mind, his feeling about the world (his attunement).

Nostalghia ("Nostalgia") (1983)

A Russian poet and musicologist named Gorchakov is in Italy to research the life of an eighteenth-century Russian composer named Sosnovsky who had done most of his work while living in Italy. Because of his talents, Sosnovsky, who was a serf, was allowed to go abroad to receive a musical education. Although he could have remained in Italy and lived the life of a free and successful musician, he chose to return to his native land, where he eventually committed suicide. The relationship between Gorchakov (Tarkovsky's alter ego) and Sosnovsky is mystorical in connecting the artist to a Career paradigm. An example of the "call" received from current news events is Gorchakov's relationship with the madman Domenico, whom he first learned about through news reports about the man who imprisoned his family in their home for seven years in an effort to protect them from apocalypse. Domenico ultimately commits suicide by burning himself to death while standing on top of a statue of Marcus Aurelius in Rome.

Unlike the mosaic structure of *Mirror*, this film is unified in time, place, and action (although there are some flashbacks and visions). The setting is a spa village in the region of Tuscany. Gorchakov and his beautiful Italian interpreter Eugenia stay at the Bagno Vignoni, near a monastery chapel they visited in connection with the research. Abandoned by Eugenia, who leaves after an emotional scene in which she realizes there is no chance for a romantic relationship with Gorchakov, the poet performs a ritual assigned to him by Domenico: he has to carry a lighted candle across the length of the outdoor bath without the flame going out.

Stalker (1979)

This film is based on a science fiction story about the visit of a spaceship to Earth for a "roadside picnic." The litter left behind by these creatures possessing a vastly advanced technology created a "Zone" possessing a mysterious power, in Tarkovsky's adaptation, with unstable, shifting traps that kill intruders. Somewhere in the Zone, however, is a room that will grant to visitors who reach it their most profound wish. In our context the Zone exemplifies both the Sender function and the space of the *barre* (it is an emblem of chora). The protagonist, the "stalker" (meaning something like "deerstalker" as in Fennimore Cooper), is a guide who is able to lead others to the wish room, although the ethics of the Zone forbid him to receive himself any benefits from the Zone. His predecessor, nicknamed "Porcupine," broke this code by asking the Zone to restore his deceased brother to life. Instead the Zone made Porcupine immensely wealthy, which is to say it granted his deeper wish—which caused Porcupine to commit suicide. That the narrative is a parable is indicated by the characters names—Stalker, Writer, Scientist (personification of principles or worldviews). Stalker evades the guards posted to keep people out of the Zone and leads his clients to the wish room, only to have both of them refuse to enter, for different reasons. The film was shot on the grounds of the ruins of an abandoned hydroelectric plant in Estonia, and much of the film is an exploration of this entropic landscape.

The Image

The exemplary status of Tarkovsky's films for the wide image is found not in his plots as such but in the atmosphere of the settings. His goal as a filmmaker is to create a diegesis whose atmosphere evokes his state of mind as *auteur*. Obviously, he says, his films have nothing to do with "entertainment." To experience this atmosphere, of course, one must see the films, but for our purposes I will cite a few passages from the screenplays to itemize the qualities of the setting that show how Tarkovsky personalized the default mood of his culture.

From Mirror

"On the way back to Yurievets it was completely dark and it rained. I could not see where I was going and fell into the nettles from time to time, stinging my legs, but I said nothing. Mother walked ahead. I could hear her splashing in puddles, and the rustle of bushes as she brushed past them in the darkness. Then I heard a sobbing. I stopped to listen, looking around in the impenetrable darkness. But I could hear nothing, apart from the regular sound of the rain and the plash of the river just beyond the bushes" (Tarkovsky, 1999: 289).

From Nostalghia

"The season has ended. The last residents in the Two Palms Hotel have gone their separate ways. The hot spring does not bubble. There is no steam hanging over the hot pool. The pool is empty, its bottom covered with waterweed. The sides of the pool, and the stones lying on its bottom, are covered with a layer of calcium. Here and there, puddles remind you of the bottom of a rockpool at low tide. An elderly workman in wellingtons is busy with a rake in the far corner, beneath the spreading pendulous branch of a fig tree that has already lost most of its leaves" (497).

From Stalker

"Close at hand, with its headlamps buried in grass, an ambulance looms, dented, its paintwork peeling. Half-rotted stretchers lie nearby, and a pile of decaying blankets. There are rolls of bandages, grey with mud. And on the opposite bank, where a dozen tanks form a mound, it is even worse. The iron monsters are in disarray, their cannon pointing in different directions. Some have managed to lose their caterpillar tracks, some are up to their turrets in mud" (392).

"They walk and walk, and then a dark spot appears ahead of them in the mist; they pass beneath the echoing vaults of another tunnel, knee-deep in water. The mist is much thinner here, and the concrete vaults are visible in the grey light. They are steaming with condensation" (399).

> "And now they are standing in front of the doorway, which is broad
> as a barn door, in the threshold of the room: a completely empty ex-
> panse. There are black puddles on the cement floor; the evening sky
> shines through the perforated ceiling" (410).

Template   It is possible now to outline Tarkovsky's "whatever," his state of mind
as a singular image of Russian nostalgia. While the films include a variety of settings, portrayed with beautiful cinematography, the features inventoried here
identify a pattern that recurs and is insisted upon in the work. The template is
the one generated earlier for *wabi-sabi,* that we will adopt ourselves as a kind of
worksheet for the preparation of our mystorical emblem.

The Material Register

1. Things

The action is set in such places as a monastery chapel, a hotel and spa baths
that are hundreds of years old; a devastated series of industrial-scale concrete buildings with grounds strewn with unusable equipment.

2. Material Attributes or Properties

The landscapes and settings repeatedly display watery places, partially sub-
merged grounds or flooded floors, broken walls, mud puddles, damaged
equipment, buildings, interiors that are worn, old, or wrecked, unkempt,
cluttered, cold, wet, dark, damp.

3. Atmosphere

The experience of the atmosphere is partly determined by the themes and
action of the narratives. Thus in *Mirror* the setting evokes a sense of mystery
and age, while in the other two examples the effect is of decay, ruin, destruction, danger.

The Spiritual Register

4. Feeling

Yearning, longing, disappointment, dissatisfaction, loss.

5. Worldview (Metaphysics)

As noted previously, while the feeling may be inferred from the material register, the resulting attitude to "how things are" in the world, as well as what
actions one should take as a result, is very difficult to anticipate based solely
on the image. Tarkovsky explained in his writings that the world and the
people in it are dependent, unfree, their actions doomed, without possibility for happiness, death being the final outcome regardless of effort. Art masterpieces "range themselves at the sites of possible or impending historical

cataclysms, like warning signs at the edge of precipices or quagmires. They define, hyperbolise and transform the dialectical embryo of danger threatening society, and almost always become the herald of a clash between old and new" (Tarkovsky, 1986: 53).

6. Morality (Spiritual Value)

Love (as expressed in Tarkovsky's journals): a commitment to the brotherhood of humanity, to maintain hope, act *as if* human goals were attainable; affirmation of self only through sacrifice. There is no *necessary* relation of this ethic to the water-saturated settings.

As it turns out Tarkovsky's particularizing of "nostalghia" resembles the *wabi-sabi* ethic, with both sharing the connection between an aesthetic attention to the signifiers in the material world of the passage of time, and an ethics that accepts the irreparability of individual death. If the primary lesson for the Emer-Agency is this status of art as "ciphers of catastrophe," the lesson for the wide image is in the relationship among the default mood of a culture, the details of the maker's individual experience of the popcycle, and the ontology and ethics that may be inferred from this combination. The basic rule is to extrapolate from these relays to discover one's own situation. What is my default mood? What are the "lumps of time" and the image facts that may reveal to me my own whatever?

Comment

- One of the difficulties in moving from literacy to electracy in the register of Career or disciplinary knowledge is this shift in state of mind from skepticism (the default mood of science) to yearning (the default mood of imaging). A common theme in critique is a condemnation of "nostalgia" as politically reactionary or quietist. In electracy, however, in which mood is augmented by the digital prosthesis to gain the power of categorization, nostalgia (yearning, longing) provides the image equivalent of universal communication achieved by abstraction in literacy. Like "problem," nostalgia may serve the ends of either propaganda or art, producing either the closed or the open mind. In any case it is not a case of either/or but both/and (both science and art, so to speak), as expressed in the phrase "the desire for knowledge." There is no knowledge without a desire to know, and this desire is an emotional passion in the family of yearning.

Seance

My remake of the Marlboro cowboy emblem returns to the sign currency of the frontier, the American West, and follows a conductive trajectory away from the default defense of masculine virility toward the gap mapped by art. A device relevant to this divagation is described in Helene Cixous, *Three Steps on the Ladder of Writing*. What Cixous means by "writing" is somewhat different from the ordinary sense of the term, other than and prior to the distinction between critical and creative work; something more essential—a poetic or lyrical quality operating within literacy that is to words what mathematics is to numbers. Much could be said about Cixous's *Ladder*, but for now I will focus on its first lesson that she learned from the authors who "called" to her, to whom she was drawn or attracted almost magnetically: "In the beginning each one of them had an inaugural scene, from which writing sprouted. Because it is always a question of a scene, with a picture. The picture is the open door we must go through" (Cixous, 1993: 8). In our context this door connects our quotidian circumstances in the Restricted Economy with the collective forces of the General Economy. In terms of Agamben's task, the lesson concerns moving outside the limitations of my individual biography in order to discover the condition of singularity.

Tarkovsky declared that "the aim of art is to prepare a person for death, to plough and harrow the soul, rendering it capable of turning to good" (Tarkovsky, 1998: 43). The first lesson of writing for Cixous is learned in the School of the Dead. It has to do with what we know "when we are small." The first apprenticeship concerns a cemetery and a witnessing of death. For Kafka this lesson was associated with "a reproduction of Alexander's Battle" that hung on the wall of his schoolroom. For Tsvetaeva it was the picture in her mother's room of "The Duel," representing the death of Pushkin. "Writing, in its noblest function, is the attempt to unerase, to unearth, to find the primitive picture again, ours, the one that frightens us" (Cixous, 1993: 9). The "ladder of writing" has the eidos or shape of the letter "H". "H: you see the stylized outline of a ladder. This is the ladder writing climbs" (4). The H is not only a picture of a ladder with one rung (a part for the whole), but also a graph of how two languages conjoin: "This is what writing is: I one language, I another language, and between the two, the line that makes them vibrate; writing forms a passageway between two shores" (3). Cixous shows us how to generate an experience of the middle voice, using the "I-I" system of autocommunication.

THE ULMER FILE
The School of the Dead

What is the lesson learned from the School of the Dead, our first masters, according to Cixous, who unlock the door to the other side ("We are witnesses to an extraordinary scene whose secret is on the other side") (9)? In Cixous's examples the scene of the first meeting with the dead is associated with a reproduction of some famous death found in one's environment. For me this picture is "Custer's Last Stand" by F. Otto Becker reproduced as an advertisement in more than a million copies by Anheuser-Busch and hung in barrooms across America in the years from 1885 to the 1950s. One such copy hangs over my desk (acquired at an antique auction). In 1904 Blanche Boies, a disciple of the prohibitionist Carrie Nation, mutilated with a woodcutter's axe a copy of the lithograph advertisement that was on display in the Kansas statehouse (Connell, 1984: 366).

> "Although Becker started with Cassilly Adams [an earlier painting of the event], the finished product became very much his own. The original and Becker's litho both equip Custer with a sword, but in Adams' painting he uses it to thrust while in Becker's version he assumes his stance dead center and wields it like a flail. . . . Concerning Indians, Becker was less exact. It is hard to guess what he had in mind. Obviously he did not know these people. Several of his braves are dressed like Apaches and one or two look like Aztecs carrying Zulu shields. In the foreground, however, whether it is technically correct or not, Becker provided an absolutely horrifying lesson in the art of scalping: A fierce black warrior with a knife between his teeth kneels on a cavalryman's back to peel away the top of his head, distorting the features until the Anglo face looks Oriental" (365).

Comment

- This passage is useful for pointing out how connections arise across the mystory levels. Describing the Becker painting, Connell characterized Custer's stance and gesture as wielding the sword "like a flail." "Flail" triggers a sting of recognition for me because it corresponds to the metaphor Plato used to explain how the space of chora winnowed chaos into the categories or elements of Earth, Air, Fire, Water. The inclusion of the painting in my mystory had other motivations, but this thread of winnowing confirms the appropriateness of the choice.

The description that best captures what frightened me (the effect that makes the painting into a door to the other side) is by Iron Hawk (cited in Black Elk's autobiography), who participated in the battle. "I saw something funny. Two fat old women were stripping a soldier, who was wounded and playing dead. When they had him naked, they began to cut something off that he had, and he jumped up and began fighting with the two fat women. He was swinging one of them around, while the other was trying to stab him with her knife. After awhile, another woman rushed up and shoved her knife into him and he died really dead. It was funny to see the naked Wasichu fighting with the fat women" (Neihardt, 1961: 128). My first encounter with this scene was through a cemetery that led me to the painting—the cemetery at the Custer National Battlefield Monument, with the headstones scattered over the Montana hillside marking the places where the soldiers fell—which I visited with my family when I was ten years old. This sacralized place of death evoked "history"—the promise of time before me and after me—showing the aporia of the human condition (our temporality). I identified then with the soldiers, not the Indians. The conductive series from this scene follows a chain of signifiers through the popcyle to produce a pattern for a mystorical emblem.

Noon Star (Emblem)

An emblem emerges through the repetitions in the sequence of scenes gathered by means of an associative passage through the popcycle: *what resembles, assembles.* The mystorical emblem is a variation on the religious and commodity versions in that the logic of the chain is provided by personal experience, however contingent it might be, of the popcycle institutions. In my case, the personalization of the default "cowboy" is influenced by my childhood growing up in Miles City, in Custer County, Montana, a town that began as a cluster of saloons and brothels to service the troops at Fort Keough, established in 1876 after Custer's Last Stand, commanded by General Miles, whose orders were to put an end to the Indian threat in the region. Scenes from each of the popcycle discourses are juxtaposed—the stories of the battle of the Little Big Horn for community History, the film *High Noon* for Entertainment, my piano lessons from Family. The source of the epigraph is a theoretical text, representing my Career discourse.

Naming   "In Dakota Territory the Arikaras christened Custer Son of the Morning Star, or Child of the Stars. At least that is how he might have received the name. Maybe the Crow scout White Man Runs Him, who also was known as Son of the Morning Star, conferred this—his own name—upon Custer. No matter how he got the name, he liked to be called Son of the Morning Star. Without doubt he liked it better than several names the troopers called him: Hard Ass, Iron Butt, Ringlets" (Connell, 184).

Marching Song   "*Garry Owen:* An Irish quick-marching or drinking song, it was adopted by the regiment as its fighting song about 1867. Its first introduction to war was at the Battle of the Washita. Popular use quite naturally brought about a popular nickname for every Seventh Cavalry trooper—*Garry Owen*—which they quite proudly accepted" (Frost, 1964: 183).

Disaster   "If disaster means being separated from the star (if it means the decline which characterizes disorientation when the link with fortune from on high is cut), then it indicates a fall beneath disastrous necessity. Would law be the disaster? The supreme or extreme law, that is: the excessiveness of uncodifiable law—that to which we are destined without being party to it. The disaster is not our affair and has no regard for us; it is the heedless unlimited; it cannot be measured in terms of failure or as pure and simple loss" (Blanchot, 1986: 2)

272 PART V   Emblems of Wide Scope

Lessons   Mrs. Klamm gave piano lessons at the home of her friend, Mrs. Benson, in a house behind the Presbyterian church in Miles City. Having recently visited the Custer Battlefield National Monument with my parents, I asked if I could learn to play "Garry Owen." I practiced it for several weeks. At the end of the lesson one day, after I played the song through without a mistake, Mrs. Klamm pasted a silver star in the upper right-hand corner of the sheet music, to indicate the successful completion of that project. On the way home I had to watch out for a bully named Gerard, who ruled the streets of my neighborhood. He had chased me several times, and I had learned to avoid using the underpass of the Northern Pacific Railroad, since the time he jumped me there. He was typical in being very large and mean, but untypical in declaring to his victims that he was just doing to them what others did to his own younger brother, a frail and diminutive boy who had spent a year in bed while he had Scarlet Fever, or so I had heard. Gerard wore an army surplus jacket, had thick unwashed hair, rarely bathed, and seemed to have no parental supervision or care. To cross paths with Gerard was just about the worst thing that could happen.

High Noon   *High Noon,* Screenplay by Carl Foreman, from the story *The Tin Star* by John M. Cunningham, Produced by Stanley Kramer, Directed by Fred Zinnemann (1952). The cast: Will Kane (Gary Cooper), Amy Kane (Grace Kelly), Jonas Henderson (Thomas Mitchell), Harvey Pell (Lloyd Bridges), Helen Ramirez (Katy Jurado), Judge Percy Mettrick (Otto Kruger), Mart Howe (Lon Chaney), Ben Miller (Sheb Wooley), Jim Pierce (Robert Wilke), Jack Colby (Lee Van Cleef), winner of several Academy Awards.

> "The gunfight is the center of the film's formal structure, the iconic moment toward which the clock-driven narrative inexorably drives and its moral resolution as well. Only the gunfight can prove that Kane really does 'know Indians' and is therefore morally entitled to set his will against that of the townspeople [who refused to support him in his fight with the gang]. The gunfight itself has a ritual quality. Kane's preparations and his solitary walk up the empty street tell us not only that he must fight Miller but that he has to do it in a certain way, playing by certain rules. Even Miller and his henchmen move in formal order and make symbolic gestures, the most significant of which is a gunman's shattering a shop window to steal a woman's bonnet—an act that validates Kane's prediction that if Miller wins neither women nor property will be safe, and that coincidentally warns Kane of the gang's presence. The ritual proceeds through passages of quick-draw confrontation, chases, and ambushes. . . .
>
> "In the classic town-tamer Western, Kane's personal redemption would have been mirrored in the triumph of the community. But the social implications of Kane's victory are anti-canonical. Instead of vindicating Kane discredits the community, which proves itself unworthy of the sacrifices he had made for it. At the end, Kane contemptuously drops his badge in the dust at the mayor's feet and rides out of town. The people have been saved, but they have less value than the man who saved them" (Slotkin, 395).

The Sidereal   "Lucidity, ray of the star, response to the day that questions, and sleep when night comes. 'But who will hide from the star that never sets?' Wakefulness is without beginning or end. To wake is neutral. 'I' do not wake: someone does, the night does, always and incessantly, hollowing the night out into the other night where there can be no question of sleeping. There is no waking save at night. Night is foreign to the vigilance which is exercised, carried out, and which conveys lucid reason toward what it must maintain in reflection—in the preservation, that is, of its own identity. . . . Something wakes: something keeps watch without lying in wait or spying. The disaster watches. When there is such watching—when sleeping consciousness, opening into unconsciousness, lets the light of the dream play—then what watches (the wake, or the impossibility of sleep at the heart of sleep) does not illuminate with an increase of visibility, of reflecting brilliance. Who watches? The question is obviated by the neutrality of the watch: no one watches. Watching is not the power to keep watch—in the first person; it is not a power, but the touch of the powerless infinite, exposure to the other of the night, where thought renounces the vigor of vigilance, gives up worldly clearsightedness, perspicacious mastery, in order to deliver itself to the limitless deferral of insomnia, the wake that does not waken nocturnal intensity" (Blanchot, 1986: 48–49).

Award Ceremonies   The chain of silver stars on my sheet music are asterisks (*astres*) on the props of my identity: C = Custer County High School—the letter "C" on the football letterman's jacket; A = the "A" grades on the report cards from school; R + D = Dr (PhD) on the diploma from graduate school. What does that spell? C*A*R*D: Stop (post) gap (card). They were the carrot and the stick of my ambition.

Showdown   "CUT to a medium shot of the action. Will starts out the doorway. Immediately Frank pushes Amy aside and points his gun at Kane. Both men fire simultaneously.

"CUT to a close-up of Will. He is hit in the arm and staggers to his knees, still firing his gun. The camera then pulls back to reveal that Miller has fallen face down, dead.

"As Will starts to pull himself up, Amy rushes to him and embraces him.

"CUT to a long, high-angle shot of the scene. The empty street suddenly fills with people rushing out of buildings. They run toward Will. He gets up slowly, shaking away those seeking to aid him, except for Amy.

"The camera closes in on him. He glares disgustedly at the townspeople. Then in a defiant gesture he takes the tin star from his vest and throws it to the dusty ground.

"CUT to a close-up of the star in the dust.

"CUT back to a medium shot of the action. Young Johnny drives up in a buckboard. He gets down and hands Will the reins. Will looks around him at the mob of people. Then he assists Amy onto the wagon, climbs up himself, and drives off without looking back.

"FADE OUT" (Maynard, 1974: 58)

Noonscape   "Among [Edward] Hopper's several paintings of solitary figures are those of women alone, often nude or in a state of undress, poised before a window or waiting in a doorway—for example *High Noon* (1949). These paintings are also concerned with the symbolism of time and are more appropriately considered in that context. On the whole, critics have often misinterpreted these solitary figures as symbols of loneliness, rather than comprehended Hopper's personal preference for quiet and solitude" (Levin, 1980: 42).

Star   "As a light shining in the darkness, the star is a symbol of the spirit. Bayley has pointed out, however, that the star very rarely carries a single meaning—it nearly always alludes to multiplicity. In which case it stands for the forces of the spirit struggling against the forces of darkness. This is a meaning which has been incorporated into emblematic art all over the world. For this reason, 'identification with the star' is possible only to the chosen few. Jung recalls the Mithraic saying: "I am a star which goes with thee and shines out of the depths." Now individual stars are often seen in graphic symbolism. Their meaning frequently depends upon their shape, the number of points, the manner of their arrangement, and their color (if any). The 'flaming star' is a symbol of the mystic Centre—of the force of the universe in expansion. The five-pointed star is the most common. As far back as in the days of Egyptian hieroglyphics it signified 'rising upwards towards the point of origin', and formed part of such words as 'to bring up', 'to educate', 'the teacher'. The inverted five-pointed star is a symbol of the infernal as used in black magic" (Cirlot, 1962: 295).

The Categorical Star

My remake of the Marlboro ad in "Noon Star" located a particularizing nuance in the default norm of masculine identity. My cowboy is not generic, but is Will Kane played by Gary Cooper in *High Noon* and modified by juxtaposition with the other documents of the mystory. The key to the categorical power of the image is the holistic reach of its mood (at one end of the spectrum of our emblem template), and the formal operation of signifiers (few shapes and sounds, many objects and words) that cause them to repeat across the sensory realm. The analogy we have been developing throughout our quest is that between allegory and mystory, specified in the present assignment between the emblem and the wide image. A formal quality of emblematic figures in allegorical narratives is just this capacity to gather the features of many discourses into one image. The paradigm for this power is the Lion in Chretien de Troyes's *Yvain, ou le chevalier au lion*.

> "The sign 'lion' functions in Chretien's *Yvain* as a remarkable shifter between several discourses: that of an allegorical moral system, that of a natural or 'physical' system, and that of a new and purely social system that we may call heraldic or totemic. . . . The lion had already become by Chretien's time, the emblem of the emblematic and Chretien takes great pleasure in 'shifting' the lion's discursive status before our very eyes. If, at first, the lion in the woods signifies Yvain's

redeemed animal nature, as soon as Yvain disguises his identity during his quest in the social world for renewed honor and becomes an unnamed *chevalier au lion*, the lion becomes inescapably a heraldic emblem, even though he is not yet painted on Yvain's shield. However, Chretien holds his audience on the boundary between cognitive systems as long as he can, refusing to let the lion become a passive bearer of significations" (Vance, 105–106).

This semiotic metastability of the lion, as Vance calls the emblem effect, applies also to the star in my emblem. As Daly explained, the initial juxtaposition of text and picture produces an enigma (whose pure form is the ready-made). The enigma is resolved in the epigram. The mystory works with four sources (the popcycle) distributed over the three parts of the emblem. Thus the motto and picture are supplied by Family, Entertainment, Community, and the epigram by Career. In making "Noon Star" out of my mystory, the great insight came through the juxtaposition of Will Kane's badge (his sheriff's star) with the silver stars on my sheet music. This combination was reinforced in the History documents by Custer's demotion after the Civil War. He had been the youngest general in the Union army, but his rank was adjusted to colonel after the war (he lost his stars). His fate as a glory-seeker confirmed the rightness of Kane's repudiation of his badge and its office. These stories showed me figuratively the terms of my own ambivalence about the competitive culture of American identity formation. What this scene might mean is suggested by the citations from *The Writing of the Disaster* by the French writer Maurice Blanchot.

I will explore the mood (feeling, metaphysics, morality) of my emblem in the next chapter. Meanwhile, Vance also reminds us of the difference between the literate and electrate categorization that we introduced in the beginning of the book with the contrast of the definition of the thing (Aristotle) and the counter-definition of formless (Bataille). The issue is over the kind of properties assigned to the work of classification and hence of sorting reality into an order. Definitions select the features of substance that carry the idea of an entity; descriptions select the features of accident that evoke the image of an entity. "Accidental" properties, in Aristotle's terms, are those that may be present in a thing but that are not necessary to its being (a horse is an animal regardless of its color, the number of flies it may swat with its tail, or the sweat on its back after a hard run). The emblem as a hybrid of picture and text is an image and an idea; in it the image and the idea exchange effects and enter into the tangle of a felt.

Comment

- The associative chain from my mystory provides the materials for an emblem, but still has to be designed on the website. "Noon Star" is only words in this version, but on the Web includes graphics (for example, an animated gif made from stills grabbed from *High Noon*, showing Kane (Cooper) taking the tin star off his vest and throwing it onto the street). Nor is it art, although the effect of recognition is partly aesthetic (the repetition of signifiers). "Recognition" itself is triggered by coincidence, synchronicity, the uncanny effect of discovering a relationship in time or space revealed by the cognitive map of the mystory.

- The "event" of insight (epiphany) came when I juxtaposed elements from each of the popcycle stories and noticed the repeating star motif. What did it mean? The answer was provided by Cooper in *High Noon*, when he throws down the star, emblem of my alienation from the system by which the community enforced its value system and way of life.

- What is the atmosphere of this scene? It is evoked by the tension of the showdown, representing the competitive nature of middleclass existence. Cooper's act of doing his duty even while discarding the value (star) captured the feeling of my alienation exactly. In the structural portrait (Cooper : Miller :: Ulmer : Gerard) I did not come out as well against Gerard as Cooper did against Miller. In the official value system "discretion is the better part of valor." In the unofficial value system, to dodge a fight is to be a coward.

- What is the nature of the world remembered in this emblem? A fight to the death between rivals. How should we behave? Do your duty anyway, without regard for success or failure.

- The five-pointed star is one of my wide images (you have as many as four or five). That its hieroglyphic meaning is "teacher" confirmed the rightness of the pattern. It is appropriated as a found icon in the encyclopedia and given its singular nuance through the relationships that emerge in my mystory.

OFFICE

1. The final major assignment is set here—the making of an emblem in which to represent a version of the wide image. The wide image exists as a pattern that you discern in the four separate websites of the mystory. The first step to find the wide image is to look for signifiers, details, fragments that repeat across any two (or more) levels of the sites. This is why it is necessary during the documenting of each discourse to use material details, signifiers that address the senses, rather than abstract descriptions or interpretations. Even when you do use abstractions, such as citations from specialized works in a career field, the citations work as aphorisms, with the effect more of an image than an explanation. The wide image is an emergent pattern, not in any one quarter, but a constellation that appears within a field of relationships.

2. There is no one form or genre for the wide image. It may be expressed and applied in any form and in ways limited only by imagination, technology, and craft. It is embodied here in the emblem, for reasons that should be apparent from the narrative journey that led to it. You will recognize the template as the one generated in the first chapter in the discussion of haiku reason, for the *wabi-sabi* Japanese default mood.

Holton and others say that the image of wide scope consists typically of a core group of four to five related primary images, and a secondary proliferation of these into an array of 50 to 100 variations. These images give access to the themata that are the core set of themes, the abstract version of the orientation to the world. The mystory simulates the wide image made retroactively by the formation of an emblem that provides a personalized rendering of a cultural default mood, rendering both sensory detail and the atmosphere of the maker's attunement to life.

3. The template derived from *wabi-sabi*, with its six parts, three each for the tenor and vehicle of a metaphor, is to the wide image what the outline is to an argument. The outline, that is, is a generative structure, which is the operational rationale for the rule of two. In an outline there must be two of everything (I; A, 1, 2; B, 1, 2. II; A, 1, 2; B, 1, 2, etc.). The rule forces the maker to think beyond the surface, beyond the first thing that comes to mind, in order to meet this demand. It is easy to think of one thing for each division, but to find something to pair it with takes more effort, which provokes creativity. Similarly, with the *wabi-sabi* template, to need to fill in each slot locates some dimensions of thought and feeling that you might have overlooked, and motivates you to look more closely at the relationship between the outside and inside of experience. To put your feeling about how the world is (metaphysics) into a sentence or two is artificial and reductive, of course, but the effort may clarify your self-understanding. Similarly, to restate your behavioral stance in the world as a morality may provide some coherence to a sequence that otherwise may seem like "one damn thing after another" (as has been said of history itself). The educational consequence of designing an externalization of your grounding mood or attunement is meant to affect your life development the way the invention of the compass and map affected travel. To put it into an emblematic phrase, a wide image is the compass of creativity. This is our claim, but you are the test.

4. The emblem shows how to work with the problem of the spectacle: the ad form and institution provide a good entry into electracy. A comparison from the previous shift in the apparatus might be with the way scientific method retained the systematic procedures of ritual but dropped the religious context. Similarly, the wide image mystory retains the emblem form of advertising but drops the commodity context. Making the wide emblem is meant to give you some fluency in the electrate rhetoric emerging within Entertainment. The next step is to use this fluency in order to testify in the formation of public policy (the magic tool helps the hero overcome the conflict or defeat the villain in a narrative). The practical fact is that Entertainment is a powerful force in setting the public policy agenda of our society (in the spectacle image and actuality merge). We have indicated all along, however, that an egent may not be the hero of the virtual civic sphere, but the donor. Once you understand what a wide image is by acquiring your own, pass it on. The proverb about teaching people to fish, rather than giving them a fish, is relevant to the EmerAgency. The point is not to tell people what to do, but to promote a more creative culture.

Chapter 10

The Ideal of Value

10—The road back: the subject uses his new wisdom to deal with the consequences of his actions, and declares a desire to return to the ordinary world.

STUDIO

Happiness

Agamben set a test for the egents to separate the body in its linguistic nature from the pornography and commodification that dominate the bourgeois body. In terms of practical consulting this test suggests that the EmerAgency approach policy issues at the level of values that circulate in the culture determining the way the policy makers focalize an issue. One way to approach this call for a paradigm shift in values and identity is to take up the question of the happiness promised through the whatever of the image.

Exercise: Personals

Make an emblem representing a personal idea of happiness or well-being.

- Advertisements appeal to us by presenting emblems of well-being, security, satisfaction. Corporations use their VALS research to target our default moods and associate them with their commodities. Use the emblem form to displace these appeals with your own image of "happiness." Substitute your own image or props related to your own situation for the commodity promoted in ads.

- Chris Marker's deconstructive documentary, *Sans Soleil* ("Sunless"), shows where an emblem of happiness may lead when it is extended into an art meditation on a fetishized scene. His two-hour film begins with a photograph of three little girls taken on a road in Iceland, which the narrator explains is an image of happiness. The film attempts to create an associative chain that would allow the maker to understand this image or find its meaning by linking it with other images in order to produce a narrative or argument. In this search for links Marker passes through the popcycle, selecting Alfred Hitchcock's *Vertigo* in Entertainment, and the assassination of revolutionary leader Amilcar Cabral, who drove the Portuguese out of Guinea, for

History. These scenarios are embedded in a travelogue featuring the narrator's ethnographic record of many rituals and ceremonies in the daily life of Tokyo, Japan. "Sunless," a title borrowed from a suite of songs by Mussorgsky (played on the sound track), turns out to describe the mood of the film, which is "happy" in the mode of blues or *saudade*. The aesthetic of the film reflects haiku reason, in an explicit allusion to the journal or pillowbook of a woman who recommended looking for "things that quicken the heart." He cites a letter written by a kamikaze pilot to his family before his last flight, in which the pilot explains that despite everything, deep in his heart he is happy. Late in the film it is revealed that the town in Iceland where the three girls lived was buried in ash when a volcano erupted nearby.

This apprenticeship of the wide image takes us only to the end of the second act in narrative structure. The third act (*final confrontation with the opponent; returning with the elixir*) is left to the next project, a consultation on a public policy issue. This introduction to the EmerAgency is a beginning, a start on an electrate practice. What remains to be accomplished in this book, to conclude the second act, is this return to the ordinary world, which involves extending the insights of the emblem to a fuller examination of our own state of mind, the mood of our daily life, and its possible correspondence or conflict with the mood of the wide image. To what extent have I simply accepted the default mood of my culture? An effect of learning cyberpidgin is that its syncretic formations of pop icons and states of mind, crossing the borders of "own" and "other," make me aware that I must already have a "state of mind," and my own pop fetishes, in the same way that learning a second language made me conscious for the first time that the grammar of English that I had been studying in the K-12 years (School) was the one I used as a native speaker of English. To try to notice one's own guiding cultural frame and default moods is not unlike trying to hear a regional spoken "accent" in the sound of one's own voice.

An imported state of mind—*wabi-sabi* or *saudade* (the samba feeling) for example—calls attention to the existence of a "native" state of mind that perhaps remained an unrecognized, unacknowledged atmosphere of my existence. I know *saudade* only intellectually, although even for a native Brazilian *saudade* is as much a myth as it is for me (Vianna, 1999). Brazil used samba (the same may be said of Argentina and tango) the same way Philip Morris used the cowboy— as an attractor for collective identity. This exploitation of sign value has a positive side, as Agamben pointed out. One implication is that there is nothing inherently progressive or liberating in sign currency, as proven by the "conquest of cool" (the appropriation of Afro-Caribbean value by advertising). Yet the fact that samba was appropriated self-consciously to help construct Brazilian national identity, or that "cool" was appropriated to sell commodities, is proof that these signifiers and their moods are detachable (the gram), writable in cyberpidgin. The lesson is that states of mind are not determined, necessary, not essences, but historical cultural defaults. Also, bourgeois commodity culture (the spectacle) is dynamic, tapped directly into sign currency, and will continue to attempt to usurp the Sender's position to control the imagined community. A third lesson is that "blues" is the default mood of the Black Atlantic, and that every part of the Americas has its own version of this mood and behavior. The emergence and spread of values and the moods that carry them, however, has a complex history. To find/invent the wide image one must sort out and map the personal relationship to the default moods of historical culture.

The givens are both collective and individual. Within the syncretic framework, *wabi-sabi* or blues posed the question of what I brought to the "table" myself, what I had available for trade, what I contributed to the hybrid. The exotic is a negative experience of the homely. What was my native state of mind that was to be enhanced and syncretized by means of the prosthesis of the unconscious? There are two sides to the barre, the gap is crossed in both directions, two semantic domains between which the signifier floats (and this "two" is an open series). To this extent my experience is dialectical (literate), making the odyssean journey away to the "exotic" and back, discovering my native place for the first time upon the completion of the circuit (the uncanny)—which is to say that my experience (necessarily, for now) is organized as "selfhood." The "uncanny" is an effect of position. I write pidgin, but not yet creole. My search was assisted by the living testimony of my own children, in whose development I could see the work of the superego (the potential monster or ker of my introjected others) and my own part in this serial mourning of interpellation.

Commodity Ritual

I recall being at the kitchen table with my son, Lee (aged 17). Outside, the dogwoods waved a thousand handkerchiefs at the thunderheads over the park. Lee told me he wanted a sports car. These words—*sports car*—refer but not to an automobile, or not only to that. Having a sports car would make him happy. He thought of it as an event in the ritual marking the closure of School. Graduation was his leverage. We have different standpoints. Between us is the nature of "experience." What do I know about it? Have I learned anything from the combination of living and studying about living that is worth passing along to my son? In my son's mystory I am not Donor, nor even Mentor, but perhaps a Sender. I try to think Family in the middle voice. What are my rights, duties, and responsibilities regarding the condition before one owns a sports car, and after one no longer cares about sports cars? Such is the gap this genealogy of morals must fill.

Sports car. I hope Wittgenstein was right, that even if some things may not be said, they at least may be shown. I began to tell Lee a cautionary tale, a *moral allegory*, about a sports car—a tale about the summer of 1967, just before I entered graduate school, when I decided to drive my TR3 from Miles City, Montana, to Mexico City. I had not thought about this journey for many years. It is a surprising beginning, since the first thing it revealed is that I once owned a sports car. My mother used every rhetorical device she knew to dissuade me from making the trip. She was certain that I would be killed, if not in a car wreck, then by bandits. "Even if you do make it to some godforsaken place called Mataturista, then what?" she wailed. My son sensed a contradiction. "Sports car" and "English Professor" did not belong together in his cognitive schemas. I wondered myself: when and why did I turn against my sports car?

REMAKE/ULMER FILE
Remarkable Meetings

Who are my primal acquaintances? What is my cyberpidgin vocabulary? This question is explored through an improvisation on a book passed along to me by a friend in college: G.I. Gurdjieff's *Meetings with Remarkable Men*. The mystic philosopher and teacher Gurdjieff embodies my Xanadu complex, my fantasy about the life of a "sage" and the assumption that wisdom is exotic, to be found elsewhere. The uncanny lesson of mystory—so hard to learn—is that I already live in Xanadu.

> "Of the questions often put to me by people of various classes and differing degrees of informedness, the following recurred most frequently: What remarkable men have I met? What marvels have I seen in the East? Has man a soul and is it immortal? Is the will of man free? What is life, and why does suffering exist? Do I believe in the occult and spiritualist sciences? What are hypnotism, magnetism, and telepathy? How did I become interested in these questions? What led me to my system, practiced in the Institute that bears my name?" (Gurdjieff, 1963: 30).

Gurdjieff's belief that an ancient wisdom might still exist among certain remarkable people living in the Middle East and Central Asia sent him on a journey that lasted many years and passed through many countries. Of the men he described in his autobiography, none were particularly famous; indeed most were obscure, but they shared a commitment to understand the deepest mysteries of life. The first such life Gurdjieff narrated was that of his father. What was the attraction of this book? The exotic setting might have had something to do with it: "From Thebes we traveled up the Nile to its source, and went on into Abyssinia, where we stayed about three months; and then coming out to the Red Sea we passed through Syria, and finally reached the ruins of Babylon" (225). *Thebes, Abyssinia, Babylon*. The initial terms of the remake are simple enough, with a modest expansion of the object of encounter: to reflect on and represent a meeting with a person, place or thing that might constitute an "encounter." The guiding question: "is experience possible?"

On the Road   Spring break, 1964. I went to California with some friends, driving from Missoula, Montana, to San Francisco. I was a sophomore in college. Standing on a corner waiting to cross a street near the campus of the University of California at Berkeley I saw approaching me a young man who projected an image that was the prototype of "cool." I experienced in a material way for the first time my own nature as yahoo, rube, yokel. His madras shirt (the first time I saw such a thing), his Mexican sandals, his long hair, his sunglasses, his walk. He had a "look." That I would not be the hero of my own story became a possibility, if being a hero had anything to do with style or fashion. I am familiar now with the theory of the mirror stage; that my identity is a form of alienation; that my experience of having a coherent self results from the internalization of an image, an ego ideal. That contradictory feeling of amazement triggered by the California paragon, embodied archetype—part jubilation as of a promised wholeness combined with the intuition of my own fragmentation—expressed an irreducible lack (the human condition). The light changed a number of times after this revelation passed, leaving in its wake an emptiness, a vacuum or vortex of instability ("there is no transcendental self, stable subject, or soul"). The inchoate hypothesis that had brought me to California in the first place seemed to have been confirmed: life really was "elsewhere" (but it is impossible to get "there").

The real issue is not the sports car, but what such a car promises (the difference between use and exchange value). Why go to Mexico? It would not do to drive to North Dakota, for example, since the state was full of my relatives. I could not grasp my own locale as being a "place" (this is my stupidity—ATH). It was impossible for me to think of writing with any pleasure a sentence like the one I found in Gurdjieff even though what it says was literally true, describing a trip I took with friends the summer after graduating from high school: *From Miles City we traveled up the Yellowstone to its source, and went on into Wyoming, where we stayed about three weeks; and then coming out to The Great Salt Lake we passed through Nevada, and finally reached the casinos of Las Vegas.* I could not "here." The motive for the trip was nothing more than a blind urge to "go forth." Later, I understood the action as a response to cultural training in the idea of adventure. The attraction of Mexico included a negative polarity, a repulsion from Montana: part quest, part flight.

"For the most trivial event to become an adventure," wrote an existentialist, "all you have to do is to start telling about it. This is what deceives people: a man is always a teller of stories, he lives surrounded by his stories and the stories of others, he sees everything which happens to him through these stories; and he tries to live his life as if it were a story he was telling. But you have to choose: live or tell" (Sartre, 1965: 58). It is difficult to accept the absoluteness of this alternative. I know it is not necessary to live something first in order to have anything to tell. The lesson of cyberpidgin, moreover, is that electrate people (those becoming image) are able to "tell live" (in real time). Lee believed in experience, and above all in that definitive kind of experience—adventure. My trip to Mexico is proof that, once upon a time, I believed in it too. I want to tell him a story, a parable perhaps, to prompt him to undertake his own critique of experience (to discover its nature, possibilities, limitations). At the same time I lack confidence in my knowledge. Nonetheless, without intention, I have re-created for my sons the same environment (Family) that produced in me certain states of mind about which I am the most ambivalent. I fear that I have given them the *ascetic ideal.*

The Ineffable   What were the selling points of a TR3? Disc Brakes; 1991 cc. Engine (100 horsepower; overhead valves; aluminum rocker pedestals; 110 mph top speed; acceleration 0–50 in 8 seconds); Gearbox (4 speed; short throw; synchromesh in 2nd, 3rd and top); Frame (rigid X for stability; Sheffield steel); Racing Clutch. All of this and more: the signature of the Noumenon. The whole is greater than the sum of its parts.

I understood in retrospect what happened after I saw my first Californian as an event of FETISH. In a magic-based culture, when people set out on a project, they commit to adopting the next thing that catches their attention as the god guaranteeing success. The next thing that penetrated the defenses of my perception—the god that would deliver to me the jubilation promised by the California look—was *the sound a TR3 makes accelerating through a series of gear changes*. The weather was Mediterranean spring (the effect increased by the contrast with Missoula which in those days was overcast for months at a time due to being located in a mountain valley with pulp mills at both ends—"atmosphere inversion"). We rode along the highways of California with the windows down taking in the eucalyptus breezes. I had never seen so many sports cars (almost as many sports cars in California as pickup trucks in Montana).

In high school I liked the sound of a Chevy V-8 dual exhaust with glasspack mufflers. The family car was a '57 Chevy hardtop, and somehow my father agreed to install glasspacks. One of the greatest pleasures of those days was to start accelerating several blocks away from my girlfriend's house, then just as I passed the house let off the gas to allow the pipes to roll a rattle of controlled backfires. I simply could not get enough of this sequence and repeated it frequently. But that was in high school. In college, already imagining an escape from Home, the sound of a 4-cylinder engine, made in *England* had a kind of elegant power that erased the '57 Chevy. I heard MGs, Austin Healeys, and other makes and models along the California roads. When I heard the TR3 accelerating through the gear changes the void created by the madras shirt became a shrine for a new desire.

Genealogy of Morals

In the context of this desire to connect my own state of mind, the experience of my inner atmosphere, to cultural or civilizational values, I returned to some passages in Nietzsche that had troubled me, and that I had marked for further inquiry. I knew better than to ask the question, "what is the Gay Science?" Gilles Deleuze reminds us that Western metaphysics operates by means of the question "what is . . . ?", a practice that we take for granted, but whose invention created the beginnings of Philosophy (Deleuze, 1983: 75). This habit in itself constitutes one of the West's default moods: definition, conceptual thinking, sufficient reason as a state of mind. The purest embodiment of "problem" is cognitive science. What we really are asking with this question ("what is?") according to Nietzsche, is "what is it for me?" (for us, for everyone that sees)—a question of perspective, of standpoint. A better question, Nietzsche said, is "which one?" meaning, "what are the forces which take hold of a given thing, what is the will that possesses it? Which one is expressed, manifested, and even hidden in it?" (77). A choral problem solving applied to public policy formation poses this question to a disaster that has prompted a community to wonder "why." Instead ask: "which one?"

The question posed by Nietzsche is one that I took up again in my turn, to ask it for myself, in my own case, my own standpoint. This point is located in *The Genealogy of Morals*, the preface, the first number.

> "As one divinely preoccupied and immersed in himself into whose ear the bell has just boomed with all its strength the twelve beats of noon suddenly starts up and asks himself: 'what really was that which just struck?' so we sometimes rub our ears 'afterward' and ask, utterly surprised and disconcerted, 'what really was that which we have just experienced?' and moreover: 'who "are" we really?' and, afterward as aforesaid, count the twelve trembling bell-strokes of our experience, our life, our "being"—and alas! miscount them.—So we are necessarily strangers to ourselves, we do not comprehend ourselves, we 'have' to misunderstand ourselves, for us the law 'Each is furthest from himself' applies to all eternity—we are not 'men of knowledge' with respect to ourselves" (Nietzsche, 1967: 15).

My son's request for a sports car constituted just such bell strokes, and prompted a moment of uncanny recognition of another chain of signifiers constellated in my emblem: *high noon. The Genealogy of Morals* for me is an uncanny book anyway, in that the effect it creates is a combination of the familiar and the unfamiliar. I am testifying, not arguing. Fredric Jameson observed that the ideologeme of the nineteenth century was "ressentiment," whose metaphysician was Nietzsche (Jameson, 1981: 59).

> "'The slave uprising in ethics begins when *ressentiment* becomes creative and brings forth its own values: the ressentiment of those to whom the only authentic way of reaction—that of deeds—is unavailable, and who preserve themselves from harm through the exercise of imaginary vengeance.' Nietzsche's whole vision of history, his historical master narrative, is organized around this proposition, which diagnoses ethics in general and the Judeo-Christian tradition in particular as a revenge of the slaves upon the masters and an ideological ruse whereby the former infect the latter with a slave mentality—the ethos of charity—in order to rob them of their natural vitality and aggressive, properly aristocratic insolence" (201).

I wondered whether this might not be the name of the atmosphere that drove me out of my hometown (ignorant of being a carrier myself). There was something familiar about the ascetic ideal, even if I did not recognize (or acknowledge) in myself the attributes of ressentiment. But what really is the relationship between the ascetic ideal and ressentiment? Max Scheler departed from Nietzsche's analysis of this state of mind to the extent that he rejected its use to characterize Christian morality. Rather, ressentiment is the condition of the bourgeoisie.

"Ressentiment is an incurable, persistent feeling of hating and despising which occurs in certain individuals and groups. It takes its root in equally incurable 'impotencies' or weaknesses that those subjects constantly suffer from. . . . Any feeling of ressentiment stemming from the impotency in a ressentiment-subject is accompanied by hidden feelings of self-disvalue over against others. . . . The constant state of ressentiment is distinguished sharply from furious reactions or outbursts of anger" (Frings, in Scheler, 1994: 6–7).

My remake of Gurdjieff is Nietzschean.

The Alienated Sage

What was the relationship between my Career commitment to academic scholarship and my inner experience, my state of mind? The story I told myself consciously seemed benign enough, but I also knew about the Imaginary order of identity—the ego and its flattering self-image. How did it come about that as a young man I identified with an image of "the wise old man"? In my "Custer" phase I wanted to be a soldier. But at some point I wanted to be a sage the way my friends wanted to be doctors, lawyers, or cowboys. Of course, the difference between my ambition and theirs is that to think oneself wise is to be a fool (ATH)—the goal is its own refutation. The model of the sage has existed in the Western tradition at least since the Hellenistic period, known as the era of the epigones. Philosophy turned its attention then to descriptions of the "normal man" who is *sure of his happiness* whatever the fortunes of the world might bring (Windelband, 1958: 164).

"The most prominent characteristic in the conception of the 'wise man' is therefore 'imperturbability (ataraxy).' Stoics, Epicureans, and Skeptics are unwearied in praising this 'independence of the world' as the desirable quality of the wise man; he is free, a king, a god; whatever happens to him, it cannot attack his knowledge, his virtue, his happiness; his wisdom rests in himself, and the world does not trouble him. The normal man, for this period, is not he who works and creates for the sake of great purposes, but he who knows how to free himself from the external world, and find his 'happiness in himself alone.' The inner isolation of individuals, and indifference toward general ends, find here sharp expression; the 'overcoming of the outer world' conditions the happiness of the wise man. But since he has no power over the world without him, he must overcome it 'within himself.' Wisdom is shown in the relation which man maintains to his passions. It is essentially freedom from passions or emotions, 'emotionlessness' (apathy). To rest unmoved within one's self, this is the blessing of this 'wisdom'" (165).

The sage is "cool." Did the Ph.D. represent for me a fetish capable of granting me this kind of freedom? Such a confusion was possible because in fact I could not recall having ever met a sage in person. My ambition was not formed conceptually, but intuitively, as a desire to rid my experience precisely of the pain of comparative living (without having a name for the mood that saturated my culture). The cyberpidgin project to record meetings with remarkable persons, places, or things, was motivated by Gurdjieff's insight into the nature of the sage—that wisdom does not declare itself as such; that it might be anywhere; that it is not housed at the terminus of the search, but is the environment, the diegesis with its primal acquaintances composed in the telling of the disappointed search, the atmosphere, a mood. The felt wisdom is an aftereffect, the blow is belated. Wisdom is not a condition of "having," but of "being." It is not a pose, a mask, a helmet, a problem.

The times are right for remaking "wisdom" as a mode of knowledge, judging by a recent book by Francisco Varela, whose *Ethical Know-How* is said to emphasize "enaction": "cognition as the ability to negotiate embodied, everyday living in a world that is inseparable from our sensory-motor capacities. Apart from cognitive science, the bodies of thought that enable this link are phenomenology and the 'wisdom traditions': Confucian ethics and Buddhist epistemology" (Varela, 1999). To this list Varela adds psychoanalysis, characterized as "the only Western tradition centrally concerned with a pragmatics of human transformation" (64). He cites Lacan saying that "the unconscious is ethical at its core." Cognitive science acknowledging psychoanalysis? A straw in the wind. The mnemonic training of manuscript culture could be added to this inventory.

> "This basic connection between the process of sensation which ends in memory, and that of human emotional life is fundamental for understanding the crucial role memory was thought to have in the shaping of moral judgment and excellence of character. In his *Nichomachean Ethics,* Aristotle says that ethical excellence, 'character' ('ethos') results from habituation or repetition. The organism's 'hexis' or 'habitus' is developed by the repetition of particular emotional responses or acts performed in the past and remembered, which then predispose it to the same response in the future. Vices and virtues are both habitual dispositions, formed in this way" (Carruthers, 1990: 68).

The Writing on the Wall   Even as I explained what I could recall about the engineering features of the TR3, the effort to form a cautionary tale, a parable, triggered some related memories. While it was true that I was nearly killed several times on the roads of Mexico, what came back to me now was the neglected fact that during that summer of 1967, as fortune would have it, I met David Alfaro Siqueiros. The significant story of the summer was not about the car, but about the unforeseen meeting with this artist. Camping out near the beach at Mazatlan (Mataturista to my mother) I met two young men (brothers) from San Francisco who were on their way to do a documentary on Siqueiros. They had a letter of introduction from some friends of friends who knew people who knew Siqueiros from the time of the Spanish Civil War. Since my Spanish was better than theirs (they did not speak Spanish), they invited me to join them as interpreter.

Lee had never heard of Siqueiros, no more than had I in 1967, despite my college education. The three great muralists of Mexico: Orozco, Rivera, Siqueiros. Siqueiros led an attempt on the life of Trotsky, who was living in exile in Mexico, I explained. That got some attention. He was not the one who actually assassinated Trotsky, but he and his men sprayed a few hundred rounds of ammunition into the rooms of the fortified compound where Trotsky was living. I know more about the biography now, having done some research 30 years later. My companions asked Siqueiros some questions about this incident, but many of the details were lost on me. The clearest recollection I have was of him telling us that time had proven right his decision to devote so much of his life to politics, while his rival Rivera stuck to his painting. Who had the last laugh, since here Siqueiros was, still at work, while Rivera was in the grave long since?

The Ascetic Ideal

The sage rejects experience as a value (that was how I understood it). What was the appeal of this ideal for me? A more immediate question concerned the relationship between my choice of an academic career and this historical ideal. Nietzsche stated concisely something that I had to acknowledge. When I made the decision to go to graduate school what image did I have of the scholar? Did I really perceive scholarship as a path to wisdom? A few months in graduate school should have disabused me of that misunderstanding. The Vietnam War filled the news. Going through the motions of political protest my thought was: if I can finish the degree, I will exist (the post card, stop gap). The degree seemed more real than did the war. Certainly there was some confusion about the virtues of poverty, humility, chastity, and no understanding at all of what scholars actually did. "The 'desert' where the strong, independent spirits withdraw and become lonely—oh, how different it looks from the way educated people imagine a desert! [. . .] For them it is not nearly romantic or Syrian enough, not nearly enough of a stage desert!" (Nietzsche, 1967: 109).

In my romantic vision of the desert I fantasized about Nietzsche himself as a sage, as a paradigm. I saw not the rejection of experience, but sageness as a certain kind of experience. What motivated me to read *The Genealogy of Morals*, for example? The inspiration occurred aboard the "student ship" I took home from Europe after a year abroad (1966)—where I learned Spanish. It was a sunny day. The initial fear aroused by the incompetence of the Italian crew had passed (on the way out of the harbor we collided with a stationary buoy and had to return to dock for repairs). My stomach had adjusted to the rolling motion of a small ship on high seas. I ventured out among the sunbathers on deck. There they were, a woman in a bikini (top untied) and a copy of *Genealogy*, both lying open and face down. If it had not been for Nietzsche I never would have introduced myself. Only later did I remark the epigraph, from *Zarathustra*, that begins the third essay of *Genealogy*, asking "what is the meaning of ascetic ideals?": "Unconcerned, mocking, violent—thus wisdom wants 'us'; she is a woman and always loves only a warrior."

On a subsequent trip to France I sought out Eze, "perched like an eagle's nest on a spike of rock towering 1,550 feet above the sea," as a tourist guide explains. "Such a setting attracts painters and tourists in search of the picturesque.

Nietzsche first thought out his masterpiece *Thus Spake Zarathustra* on the picturesque mule path that winds down to the Lower Corniche. The path leads through pine woods and olive groves to the seaside resort of Eze-Bord-de-Mer" (Michelin, 1967: 68). Nietzsche admitted the attraction of such "deserts," his personal favorite being "the Piazza di San Marco, in spring of course, and morning also, the time between ten and twelve" (Nietzsche, 1967: 109). But then he spoke directly to me, cutting through these mirages, forcing me to acknowledge that *The Genealogy of Morals is a refutation* of the ideal of the Wise Man, the sage, the ascetic ideal, the romantic version of which contributed to my decision to go to graduate school. The refutation in part is also the promise of self-overcoming. The lesson: no aphorism of thought without the anecdote of life. No telling without living. No direct access to either wisdom or experience, but always the gap between the two.

The Fugitive   This direct sting touched on a quality of my behavior as a scholar that was a puzzle and a trouble—my compulsion to work ceaselessly, to research and write and then to publish (manifested in this very book—why am I doing this? What compels me to explain myself "to myself"?). I rationalized it as the desire to know, to understand, or as a career responsibility to keep up with current work. At the same time, I counseled graduate students on the role that "obsession" played in the composition of a book (finding no better name for my own "productivity"). "Oh, what does science not conceal today! How much, at any rate, is it 'meant' to conceal! The proficiency of our finest scholars, their heedless industry, their heads smoking day and night, their very craftsmanship—how often the real meaning of all this lies in the desire to keep something hidden from oneself! Science as a means of self-narcosis: 'do you have experience of that'"? (147). Yes. I recognize this portrait of the choleric type in alchemical psychology, "head smoking day and night." Here again was "problema" as armor, protection, shield of the unavowable. The research question, the interrogation, now exposed itself as a state of mind. What was this "desire" in the "desire for knowledge" (distinguished from "the love of wisdom")?

Narrative "recognition" (anagnorisis) is a temporal circuit connecting error, secret, and lie with truth. I certainly did have this feeling of being self-deceived. Nietzsche anticipated the underground life in his "educated desert": "A voluntary obscurity perhaps; an avoidance of oneself; a dislike of noise, honor, newspapers, influence; a modest job, an everyday job, something that conceals rather than exposes one; an occasional association with harmless, cheerful beasts and birds whose sight is refreshing [. . .] Perhaps even a room in a full, utterly commonplace hotel, where one is certain to go unrecognized and can talk to anyone with impunity. Oh it is lonely enough, believe me!" (109). Which sage was it who advised, "live hidden"?

Reading an out-of-date guide to the Caribbean, I found the hotel in Haiti that might be the educated desert, setting for my Nietzschean remake of Gurdjieff. The name of the hotel is "Montana" (hence addressed to me, home away from home, uncanny) listed among those "best for the budget."

"Montana, between Port-au-Prince and Petionville, is estate-like, surrounded by a hillside garden with well-tended flowers growing in a setting of palm trees and bougainvillea. Even the dining room has a tropical look, with large philodendron plants growing against a wide stone wall. Those seeking a good buy like it here, enjoying the pool which avoids that sterile resort look, with its surrounding flowers and sundeck area. It's no more than 50 feet from the water to your bedroom. Rooms, 53 in all, are decorated, with a native mahogany decor contrasted with bold, strong colors used in draperies and bedspreads. Each unit has a balcony, private bath, and air conditioning. The cuisine, a mixture of French and Haitian, is good, and at your four-course dinner you are likely to be served everything from Haitian rice and beans to coq au vin or filet mignon" (Porter, 1982: 278).

Would the woman from the student ship be waiting by the pool? Not likely, in Haiti. For one thing, Haiti manifests that peculiar binary, revolution and tourism, that Dean MacCannel said organized the modern world. Some commentators observe that Haiti's revolution was untimely, coming too soon, causing the island to be isolated from the stage of capitalist development that might have saved its economy. Meanwhile, it shows the limits of tourism. It answered the question of whether it is possible for a place to become so *other* that it loses its status as "exotic." Haiti no longer is included in the tourist guides to the Caribbean, just at the moment when "we are all Caribbeans now in our urban archipelagos" (Clifford, 1988: 173).

Predestination

What could I be hiding from myself? Some further research on the ascetic ideal provided one possible answer: religion. Deleuze noted Nietzsche's view that "three anecdotes are sufficient to define the life of a thinker: one for the place, one for the time, and one for the element" (Deleuze, 1983: 110). Empedocles and his volcano is the example. I reopened the case of my personal background and setting, to look closer to home for a source of my desire to be a sage. This mystorical move forced me to reconsider my upbringing in my father's religion—the Presbyterian Church. "Thought does not need a method but a paideia, a formation, a culture" (110). This upbringing was so repressed I had to reread Max Weber to remember it—his account of the birth of the spirit of capitalism in the Protestant Reformation in general, and Calvinism in particular.

In Weber's account of Protestant experience, the quality of the Protestant inner life, I found my equivalent of the default moods of *saudade* or dharma. "In its extreme inhumanity this doctrine [of predestination] must above all have had one consequence for the life of a generation which surrendered to its magnificent consistency. That was a feeling of unprecedented inner loneliness of the single individual. In what was for the man of the age of the Reformation the most important thing in life, his eternal salvation, he was forced to follow his path alone to meet a destiny which had been decreed for him from eternity. No one could help him" (Weber, 1958: 104). No wonder I preferred *saudade* or blues, "happy to be feeling," and forgot about Calvinism. This recognition was not the bliss of satori, but the horror of anagnorisis.

The ascetic ideal of the Protestants arose independent of capitalism. As Weber explained, the distinctive "spirit" of capitalism (the "state of mind") concerns the inner feeling of "duty" to one's "calling," whatever it might be. Within Protestantism, I experience my work as a calling in the religious sense, and I feel obligated, responsible, duty-bound to do it for its own sake, ceaselessly, restlessly, continuously. I may never write enough articles or make enough money for that matter, because the performance is not motivated by such products. The commitment to the ascetic ideal within this spirit was total, "turning with all its force against one thing: the spontaneous enjoyment of life and all it had to offer" (166). Leisure and enjoyment do not contribute to the greater glory of God. To waste time is the deadliest of sins. The special feature of Calvinism that contributed most to capitalism was the systematic rationalization of conduct: the destruction of spontaneous enjoyment was not left to chance, but was systematized in what Foucault called a "technology of the self." I recognized in this description my upbringing, however secularized and routinized and benign it might have been, however reduced, naturalized, or repressed, as a training in asceticism. I had to admit that these same values organized the *paideia* in which my sons were raised. I had a Protestant body, against which my educated mind was helpless, since this mind was unaware even of being embodied. I am not arguing, but testifying.

Weber's account clarified several features of my own experience, while tearing away the romantic self-image I entertained of my desert. Presbyterianism is absent from my conscious life now, not part of my waking behavior, just as religion in general is no longer necessary for the success of capitalism. We did not have our sons baptized—a gesture directed against that repressed part of my childhood. But the *paideia* or ethos persisted at another level. "The idea of duty in one's calling prowls about in our lives like the ghost of dead religious beliefs" (182). The behavior now is compulsive and conducted without any attempt at justification. It is, precisely, a value. Or, as Nietzsche might say, it is misunderstood, carried out in the name of mundane passions that are in fact irrelevant to it. "No one knows who will live in this cage in the future, or whether at the end of this tremendous development [of capitalism] entirely new prophets will arise" (182). One cannot help but hear the pun on profits. Nietzsche, as Deleuze made clear, sought a new image of thought altogether. The sports car (a commodity desire) was a fanciful key meant to unlock the ascetic cage—a figment of the gay science, the joyful wisdom. Mexico.

Exercise: Noticing Default Moods

Document or put into a narrative what you notice about the relationship between the behaviors you perform within a particular institution, your state of mind in this performance, and the official or stated purposes or objectives of that institution.

- The goal is just to notice the connections or disparities among actions, states of mind, and beliefs, to map the sources and influences of "default moods," such as the Protestant spirit of capitalism that I discovered in my mystory. Any mix is possible from clear coordination through contradiction to complete disconnect. A typical example might be in sports, institutionalized in School, professing the belief that "it is not who wins, but how you play the game" (expressing a respect for the individual that comes perhaps from religion), conducted in an atmosphere of "win at all costs" (from capitalism).

The March of Humanity

Why was a journey in search of wisdom so appealing to me, at least in principle? What had happened in my experience that justified the alternative of ataraxy? And considering this appeal, why had I done so little to act upon it? In any case, I had not attempted to meet with any remarkable persons, although some had crossed my path (such was one lesson to be learned from Gurdjieff). When I met Siqueiros he was famous enough, whether or not he turned out to be remarkable. A typical passage in the history books reads:

> "Of the three masters of the new Mexican mural art, Siqueiros has the most revolutionary temperament. Compared with Rivera's classically equilibrated composition and Orozco's controlled drama, Siqueiros' murals impress by vehemence of their passionate movement, which often seems almost to burst out of the architectural framework. This potent vitality of form and color stems from the artist's ardent participation in the social and political problems of his country. His murals were conceived in the service of the nation, and from that fact they derive the magniloquence of their language and the explosive force that their themes assume" (Hans L. C. Jaffe, 1967).

When our little documentary group found Siqueiros in 1967 he was at work on his final monumental undertaking, "The March of Humanity." One commentator described this work as the most ambitious and most questionable of Siqueiros' career, overblown and unremittingly oppressive, tainted by the rationale of its sponsor, Manuel Suarez, who had declared, "Let us make tourism an even more important form of expression; let us make it grow by means of art" (Rochfort, 1993: 217). In 1967, seeing the work in pieces, spread around the large open yard, it was hard to get any sense of what it might become. We were given to understand that it was being prepared for a building that was to be part of the Olympics, scheduled to be held in Mexico in 1968.

Everything about "The March of Humanity," or at least its costly, inaccessible setting in the Polyforum associated with El Hotel de Mexico (part of a redevelopment project in Mexico City), commentators declared, contradicted the principles of a revolutionary socialist artist that motivated Siqueiros throughout his controversial career. Had he outlived Rivera for this—to decorate a tourist pavilion? My thought was: you see how the future is open. Now I recognize the irony of the convergence of this polarity: revolution; tourism—a rhizome. The riddle given to me as a test, to determine whether the tale is about me, or whether I join the anonymous perished ones, sacrificed for narrative—"What is the difference between a revolution and a tourist attraction?" "Which one?"

The Wall   The signature method I used as my daemon, to certify certain research decisions, confirmed the value of a second—virtual—visit to Siqueiros, to make up with research what I neglected in person (to supplement experience with knowledge). Perhaps this was the appeal of research, as a virtual "meeting with a remarkable person"—a secondary encounter. "Ulmer," subjected to a macaronic anagrammatic antonomasia, produced in French "le mur" (the wall), as in Lacan's phrase "le mur du langage." "Mural" in any case anagrams nearly directly into "ulmer" (ulmar). "The fresco technique is ideally suited to the esthetic requirements of mural painting, a painting style which must be thoroughly in harmony with the surrounding architecture. Modeling is usually kept to a minimum. Flat color areas and a strong linear pattern are typical. The fresco mural is part of the interior or exterior wall surface of a building and must be controlled by its location, by considerations of scale, and by its readability from many different angles and distances. Clarity and simplicity are essential" (Jensen, 1964: 14–15). I hear my name, and hence my destiny (the wide image as a marker of predestination) in everything to do with walls and therefore with any murals that come my way.

Ken Hillis on the Wall

"In *The Civilizing Process*, Norbert Elias identifies the construction of a fictional and invisible 'wall'—a spatial metaphor underpinning modern identity that demarcates the interiorized self from objects and other individuals outside 'it.' Over the past seven hundred years, this 'wall' has helped insert a pause between the brain's command and the hand's carrying out of this command, a break inserted into the seamlessness of eye-hand coordination. This separation permits the rise and ongoing refinement of modern social relationships and capitalist economies based on differentiation of labor skills. In an economy based on division of labor, it is unproductive for individuals dependent on one another for goods and services to kill each other spontaneously during heightened emotional states. This 'wall' helps create a critical distance and a cooling off period that minimizes bodily harm and social disruptions. Elias writes of, 'an eternal condition of spatial separation between a mental apparatus apparently locked 'inside' man . . . and the objects 'outside' and divided from it by an *invisible wall*.' . . . VEs [virtual environments] are an attempt to supersede the modern constraints imposed by this distance or 'wall' between subject and object, and by extension between subject and society, which comes to be experienced as 'external' to, or other than, the subject. Users, immersed and interactive, can forget momentarily that they are interacting with representations of other people and things, and that the transparent screen in many ways reifies Elias's wall even as it appears to offer a way to vault over it" (Hillis, 1999: 105).

This is the "wall" that is articulated in the barscreen of our widesite. The wide image may be thought of as a series of murals decorating the border of identity. The work that caught my eye in this second visit was not "The March of Humanity" that I saw in progress in 1967, but the masterpiece created for the Electrician's Syndicate, Mexico City, "Portrait of the Bourgeoisie." The site was a stairwell, and Siqueiros and his team of collaborators transformed the space, destroying the cubed construction of the architecture using Baroque perspective, deformative techniques and a continuous design imposed across the walls and ceilings of the site. The theme (anticapitalist, antifascist treatment of the conflict with National Socialism, reflecting the moment of its making, 1939) first got my attention because of its resonance with my default state of mind (the spirit of capitalism): "The painting virtually explodes in its depiction of the rampant chaos and destructive forces unleashed by the capitalistic system " (Hurlburt, 1989: 234). Did I recognize this portrait?

"They represent the actual process of capitalism toward its death," Siqueiros declared in his legend for the painting, stating his Marxist standpoint. His Marxist-Leninist standpoint. "The demagogue moved secretly by the force of money, propels the masses toward a great holocaust. A monstrous mechanism, crowned by the imperialist eagle, concludes the general function of capitalism, transforming the blood of the workers—who form the infrastructure of the real economic system—into the flood of gold that nourishes the benefiting incarnations of world imperialism, generator of war" (234). His misunderstanding is typical, Weber could say, of those who fail to see that it is not greed that constitutes the spirit of capitalism (such vice is a powerful force in every form of economy) but the domination of one's inner world by the obligations of duty experienced as a spiritual calling. The sublime force of ideology. The disaster outside is the only perceptual condition adequate to serve as an image for the feeling in me that leads to the conduct known as morality. *The disaster of duty.* The castastrophe of obligation, against "myself."

Then there are the ironies of the confusions relating Nietzsche's overman to the Nazi superman. I was no less bourgeois for having sought refuge in graduate school from the petty hypocrisy of small-town mainstreet. The English Puritans came to America in the first place to escape what they saw as the hypocrisy of the establishment, only to form a new establishment. The feeling of this duty inside (the society in me) could recognize itself, its destructive nature but also its creative potential, through a mystory, portraying the dilemmas defining each discourse, in me. "These impotencies," a scholar comments, referring to ressentiment, "generate either individual or collective, but always negative emotive attitudes. They can permeate a whole culture, era, and an entire moral system" (Frings, in Scheler, 1994: 6). They can; they may. In high school I understood my alienation as a hatred of the hypocrisy of my hometown. I now know this feeling was a default mood.

> "The world is sad, Oscar Wilde said, because a puppet was once melancholy. He was referring to Hamlet, a character he thought had taught the world a new kind of unhappiness—the unhappiness of eternal disappointment in life as it is. Weltschmerz. Whether Shakespeare invented it or not, it has proved to be one of the most addictive of literary emotions. Readers consume volumes of it, and then ask to meet the author. It has also proved to be one of the most enduring of literary emotions, since life manages to come up short pretty reliably. Each generation feels disappointed in its own way, though, and seems to require its own literature of disaffection. For many Americans who grew up in the nineteen-fifties, 'The Catcher in the Rye' is the purest extract of that mood. Holden Caulfield is their sorrow king. Americans who grew up in later decades still read Salinger's novel, but they have their own versions of his story with different flavors of Weltschmerz—'Catcher in the Rye' rewrites, a literary genre all its own" (Menand, 2001: 82).

The young man who murdered John Lennon offered a copy of Salinger's "Catcher" as his motive, explaining that Lennon had become a hypocrite.

The Whirling Square

How difficult is the task set by Agamben, to overcome the bourgeois body? Art historians repeatedly noted that Siqueiros's Stalinist themes and pronouncements were at odds with his aesthetics, experimental techniques and formal designs. It was the form of the design that enabled me to realize what the portrait of the bourgeoisie was "for me." Siqueiros, like the other Mexican muralists, applied the geometry of the Golden Section as the basis for his compositions. My recognition came with the characterization of a root-five rectangle—"the basic shape of vegetable and animal architecture and the form which permitted the solving of the mystery of the perfection of classical Greek art," associated with the "whirling square" (Hurlburt, 1989: 258). The key is the dynamic symmetry of the ratios, concerned with relationships of areas, not lines. "The whirling square has a ratio of 1.618:1 or 1:0.618. This relationship is usually abbreviated to phi and referred to as the 'golden section'" (Barratt, 1980: 108). Dynamic rectangles and squares have been important in traditions of sacred geometry around the world, because they express the order that underlies change: difference and unity are equally valuable. "The square root of 2 is an irrational function and a universally applicable relationship. Since everything in the natural world undergoes change, this root, being invariant, is by definition supernatural or supra-rational, that is to say, it is a symbol of the archetypal realm" (Lawlor, 1982: 28). The square collects Siqueiros into the set of my primal acquaintances, where he is honored for having painted a portrait of *my people*.

The invariant principle: wasn't this Einstein's themata? The use of sacred geometry indicated that Siqueiros also shared the ascetic ideal, experienced specifically as the feeling, emotion, desire to improve the world as we find it. "He therefore opposes knowledge to life and to the world he opposes another world, a world-beyond, the truthful world. The truthful world is inseparable from this will, the will to treat the 'world' as appearance. Thus the opposition of knowledge and life, the distinction between worlds, reveals its true character: it is a distinction of moral origin. And we always come up against the 'virtuism' of the one who wills the truth [. . .] He wants life to become virtuous, to correct itself and to correct appearance, for it to serve as the way to the other world. He wants life to repudiate itself and to turn against itself. Thus behind the moral opposition there stands another kind of contradiction, the religious or ascetic contradiction" (Deleuze, 1983: 96). Yes, like this Stalinist artist, I experienced in myself a desire, a duty, an imperative, a need to improve the world (an obligation I had never understood how to meet). I am testifying, not arguing. I am saying: here is the felt duty. The EmerAgency is a whirling square. It is my attempt to pass Agamben's test.

Michel Serres showed me something about my dilemma, my aporia, in the fables of Aesop and La Fontaine—the stories about the fox, the wolf, and the cheese, which is not really cheese but a reflection of the moon in the water at the bottom of a well (behold!). There are three in the story, Serres explains, "two idiots and the moon. Who is the stronger, who is the stupider? The answer to the question spins like a top" (Serres, 1982: 75). The fable says something about the game of truth or of justice, in terms of game theory, prisoners' dilemma, the balance beam of an assay scale (the scales of justice) evoked in the machinery of the well. I read it as a comment on the imitation game of life. "I don't want to play any more. Neither at the game of who is smarter nor that of the truth. For you can die of hunger, of cold, of drowning, while playing. I want to eat some good cheese. Not the best, nor the true, seen in the mirrors as images. I want to be wise. And I want my little piece of the banquet, the object" (75). Who speaks, with what tone, in this passage? What I hear is: perhaps you did not want to be wise, *but only to be old?* In this thought two diagrams converged: the battlefield map in the tourist guide to the Little Bighorn memorial, and Walter Benjamin's personal labyrinth. To be wise is to have prepared in advance, like a celebrity's obituary, this diagram of destination. The wisdom effect (learning how to die). It was not what I expected.

Mataturista

He crossed the border at Juarez around dinner time (the customs officers remembered his baby blue TR3). After getting something to eat and drinking three cups of coffee, he decided to continue on that night to Mazatlan rather than getting a motel room. The highway from Juarez to the ocean is nearly a straight line, a diagonal on the map, heading south and west to the Pacific coast (you could treat it as phi for an undrawn square). It was a mistake, a misjudgment, to try to make this last leg of the trip without a good night's sleep, having already driven from Montana, sleeping out at rest stops, placing his sleeping bag beneath picnic tables in case of rain. His mother's cautionary tales about people murdered in their sleep who were foolish enough to take naps at rest stops kept him awake ("suppose you get to Mataturista; then what?").

The TR3 pulled away from the diner, shifting through the gear changes. He hit the electric overdrive and cruised toward the setting sun. In the dark, not a car going either direction, the engine stroking smoothly, powerfully, with its characteristic whine, the Triumph riding low. No doubt he had been overdriving his headlights, the straightness of the road giving him the illusion that he could see all the way to the city. Two-lane blacktop, with no shoulder, running through what seemed in the dark to be desert all the way. Just desert. He practiced his Spanish verbs to keep awake: quiero, quieres, quiere, queremos, quereis, quieren. *It happened all in an instant, just a brightness at first in the yellow beams. An image, as if in slow motion (trying to picture it) of several peasants in their white workclothes, waving, waving their arms; one with a sack, waving (the scene set in motion long before he saw it), waving ambiguous surrender or greeting or warning (Goya, "Third of May 1808").*

He had been in a trance, if not actually asleep (a trick learned driving gravel trucks for his father every summer). The farmers, the peasants, crowded on the tractor watched the headlights since they first appeared on the horizon, mistakable at first for fireflies, if there had been any fireflies in the moonless night (the tin moon of Lorca and Plath). The peasants stood on the back of this tractor, the tractor of socialist realism, giant wheels turning, with no lights at all (not on the front, not on the back, neither white nor red,) moving at the speed at which a field might be plowed, so that the TR3 closed the gap between them quickly, speedometer right on 75, the white shirts and pants flapping now like reflectors in the full high beams of the oncoming sports car, blinking on like a revelation, pulsing with the synchronized gestures of spectators, handkerchiefs out, as if cheering with a rush of motor wind at that moment of material illumination.

OFFICE

1. The chief exercise here is to compose an emblematic scene of happiness, or that promises happiness: a self-addressed ad. "Happiness" is the name of a state of mind that is one of the most abstract or general of moods, not to be sought directly, the sages often remind us: it is the byproduct of other enactments. The American constitution guarantees the pursuit of happiness, which is perfect for a pluralist society since there are so many ways to live this ideal. Tarkovsky's parable, *Stalker,* warned about the lack of self-knowledge regarding our wishes, split between the ideal and the abject (untransposed, in Bataille's formless). You may find that the VALS (values and lifestyles) research of the agencies is not far off when you try to embody in a situation the feeling of well-being. You are dealing here with one of the oldest question of philosophy, asking about what constitutes the good life.

2. The final remake is also an Ulmer File, intended as a relay for your inquiry into your own state of mind and the default moods of your situation. The goal of the mystory map is to foreground the very frame through which we experience and understand the world and ourselves. The frame is out of sight and out of mind, taken for granted. Literate critique approaches this self-awareness through conceptual analysis, itemizing the identity categories of ideology. Electrate imaging supplements this analysis

with emotional and aesthetic production. I could see and understand intellectually and aesthetically the moods of exotic others (of Japan or Brazil), which were attractive for the very reason that they were "something"—they had a shape and a being. In my alienated condition I was unaware of my own identity that was as shaped and as informed by mood, belief, custom, accent, as were those exotic states I admired.

3. The uncanny detour away from home and back raised my awareness and understanding of my own position on the map. First I had to relearn the belief system introjected during my upbringing, this time in academic terms. I had learned the spirit of Protestantism and capitalism, for example, through participation in a habitus, which I accepted uncritically and as the way of the world. I was never given explicit instruction in intellectual foundations of these institutions. With this information as a guide it was easy enough to discover in my attitudes, opinions, beliefs, and habits the worldview and mood of the Protestant spirit of capitalism. Duty: it is one of the great virtues of the American character, and also one of its great vices. Paradox. Aporia. What is one to do? The wide image is a compass, a map, perhaps even an oracle.

4. To summarize: if electracy does for the body what literacy did for the mind (provide a prosthesis to augment and extend certain features of intelligence native to the human organism), I have to understand what it means to have a bourgeois body. As one historian put it, when a society really wants to be sure to remember something, it stores it in the body of its subjects. An assumption of this book (typical of rhetoric primers) is that at the core of human experience is something traditionally called "values." Your worldview (beliefs about how the world works and what actions are appropriate), whether examined or unexamined, was learned or constructed through a kind of cultural "osmosis." What we are calling attunement refers to the way mood mediates between this worldview and your actions in daily life. It is the cognitive map you use to negotiate the relation between your personal experience and the collective history.

In practical terms, what is meant by the term "enthymeme" is that all narratives and arguments include in their structure the places of your worldview. You always arrive late at the scene of a story or exposition. They appeal to you (hail you) by grounding their premises on your worldview (to the extent that you are part of the imagined community for that work). This ability of a story or explanation to appeal to you is due to the existence of the default moods of a culture. These moods are not whims or emotions but have their origin in the institutions associated with the categories of our identity: race, ethnicity, religion, economics, gender, sexuality, nation, and the like. To say that someone is a W.A.S.P., for example, is to evoke a set of collective identity formations of White, Anglo-Saxon, Protestant civilization. The same is true for a Black, African, Muslim civilization, and so forth through all the permutations of the categories. The mix of beliefs and behaviors expressive of each instantiation of each category produces even at the level of default moods an emergent and therefore unpredictable (complex) attunement. This attunement is also called "home." To understand what it means to be the "other" of a worldview you need only enter a booster store selling the paraphernalia of a rival sports team. Or, for a more profound example, listen to a propaganda tape made by an enemy of your nation, such as Osama bin Laden (in our case).

5. The relevance of the ideological and rhetorical condition of "home" for the Emer-Agency is twofold: first, the quest for the wide image involves discovering the particular, singular nuance that an individual gives to the default cultural resources. A wide image, that is, is a compromise formation of biology and culture (drives and desires).

This nuance is your style or "symptom" (*sinthome*, to use Lacan's term)—the pure pattern of signifiers that means nothing in itself, but is the expression of your coherence (identity, difference). The claim is that when you are being productive (at anything) and enter into the state of "flow," the mood or emotional tone of this experience is a manifestation of the wide image. Second, your service as an egent involves mapping the field of connections relating community difficulties, public policy, and worldview (values, attunements). The claim (which we will not be able to test fully in this book) is that the internet opens a new dimension, a virtual civic sphere, with the potential (through the fifth estate) to give citizens access as witnesses to the process by which a society selects which circumstances constitute problems, and what policies are appropriate to guide the search for solutions and remedies.

As you work on putting your mystory pattern into an emblem, keep in mind that the result is the magic tool that prepares you to consult on a public policy question. The EmerAgency experiment proposes that egents address policies at their roots—in worldviews. An egent consults by testifying to a value. Here it is: in me. Problems B Us. We will get at least an introduction to this next phase of consultation in the conclusion to the book.

CONCLUSION: CULTURE WARS OR SYNCRETISM?

Do your duty; shake your booty.

STUDIO
The Gift of Aporia

In the emblem we have a magic tool (a map of our creative imagination), but have not really attempted to apply it to a policy consultation. The historical problem of colonialism, and the more local issue of binge drinking, have stood in for a public problem that an egent might choose for herself. That consulting practice will require a new project. For now, we can get a feeling for the next stage by an exercise that tests the openness of the inside that we learned from composing a wide image. An egent is a witness, participating through the connectionist network of the internet in the virtual corporate gaze of a fifth estate. The slogan of the EmerAgency is "Problems B Us." An egent treats a public issue not as "problem" but "aporia." The difference is that conventional consultants look for that aspect of social difficulties that lends itself to pragmatic solutions, while inventional consultants (egents) might look at the same difficulties but call attention to that in them which is impossible. Most of the theorists in our repertoire, as summed up by Heidegger, consider the human condition itself to be aporetic, irreparable. The "impossible" dimension refers to this limit-condition (the proverbial "death and taxes").

> "[Man] becomes the strangest of all beings because, without issue on all paths, he is cast out of every relation to the familiar and befallen by ATH, ruin, catastrophe. Man is 'issueless,' Heidegger says, not simply because he encounters obstacles, nor even because man becomes mired in his own paths as he loses hold of that opening to Being in which the truth of his knowing is founded. Man is 'without issue on all paths' ('pantoporos aporos') because his violent and venturesome way-making must shatter against death, 'this strange and uncanny thing that banishes us once and for all from every thing in which we are at home.' 'It is not only when he comes to die, but always and essentially that man is without issue [Ausweglos] in the face of death. Insofar as man is, he stands in the issuelessness of death. Thus Da-sein is the happening of strangeness'" (Fynsk, 1986: 121).

Exercise: Testimony

Select another news report (like the article on binge drinking) that stings you for whatever reason, as a situation of difficulty, blockage, obstacle, breakdown, impossibility. Compose a word-picture emblem selecting some specific detail of this situation and juxtaposing it with some aspect of your wide image. Treat the emblem as an allegory of "aporia."

- The goal is to mark the presence of the General Economy in daily life. Sartre called it the practico-inert. "It is this inscribed or worked-on matter that constitutes the total environment in which we live—physically and socially: its organized space, means of production, institutions, its 'social facts,' and codified patterns of behavior, in short the practico-inert. This material reality is a resistance to our projects, a limit to our knowledge, and our only possible instrumentality for living" (Barnes, 1981: 249)

- The purpose of this emblem is to map the EmerAgency updating of the ATH of tragedy as a deconstruction of instrumental consulting. The collective disaster helps reveal the individual "foolishness" (and vice versa). The theory is that any practical solution to the breakdowns or disasters in the civic realm is limited finally by two other dimensions of disaster that calculative thinking neglects: the ultimate limitation on human capacity at the macro level of cosmology; and the fundamental incompleteness—the wound—of individual identity. The goal of this exercise is to test the affective capacity of the wide image precisely in its nature as "wide"—its ability to mediate your relation to world situations outside your biography.

- The basic strategy for now is to use the news scene as a metaphor evoking your own feeling of "I'm stuck." Read the newspaper or watch television with a personal issue in mind, and try to find a reported event that seems to work as a "structural portrait" of your situation. Your testimony on a policy issue is expressed in this metaphor that uses a documentation of the external circumstances of a social problem or disaster as a figure or analog for your inner experience. The binge drinking example related directly to the world of college students, just as colonialism obviously is relevant to all of us. However, since the testimony is figurative, not literal, the news event and its policy context need not apply literally to your situation.

Our theory places the paradoxical figure of aporia into tension with the logic of problem, defined etymologically with respect to "projection, or protection, that which one poses or throws in front of oneself, either as the projection of a project, of a task to accomplish, or as the protection created by a substitute, a prosthesis that we put forth in order to represent, replace, shelter, or dissimulate ourselves, or so as to hide something unavowable—like a shield" (Derrida, 1993: 11–12). As a state of mind, "problem" is a modern "fetish." Derrida's example is the ghost of Hamlet's father, who calls Hamlet out of his normal world into the special world of tragedy: crime, revenge, duty, and death. The ghost appears fully encased in armor, and Hamlet alone recognizes the identity of the spirit. This context brings out the dimension of "denial" or "defense" in problem-solving.

With *problem* one knows what to do; there is a method for working the puzzle. *Aporia*, however, Derrida defined as "the point at which the problematic task becomes impossible and where we are exposed, absolutely without protection, without problem, and without prosthesis, without possible substitution. . . . in this place of aporia, there is no longer any problem" (12). Some synonyms for what "aporia" names are "barred path"—the feeling of "I'm stuck, I cannot get out, I'm helpless" (13). Such is the movement required for the education of mood. We started with ordinary homesickness (or even boredom), to aporia (to discover within homesickness the generator of aporia). The exercise should use the news event to locate this feeling of "stuckness" or "limit."

The Rhetoric of Aporia

- The aporia in narrative structure maps and symptomizes the political unconscious—a contradiction in the cultural resources of the community, according to Jameson. "We have implied that the social contradiction addressed and 'resolved' by the formal prestidigitation of narrative must, however reconstructed, remain an absent cause, which cannot be directly or immediately conceptualized by the text. It seems useful, therefore, to distinguish, from this ultimate subtext which is the place of social contradiction, a secondary one, which is more properly the place of ideology, and which takes the form of the aporia or the antinomy: what can in the former be resolved only through the intervention of praxis here comes before the purely contemplative mind as logical scandal or double bind, the unthinkable and the conceptually paradoxical, that which cannot be unknotted by the operation of pure thought, and which must therefore generate a whole more properly narrative apparatus—the text itself—to square its circles and to dispel through narrative movement, its intolerable closure" (Jameson, 1981: 82–83). For Jameson, a Marxist, the social contradiction is class conflict. In narratology, "class" or the other ideological norms constitute "power"—the values that motivate the standpoint that controls the narrative world.

- For Derrida the aporia is not necessarily a bad or negative condition, but a "promise" of an alternative logic. "I believe that we would misunderstand [aporia] if we tried to hold it to its most literal meaning: an absence of path, a paralysis before road-blocks, the immobilization of thinking, the impossibility of advancing, a barrier blocking the future. On the contrary, it seems to me that the experience of the aporia, such as de Man deciphers it, gives or promises the thinking of the path, provokes the thinking of the very possibility of what still remains unthinkable or unthought, indeed, impossible. The figures of rationality are profiled and outlined in the madness of the aporetic" (Derrida, 1986: 134). The way out here is the deconstruction of contradiction itself, to expose all contradictions based on the articulation of oppositions (e.g. performative/constative speech acts, science/rhetoric, truth/persuasion) as secondary to a "prior" unity (truth is irreparably a rhetorical construction, etc., including the truth of Marxist dialectical materialism).

- Richard Dyer ascribed the "charisma" or aura of star celebrities—the truly iconic ones—to the stars' capacity to embody the aporetic condition of the practico-inert. "Marilyn Monroe provides another example. Her image has to be situated in the flux of ideas about morality and sexuality that characterized the fifties in America and can here be indicated by such instances as the spread of Freudian ideas in postwar America (registered particularly in the Hollywood melodrama), the Kinsey report, Betty Friedan's *The Feminine Mystique,* rebel stars such as Marlon Brando, James Dean, and Elvis Presley, the relaxation of cinema censorship in the face of competition from television etc. (In turn, these instances need to be situated in relation to other levels of the social formation, e.g. actual social and sexual relations, the relative economic situations of men and women etc.). Monroe's combination of sexuality and innocence is part of that flux, but one can also see her 'charisma' as being the apparent condensation of all that within her. Thus she seemed to 'be' the very tension that ran through the ideological life of fifties America. You could see this as heroically living out the tensions or painfully exposing them" (Dyer, 1991: 58–9).

Comment

- We are exploring the state of mind that the French poet Baudelaire, inventor of the modern image, called "spleen." The testimony metaphor uses a kind of Method acting in which you identify with the event by finding a scene of frustration in your own life experience. The point is not to claim that your situation is as serious as, say, that of victims of land mines in Afghanistan or Vietnam, but that an image of a child with a prosthetic leg evokes how you felt in your given circumstances.

There is more to say about giving and receiving the gift of the magic tool. No one may receive it in the abstract, through an explanation. It happens as an event of recognition, as an experience of tuning. It is uncanny, a surprise, a secret that should or could have remained hidden but now comes to light. The norm, the natural standpoint, dictates a certain way of doing things, a certain attitude, behavior, preferences, with which it seems best to conform (go along to get along). What if we enter a time of emergency (we are in such a time now), a time when every human resource is needed?

The purpose of the widesite is to prepare the place in which the magic tool may be found as a gift. The Donor or Sender, that is, must give the magic tool without "return." Derrida insists on this aporia of the gift: that to be a gift there must be no calculation or contract. Into the calculative logic of explanation must be insinuated the paradoxes of aporetics (irreducible dilemmas). "Everything seems to lead us back toward the paradox or the aporia of a nuclear proposition in the form of the 'if . . . then': if the gift appears or signifies itself, if it exists or if it is presented as gift, as what it is, then it is not, it annuls itself" (26). But such twists are the materials of conduction. The "tool" is just this moment of encounter, of extimacy, between outside and inside, and the realization that metaphor and metonymy, figuration, (poetry and design) are the divination system with the uncanny capacity to find and map the borders of identity.

LECTURE
Master-Slave (Again)

Let us continue our provisional testimony on our postcolonial situation, then, since it is relevant to globalization and cyberpidgin, and as a transition to the third act of our narrative allegory, the final encounter with the villain of trouble, the practico-inert monster. The evolution of morals continues, a reality that confronts our society with an aporia. The transvaluation of values that Nietzsche recorded in his genealogy refers to the first major syncretism of the Western tradition, the hybridization of the Greco-Roman and Judeo-Christian civilizations that produced Augustine, and that in Nietzsche's view resulted in the triumph of slave values and the cultural mood of ressentiment. Another turn of the spiral of history has brought about a period of transvaluation of values, in which the Western system of vices and virtues is undergoing revision through syncretism with the civilization enslaved during the colonial period, adding the Black Atlantic to the mix. In electracy the Americas are becoming Greco-Roman-Judeo-Christian-Afro-Caribbean (JewGreekCreole). As it was in the previous period of syncretism, the body is at stake in the struggle over morals. It is ironic, or paradoxical, or lucky—depending on one's point of view—that at the very moment when the Western dream of transcendence of the body produced a technology (VR) capable of leaving behind the filthy "meat" of the flesh (wetware) to realize the omnipotence of the mind, that the African body emerged in our behavior in a way that inverted the VR hierarchy in favor of the embodied flesh. Against ressentiment and Duty the syncretized West proposes a new mood that comes in two flavors: *cool* and *funk*.

Deconstruction   The insight of syncretism is that the outcome of this conflict will not be the triumph of one or the other (duty OR funk), but a hybrid that is a new, unforeseen, state of mind, different from both of its sources. Moreover, the very binary terms in which this process is stated shows that we are still treating the question by means of concepts (literacy) rather than images (electracy).

Deconstruction brings into thought the generative site of Western metaphysics, meaning specifically the operation by means of which literacy categorizes or classifies the world.

> "With regard to concepts in bipolar opposition—that is, to metaphysical concepts, to the aporias that become visible in the formation of concepts, and to the conflicting strata of argumentative and discursive totalities—the infrastructure is the 'open matrix' in which those oppositions and contradictions are engendered. Derrida defines infrastructure when he writes, 'Here structure means the irreducible complexity within which one can only shape or shift the play of presence or absence: that within which metaphysics can be produced but which metaphysics cannot think. The infrastructures which as we shall see are irremediably plural, represent the relation—connection, ratio, rapport—that organizes and thus accounts for the differences, contradictions, aporias, or inconsistencies between concepts, levels, argumentative and textual arrangements and so on that characterize the discourse of metaphysics" (Gasche, 147).

"Infrastructure" as used here could be applied also to the function of chora (space, place, receptacle) in its original use in Plato's *Timaeus*, as the place in which chaos was sorted into the fundamental kinds of what is—Earth, Air, Fire, and Water. The metaphorical status of chora recalls Derrida's focus on the nature of language. Another way to state the insight of "infrastructure" is to note the process Derrida called "white mythology," the erasure or forgetting of the metaphorical or figurative (rhetorical) generation of concepts. Our deconstruction of consulting is designed to move the thinking about our historical moment from literate to electrate categories.

To clarify the relevance of this transvaluation to the invention of the image apparatus it is useful to remind ourselves of the mind-body (spirit-matter) hierarchy coming from both the Greek and Hebrew traditions of our civilization, for this dichotomy-hierarchy is what is undergoing transformation in the new syncretism. David Hawkes provides the further insight, central to our concern with the image in the spectacle, that the spirit-matter hierarchy included a third term—representation—such that the condemnation of the body extended to iconic signs.

David Hawkes on the Iconoclasm of the Western Tradition

"After Plato, Helenic thought generally takes for granted the superiority of the ideal over the material. This means that the mutually definitive binary opposition between ideas and matter has become a hierarchy, in which the former pole is privileged over the latter. We can see some of the consequences of this in Aristotle's *Politics*. In that work, all forms of power are justified by analogy with the mind/body hierarchy: 'It is then in an animal . . . that one can first discern both the sort of rule characteristic of a master and political rule. For the soul rules the body with the rule characteristic of a master, while intellect rules appetite with political and kingly rule, and this makes it evident that it is according to nature and advantageous for the body to be ruled by the soul, and the passionate part [of the soul] by intellect and the part having reason, while it is harmful to both if the relation is equal or reversed.' From the presupposition that the mind's subjective ideas are naturally superior to the objective material body, Aristotle proceeds to deduce the necessary dominance of masters over slaves, of Greeks over barbarians, and of men over women. A bias in the relation of the ideal to the material gives credence to the claim that certain human beings are fit only to be ruled by others, as well as to the assertion that certain forms of consciousness are systematically false. . . .

"The Hebrew tradition, which along with Hellenic thought is the primal influence on Western philosophy, also ascribes false consciousness to a misconstruction of the relations between the elements of the totality. In the Hebrew Bible, the Israelites are distinguished from the gentiles by the prohibition on material representations of their deity. Due to the attraction which sensual things hold for fallen humanity, such representations will inevitably become fetishes; that is, people will forget that they are merely representations, and idolize them, venerating them as though they were incarnations of the divine. Yahweh makes this clear when, in the first two commandments, He makes the abandonment of images a precondition of monotheism. . . . Representations of the deity are thus incompatible with Judaic monotheism, which asserts that the source of all meaning is an absolute *logos* which is necessarily incorporeal" (Hawkes, 1996: 16–17).

The apparatus of electracy with its foregrounding of the image is irreducibly intertwined with the fate of the Black Atlantic, which is to say that the stakes in the battles over multiculturalism include a technological and even a grammatological dimension. As W. J. T. Mitchell argued in *Picture Theory*, the formal question of learning how to author in the hybrid media of text and picture is inextricable from the ideological issue of power. He makes clear that the shift from concept (word, *logos*) to image (and chora) in electracy involves a metaphysical problem.

W. J. T. Mitchell on Picture Theory

"It isn't just that the text/image difference 'resembles' the relation of self and other, but that the most basic pictures of epistemological and ethical encounters (knowledge of objects, acknowledgment of subjects) involve optical/discursive figures of knowledge and power that are embedded in essentialized categories like 'the visual' and 'the verbal' (Panofsky's opening move into the discipline of 'iconology' as a discourse on images is, as we've seen, a visual, gestural encounter with another person.) It is as if we have a metapicture of the image/text encounter, in which the word and the image are not abstractions or general classes, but concrete figures, characters in a drama, stereotypes in a Manichean allegory or interlocutors in a complex dialogue.

"The 'otherness' we attribute to the image-text relationship is, therefore, certainly not exhausted by a phenomenological model (subject/object, spectator/image). It takes on the full range of possible social relations inscribed within the field of verbal and visual representation. 'Children should be seen and not heard' is a bit of proverbial wisdom that reinforces a stereotypical relation, not just between adults and children, but between the freedom to speak and see and the injunction to remain silent and available for observation. That is why this kind of wisdom is transferable from children to women to colonized subjects to works of art to characterizations of visual representation itself. Racial otherness, (especially in the binarized 'black/white' divisions of U.S. culture) is open to precisely this sort of visual/verbal coding. The assumption is that 'blackness' is a transparently readable sign of racial identity, a perfectly sutured imagetext. Race is what can be seen (and therefore named) in skin color, facial features, hair, etc. Whiteness, by contrast, is invisible, unmarked; it has no racial identity, but is equated with a normative subjectivity and humanity from which 'race' is a visible deviation. It's not merely a question of analogy, then, between social and semiotic stereotypes of the other, but of mutual inter-articulation. That is why forms of resistance to these stereotypes so often take the form of disruptions at the level of representation, perception, and semiosis" (Mitchell, 1994: 162–163).

Heuretics

This understanding may be used on behalf of the status quo or of change. Fernand Hallyn, in *The Poetic Structure of the World*, shows the possibilities with the analysis of an historical example—the Copernican revolution. Reviewing the details of the cases of Copernicus and Kepler, Hallyn looked for the "poetics" of this discovery. "A poetics is obliged to seize the scientific hypothesis at the precise moment it emerges from its cultural milieu, but while it is still in the mixing pot of texts, prejudices, symbols, and so on. We could never hope to understand Copernicus by detaching him from this synchronic field and inserting him only in the diachronic history of astronomy" (Hallyn, 1993: 283). Such too is the problem of understanding the internet as invention.

Hallyn shows that the discoveries of Copernicus and Kepler are anticipated in the aesthetics of their respective periods. Two sets of data or two semantic fields are brought into relationship—the invention of perspective in painting parallels and anticipates the invention of the new astronomy. Or, more generally, the aesthetics of Mannerism across the arts shares a solution to the problem of representation with the one found in Kepler's new physics. Hallyn's method may be characterized as poststructural in that it goes beyond the structuralist generalization of discourse theory postulating a homologous relationship across disparate domains of a given historical period, to explore the particular details of the production of a specific hypothesis in a concrete case. "The topography of places does not explain what happens there: 'the individual who occupied that place was led to orient himself emotionally and intellectually, and the question is to determine how he did so'" (13). It is not a matter of coding, but of inference; not only conception and perception, but sensation.

Kepler's method in the particular case is found again at the level of Hallyn's historical account: "Starting with a metaphor that compares geometric knowability to musical consonance, Kepler derives a series of associations. The movement is similar to what happens in allegory, which also consists of 'weaving' a collection of applications from one semantic field onto another" (236). What Hallyn confines to the interpretive realm of historical scholarship chorography extends to invention, while substituting tangling for weaving (felt for text). Such is the goal of a relay—to extend an abductive reconstruction of the poetics of a discovery produced after the fact into a generator for making further discoveries of a different sort. Heuretics is this logic of invention. Might it not be possible to apply to new circumstances, to a new problem, the details of a solution arrived at in completely different circumstances? In one sense this question has already been answered in the affirmative. The Copernican revolution has become the hypericon of all the transformative discoveries of Enlightenment science since the Renaissance. Kant, Darwin, Marx, and Freud have all been described as the "Copernicus" of their respective domains. Kuhn's theory of scientific revolutions suggested that a case such as that of Copernicus functions as an exemplar that tacitly embodies the rules of a paradigm.

The heuretic strategy is to accept these precedents as the basis for an experimental method; to propose that any problem I may pose for myself may be organized in the style of a Copernican revolution. But this "revolution" is itself a metaphor of "turning about." We continue the evolution of the meaning of "revolution" from the shape of one's path in a gravity field to "seance" (table turning). The structure of the poetics is homologous with that of the riddle form, involving the juxtaposition and interference of two apparently unrelated semantic domains. In principle the instructions say *to juxtapose the semantic domain of a given problem with the semantic domain of contemporary aesthetics*. Guidelines for the representation of the problem may be derived from the principles of representation discernible in the arts of my moment. Here is a procedure to meet Jameson's suggestion to look for a new collective logic in the aesthetics of our time.

The Next Copernican Revolution?   The interest of Hallyn's study is that it shows in detail the specifics of the intertext in a prototypical case of problem solving. We may adapt this case to the terms of internet invention: the metaphorical relationship must be found between the attributes of a given problem category and those of contemporary aesthetics—between the rhetoric of electracy (as the problem in my discipline field) and funk (a contemporary aesthetics). Is the EmerAgency a "Copernican revolution" in problem solving? At the very least, it is an uprising of aporia formation. The challenge is that each successive such revolution has been the scene of a traumatic wound. The previous blows to our collective self-image as human came from Copernicus, Darwin, and Freud: we are not at the center of the universe; we are descended from apes; we do not know what we are doing in most of our actions. And Derrida reminds us that Marx should be included in this series, for showing us that our ideals are but masks for power.

To be a "Copernican" revolution, our approach to problems involves a shift in point of view, such as that reflected in Kant's epistemology. As Copleston explained, Kant reasoned that whether the sun turns about the earth or vice versa does not affect the observed phenomena, which would be the same in either case. "The question is whether there are not astronomical phenomena which can only be explained on the heliocentric hypothesis [. . .] In an analogous manner, Kant suggests, empirical reality would remain what it is even on the hypothesis that for objects to be known they must conform to the mind rather than the other way about" (Copleston, 1960: 20). We may extrapolate to our own immediate question, the genealogy of electrate morals, to ask whether there are not value questions (questions of identity) that can only be explained by the funky hypothesis. This shift in perspective, we must remember, is culturally traumatic.

The Funk

The opposition between the Western and the African cosmologies is an open and explicit conflict in contemporary culture. What policies are being formulated to manage and administer this process? The point to keep in mind throughout this discussion is that what appears to be (and is) a struggle between opponents is also a hybrid merger. In our context (the history of the apparatus) we can see that the JewGreekCreole syncretism is a source of optimism about electracy, given the correspondence of imaging and creative thinking (but not everyone agrees).

Rickey Vincent on Funk

"There are many aspects of The Funk that are intimately tied to an African value system that has been propagated through black culture since the Middle Passage. Funk is deeply rooted in African cosmology— the idea that people are created in harmony with the rhythms of nature and that free expression is tantamount to spiritual and mental health. If we were to look into this African philosophy, the African roots of rhythm, spiritual oneness with the cosmos, and a comfort zone with sex and aspects of the body, we would find that funkiness is an ancient and worthy aspect of life. Thus, funk in its modern sense is a deliberate reaction to—and rejection of—the traditional Western world's predilection for formality, pretense, and self-repression.

"In traditional Western society the maintenance of rationality, civility, and pomp, with deliberate disregard and disdain for the natural urges of the body and soul, has become a goal unto itself. The influx of technology has in many ways provided a further impetus for most Westerners to obsess with the aesthetics of curbing their instincts. One of Toni Morrison's characters in *The Bluest Eye* looks at the situation facing upstanding 'white' Americans: 'They learn how to behave. The careful development of thrift, patience, high morals, and good manners. In short, how to get rid of the funkiness. The dreadful funkiness of passion, the funkiness of nature, the funkiness of the wide range of human emotion. Wherever it erupts, this funk, they wipe it away; where it creates, they dissolve it, wherever it drips, flowers or clings, they find it and fight it until it dies. They fight this battle all the way to the grave.' This vengeance against nature is also manifest in the obsessively cruel and sexually violent treatment of blacks by whites throughout American history" (Vincent, 1996: 4–5).

The creolization of African and Western embodiment took place, it must be remembered, within the destroyed, blasted conditions of colonialism, commodification, and slavery. The result is that the new body manifests itself in two versions or moods—cool and funk—which are often found together, but which are not the same thing. While "cool" was a state of mind of dignity and wisdom in Africa, as we know from Robert Farris Thompson's history, after the middle passage it was put to work in the Americas as an attitude of defense, especially a defense of Black masculinity. "Some African-American males have channeled their creative energies into the construction of a symbolic universe. Denied access to mainstream avenues of success, they have created their own voice. Unique patterns of speech, walk, and demeanor express the cool pose. This strategic style allows the black male to tip society's imbalanced scales in his favor. Coolness means poise under pressure and the ability to maintain detachment, even during tense encounters" (Majors and Billson, 1992: 2). The problem is not with Street cool, but in the popcycle circulation of cool from Street to Entertainment.

Cool   The spectacle, like the sage, is cool. There is a perfect fit, that is, between the cool pose of Black masculinity that came to define the etiquette and ethic of Street discourse and the defensive function of Entertainment discourse, protecting against compassion fatigue by a kind of artificial PTSD (post-traumatic stress disorder). "Cool" is a practice of impersonation that accords with the becoming-image that is the emerging subject of electrate people. The dilemma is that "cool," separated from funk, is ressentiment by other means. "For some black males, cool pose represents a fundamental structuring of the psyche—the cool mask belies the rage held in check beneath the surface. For others it is the adoption of a uniquely creative style that serves as a sign of belonging and stature. Black males have learned to use posing and posturing to communicate power, toughness, detachment, and style—self" (8). Cool in the blasted conditions of Street discourse marginalized in the Western value system, manifests itself in the behavior of the barroom and brothel. The coolest one is the tough pimp, an atmosphere circulated in "Blaxploitation" films and Hip Hop. Cool pose is not specific to the United States, but is found in machismo throughout the Americas. The tango man, for example, is as cool—as macho—as they come.

> "This is the story of the guapo or compadrito, those men of different skin shades but the same dark fate who cultivated courage—courage as a skill and as a value. In Borges's words, these guapos were specialists in progressive intimidation, 'veterans in winning without having to fight.' With a few knife fights over questions of honor, few words but plenty of bad attitude, they established a reputation and territory for themselves on the outskirts of the city. . . .
>
> "Whether the guapos cared or not about their women it is hard to tell; they learned to look tough, to despise life, and to disdain women. Perhaps they disdained women defensively because women were unattainable or difficult to keep. Perhaps they came to despise life from fighting over women in order to keep on being men, despite their class. The macho identity was born out of this contradiction, and women's identities were born out of the competition among men: Macho men of different colors and classes pulling at women from different directions shaped women's nameless identities" (Savigliano, 31).

Teen Spirit What happens when the bourgeois body becomes cool? The spread of cool through the popcycle is evident in the symbiotic relationship between teenage Street behavior, including lifestyle consumption patterns, and entertainment. Cool is the channel of communication for the Sender and Receiver of value or sign currency, the emblem of which is Joe Camel. Cool is compatible with an emblematic language of gestures. The arguments over authenticity and "selling out" show a failure to understand the inevitability of this circulation in the spectacle.

Marcel Danesi on Adolescent Style

"The symbolic and behavioral feature that distinguishes teenagerhood is coolness. The expression cool comes out of the jazz club scene of the 1930s. When the air in the smoke-filled nightclubs of that era became unbreathable, windows and doors were opened to allow some 'cool air' in from the outside to help clear away the suffocating air. By analogy, the slow and smooth jazz style that was typical of that late-night scene came to be called 'cool.' Cool was subsequently extended to describe any physically attractive, male jazz musician or aficionado who patronized such clubs. Recently, the makers of Camels cigarettes have strategically revived the nightclub coolness theme in their magazine ads and billboards. In one ad, a camel, dressed in a 'nightclubbish' white jacket, is enjoying the cool breeze coming in off the seashore. A cigarette is placed gingerly between his lips, dangling suggestively from the side of his mouth. He holds a rose in his hand, a symbol of love. He's obviously 'making eyes' at someone. The camel conveys an image of total coolness, recalling the socialite smoothness and finesse embodied by thirties and forties cinema stars, especially Humphrey Bogart in *Casablanca*.

"Coolness entails a set of specific behavioral characteristics, that vary in detail from generation to generation from clique to clique, but which retain a common essence. It is firmly anchored in a symbology—a set of discernible bodily movements, postures, facial expressions, voice modulations, and so on—that is acquired, and takes on strategic social value, within the peer context. First and foremost, coolness implies a deliberately slow and lackadaisical form of bodily locomotion, accompanied by a nonchalant and unflappable countenance. One is never to be seen in a state of hurriedness, embarrassment, or timidity. The walk is laggard, to the point of being a saunter or a stroll. The head is always tilting or gyrating in a deliberately slow, semicircular motion. The face is unperturbed, unexcited, composed. The cool teen never shows any intense emotion. Being cool involves a control over emotionally induced body states. Losing one's cool, as the expression goes, is to be avoided at all costs" (Danesi, 1994: 37–38).

Lifestyle, Street, and spectacle exist in a loop in which, through the experience of becoming image, is forming the subject of the electrate apparatus. As one "futurist" explains, "why is it important to listen to the progressive street cultures? Because these are the mind-sets—the collective thinkers and influencers—that are behind youth's latest infatuations with digital pets, beverages with floating objects, wash-in glitters and mascara hair colors, electronic music that can't be found on any contemporary radio station—and the list goes on. Through 'Mindtrends,' our biannual trend report, we track the movements among the progressive mind-sets and interpret them into actionable opportunities for marketing, new product development, brand management and advertising. The tracking of so-called 'trends' and 'what's cool' is a hot topic these days, mainly because mainstream businesses have been trying to crack the tastes, preferences, and styles of the elusive and fickle youth culture. It's understandable why. With over $36 billion of expendable income—and yes, they are spending those dollars—everybody wants a piece of the 'cool' spenders" (Lopiano-Misdom and De Luca, 1997: xii). The Marlboro cowboy is cool in this sense.

Comment

- A question for the EmerAgency is whether it is possible to interrupt the commodity creativity popcycle and redirect its associative dynamic toward the function of the fifth estate (collective self-knowledge).

- The source of the problem with cool is its effect relative to the defensive condition of the society of the spectacle. Cool reduces affect and continues in its own way the literate and bourgeois alienation from the body, while funk counteracts this alienation. The aporia remains, nonetheless, of how to design cybercreole, to provide a rhetorical practice adequate to the overload of bad news in the era of global information.

The Corporate Actant

Within the spectacle, or the emerging electrate apparatus, subject formation and the experience of being a person and having an identity are transforming along with the transformations of technology and institutional practices. If Socrates represents for us the prototype or even the first full embodiment of a literate person, who or what fills an equivalent position for electracy? A first response to this question often produces the names of stars or celebrities, especially Elvis Presley or Princess Diana. It is true that stars are the vanguard of electrate experience, in that they have entered the special world of the spectacle and become image, in which their look separates from their bodies to participate in the field of the gaze. In interviews celebrities often describe or even complain of the split in their experience between their physical personal existence and the nearly autonomous life of their image. Mariah Carey was once cited in a newspaper article, in response to a flurry of rumors about her love life, as saying that *her image was having more fun than she was.* An important authoring skill in electracy concerns learning to "write" in the virtual sphere with this disembodied projection of one's "self."

Meanwhile, at the collective level the new subject formation is that of the corporation itself. Theorists have argued that within the spectacle diegesis, a collective entity such as a corporation may function as an actant.

Algirdas Greimas, The Commercial Company as Collective Actant

"Legal discourse defines a commercial company both in its 'being' and with regard to its 'doing.' The company is indeed an object of discourse, that is to say, an 'entity,' but it is also a 'moral person.' Yet, at the same time this 'person' can receive successive predications, it is supposed to behave in a certain way and obey a certain number of explicit rules.

"Such discursive objects are called 'actants' in semantics. They have qualitative configurations that define their specificity, and they are also defined by the domain of their functions. In the broad sense of the term, an actant can be either the linguistic representation of a human person or the character of a story or again an animal or a machine.

"Furthermore, an actant must be individualizable: a person can be represented in discourse as John Doe, born the . . . , domiciled . . . , etc. a machine can be constructed by. . . . , in use since . . . , situated, etc. We shall designate by the term 'actors' those that represent the corresponding actants, by their typical behavior, and at the same time are distinguished by a specific historical anchoring (inscription in space and time, name, etc.).

"On the whole, the commercial company corresponds to such a definition: it appears as a characterized actant in the legal text. It is a collective actant, and the actors it subsumes are also collective actors.

"The problem we are dealing with here is that of the status of the 'moral person,' as opposed to the 'physical person.' Contrary to what is generally thought, these are not characteristics of individuation: its uniqueness and its historicity make it possible to determine the individual actant in relation to the collective actant. The latter can also be individualized and generate individual actors" (Greimas, 1990: 114–115).

The paradigmatic instance of corporate identity formation is found in the advertising campaign mounted by Apple Computer, the "Think Different" series. The template for this campaign, taking to an extreme the rhetorical device of the "testimonial," was an appropriated publicity still of a celebrity, famous for achievements in film, television, popular music, fine arts, plus a few figures from science and politics who had become media icons (such as Einstein and Gandhi). The full-page photograph was "aided" by the company logo (the rainbow-colored apple with a bite out of it) and the campaign slogan, "think different." The sheer excess of the number of such figures featured in the series (it seemed that no pop icon was left out) suggested a certain desperation, at the level of subject formation, of the desire to be, to exist as a moral person. Or, we could say that the ad campaign performs in the spectacle the same gathering of the "hodge-podge of identifications" from which the subject assembles the ego.

In the context of identification as impersonation, the archive of constantly changing stars juxtaposed with the company name indicates a failure of internalization, of "introjection," as if each act of introducing the outside icon into the inside of the entity failed (there was no inside), and therefore was repeated with a sequence of different icons, to give an effect of "papering over" or of graffiti. An analogy for corporate simulation of "self" might be with the replicants in *Bladerunner* who sustain the illusion of being individuals by the accumulation and simulation of family photographs and their related memories. As a symptom of electrate subject formation, corporate identity design demonstrates the prominence of surface (neither the transcendence of spirit nor the depth of self). The reason for dwelling on corporate identity is that the EmerAgency test posed by Agamben requires us to challenge advertisers for the position of Sender in the national narrative.

Exercise: Corporate States of Mind

In a newspaper column on the Enron scandal, Maureen Dowd described "Planet Enron" as not just one company, but a state of mind, which she summarized as that of a "platinum card aristocracy." Compare the way a corporation advertises its product and the way it represents itself on its website (if it has one). Use the wabi-sabi *template to try to identify the state of mind of the corporation.*

Value Reserves

Studies have shown that a strategy of much corporate advertising is a "parasitical" drawing upon the value resources of a culture—the same resources that the Sender communicates to the Receiver in a narrative—to create a connection in the spectacle between the company and a fundamental value of the society. It might seem at first that corporate identity attempts to circumvent the quest and appropriate directly for itself the object of value. In fact, corporations position themselves as Senders, communicating the object of value (ornamented with commodities) to consumers positioned as Receivers. This practice exploits the switch in the semantics of "value" between mores and system: value as "ideal belief" and as "position in a network." It is ironic that the kind of "personhood" the corporations attempt to replicate is that of a "self"—a literate identity. Hence, they seek sign values associated with "authenticity," which they narrow down essentially to two kinds of community scene: main street of rural small-town America, and the inner city "hood" or ghetto. The electrate aspect of advertising is not the signifieds thus created, the simulation and promotion of "self," but the formal creation of the ad as a space in which to transfer meanings from one domain to another.

Example: Reebok "Blacktop"

"It may be useful to walk through (Roland Barthes's) formal grid for tracking the signifier, using an example from a Reebok campaign for the Blacktop shoe. The campaign drew on the referent system of 'the blacktop'—a social and cultural space where inner-city youth play basketball. Appropriating signifiers for the purpose of constructing sign values tends to fetishize the signifier. What does this mean? Reebok's Blacktop campaign lifted the photographic image of the chain-link fence and turned it into a signifier of inner city alienation. Similarly, Reebok has stolen and hollowed out rapper images in the form of the MC and the DJ and the 'fatboys.' When Reebok took the name of the socially structured space of the asphalt basketball court—the blacktop—and appropriated it as the name for their shoe, they not only sought to inflate the sign value of their shoe, they also turned the blacktop as a social and cultural space into what Barthes called a second-order signifier. Inside the semiotic space of the Reebok ads, the Blacktop (as defined by the chain-link image, the stylized MC image, etc.) has been turned into a reified signifier that marks the 'place where legends are made' by Reebok. . . . Sign values depend, then, on a system of cultural cannibalism" (Goldman and Papson, 1996: 8–9).

Reflecting the principle that it takes a collective entity to deal with a corporate agent, the EmerAgency gathers its egents into a collective actant, not through legal incorporation, but through participation in the consultancy enabled by the internet. The point is not to critique Entertainment discourse but to learn from it how to image. If individual egents see themselves as protagonists learning to interact with donors, collectively the EmerAgency is itself a donor or even a Sender. The fundamental issue to be witnessed by The EmerAgency as fifth estate concerns the effect of corporate sponsored entertainment to strip funk from cool, to retain the defense and ignore the body, thus preserving the public in its anelectrate condition. It is the difference between closing or opening the "hole of being" (the difference between propaganda or art). Either way, what we want to learn is the rhetoric of imaging, to appropriate it for our own purposes of education and the virtual civic sphere. The Funk is its own "thang" that may or may not coexist with cool. The categorical dimension of funk, as we argued in the case of duende, is not the dance, nor the lifestyle, but the mood.

Rickey Vincent on Rooster-Poot Funk

"Funk is a means of release that cannot be denied. *Village Voice* writer Barry Walters explained the Funk as well as anyone could: 'Trying to put that *thang* called funk into words is like trying to write down your orgasm. Both thrive in that gap in time when words fall away, leaving nothing but sensation.'

"Funk is impossible to completely describe in words, yet we know the funk vibe when we see it. Funk is that low-down dirty-dog feeling that crops up when a *baad* funk jam gets to the heated part, and you forget about that contrived dance you were trying, and you *get off your ass and jam*. Funk is that geeked feeling that comes over you when a superstar steps into the room—or onto the stage—and everyone is hyped; The Funk hits you in competition, when that last shot you made was your best, yet you still dig down for that extra level for the overdrive that you didn't know was there; you know The funk when you're on a date and it's time to make your move—the funk is a rush that comes all over your body. Scientists have yet to discover that particular funk gland, but rest assured there are plenty of bodily excretions associated with it.

"Funk is that nitty-gritty *thang* that affects people when things get heavy. Funk can be out of control, like the chaos of a rebellion, or instinctively elegant, like that extended round of lovemaking that hits overdrive. Funk is what you say when nothing else will do. 'Funk it!' George 'Dr. Funkenstein' Clinton, the most heralded authority of funk philosophy, reduced The funk to its barest essence: 'Funk is whatever it needs to be, at the time that it is'" (Vincent, 1996: 3–4).

From Thing to *Thang*

A crucial moment in the invention of literacy was Aristotle's formulation of the "thing" in the practice of definition. Now the *thang* is similarly important for electracy. The Funk is *whatever,* negotiating the treacherous passage between pornography and the commodity ushering the bourgeois body (my body) to the grave, as Agamben said. Another slogan is, *Free Your Ass, And Your Mind Will Follow* (234). The guitarist James Blood Ulmer (this signature is my conductive link to the movement) declared that "Jazz is the Teacher, and Funk is the Preacher" (28). What is the lesson? Not pose, but duende. Not 'tude (no matter how *baad*), but mood.

Rickey Vincent on Funk as Mood

"The earliest English language dictionaries refer to the term *funk* as a 'cowering fear,' a 'somber emotional state,' or a depressed mood. This concept derived from the Flemish word *fonck,* a term for fear or dismay. Considering the situation facing black Americans at the turn of the twentieth century, the somber state of funk, even in its oldest European definition, could apply to black Americans as a form of melancholy not unlike the blues.

"Older linguistic references to *funky* come from the word root *fumet,* a French word for a musty smell, which is also clearly derived from the Latin root of *fume, fumus,* which means 'smoke.' Old English definitions of the term involve a 'strong smell' or 'big stink,' which has been the most common vernacular use. . . .

"Eventually the notion of 'funkiness' in terms of body odor was associated with 'funky music,' and the currency of the term most likely came into use among jazz musicians. . . . A significant discussion of the origins of the words funk and jazz is put forth by art historian Robert Farris Thompson. In his 1983 book *Flash of the Spirit,* Thompson asserts that the slave trafficking in the West Indies did not decimate African linguistic patterns completely, and that Kongo civilization and art were not obliterated in the New World. Thompson maintains that the black slang term *funky* always referred to 'strong body odor' (never to depression or fear), which is closer in meaning to the Central African Ki-Kongo word *lu-fuki*. . . .

"Similarly, Thompson discusses the origins of *jazz* as a 'Creolized' term for sex that was applied to the Congo dancers of New Orleans. Thompson maintains that many African-derived words described by etymologists as 'origin unknown' are African in origin, and that in particular, *jazz* came from the creole *jizz*, which is related to *dinza*, the Ki-Kongo word for 'ejaculation'. . . . Over the years, African slaves and their American counterparts developed a form of pidgin language that spread around the region, evolving into a hybrid, or Creole. According to Smitherman, 'this lingo involved the substitution of English for West African words, but within the same basic structure and idiom that characterized West African language patterns.' . . .

"If indeed what Thompson suggests is true, that the 'smell' of a man of integrity carries a blessing, then what is considered good in the West (no scent) versus what is considered good in Africa (heavy scent) reveals something profound about the differing frames of reference" (32–34).

Exercise: Mood Spectrum

Assess your mystory and wide image emblem in terms of cool and funk as default moods. On the widesite select three representative images of your personal VALS (text and picture) and arrange them on a scale with the ascetic ideal of duty at one extreme and funk embodied moment at the other. Find a news event to serve as a metaphor of what it feels like to be your body.

- The idea is to gain some relative sense of where you are in the spectacle process of becoming image. The wide image must be sorted and distinguished from the VALS of the establishment and the new syncretic mood of popular culture. At the same time, the yearning that connects with the blues (and funk) must be formatted, personalized, and not just emulated in an acceptance of the default. One of the paradoxes of our situation of virtual embodiment is that the very becoming image that puts us in our bodies also makes us dissatisfied with them. An effect of what Bukatman calls "terminal identity" is this movement of the subject away from the organic body into a cyborg symbiosis between bodies and machines.

How to Forget a Cowboy

The Protestant body sweats, but is not funky. It is said that when Haitians, for example, want to escape from the gods of Vodou, the loa, they convert to Protestantism. What happens when the dominant and emergent apparatuses come into conflict is evoked in the scene of Galileo being shown the "tools" (the tor-ture devices of the Inquisition). The institution of School (which is to literacy what religion is to orality) is not likely to be any more receptive to electrate funk than was the Medieval Church to empirical astronomy. The EmerAgency role, positioned at the crossroads of the popcycle, witnessing the circulation of values on the axis or route of communication from society through the Sender to the Receiver, is to testify to the technological and apparatus dimension of this mo-ment of transvaluation of values. The trauma that always accompanies decenter-ing is located in our riddle in the "body" (one of the few things about which there is some consensus across our field of study). *Free your ass and your mind will follow.* We understand what this slogan means in Entertainment. Who knows what it foretells about the rest of the popcycle, and about electracy as a worldview, but such is the funky "telescope" through which we are invited to look. The electrate apparatus challenges a fundamental presupposition of the literate world view. The presupposition is reflected in the normative hierarchy of mind over body, reason over emotion, spirit over flesh, and the other pairs that this binary oppo-sition entails, including an iconoclasm that traces its heritage to both the Judeo-Christian and Greco-Roman branches of the Western tradition. A syncretic slogan for the EmerAgency that acknowledges both the old and the new virtues may be: *do your duty; shake your booty.*

Any picture, any scene, any text, is a site of tension, open to a struggle for con-trol of meaning, which we know means a struggle over the narrative chain of signi-fiers, since any item or signifier means only in relation to another signifier. To return to our remake of the Marlboro ad, what does "cowboy" signify? The post-colonial period in recent American history has seen an explicit debate over our na-tional identity. John Fiske described this situation in relation to one instance, an exhibition entitled "The West as America, Reinterpreting Images of the Frontier, 1820–1920," mounted at the National Museum of American Art of the Smithson-ian Institution (Fiske, 1993: 162). The art displayed included the usual master-pieces and monuments celebrating and commemorating the settlement of the frontier. The captions displayed on the wall plaques created by the curators, how-ever, undercut the default ideological reception of the exhibition with commen-tary and critique of this westward expansion as imperialism, racism, sexism, and genocide, thus inserting into the discourse the point of view associated in the pop-ular press with "political correctness." In the political debates provoked by the ex-hibition, various leaders and pundits called for state control of the culture. As Fiske noted, the idea that the images of the culture need to be controlled for propagan-da or ideological reasons is an old one in our nation. He gives as an example a statement from 1845, cited in the exhibition catalogue.

> "Someone has said, give me the writing of the songs of a country, and you may make its laws. I had almost said, give me the control of the art of a country, and you may have the management of its administrations. There can be no greater folly than that committed by our statesmen, when they treat art and literature as something quite aside from great national interests. . . . Art is too often looked

upon as an abstract thing, designed only for men of taste and leisure. . . . Every great national painting of a battlefield, or great composition, illustrating some event in our history—every engraving, lithograph and wood cut appealing to national feeling and rousing national sentiment—is the work of art; and who can calculate the effect of all these on the minds of our youth?" (168).

Formless

What is the wound or blow delivered to the collective ego of Western humanity by the Funk? The blow has been a long time in landing, with one of its early manifestations being that most disturbing dialogue by Diderot, *Rameau's Nephew*. The nephew explains to the philosopher his cynical theory of education. He proposes to educate his son not in the ideals "of ancient Sparta," but in the actual practices of contemporary Parisian life, all the tricks and treacheries needed to become rich and powerful. "I was appalled to think of what his child would become under such a tutor," mused the philosopher. "It was clear that if he was brought up on a system so exactly framed on our actual behavior, he would go far" (Diderot, 1964: 75). Showing his aptitude for impersonation, the nephew demonstrated his art of flattery: "I have a flexibility of spine, a way of twisting it, of shrugging or sagging, of stretching out my fingers, of nodding and shutting my eyes, of being thunderstruck as if I heard a divine angel's voice come down from heaven—this it is to flatter" (42).

The "aura" of the nephew in intellectual circles is due in part to Hegel's reading of him as the exemplar of "alienated man" (Trilling, 30). Hegel's siding with the nephew against the philosopher marked a turning point in the value structure in European society. Hegel associated the philosopher in this dialogue with the type of the "honest soul" representing the values of traditional morality, a vision of "happiness" through the noble life associated with order, peace, honor, beauty (39). In his commentary Lionel Trilling noted that in the twentieth century while most parents still held out hopes of the "noble life" for their children (*Amen*), the culture told a different story about the possibility and nature of happiness. That the hope persists may be seen in Wiliam J. Bennett's *The Book of Virtues*, with its goal of reviving the identity experience of "character."

William Bennett on Moral Literacy

"The vast majority of Americans share a respect for certain fundamental traits of character: honesty, compassion, courage, and perseverance. These are virtues. But because children are not born with this knowledge, they need to learn what these virtues are. We can help them gain a grasp and appreciation of these traits by giving children material to read about them. We can invite our students to discern the moral dimension of stories, of historical events, of famous lives. There are many wonderful stories of virtue and vice with which our children should be familiar. This book brings together some of the best, oldest, and most moving of them" (Bennett, 1993: 12).

These are not the virtues of cool nor of funk either. Bennett is right about the moral dimension of stories, and one feature of the mystory is to make a map of the stories that have hailed us with their morals. But Bennett's goal is an example of nostalgia in a reactive sense. The road to absolute knowledge requires passage through the nephew's alienated state of mind, Hegel argued. In our post-enlightenment moment, no longer accepting the possibility of absolute knowledge, the issue for the EmerAgency is that of "value"—the sending and receiving of the object of value. The question is: What values are most native to electracy? The road to electracy passes through funk. It is not a question of being "against" virtue, but of grasping virtue within the point of view of the apparatus.

Syncretism   The strategy of EmerAgency online consulting in the role of Sender during this period of syncretism associated with the emergence of electracy may be plotted by analogy with the previous period of syncretism that led to conversion of the Roman Empire to Christianity. The signature linking Funkmeister George Clinton and former President Bill Clinton is a symptom of the coming community, as is the photo-op picture of Bill playing jazz on his sax during the election campaign. In our context, the scandal of the Clinton presidency shows that Bill was funky as well as cool. In the coming community will the Monica Lewinsky affair be an *asset* to Clinton's legacy? Remember Diogenes, the funkmeister of Ancient Athens, who asked to be buried standing on his head, because soon down would be up? Identity, both individual and collective, is an imagined idea, mediated and sustained by a consistent and continuously updated narrative (Giddens, 1991). The identity of an individual, a nation, an empire, a civilization, may be altered by altering the story it tells about itself, as W. J. T. Mitchell points out, using the example of the film *JFK*.

> "The narrative work of JFK is rather like that of Desert Storm. It manages to unwrite one scenario (the Warren Commission's story of Lee Harvey Oswald 'acting alone' for personal, private, and unknowable reasons) and to put in its place an alternate script: that Lee Harvey Oswald was a 'patsy' who was set up with an elaborately constructed 'communist sympathizer' dossier to divert attention from the real assassins, who were in the employ of the CIA. This complex secret narrative is framed and motivated by a larger story: that the CIA, the U.S. intelligence community, and the whole range of interests summarized by Eisenhower's 'military-industrial complex' saw Kennedy as a threat to their increasing dominance over America's Cold War economy" (Mitchell, 1994: 406).

This process of forgetting one route through a body of information while recollecting an alternative route is exactly the one used by Christians against the pagan metaphysics of Rome, which Mary Carruthers describes as an "attunement" of "mental tone." In her example, the associative path of memory is literalized in alternative routes of processions from one monument to another in the streets of Rome. One "forgets" not by erasure but by remotivation, appropriation, recontexualization. Syncretic appropriation, Carruthers says, is a kind of Gestalt shift, using the same focalizing capacities of the sensorium that allows one to see an ambiguous shape first as a duck, then as a rabbit. The ambiguous eidos is the paradoxical case, a crossroads of two different semantic domains, even two different cosmologies.

Mary Carruthers on Christian-Pagan Syncretism

"By the seventh century the first pagan temple to be 'converted,' the Pantheon, was dedicated as Santa Maria ad Martyres, and incorporated into the national liturgy of Easter. And around the same time, the Christian procession of the Great Liturgy on April 25 replaced the old civic procession of Robigalia, appropriating not only the date but also the route and the goal (civic supplication and penitence) of its pagan original.

"These appropriations were carried out with a profound understanding of how human memories work. The Pantheon was inserted into a different social network by being attached to a closely related web of memories which overlay the first, blocking and reforming them. And what remained recognizably the same in the two webs is as important to understanding why the appropriation worked effectively as is the difference between them. . . .

"Things that are completely different and separate do not block each other: they act instead as two distinct memory sites. Where two or more competing patterns exist in one site, however, only one will be seen: the others, though they may remain potentially visible, will be blocked or absorbed by the overlay. What will block out every pattern but one is our *intentio*, the mental 'tone' we select, whose vibrations, like those of the taut strings of an instrument, create the patterns which connect a particular experience into everything else we know and enable us to see the Great Liturgy instead of the Robigalia. If the people of a city come conventionally (habitually) 'to see' the Great Liturgy, it matters not at all that some in the crowd may for a time persist in 'seeing' the Robigalia procession, or some particular story of their own devising" (Carruthers, 1998: 56–57).

Comment

- Carruthers's use of the tuned string (ficelle) alludes to the music of the spheres, which is the Pythagorean cosmology of correspondences that also informs Plato's *Timaeus* and the theory of chora as the mediation that sorts chaos into order (or one order into another).

- The circulation that promotes and demotes dominant and subordinant moods, and that leaves private eccentric moods free to persist and develop, is the popcycle of invention that allows a wide image to become a paradigm.

- Syncretism with the Black Atlantic in this context may be seen as the return of the pagan body cast in Christian morality as "debauched."

As our commentators noted repeatedly, funk, blues, and the rest are not confined to music, but name a value system, a cosmology, that is in some respects antithetical to the dominant world view of the West. The value currency of the Funk mood is "formless" (*informe*), as opposed to Greek form or Hebrew logos. Identity and behavior in electracy are not guided or judged by ideals, principles, elements, or transcendence of any sort. The virtues of the "honest soul" have only become less relevant since the time of Diderot. We have to imagine instead the mores of a "base materialism," in a society that understands itself in what is abject, through monuments that are repulsions more than attractions. And here is where the battle lines of a culture war will be and are being drawn. The theorist of this "lowering" of everything that is elevated or ideal is Georges Bataille, who advised us to consider blobs of spit and the big toe if we want to have an impact on public problem solving. The cartoon version is *Southpark*. The slogan of this formless mood is "no more transpositions" (Bois and Krauss, 1997: 172). It is important to cite the philosopher, since the relay of funk may seem like too much "fun" to threaten anyone.

Yve-Alain Bois on Formless

"'Affirming that the universe resembles nothing and is only *informe* amounts to saying that the universe is something like a spider or spit,' Bataille wrote in the famous article '*Informe*,' an entry in the *Documents* 'critical dictionary. . . .'

"'Whatever it [the *informe*] designates has no rights in any sense and gets itself squashed everywhere, like a spider or an earthworm.' The *informe* is what must be crushed (or spat out), because it has no right in any sense, because it does not make any sense, and because that in itself is unbearable to reason. The *informe* is the unassimilable waste that

> Bataille would shortly designate as the very object of heterology. To say
> that the universe is *informe* is to say that it makes no sense and thus that
> it should be crushed like a spider or expectorated like mucous.
> Bataille's double proposition is thus not contradictory, the 'something
> like' not referring to a resemblance but to an operation; the spit or the
> crushed spider are not themes (even though it is evident that Bataille
> chose them as examples because, besides their character as reject, they
> escape from geometry, the idea, morphology). Metaphor, figure,
> theme, morphology, meaning—everything that resembles something,
> everything that is gathered into the unity of a concept—that is what the
> *informe* operation crushes, sets aside with an irreverent wink: this is
> nothing but rubbish" (79).

To put it in grammatological terms, literacy did not have enough computing
power to think formless, or to exploit the holistic moods of categorical images.
The mathematical order of chaos emerged only within the patterning made legible by the computer. We will take up the task of applying formless funk to specific cases of public policy formation in a sequel to *Internet Invention,* through the
online EmerAgency. Meanwhile, it is not the job of the EmerAgency to dictate
what or which story attunes a community, but rather to be sure that within that
process the latter possibility mentioned by Carruthers is represented within the
popcycle: the story *of one's own devising* (as distinct from the alternatives provided
by the default cosmologies), which is the opening for the story of the wide
image. The effect of this possibility should be at once critical and creative: critical by revealing the choral or sorting operation of the spectacle, and creative by
awakening the individual netizens to the potential of their own state of mind
through the wide image.

What Next?

Act III, 11—Resurrection: the villains make one last unsuccessful attempt to
defeat the subject. 12—Return with the elixir: the subject returns with a
token of the journey.

Assignment: A Consultation (Postponed)

Make a website consultation on the public policy issues related to a current world crisis.

OFFICE

1. Even if we did not manage to carry our project into the third and concluding act of
   the narrative allegory guiding our experiment, we did come full circle to achieve at
   least a formal closure. I am thinking of the return at the end to Bataille's formless

operations, continuing the counter-definition practice used at the beginning of the book as a transition from topos to chora, word to image rhetoric. In any case, the real insight into electracy provided by the narrative form was not the linear one of plot resolution, but the nonlinear one of the atmosphere of setting.

2. How would I design an emblem blending the space of my mystory and that of a news event? To stay with the Binge Drinking call, imagine the following emblem: the picture is a row of beer bottles on a bar, with the labels modified to include the five-pointed star, as the logo for "Last Stand" or "Showdown" beer. The motto is a phrase from a philosopher defining "aporia" (perhaps a phrase from Heidegger, about Da-sein as the happening of strangeness). The epigram is information on binge drinking—specifically, statistics on how many drinks it takes for an average person to suffer alcohol poisoning. The design plays on the multiple meanings available in the phrase, "know your limits." The first meaning suggests the Greek maxim, "nothing in excess," perhaps stated as a warning to "drink responsibly." The unofficial meaning in underground values is to find out how many beers you can drink before you pass out. In the context of *Noon Star*, this ambiguity may produce a critical effect, since my emblem denounces the overvaluation of competition.

3. The next stage of EmerAgency consulting is taken up in a book entitled "Electronic Monumentality: Consulting the Internet Memory." The point of departure is a consultation on the question of a monument or memorial commemorating September 11, 2001. It moves the mystory testimony into a new practice called the MEmorial. A testimonial form of choragraphy is tested in a collaboration with the Florida Research Ensemble in "Miami Miautre: Mapping the Virtual City." The MEmorial takes up where the wide image leaves off. For example, alcohol-related accidents kill 1,400 college students each year. A MEmorial would not treat these deaths in terms of virtue and vice, but in a formless way as a sacrifice on behalf of an untransposed value important to American national identity.

Works Cited

Abrams, M. H. (1971), *Natural Supernaturalism: Tradition and Revolution in Romantic Literature* (New York: Norton).

Agacinski, Sylviane, "Another Experience of the Questions, or Experiencing the Question Other-Wise," in Cadava.

Agamben, Giorgio (1993), *The Coming Community,* Trans. Michael Hardt (Minneapolis: University of Minnesota Press).

———(1993a), *Stanzas: Word and Phantasm in Western Culture,* Trans. Ronald L. Martinez (Minneapolis: University of Minnesota Press).

Alexander, Caroline (1994),*The Way to Xanadu: Journeys to a Legendary Realm,* (New York: Knopf).

Algra, Keimpe (1995), *Concepts of Space in Greek Thought* (Leiden, N. Y.: Brill).

Anderson, Elijah (1999), *Code of the Street: Decency, Violence, and the Moral Life of the Inner City* (New York: Norton).

Arieti, Silvano (1976), *Creativity: The Magic Synthesis* (New York: Basic Books).

Armstrong, Nancy (1990), "The Occidental Alice," *Differences 2.*

Artaud, Antonin (1958), *The Theater and Its Double,* Trans. Mary Caroline Richards (New York: Grove).

Auster, Paul (1988), *The Invention of Solitude: A Memoir* (New York: Penguin).

Babington, Bruce, and Peter William Evans (1985), *Blue Skies and Silver Linings: Aspects of the Hollywood Musical* (Manchester, N.Y.: Manchester University).

Bakhtin, M. (1984), *Problems of Dostoevsky's Poetics,* Ed. C. Emerson (Minneapolis: University of Minnesota).

Bal, Mieke (1997), *Narratology: Introduction to the Theory of Narrative,* 2nd ed. (Toronto: University of Toronto).

Ballard, Bruce W. (1991), *The Role of Mood in Heidegger's Ontology* (New York: University Press of America).

Bancroft, Anne (1979), *Zen: Direct Pointing to Reality* (New York: Thames and Hudson).

Barnes, Hazel E. (1981), *Sartre and Flaubert* (Chicago: University of Chicago).

Barratt, Krome (1980), *Logic and Design in Art, Science, and Mathematics* (New York: Design Press).

Barthes, Roland (1977), *Image, Music, Text,* Trans. Stephen Heath (New York: Hill and Wang).

———(1981), *Camera Lucida: Reflections on Photography,* Trans. Richard Howard (New York: Hill and Wang).

———(1982), *Empire of Signs,* Trans. Richard Howard (New York: Hill and Wang).

Basho, Matsuo (1996), *Back Roads to Far Towns,* Trans. Cid Corman and Kamaike Susumu (Hopewell, N.J.: Ecco Press).

Bataille, Georges, et al. (1995), *Encyclopaedia Acephalica* (London: Atlas).

Baudelaire, Charles (1964), *Baudelaire*, Ed. Francis Scarfe (Baltimore: Penguin).

Beaujour, Michel (1991), *Poetics of the Literary Self-Portrait*, Trans. Yara Milos (New York: New York University).

Benedikt, Michael, Ed. (1991), *Cyberspace: First Steps* (Cambridge, Mass: MIT).

Benjamin, Walter (1969), *Illuminations*, Trans. Harry Zohn (New York: Schocken Books).

——— (1978), *Reflections: Essays, Aphorisms, Autobiographical Writings*, Trans. Edmund Jephcott (New York: Harcourt).

Bernabé, Jean, Patrick Chamoisseau, and Raphael Confiant (1993), *Éloge de la Créolité*. Trans. M.B. Taleb-Khyar (Paris: Gallimard).

Berry, Laurie (1996), "Mockingbird," in Jerome Stern, Ed., *Micro Fiction: An Anthology of Really Short Stories* (New York: Norton).

Birnbaum, Daniel (2000), "Stickup Artist," in *Artforum*, November.

Birney, Hoffman (1934), *Grim Journey*, (New York: Minton, Balch).

Black Elk, Wallace H., and William S. Lyon (1990), *Black Elk: The Sacred Ways of a Lakota* (San Francisco: Harper & Row).

Blanchot, Maurice (1986), *The Writing of the Disaster*, Trans. Ann Smock (Lincoln: University of Nebraska).

Bois, Yve-Alain, and Rosalind E. Krauss (1997), *Formless: A User's Guide*, (New York: Zone).

Boltanski, Christian (1988), "Interview," in *Bomb* 26 (1988–89).

——— (1988a), "Little Christians: Interview," *Artscribe International* (Nov/Dec).

Bordowitz, Gregg (1994), in Sappington and Stallings, pp. 25–43.

Briggs, John (1990), *Fire in the Crucible: The Self-Creation of Creativity and Genius* (Los Angeles: Tarcher).

Briggs, John, and Richard Monaco (1990), *Metaphor: The Logic of Poetry* (New York: Pace).

Brotchie, Alastair (1995), "Introduction," in Bataille et al. (1995), 9–27.

Broughel, Barbara (1987), "The Blob," in Steve Gallagher, 16–17.

Broughton, Simon, et al., Eds. (1994), *World Music: The Rough Guide*, (London: Rough Guides).

Brown, Joseph Epes, Ed. (1971), *The Sacred Pipe* (New York: Penguin).

Buci-Glucksmann, Christine (1994), *Baroque Reason: The Aesthetics of Modernity*, Trans. Patrick Camiller (London: Sage).

Buck-Morss, Susan (1989), *The Dialectics of Seeing: Walter Benjamin and the Arcades Project*, (Cambridge: MIT Press).

Bukatman, Scott (1993), *Terminal Identity: The Virtual Subject in Postmodern Science Fiction*, (Durham, N.C.: Duke).

Bullock, Alan, and Oliver Stallybrass (1977), *The Harper Dictionary of Modern Thought*, (New York: Harper & Row).

Cadava, Eduardo, Peter Connor, and Jean-Luc Nancy, Eds. (1991), *Who Comes after the Subject?* (New York: Routledge).

Carruthers, Mary (1990), *The Book of Memory: A Study of Memory in Medieval Culture* (New York: Cambridge).

——— (1998), *The Craft of Thought: Meditation, Rhetoric, and the Making of Images, 400–1200* (New York: Cambridge).

Carson, John (1987), "Darby O'Gill and the Little People," in Gallagher, 26–29.

Castleman, Harry, and Walter J. Podrazik (1982), *Watching TV: Four Decades of American Television* (New York: McGraw-Hill).

Charters, Samuel (1999), "From *The Poetry of the Blues*," in Steven C. Tracy, Ed., *Write Me a Few of Your Lines: A Blues Reader* (Amherst: University of Massachusetts), 352–360.

Chekhov, Michael (1985), *Lessons for the Professional Actor* (New York: Performing Arts Journal Press).

Cirlot, J. E. (1962), *A Dictionary of Symbols*, Trans. Jack Sage (New York: Philosophical Library).

Cixous, Helene (1991), *Readings: The Poetics of Blanchot, Joyce, Kafka, Kleist, Lispector, and Tsvetayeva*, Trans. Verena Andermatt Conley (Minneapolis: University of Minnesota).

———(1993), *Three Steps on the Ladder of Writing*, Trans. Sarah Cornell and Susan Sellers (New York: Columbia).

Clifford, James (1988), *The Predicament of Culture: Twentieth-Century Ethnography, Literature, and Art* (Cambridge, Mass: Harvard University).

Cooper, Lane (1960), *The Rhetoric of Aristotle* (New York: Appleton-Century-Crofts).

Copleston, Frederick, S.J. (1960), *A History of Philosophy, Volume 6: Modern Philosophy Part II, Kant* (New York: Doubleday).

Core, Philip (1984), *Camp: The Lie That Tells the Truth* (New York: Delilah Books).

Courtine, Jean-Francois, (1991), "Voice of Conscience and Call of Being," in Cadava.

Crowell, Steven G, (1990), "Dialogue and Text: Re-marking the Difference," in Maranhao.

Cushman, Robert F. (1976), *Cases in Civil Liberties*, 2nd ed. (Englewood Cliffs: Prentice-Hall).

Dabakis, Melissa (1988), "Re-imagining Women's History," in Melissa Dabakis and Janice Bell, Eds., *Rosa/Alice. May Stevens: Ordinary Extraordinary* (New York: Universe Books).

Daelemans, Sven, and Tullio Maranhao (1990), "Psychoanalytic Dialogue and the Dialogical Principle," in Maranhao.

Daly, Peter M. (1988), "Modern Advertising and the Renaissance Emblem: Modes of Verbal and Visual Persuasion," in Karl Josef Holtgen, Peter M. Daly, and Wolfgang Lottes, Eds., *Word and Visual Imagination: Studies in the Interaction of English Literature and the Visual Arts* (Erlangen: Universitatsbund Erlangen-Nurnberg).

———(1998), *Literature in the Light of the Emblem: Structural Parallels Between the Emblem and Literature in the Sixteenth and Seventeenth Centuries*, 2nd ed. (Toronto: University of Toronto).

Danesi, Marcel (1994), *Cool: The Signs and Meanings of Adolescence* (Toronto: University of Toronto).

Deleuze, Gilles (1983), *Nietzsche and Philosophy*, Trans. Hugh Tomlinson (New York: Columbia University Press).

———(1990), *The Logic of Sense*, Trans. Mark Lester (New York: Columbia).

Deleuze, Gilles, and Felix Guattari (1987), *A Thousand Plateaus: Capitalism & Schizophrenia*, Trans. Brian Massumi (Minneapolis: University of Minnesota Press).

Derrida, Jacques (1979), "Living On/Borderlines," Trans. James Hulbert in Bloom et al., *Deconstruction and Criticism* (New York: Seabury).

———(1986), *Memoires: For Paul De Man*, Trans. Cecile Lindsay, Jonathan Culler, and Eduardo Cadava (New York: Columbia University).

———(1991), "'Eating Well,' or the Calculation of the Subject," in Cadava.

———(1992), *Given Time: I. Counterfeit Money*, Trans. Peggy Kamuf (Chicago: University of Chicago Press).

———(1993), *Aporias*, Trans. Thomas Dutoit (Stanford: Stanford).

———(1994), *Specters of Marx: The State of the Debt, the Work of Mourning, and the New International*, Trans. Peggy Kamuf (New York: Routledge).

Diderot, Denis (1964), *"Rameau's Nephew" and Other Works*, Trans. Jacques Barzun, Ralph H. Bowen, (New York: Bobbs-Merrill).

Diggs, Stephen (1997), "Alchemy of the Blues," *Spring: A Journal of Archetypes and Culture*, 61.

Douglass, Frederick (1997), *Narrative of the Life of Frederick Douglass, an American Slave: Written by Himself* (New York: Signet).

Dreyfus, Hubert L., and Stuart E. Dreyfus (1986), *Mind over Machine: The Power of Human Intuition and Expertise in the Era of the Computer* (New York: Free Press).

duBois, Page (1991), *Torture and Truth* (New York: Routledge).

Duchamp, Marcel (1973), *Salt Seller: The Writings of Marcel Duchamp*, Michel Sanouillet and Elmer Peterson, Eds. (New York: Oxford).

Dyer, Richard (1991), "Charisma," in *Stardom*, Christine Gledhill, Ed. (New York: Routledge).

Eady, Cornelius (2001), *Brutal Imagination* (New York: Putnam).

Eagleton, Terry (1987), *Saints and Scholars* (London: Verso).

Eco, Umberto (1982), *The Aesthetics of Chaosmos: The Middle Ages of James Joyce*, Trans. Ellen Esrock (Cambridge, Mass.: Harvard).

———(1984), *Semiotics and the Philosophy of Language* (Bloomington: Indiana University).

Ellis, Sarah (2001), *"Beyond the Pawpaw Trees*—Palmer Brown," in *Lost Classics*, Ed. Michael Ondaatje et al. (New York: Anchor).

Erdelyi, Matthew Hugh (1985), *Psychoanalysis: Freud's Cognitive Psychology* (New York: W. H. Freeman).

Erickson, Thomas D. (1990), "Interface and Evolution of Pidgins," in Laurel.

Evans, Dylan (1996), *An Introductory Dictionary of Lacanian Psychoanalysis* (New York: Routledge).

Evers, Inge (1987), *Feltmaking: Techniques and Projects* (Asheville, N.C.: Lark).

Fisher, Shirley (1989), *Homesickness, Cognition, And Health* (Hillsdale, N.J.: Lawrence Erlbaum).

Fiske, John (1993), *Power Plays, Power Works* (New York: Verso).

Fletcher, Angus (1964), *Allegory: The Theory of a Symbolic Mode* (Ithaca, N.Y.: Cornell University).

Fletcher, John, and Andrew Benjamin, Eds. (1990), *Abjection, Melancholia, and Love: The Work of Julia Kristeva* (London: Routledge).

Foreman, Richard (1976), "How to Write a Play," *Performing Arts Journal*, 1:84–92.

Foss, Bob (1992), *Filmmaking: Narrative and Structural Techniques* (Los Angeles: Silman-James Press).

Fowler, Christopher (1984), *How to Impersonate Famous People* (New York: Crown).

Freud, Sigmund (1958), "The 'Uncanny'," in *On Creativity and the Unconscious* (New York: Harper and Row).

———(1963), *Dora: An Analysis of a Case of Hysteria* (New York: Collier).

———(n.d.), *Psychopathology of Everyday Life* (New York: Mentor).

Frey, Patrick (1989), "Whereof one cannot speak, thereof one should not be silent," *Parkett*, 19.

Frost, Lawrence A. (1964), *The Custer Album: A Pictorial Biography of General George A. Custer* (Seattle: Superior Publishing).

Fry, Edward F. (n.d.), *Cubism* (New York: McGraw-Hill).

Fynsk, Christopher (1986), *Heidegger: Thought And Historicity* (Ithaca, N.Y.: Cornell University).

Gallagher, Steve, Ed. (1987), *Picture This: Films Chosen by Artists* (Buffalo, N.Y.: Hallwalls).

Gamman, Lorraine, and Merja Makinen (1994), *Female Fetishism* (New York: New York University).

Garber, Marjorie (1992), *Vested Interests: Cross-dressing and Cultural Anxiety* (New York: Routledge).

Garcia, Jerry (1995), *Harrington Street* (New York: Delacorte).

Gasche, Rodolphe (1986), *The Tain of the Mirror: Derrida and the Philosophy of Reflection* (Cambridge, Mass.: Harvard).

Gelernter, David (1994), *The Muse in the Machine* (New York: Free Press).

Genet, Jean (1985), "Something Which Seemed to Resemble Decay . . . ," in *Antaeus* 54:108–116.

Genette, Gerard (1982), *Palimpsestes: La Litterature au Second Degre* (Paris: Seuil).

George, Nelson (1998), *Hip Hop America* (New York: Penguin).

Gibson, William (1984), *Neuromancer* (New York: Ace Books).

Giddens, Anthony (1991), *Modernity and Self-Identity: Self and Society in the Late Modern Age* (Stanford, Calif.: Stanford University).

Gilroy, Paul (1993), *The Black Atlantic: Modernity and Double Consciousness* (Cambridge, Mass.: Harvard).

Goldman, Robert, and Stephen Papson (1996), *Sign Wars: The Cluttered Landscape of Advertising* (New York: Guilford Press).

Goodwin, Andrew (1992), *Dancing in the Distraction Factory: Music Television and Popular Culture* (Minneapolis: Minnesota).

Goody, Jack (1977), *The Domestication of the Savage Mind* (New York: Cambridge).

Greenberg, Alan (1994), *Love in Vain: A Vision of Robert Johnson* (New York: Da Capo).

Greenblatt, Stephen (1988), *Shakespearean Negotiations: The Circulation of Social Energy in Renaissance England* (Berkeley: University of California).

Greimas, Algirdas Julien (1987), *On Meaning: Selected Writings in Semiotic Theory*, Trans. Paul J. Perron and Frank H. Collins (Minneapolis: University of Minnesota).

———(1990), *The Social Sciences: A Semiotic View*, Trans. Paul Perron and Frank H. Collins (Minneapolis: University of Minnesota).

Gross, Elizabeth (1990), "The Body of Signification," in Fletcher.

Grossmann, Reinhardt (1983), *The Categorical Structure of the World* (Bloomington: Indiana University).

Guillermoprieto, Alma (1990), *Samba* (New York: Vintage).

Guralnick, Peter (1998), *Searching for Robert Johnson* (New York: Plume).

Gurdjieff, G.I. (1963), *Meetings with Remarkable Men* (New York: Dutton).

Haar, Michel (1993), *The Song of the Earth: Heidegger and the Grounds of the History of Being*, Trans. Reginald Lilly (Bloomington: Indiana University).

Haineault, Doris-Louise, and Jean-Yves Roy (1993), *Unconscious for Sale: Advertising, Psychoanalysis, and the Public*, Trans. Kimball Lockhart with Barbara Kerslake (Minneapolis: University of Minnesota Press).

Hakken, David (1999), *Cyborgs @ Cyberspace? An Ethnographer Looks to the Future* (New York: Routledge).

Hallyn, Fernand (1993), *The Poetic Structure of the World: Copernicus and Kepler*, Trans. Donald M. Leslie (New York: Zone).

Harrison, Ted (1992), *Elvis People: The Cult of the King* (London: Fount).

Hass, Robert (1984), *Twentieth-Century Pleasures: Prose on Poetry* (Hopewell, N.J.: Ecco Press).

Havelock, Eric A. (1967), *Preface to Plato* (New York: Grosset and Dunlap).

———(1978), *The Greek Concept of Justice: From its Shadow in Homer to its Substance in Plato* (Cambridge, Mass.: Harvard).

———(1986), *The Muse Learns to Write: Reflections on Orality and Literacy from Antiquity to the Present* (New Haven, Conn.: Yale).

Hawles, David (1996), *Ideology* (New York: Routledge).

Heidegger, Martin (1966), *Discourse on Thinking*, Trans. John M. Anderson and E. Hans Freund (New York: Harper & Row).

———(1995), *The Fundamental Concepts of Metaphysics: World, Finitude, Solitude*, Trans. William McNeill and Nicholas Walker (Bloomington: Indiana University).

Hermassi, Karen (1977), *Polity and Theater in Historical Perspective* (Berkeley: University of California).

Hillis, Ken (1999), *Digital Sensations: Space, Identity, and Embodiment in Virtual Reality* (Minneapolis: University of Minnesota).

Hirshfield, Jane (1998), *Nine Gates: Entering the Mind of Poetry* (New York: HarperCollins).

Hodge, Robert, and Gunther Kress (1988), *Social Semiotics* (Ithaca, N.Y.: Cornell University).

Hodges, Andrew (1983) *Alan Turing: The Enigma* (New York: Simon and Schuster).

Holman, C. Hugh (1972), *A Handbook to Literature*, 3rd ed. (New York: Bobbs-Merrill).

Holton, Gerald (1973), *Thematic Origins of Scientific Thought* (Cambridge, Mass.: Harvard).

Hurlburt, Laurance P. (1989), *The Mexican Muralists in the United States* (Albuquerque: University of New Mexico).

Jaffe, Hans L. C. (1967), *20,000 Years of World Painting* (New York: Abrams).

Jameson, Fredric (1972), *The Prison-House of Language: A Critical Account of Structuralism and Russian Formalism* (Princeton, N.J.: Princeton).

———(1981), *The Political Unconscious: Narrative as a Socially Symbolic Act* (Ithaca, N.Y.: Cornell University).

———(1985), "Class and Allegory in Contemporary Mass Culture: *Dog Day Afternoon* as a Political Film," in Bill Nichols, Ed. *Movies and Methods: Volume II* (Berkeley: University of California).

———(2000), "Third-World Literature in the Era of Multinational Capitalism," in Michael Hardt and Kathi Weeks, Eds., *The Jameson Reader* (Oxford: Blackwell).

Jensen, Lawrence N. (1964), *Synthetic Painting Media* (Englewood Cliffs, N. J.: Prentice-Hall).

Jesse, Anita (1994), *Let the Part Play You* (Burbank, Calif.: Wolf Creek).

Joyce, James (1966), *Ulysses* (New York: Vintage).

Katz, Ephraim (1979), *The Film Encyclopedia*, (New York: Perigee).

Kearney, Richard (1988), *The Wake of Imagination: Toward a Postmodern Culture*, (Minneapolis: University of Minnesota).

Koestler, Arthur (1964), *The Act of Creation: A Study of the Conscious and Unconscious in Science and Art* (New York: Dell).

Koon, George William (1983), *Hank Williams: A Bio-Bibliography* (Westport, Conn.: Greenwood).

Kopf, Biba (1987), "Bacillus Culture," in Charles Neal, Ed., *Tape Delay* (Harrow, England: SAF).

Koren, Leonard (1994), *Wabi-Sabi: For Artists, Designers, Poets and Philosophers* (Berkeley, Calif.: Stone Bridge).

Krane, Susan (1989), *Houston Conwill: "The New Cakewalk": A Traveler's Guide* (Atlanta: High Museum).

Krips, Henry (1999), *Fetish: An Erotics of Culture* (Ithaca, N.Y.: Cornell University).

Kristeva, Julia (1982), *Powers of Horror: An Essay on Abjection*, Trans. Leon S. Roudiez (New York: Columbia).

Krol, Ed (1992), *The Whole Internet* (Sebastopol, Calif.: O'Reilly).

Kuhn, Annette (1995), *Family Secrets: Acts of Memory and Imagination* (New York: Verso).

Kurzweil, Raymond (1992), *The Age of Intelligent Machines* (Cambridge, Mass.: MIT).

Laplanche, J., and J.B. Pontalis (1973), *The Language of Psycho-Analysis* (New York: Norton).

Laurel, Brenda, Ed. (1990), *The Art of Human-Computer Interface Design* (Reading, Mass.: Addison-Wesley).

Lawlor, Robert (1982), *Sacred Geometry: Philosophy and Practice* (London: Thames and Hudson).

Lecercle, Jean-Jacques (1990), *The Violence of Language* (New York: Routledge).

Le Fanu, Mark (1987), *The Cinema of Andrei Tarkovsky* (London: British Film Institute).

Leiris, Michel (1988), "The Sacred in Everyday Life," in *The College of Sociology 1937–39*, Ed. Denis Hollier, Trans. Betsy Wing (Minneapolis: University of Minnesota).

Leiss, William, Stephen Kline, and Sut Jhally (1986), *Social Communication in Advertising: Persons, Products & Images of Well-Being* (New York: Methuen).

Lemaire, Anika (1977), *Jacques Lacan*, Trans. David Macey (London: Routledge).

Levin, Gail (1980), *Edward Hopper: The Art and the Artist* (New York: Norton).

Lewis, Thomas H. (1990), *The Medicine Men: Oglala Sioux Ceremony and Healing* (Lincoln: University of Nebraska).

Lippard, Lucy R. (1990), *Mixed Blessings: New Art in a Multicultural America* (New York: Pantheon).

Lipton, Eunice (1994), *Alias Olympia: A Woman's Search for Manet's Notorious Model and Her Own Desire* (New York: Meridian).

Litz, A. Walton (1972), *James Joyce*, revised ed. (New York: Hippocrene Books).

Lock, Graham (1999), *Blutopia: Visions of the Future and Revisions of the Past in the Work of Sun Ra, Duke Ellington, and Anthony Braxton* (Durham, N.C.: Duke University).

Lomax, Alan (1993), *The Land Where the Blues Began* (New York: Delta).

Lopiano-Misdom, Janine, and Joanne de Luca (1997), *Street Trends: How Today's Alternative Youth Cultures are Creating Tomorrow's Mainstream Markets* (New York: Harper Business).

Lorca, Federico Garcia (1983), "The Duende," in Jerome Rothenberg and Diane Rothenberg, Eds., *Symposium of the Whole: A Range of Discourse Toward an Ethnopoetics* (Berkeley: University of California).

Lorin, Philippe (2001), *Five Giants of Advertising* (New York: Assouline).

Lotman, Yuri M. (2000), *Universe of the Mind: A Semiotic Theory of Culture*, Trans. Ann Shukman (Bloomington: Indiana University).

Lowes, John Livingston (1955), *The Road to Xanadu: A Study in the Ways of the Imagination* (Boston: Houghton Mifflin).

Lukacher, Ned (1986), *Primal Scenes: Literature, Philosophy, Psychoanalysis* (Ithaca, N.Y.: Cornell University).

Lyotard, Jean-Francois (1994), *Lessons on the Analytic of the Sublime*, Trans. Elizabeth Rottenberg (Stanford, Calif.: Stanford University).

McGowan, Chris, and Ricardo Pessanha (1991), *The Brazilian Sound: Samba, Bossa Nova, and the Popular Music of Brazil* (New York: Watson-Guptill).

Magill, Frank N., Ed. *Masterpieces of World Philosophy in Summary Form* (New York: Harper).

Majors, Richard, and Janet Mancini Billson (1992), *Cool Pose: The Dilemmas of Black Manhood in America* (New York: Simon & Schuster).

Mann, Wolfgang-Rainer (2000), *The Discovery of Things: Aristotle's Categories and Their Context* (Princeton, N.J.: Princeton University).

Maranda, Elli Kongas, and Pierre Maranda (1971), *Structural Models in Folklore and Transformational Essays* (The Hague: Mouton).

Maranhao, Tullio, Ed. (1990), *The Interpretation of Dialogue* (Chicago: University of Chicago).

Maynard, Richard A., Ed. (1974), *Values in Conflict: "High Noon," "The Hustler," "The Savage Innocents"* (New York: Scholastic Book Service).

Meltzer, David, Ed. (1999), *Writing Jazz* (San Francisco: Mercury House).

Menand, Louis (2001), "Holden at Fifty," *The New Yorker*, October 1: 82–87.

Michelin Green Guides (1967), *French Riviera* (London: Dickens).

Mitchell, W. J. T. (1994), *Picture Theory* (Chicago: University of Chicago).

Monk, Ray (1990), *Ludwig Wittgenstein: The Duty of Genius* (New York: Free Press).

Monte, John, Ed. (1978), *The Fred Astaire Dance Book* (New York: Simon and Schuster).

Morrison, Jasper (1999), "Looking for Atmosphere" (Interview with Jasper Morrison), Federica Zanco in *Jasper Morrison*, Charles-Arthur Boyer and Federica Zanco, Eds. (Paris: Editions Dis Voir).

Moos, David (1994), "Sample Time: Film and the Frame of Painting," in Ihor Holubizky and David Moos, *Portraits and Gods: Paintings by Tony Scherman* (Hamilton, Ontario: The Art Gallery of Hamilton).

Murray, Albert (1976), *Stomping the Blues* (New York: Da Capo).

Neihardt, John G. (1961), *Black Elk Speaks: Being the Life Story of a Holy Man of the Oglala Sioux* (Lincoln: University of Nebraska).

Nietzsche, Friedrich (1967), *On the Genealogy of Morals*, Trans. Walter Kaufmann (New York: Vintage).

Novak, Marcos (1991), "Liquid Architectures in Cyberspace," in Michael Benedikt, 225–254.

Olalquiaga, Celeste (1992), *Megalopolis: Contemporary Cultural Sensibilities* (Minneapolis: University of Minnesota).

Olson, David R. (1994), *The World on Paper: The Conceptual and Cognitive Implications of Writing and Reading* (New York: Cambridge).

Papert, Seymour (1980), *Mindstorms: Children, Computers, and Powerful Ideas* (New York: Basic Books).

Perrin, Robert (1987), *The Beacon Handbook* (Boston: Houghton Mifflin).

Peterson, James (1994), *Dreams of Chaos, Visions of Order: Understanding the American Avant-Garde Cinema* (Detroit: Wayne State).

Pickow, Peter, and Amy Appleby (1988), *The Billboard Book of Songwriting* (New York: Billboard Publications).

Pierson, Frank (1988), "Writer's Revelations," in Alan A. Armer, *Writing the Screenplay: TV and Film* (Belmont, Calif.: Wadsworth).

Porter, Darwin (1982), *Frommer's Dollarwise Guide to the Caribbean* (New York: Simon & Schuster).

Ricoeur, Paul (1985), *Time and Narrative*, Trans. Kathleen McLaughlin and David Pellauer (Chicago: University of Chicago).

Rilke, Rainer Maria (1958), *The Notebooks of Malte Laurids Brigge*, Trans. M. D. Herter Norton (New York: Capricorn Books).

Rochfort, Desmond (1993), *Mexican Muralists: Orozco, Rivera, Siqueiros* (London: Laurence King).

Roethke, Theodore (1961), *Words for the Wind* (Bloomington: Indiana University).

Rosenzweig, Phyllis (1993), "Directions—Glenn Ligon: To Disembark," Pamphlet, Hirshhorn Museum, Smithsonian Institution.

Royal, Robert F., and Steven R. Schutt (1976), *The Gentle Art of Interviewing and Interrogation: A Professional Manual and Guide* (Englewood Cliffs, N.J.: Prentice-Hall).

Rucker, Rudy (1987), *Mindtools: The Five Levels of Mathematical Reality* (Boston: Houghton Mifflin).

Sappington, Rodney, and Tyler Stallings, Eds. (1994), *Uncontrollable Bodies: Testimonies of Identity and Culture* (Seattle: Bay Press).

Sartre, Jean-Paul (1965), *The Philosophy of Jean-Paul Sartre*, Ed. Robert Denoon Cumming (New York: Vintage).

———(1966), *The Psychology of Imagination*, Trans. Bernard Frechtman (New York: Washington Square Press).

Savigliano, Marta E. (1995), *Tango and the Political Economy of Passion* (Boulder, Colo.: Westview).

Schank, Roger C. (1986), *Explanation Patterns: Understanding Mechanically and Creatively* (Hillsdale, N.J.: Lawrence Erlbaum).

Scheler, Max (1994), *Ressentiment*, Trans. Lewis B. Coser and William W. Holdheim, (Milwaukee: Marquette).

Serres, Michel (1982), *The Parasite*, Trans. Lawrence R. Schehr (Baltimore: Johns Hopkins).

Shahn, Ben (1957), *The Shape of Content* (New York: Vintage).

Shepard, Sam (1982), *Motel Chronicles* (San Francisco: City Lights).

Siegel, David (1996), *Creating Killer Web Sites: The Art of Third-Generation Site Design* (Indianapolis: Hayden).

Slomkowski, Paul (1997), *Aristotle's Topics* (New York: Brill).

Slotkin, Richard (1993), *Gunfighter Nation* (New York: Harper Perennial).

Sobchack, Vivian (1994), "Revenge of *The Leech Woman:* On the Dread of Aging in a Low-Budget Horror Film," in Sappington and Stallings: 79–91.

Spence, Lewis (1993), *An Encyclopedia of Occultism* (New York: Citadel).

Sperber, Dan, and Deirdre Wilson, (1986), *Relevance: Communication and Cognition* (Cambridge, Mass.: Harvard).

Spitzer, Leo (1963), *Classical and Christian Ideas of World Harmony: Prolegomena to an Interpretation of the Word "Stimmung"* (Baltimore: Johns Hopkins).

Stam, Robert, et al. (1992), *New Vocabularies in Film Semiotics* (New York: Routledge).

Sternfeld, Joel (1996), *On This Site: Landscape in Memoriam* (San Francisco: Chronicle Books).

Stewart, George R. (1960), *Ordeal by Hunger: The Story of the Donner Party,* new edition (Boston: Houghton Mifflin).

Stone, Allucquere Rosanne (1991), "Will the Real Body Please Stand Up? Boundary Stories about Virtual Cultures," in Benedikt: 81–118.

Swearingen, C. Jan. "Dialogue and Dialectic: The Logic of Conversation and the Interpretation of Logic," in Maranhao.

Tarkovsky, Andrey (1986), *Sculpting in Time: Reflections on the Cinema,* Trans. Kitty Hunter-Blair (Austin: University of Texas).

———(1999), *Collected Screenplays,* Trans. William Powell and Natasha Synessios (New York: Faber and Faber).

Tatar, Maria (1987), *The Hard Facts of the Grimms' Fairy Tales* (Princeton, N.J.: Princeton University).

Taussig, Michael (1993), *Mimesis and Alterity: A Particular History of the Senses* (New York: Routledge).

Taylor, Julie (1998), *Paper Tangos* (Durham, N.C.: Duke University).

Thompson, Kristin (1999), *Storytelling in the New Hollywood: Understanding Classical Narrative Technique* (Cambridge, Mass.: Harvard).

Thompson, Robert Farris (1984), *Flash of the Spirit: African and Afro-American Art and Philosophy* (New York: Vintage).

Tonkinson, Carole, Ed. (1995), *Big Sky Mind: Buddhism and the Beat Generation* (New York: Riverhead).

Transtromer, Tomas (1997), "Memories Look at Me," in *New Collected Poems,* Trans. Robin Fulton (Newcastel upon Tyne: Bloodaxe Books).

Trilling, Lionel (1971), *Sincerity and Authenticity* (Cambridge, Mass.: Harvard).

Turner, Frederick (1994), *Remembering Song: Encounters with the New Orleans Jazz Tradition,* expanded edition (New York: Da Capo).

Turner, Kay (1999), *Beautiful Necessity: The Art and Meaning of Women's Altars* (New York: Thames and Hudson).

Turner, Mark (1995), *The Literary Mind: The Origins of Thought and Language* (New York: Oxford).

Turner, Victor (1974), *Dramas, Fields, and Metaphors: Symbolic Action in Human Society* (Ithaca, N.Y.: Cornell University).

———(1982), *From Ritual to Theater: The Human Seriousness of Play,* (New York: Performing Arts Journal Publications).

Ueda, Makoto (1995), "Basho on the Art of the Haiku: Impersonality in Poetry," in *Japanese Aesthetics and Culture: A Reader,* Ed. Nancy G. Hume (Albany: SUNY).

Ulmer, Gregory L. (1989), *Teletheory: Grammatology in the Age of Video* (New York: Routledge).

———(1994), *Heuretics: The Logic of Invention* (Baltimore: Johns Hopkins).

———(1994a), "The Heuretics of Deconstruction," in Peter Brunette and David Wills, Eds., *Deconstruction and the Visual Arts: Art, Media, Architecture* (New York: Cambridge): 80–95.

Vance, Eugene (1987), *From Topic to Tale: Logic and Narrativity in the Middle Ages* (Minneapolis: University of Minnesota).

Van Dyne, Susan R. (1993), *Revising Life: Sylvia Plath's Ariel Poems* (Chapel Hill: University of North Carolina).

Varela, Francisco J. (1999), *Ethical Know-How: Action, Wisdom, and Cognition* (Stanford, Calif.: Stanford University).

Ventura, Michael (1985), "Hear That Long Snake Moan," in *Shadow Dancing in the USA* (Los Angeles: Tarcher).

Vianna, Hermano (1999), *The Mystery of Samba: Popular Music and National Identity in Brazil,* Trans. John Charles Chasteen (Chapel Hill, N.C.: University of North Carolina).

Vincent, Rickey (1996), *Funk: The Music, the People, and the Rhythm of the One* (New York: St. Martin's).

Virilio, Paul (1994), *The Vision Machine* (Bloomington: Indiana University Press).
———(1999), *Politics of the Very Worst; An Interview by Philippe Petit,* Trans. Michael Cavaliere (New York: Semiotexte).
Voytilla, Stuart (1999), *Myth and the Movies: Discovering the Mythic Structure of 50 Unforgettable Films* (Studio City, Calif.: Michael Wiese Productions).
Warner, Marina (1994), *From the Beast to the Blonde: On Fairy Tales and Their Tellers* (London: Chatto & Windus).
Waterman, Christopher Alan (1990), *Juju: A Social History and Ethnography of an African Popular Music* (Chicago: University of Chicago).
Weber, Max (1958), *The Protestant Ethic and the Spirit of Capitalism,* Trans. Talcott Parsons (New York: Scribner's).
Weiss, Allen S. (1990), "K," in *Art & Text,* 37.
White, Hayden (1999), *Figural Realism: Studies in the Mimesis Effect* (Baltimore: Johns Hopkins).
White, Stephen K. (1991), *Political Theory and Postmodernism,* (New York: Cambridge).
Williams, Raymond (1976), *Keywords: A Vocabulary of Culture and Society* (New York: Oxford).
Williamson, Judith (1978), *Decoding Advertisements: Ideology and Meaning in Advertising* (London: Marion Boyars).
Windelband, Wilhelm (1958), *A History of Philosophy: Greek, Roman, Medieval* (New York: Harper).
Witt, Elder (1988) *The Supreme Court and Individual Rights* 2nd ed. (Washington, D.C.: Congressional Quarterly).
Wittgenstein, Ludwig (1968), *Philosophical Investigations,* Trans. G. E. M. Anscombe (Oxford: Blackwell).
Wolf, Gary (1995), "The Curse of Xanadu," in *Wired,* June, 138–152, 194–202.
Woll, Allen L. (1983) *The Hollywood Musical Goes to War* (Chicago: Nelson-Hall).
Yates, Frances A. (1966), *The Art of Memory* (Chicago: University of Chicago).
Yenser, Stephen (1987), *The Consuming Myth: The Work of James Merrill* (Cambridge, Mass.: Harvard).
Zizek, Slavoj (1989), *The Sublime Object of Ideology* (London: Verso).
———(1991), *For They Know Not What They Do: Enjoyment as a Political Factor* (London: Verso).
Zulawski, David E., and Douglas E. Wicklander (1992), *Practical Aspects of Interview and Interrogation* (New York: Elsevier).

Index